ON the WORD of a JEW

ON THE WORD OF A JEW
Religion, Reliability, and the Dynamics of Trust

Edited by Nina Caputo and
Mitchell B. Hart

Indiana University Press

This book is a publication of

Indiana University Press
Office of Scholarly Publishing
Herman B Wells Library 350
1320 East 10th Street
Bloomington, Indiana 47405 USA

iupress.indiana.edu

© 2019 by Indiana University Press

All rights reserved
No part of this book may be reproduced or utilized in any form or by any means, electronic or mechanical, including photocopying and recording, or by any information storage and retrieval system, without permission in writing from the publisher. The paper used in this publication meets the minimum requirements of the American National Standard for Information Sciences—Permanence of Paper for Printed Library Materials, ANSI Z39.48-1992.

Manufactured in the United States of America

Library of Congress Cataloging-in-Publication Data

Names: Caputo, Nina, [date] editor. | Hart, Mitchell Bryan, [date] editor.
Title: On the word of a Jew : religion, reliability, and the dynamics of trust / edited by Nina Caputo and Mitchell B. Hart.
Description: Bloomington, Indiana : Indiana University Press, [2019] | Includes bibliographical references and index.
Identifiers: LCCN 2018019382 (print) | LCCN 2018021056 (ebook) | ISBN 9780253037411 (e-book) | ISBN 9780253037398 (cl : alk. paper) | ISBN 9780253037404 (pb : alk. paper)
Subjects: LCSH: Judaism—Relations—Christianity. | Christianity and other religions—Judaism. | Jews—Public opinion. | Gentiles—Attitudes. | Reliability.
Classification: LCC BM535 (ebook) | LCC BM535 .O48 2018 (print) | DDC 305.892/4—dc23
LC record available at https://lccn.loc.gov/2018019382

1 2 3 4 5   24 23 22 21 20 19

In memory of Yarnton Manor

Contents

Acknowledgments — ix

Introduction: On the Word of a Jew, or Trusting Jewish History / Nina Caputo and Mitchell B. Hart — 1

Section One: To Swear an Oath

1. Oaths, Vows, and Trust in the Bible / Robert S. Kawashima — 17

2. "And in Most of Their Business Transactions They Rely on This": Some Reflections on Jews and Oaths in the Commercial Arena in Medieval Europe / Ephraim Shoham-Steiner — 36

3. The Oath of a Jew in the Thirteenth-Century English Legal Context / Joshua Curk — 62

4. What Is an Infidel?: Jewish Oaths and Jewish History in the Making of English Trust and Tolerance / Mitchell B. Hart — 81

5. Trusting Adolphe Crémieux: Jews and Republicans in Nineteenth-Century France / Lisa Leff — 101

Section Two: The Business of Trust

6. "A Kind of Republic and Neutral Nation": Commerce, Credit, and Conspiracy in Early Modern Europe / Joshua Teplitsky — 119

7. Jewish Peddlers and Non-Jewish Customers in the New World: Between Profit and Trust / Hasia Diner — 138

8. Belonging and Trustworthiness: Jewish Businessmen in the Public Rhetoric around the "Trustworthy Businessman" in Post–World War I Germany / Stefanie Fischer — 158

Section Three: Intimacy of Trust

9. The Voice of a Jew? Petrus Alfonsi's *Dialogi contra Iudaeos* and the Question of True Conversion / Nina Caputo — 181

10 A Return to Credibility? The Rehabilitation of Repentant
    Apostates in Medieval Ashkenaz / Rachel Furst   201

11 The Jewish Physician as Respondent, Confidant, and Proxy:
    The Case of Marcus Herz and Immanuel Kant / Robert Leventhal   222

Section Four: The Politics of Trust

12 Perspectives from the Periphery: The East India
    Company's Jewish Sepoys, Anglo-Jewry, and the Image of
    "the Jew" / Mitch Numark   247

13 Between Honor and Authenticity: Zionism as Theodor
    Herzl's Life Project / Derek Jonathan Penslar   276

14 The Most Trusted Jew in America: Jon Stewart's Earnestness /
    Shaina Hammerman   297

    Index   319

Acknowledgments

THIS VOLUME BEGAN as an eight-month-long Oxford Seminar in Advanced Jewish Studies at the Oxford Centre for Hebrew and Jewish Studies in 2013–14. We'd like to thank the core seminar members who made those eight months such an intellectual and social pleasure. Our thanks to Marco Di Giulio, Todd Endelman, Stefanie Fischer, Rachel Furst, Sara Lipton, and Ron Schechter. Thank you as well to the weekly seminar and conference participants: Nicholas Cole, David Feldman, Adriana Jacobs, George Rousseau, Miri Rubin, Adam Sutcliffe, Daniel Strum, and Frank Wolf, as well as to all those who have contributed their essays to this volume.

Special thanks to Josh Teplitsky, whose participation in the seminar and the social gatherings added so much to the enjoyment of the year.

We'd also like to acknowledge and thank Martin Goodman for his support and encouragement of the seminar and Martine Smith-Huvers and Sue Forteath for their professional logistic support and their constant good cheer in the center's office.

Thanks to the staffs of the Bodleian Library and the British Library and to the Alexander Grass Chair for financial assistance.

Our thanks to the two readers for Indiana, Gil Anidjar and Rebekah Klein-Pejšová, for their careful readings and comments, and to Dee Mortensen, Paige Rasmussen, and Julia Turner for all their help in the publication process. Also, Anna Lankina was incredibly thorough and attentive to detail in her preparation of the index.

Finally, we owe our deepest gratitude to David Rechter, who facilitated the seminar and who, with his family—Lynne Hirsch, Ella, Noah, and Laura—graciously hosted and entertained us throughout the year.

ON THE WORD OF A JEW

Introduction

On the Word of Jew, or Trusting Jewish History

Nina Caputo and Mitchell B. Hart

Trust in Jewish History

What, if anything, does religion, race, or gender have to do with reliability? When and how do such differences matter when it comes to trusting the word of another?[1] Most of us living in the Western world today might take it for granted that one's Jewishness does not and should not matter when it comes to acting or engaging in the public realm. That is, the word of a Jew qua Jew is no longer, for most people, a matter of suspicion. This was, however, not always the case. Contemporary politics, in the age of Muslim travel bans and the "war on terror," bring the historical contingency of trust into sharp relief. The "trustworthy Jew" and the "untrustworthy Jew" have a history, one that reaches from the Middle Ages into the twenty-first century but that has remained largely unexplored by historians.

This collection of essays looks at when and how Jews became reliable or trustworthy in the realms of jurisprudence, medicine, politics, culture, and business and finance. As an exploration of issues of trust, it is also an exploration of mistrust and the gradations between these two positions. Neither trust nor mistrust should be viewed as unconditional or noncontingent states. Rather, the challenge is to understand the mechanics of trust, how "the Jew" and Jews move, either as subjects or objects, between trust and mistrust discursively and materially.

Thus, the question of Jews and trust as this book frames it is more generally a question of a transformation of Western or Christian society over time. While it is difficult to pinpoint just how or when it is that tolerance or acceptance occur, this book explores this process through case studies that examine how "the Jew" serves as a spur or impulse to large-scale changes in Western mentalities and practices, and explains how this occurred within specific contexts. Social, economic, and political forces shape common understandings of the character of the Jews—that is, whether they can fulfill the expectations of being "gentlemen" or respectable citizens.

This book begins with the acknowledgment of the well-known image of the perfidious and untrustworthy Jew that has been part of the Christian imagination for eighteen hundred years. In the words of Salo Baron, "That one could not trust any Jew, who, by both nature and the dictates of his law, was a cheat and a swindler, had become a commonplace in the medieval literary presentations of Jewish types."[2] Or, as Francesca Trivellato has more recently put it, "It is all too evident that Jewish communities in Christian Europe had to manage their self-image of credibility not only against reality (were individual Jews reliable or not?) but also against deep-rooted anti-Semitic preconceptions of Jews as usurers and cheaters."[3] That emancipation and the process of inclusion in the body politic slowly shifted Jews' status in western European Christian society, eventually naturalizing them vis-à-vis the laws, customs, and mannerisms of the broader society, has garnered much scholarly attention.[4] But as this scholarship has shown, the redefinition of political status rarely coincided with an immediate reassessment of previously held perceptions or prejudices. Indeed, Jews, both as communities and as individuals, successfully navigated economic and social relationships with Christians long before emancipation provided them the legal framework within which to do so, despite legal and frequently deeply ingrained cultural limitations placed on them.

Given the persistently ambivalent nature of Jewish-Christian relations, amply documented by the negative and hostile images generated about Jews by Christians in both elite and popular discourse, one might reasonably assume that a study of trust and mistrust would simply reaffirm assumptions that Christian antisemitism and reciprocal Jewish insularity are generally intractable and unyielding. Surprisingly, however, the studies in this volume tend to challenge such assumptions in complicated ways. The focus on the mechanics of trust destabilizes the sense that antisemitism, whether as an individual gut response or a more organized ideology, is generally all-encompassing and unchanging. Niklas Luhmann's observation that "trust can only be secured and maintained in the present" is useful here.[5] Trust, he argues, whether personal trust relationships or system-trust, is fundamentally contingent. Change—social, cultural, political, economic, emotional, etc.—can instantly transform distrust into trust or the reverse. On the contrary, while antisemitism (or anti-Judaism) has distinctive historical manifestations,[6] one of its defining qualities is a firm belief that Jews are, by definition, unchanging and unchangeable. As Stephanie Fischer's work aptly illustrates, trust relationships can, and at times must, exist even when that trust runs counter to ideology. Thus, while in no way denying or minimizing the extent and significance of antisemitism, the studies in this volume reveal a far more complex history of Jewish and Christian relations than a focused study of theology and ideology might suggest.

Just how normative or pervasive was the mutual mistrust between Jews and Christians in daily experience—that is, in the legal, social, and economic realms? Theologically, for Christians the Jew's purported character was not a product of contingent social or political circumstances, but was rooted in an essential or ontological irrationality and criminality that began with deicide and is renewed and reinforced continuously by the Jews' unwillingness to recognize the truth of Christianity. The essays in this volume explore the extent to which this theological idea and image of the perfidious Jew translated into the legal realm, and then into the everyday social, economic, and cultural realms of a particular society.

The reality of negative and hostile images of Jews found in elite and popular Christian sources should not and did not translate automatically into an assumption of mistrust on the part of Christians for Jews. Nor should we assume that Jews necessarily trusted one another simply out of a sense of religious or ethnic solidarity. As Trivellato has so persuasively argued, in the realm of national and transnational trade, "historians often presume rather than demonstrate that religion, ethnicity, and kinship provided the glue for cooperation in long-distance trade. . . . If trust is not a natural attribute of trading diasporas, then we need to examine what accounts for the development of cooperative business relations in different cases."[7] Thus, historians should interrogate the mechanics of trust and mistrust in everyday interactions between Jews and Christians (and, in a few cases, between Jews and other Jews).

Negotiations of trust play a role in all social relations, but a self-conscious awareness of the mechanics of trust finds expression less frequently. Organized thematically,[8] this volume includes studies that range in time from the biblical period to the twenty-first century and geographically from ancient Israel to India, and from continental Europe and Great Britain to North America. Contributors offer narratives about Jews and trust while also developing methodological and analytical frameworks that introduce readers to the general scholarship on trust.

"The principle of trust," as one contributor to this volume has observed, "constitutes the ethical ideal underlying the very possibility of civilization. Without it, collective existence is unthinkable."[9] Given such a broad, universal definition of the role of trust, one book of essays cannot hope to be comprehensive, even within particular temporal or spatial boundaries (i.e., national or religious histories). *On the Word of a Jew*, rather, brings together essays that range widely but are case histories, intended to be suggestive of a rich field of research that awaits further exploration.

The conscious efforts of Jewish elites from the Middle Ages into the twentieth century to maintain a degree of ritual, liturgical, and cultural cohesion among far-flung communities meant that members of Jewish communities functioned both as part of distinctive, insular communities and as participants in the dominant culture in which they lived.[10] Because oaths form the framework for legal institutions and contracts, an examination of how Jews participated in oath taking reveals mechanisms by which Jews at different times have balanced their efforts to preserve their standing in the community at large and in Jewish society.

Oaths simultaneously mitigate distrust and rely on a basic trust that the ritual of swearing, the solemn authority that supports the oath, and even the promised consequences of forsaking the oath will render the terms of the agreement reliable and true.

In the Bible, as Robert Kawashima shows, oaths are crucial in the making of covenants between God and humans, between individuals, and between different tribes or nations. Oaths remained of great import in postbiblical Judaism for the establishment of trust between Jews and Christians and between or among Jews themselves. Without doubt, Jews and Christians interacted on a daily basis, trading or exchanging goods and services with one another. At times this led to disagreements that could only be settled legally. In both the economic and legal spheres, trust matters. And trust and reliability had to be established between Jews and Christians when required. When a Jew had to testify in a Christian court, either as a defendant or as a witness, why would Christians believe what he or she said? Oaths, it seems, secured at least a temporary trust in the word of a Jew, even if some Christians maintained that even under oath, a Jew could not be trusted. As Thomas Kaufmann has recently written, Martin Luther, for example, mistrusted Jews—even those willing to be baptized—whether they were under oath or not.[11]

The first section of this volume, "To Swear an Oath," demonstrates that the need for an oath presumes both an absence of trust and the possibility of establishing trust. Exploring the history of the oath allows us to see the complex negotiations involved in creating and maintaining trust. At times, however, oaths could also be used to inhibit or prevent relationships forming between Jews and non-Jews. While Jewish authorities in rabbinic times had already devised ways to make the oath work against Jewish and non-Jewish relationships, particularly economic ones, Jews devised fascinating and unexpected ways to make oaths, including Christian oaths, work for them.

The Jewish oath, or the oath taken *more judaïco* (in the manner of the Jews), also made it possible for Jews to participate in Christian or secular legal systems. And in some cases, as in Angevin England until at least the last quarter of the thirteenth century, it seems that the oath of a Jew was, as Joshua Curk writes, "imbued with a level of gravitas not accorded to Christian oaths."[12] In certain times and places, the Jewish oath was clearly meant as insulting and derogatory; in others, such as early nineteenth-century France, the oath was put forth, at least by some in the judicial system, as a means by which Jewish religious rights could be protected. Moreover—and paradoxically, perhaps—the Jewish oath was deemed necessary in order to secure equality before the law, though most Jews, to be sure, did not see it this way. In the end, as Lisa Leff argues, the oath was instrumental in testing the principles of the republican French state and in confronting the judiciary with the contradiction between a special Jewish oath and the idea of civic and legal equality.

One might assume that in the premodern period, before the ideals of religious tolerance and civil equality took hold—albeit incrementally and in many places not irreversibly—the lines between Christians and Jews with regard to trust and how to establish it would be fairly clearly and rigidly drawn. However, as Ephraim Shoham-Steiner demonstrates, internal Jewish sources from the Middle Ages testify that in their attempt to earn the trust of non-Jewish business liaisons, Jews were swearing oaths by invoking the names of Christian saints. Developing between the eleventh and thirteenth centuries, this practice was intended to generate trust between Jewish and non-Jewish business associates in the medieval Franco-German mercantile setting. Jews swore oaths in the name of Christian saints despite the biblical injunction against invoking the names of foreign deities and despite the fear expressed in rabbinic commentaries that business relations between Jews and Christians would lead to just such mutual oath taking.

Thus, the subject of Jews and oaths reveals significant and at times surprising or unexpected aspects of Jewish and Christian relations from the Middle Ages into the nineteenth century. The topic of Jews and trust more generally reaches into the present, as historians and cultural critics continue to ask how trust is created and maintained, and what this process has to do with religion, race, gender, and other social factors.

The Mechanics of Trust

The growing body of scholarship on Jews and trust deals to a large extent with the world of trade and commerce, much of it focused on the Middle Ages and the early modern period. *On the Word of a Jew* broadens that focus, with essays on law, politics, intellectual life, and culture, even as it includes essays devoted to financial transactions. These categories, of course, are heuristic; in reality, they overlap, as the essays in section two, "The Business of Trust," demonstrate. Thus, an essay focused on trust and mistrust in the world of jurisprudence or politics will also include elements of the economic. For example, a dominant mode of central European Jewish political culture in the seventeenth and eighteenth centuries was intimately tied to matters of money and commerce. As Josh Teplitsky demonstrates, it is impossible to disentangle the informal but potent activities of the Court Jews on behalf of Jewish settlement, commercial rights, and collective security.

Two distinct forms of trust combined to produce this intersection of interests: a reliance by monarchs and princes on Jewish credit and services and the interdependence among Jewish agents. Neither community of trust was permanent, or free from challenge. In fact, each form of trust engendered its own subversion. Insofar as Jews were outsiders to the political system—not harboring ambitions for ennoblement or aggrandizement of territorial holdings—their position at court was nonthreatening, making them reliable agents in service of the sovereign; conversely, this outsider status cast aspersions on their loyalty and their complete identification with the needs of the state. At the same time, matters of trust and mistrust could become crucial elements in intra-Jewish struggles—in this case, between the Court Jews of central Europe—sometimes with dire consequences. Again, Jews did not always and necessarily trust or act reliably toward other Jews, just as Jews and Christians did not always and necessarily mistrust one another.

Trust between Jews and non-Jews in the world of trade and commerce was not limited to elites. In the century from the 1820s until the 1920s, one-third of world Jewry engaged in a great overseas migration, leaving Europe as well as the Ottoman Empire and parts of North Africa, and heading for lands—in North, South, and Central America, southern Africa, and the Antipodes—that had been opened up through European conquest and colonialism. All these places had no or few Jews already resident, and the participants in the great migration became the first Jews whom local people met.

Many, and in some places most, of the Jewish men arrived as peddlers, itinerant merchants who, by foot and then by animal-driven cart, went house to house, farm to farm, and to mining and logging camps selling consumer goods. They sold primarily to women who let the immigrant Jewish peddlers into their homes. The success of Jewish peddlers demanded a mutual trust, as Hasia Diner has demonstrated.[13] Jewish peddlers had to learn to trust their customers, and, equally, their Christian customers had to develop trust in these strange, foreign Jews who entered their domestic spaces.

A similar sort of trust through commerce was at work in the relationships between Jewish and Christian cattle dealers in early twentieth-century Germany. If the case of new-world Jewish peddlers shows us how informal, personal modes of trust were established between Jews and Christians, the world of German cattle dealing illuminates institution-based trust and explains how institutions produce social and economic trust in times of financial crisis. In truth, the concept of the "trustworthy businessman," a legal as well as social concept in interwar Germany, was a product of both formal and informal forces, shaped and interpreted by various actors, such as state agencies, business partners, and lobby groups. The trust between Jews and Christians in the world of German cattle dealing was in part institutionally based and in part the result of personal, informal relations. And the breakdown of this trust, a result of the economic crisis of the later Weimar years, was also the result of both formal and informal factors, including the effects of an organized antisemitic movement.

The third section of this book, "Intimacy of Trust," deals with the social and cultural dynamics of trust as a necessary component of personal intimacies across confessional lines. The first two essays explore this dynamic within the context of religious conversion, and the final essay considers the context of the philosophical category of friendship. Nina Caputo's essay offers a close reading of Petrus Alfonsi's work *Dialogi contra Iudaeos*, using this to examine the ways in which trust is established when religious conversion has opened up the possibility of profound mistrust. How is a reliable text produced? Alfonsi's case is particularly intriguing and evocative because the dialogue or disputation he constructs is between characters identified as his former Jewish self and his current Christian self. Again, what is the relationship between religion and reliability, and in this case, how is that relationship negotiated within or between the religious identities of a single individual? Rachel Furst's "Constructing Credibility" looks at issues of trust and mistrust, religion, and reliability in medieval Ashkenaz. Examining the status of legal testimony offered in a Jewish court by a Jewish convert to Christianity, Furst demonstrates how credibility functioned within the medieval Jewish community as a marker of personhood and citizenship. This study brings into focus ways in which medieval Jewish law and society shared some of these underlying assumptions with the majority Christian culture.

Trust between Jews and Christians could occur at the most personal levels, even between those who publicly evinced skepticism and even hostility toward the faith of the other. For instance, despite his well-documented remarks against Jews and Judaism, the German philosopher Immanuel Kant forged a significant philosophical and personal bond with his student and physician Marcus Herz. Their correspondence shows that Kant had the highest respect for Herz's intelligence and judgment, and turned to Herz for guidance and council, not merely in matters of philosophy, but with regard to his health and "care of self." Kant and Herz's relationship offers a striking example of the ways in which trust and intimacy, and limits and boundaries could be successfully navigated.

The final section of this book, "The Politics of Trust," deals with the role of trust in the construction of national identity and community. The essays in this section tease out themes that were implicit in earlier essays but that constitute central components of analyses of the nexus of trust and nationalism. What, for example, is the relationship between trust and honor? What role did religious identity and difference play in determining the status or designation of honorable or respectable, and thus reliable or trustworthy? Mitch Numark addresses these issues in his essay on the Bene Israel Jews in the East India Company's Bombay army during the eighteenth and nineteenth centuries. He shows that the Bene Israel Jews were at once loyal and brave sepoys (Indian soldiers) and trusted native officers. And he shows the ways in which nineteenth-century British Jews made use of the Bombay army's Bene Israel sepoys to counter arguments against the removal of Jewish disabilities, advance the cause of Jewish emancipation, and promote an image of Jews as trustworthy and brave soldiers who fight and sacrifice on Britain's behalf. Numark explores the question of Jews and trust within the context of British nationalism and analyzes the mechanisms by which Jews come to be trusted in what, in the nineteenth century, was still regarded as a Christian country or nation.

Derek Penslar, on the other hand, deals with matters of trust, reliability, and honor within the context of Jewish nationalism. Penslar explores Theodor Herzl's turn to Zionism in 1895 and his ongoing life project to attain both honor and authenticity, two overlapping yet distinct and at times contradictory affective states. Herzl's yearnings to achieve them and attempts to reconcile the tensions between them are manifest in his writings over the course of his lifetime.

Penslar's essay contributes to the examination of the concepts of trust and keeping one's word, concepts that are associated with the bases for stable interpersonal relations, which assume a reliability of performance and exchange. Socioeconomic obligations are often undergirded by more than mere instrumentality; they depend on an individual's sense of honor, a conviction that self-worth depends on following a certain code of behavior even when it is not convenient or personally beneficial to do so. Honor is often associated with honesty, but codes of honor can demand reticence, silence, and even outright dissemblance as long as such behavior is altruistic, not self-serving. Honor, therefore, can preclude authenticity.

Authenticity, of course, can be a difficult quality to determine, particularly in the realm of public figures. This might be especially true in the world of entertainment, where performing one's "self" would appear to be a sine qua non of one's profession. How, then, did a Jewish entertainer, a comedian, come to be "the most trusted man in America" in the early twenty-first century? In the volume's final essay, Shaina Hammerman explores a shifting sense of contemporary American national identity in her analysis of the former host of *The Daily Show*, Jon Stewart. What is the significance of Americans' public trust in a Jew? Hammerman builds on previous studies in the social and political sciences that demonstrate the high trust level many Americans, particularly young Americans, placed in Jon Stewart as the deliverer of news and opinion—this despite or because of Stewart's role as the bringer of fake news. This trust, in turn, appears to have had very real consequences for American political life. Stewart, she shows us, was trusted not despite of his Jewishness, but because of it. And this was part of a more complex strategy employed by Stewart that relied not only on satire and paradox but also on Stewart's persona as culturally and politically marginal and powerless.

Trust and Identity

In concluding with Jon Stewart, a case study that illustrates how Jewishness, or the performance of Jewishness, can serve to produce rather than impede trust and reliability, we do not wish to suggest a teleological arc when it comes to Jews and trust. The Jewish sepoys were trusted by the British Raj as soldiers in part because of and not despite the fact that they were Jews. Nonetheless, the essays in this volume raise fundamental questions with regard to the relationship between religious differences and trust, and the impact of large historical transformations over time on this relationship. The German historian Petra Schulte notes that "in relation to the intellectual history of the concept *fides*, the idea of trust during the entire medieval period was tightly bound up with the concept of Christian faith."[14] If a working idea of trust and trustworthiness was inextricably bound up with the Christian faith, what impact did secularization, in its many forms, have on Jewish and Christian trust? Or perhaps this is a misplaced question, since it may suggest that as we move from the medieval to the early modern and then into the modern era we can see a development from mistrust to trust. Yet we hope that the essays in this volume amply demonstrate that trust between Jews and Christians was hardly something recent or the inevitable and unique result of modernity.

At the same time, it is undeniable that at some point the notion of the perfidious Jew began to diminish and eventually even disappear, at least in the public sphere, so that the Jew could now be trusted, or be as trusted as anyone else, without the need for qualifiers such as the Jewry oath. Was it Jewishness itself that was no longer understood as an impediment to trustworthiness, though of course other nonreligious or nonethnic factors were also at play? Did the understanding of Jewish nature change, or did political and social systems as a whole undergo a fundamental transformation so that the mechanisms involved in the production of trust changed? More pointedly, did the retreat of religion—that is, Christianity—into the realm of the personal and private mean that religious difference—that is, Judaism—no longer mattered in the ways it had before?

It is not that the nature or character of the Jew had to change; rather, it is that in some places and at some point, it was character itself that ceased to matter—or at least ceased to matter in the same way as it had in the past. It was replaced, as the American historian Warren Susman argued, by the idea of personality.[15] The nature of the Jew also ceased to matter, at least for most people, because the nature of trust changed. Modernity, as Anthony Giddens and others have argued, is defined in large part by the emergence of disembedded mechanisms and expert systems, which in turn depend on trust. This means, as Giddens writes, that "trust here is vested, not in individuals, but in abstract capacities. . . . Expert systems are disembedding mechanisms because . . . they remove social relations from the immediacies of context."[16] One might argue that Giddens draws too rigid a distinction between modern and premodern modes of establishing trust. However, this does not mean that valid distinctions cannot or should not be drawn or that important developments over the centuries cannot be identified.

In the context of our discussion, one could argue that modernity—wherever and whenever that took hold—makes the character of the Jew insignificant because it makes religion, as well as ethnicity, and by now perhaps even race and gender—increasingly insignificant when it comes to establishing or maintaining notions of trust and truth in the public sphere. Today, if we find some conjunction of Jews and trust in the public realm, it is more likely to be that people will trust a Jew to do certain tasks—think doctor, lawyer, or financial investor, such as Bernie Madoff—precisely because he or she is Jewish, although in the case of medicine, according to David Ruderman, this has been true since the Middle Ages.[17] Does this trust in a Jew now signal a large-scale belief in some historical transformation in the character of the Jew?

Again, we would argue that it is more likely that such issues of character have simply ceased to matter for most people, at least when it comes to Jewishness. Granted, this may still be too linear and teleological a narrative to serve as anything but a starting point of discussion and debate.

Notes

1. A few words about the contested categories used in this and the other essays: We understand that the category "religion" is reductionist and fails to capture the complex nature and role of laws, rituals, beliefs, and practices traditionally identified as religious. We also understand that categories such as race and gender are now commonly understood to be social constructs rather than natural biological givens. As these terms appear in this volume, they reflect historical sensibilities rather than those of the essays' authors.

2. Salo Baron, *Social and Religious History of the Jews*, vol. 11 (New York: Columbia, 1967), 107.

3. Francesca Trivellato, "Sephardic Merchants in the Early Modern Atlantic and Beyond: Toward a Comparative Historical Approach to Business Cooperation," in *Atlantic Diasporas: Jews, Conversos, and Crypto-Jews in the Age of Mercantilism, 1500–1800*, ed. Richard L. Kagan and Philip D. Morgan (Baltimore: Johns Hopkins University Press, 2008), 107.

4. The scholarly literature on this topic is indeed substantial. Recent standard works include Pierre Birnbaum and Ira Katznelson, eds., *Paths of Emancipation: Jews, States, and Citizenship* (Princeton, NJ: Princeton University Press, 1995); Paula Hyman, *Gender and Assimilation in Modern Jewish History: The Roles and Representation of Women* (Seattle: University of Washington Press, 1995); David Sorkin, *The Transformation of German Jewry, 1780–1840* (New York: Oxford University Press, 1987); and Todd Endelman, *The Jews of Georgian England, 1740–1830* (Philadelphia: Jewish Publication Society of America, 1979).

5. Niklas Luhmann, *Trust and Power*, trans. Christian Morgner and Michael King, English edition (Cambridge: Polity Press, 2017), 15.

6. It goes without saying that modern racial antisemitism and theologically based demonization of Jews are not identical. For the purpose of this discussion, however, it will suffice to merge them into one category, since both identify Jews as posing a danger to human society by their very nature.

7. Trivellato, "Sephardic Merchants," 100–101. On the need for greater skepticism about the trust members of the same faith group "naturally" have for one another, see also Richard

Sosis, "Does Religion Promote Trust? The Role of Signaling, Reputation, and Punishment," *Interdisciplinary Journal of Research on Religion* 1 (2005): 1–30.

8. The essays in *On the Word of a Jew* address a question that is only now beginning to preoccupy scholars of Jews and Judaism working in English. While a large literature in sociology, anthropology, business studies, political science, and history exists on the nature and importance of trust generally, Jewish studies scholars are only beginning to explore this topic. Sarah Stein, in her work *Plumes: Ostrich Feathers, Jews, and a Lost World of Global Commerce* (New Haven: Yale University Press, 2010), notes the significance of trust, "bonds of subethnicity," and reputation for understanding Jewish trading networks; so, too, does Gideon Reuveni in the introduction to the volume he coedited on Jews and the economy ("Prolegomena to an 'Economic Turn' in Jewish History," in *The Economy in Jewish History: New Perspectives on the Interrelationship Between Ethnicity and Economic Life*, ed. Gideon Reuveni and Sarah Wobick, 1–22 [New York: Berghahn, 2010]). However, these are only passing references, not in-depth explorations. Francesca Trivellato's *The Familiarity of Strangers: The Sephardic Diaspora, Livorno, and Cross-Cultural Trade in the Early Modern Period* (New Haven: Yale University Press, 2009) is one of the few full-scale works in Jewish history that posits trust as essential—in this case, as a component in the building of early modern Sephardic economic and trading networks—and explores this theme in full. David De Vries's *Diamonds and War: State, Capital, and Labor in British-Ruled Palestine* (New York: Berghahn, 2010) also pays attention to the role of trust in the history of Jewish involvement in the diamond trade, focusing on the social and political history of the industry in Palestine.

9. Robert Kawashima, seminar paper delivered at the University of Oxford, November 2013.

10. For a sustained discussion of these dynamics in modern eastern Europe, see Richard E. Cohen, Jonathan Frankel, and Stefani Hoffman, eds., *Insiders and Outsiders: Dilemmas of East European Jewry* (Oxford, UK: Littman, 2010).

11. Thomas Kaufmann, *Luther's Jews: A Journey into Anti-Semitism*, trans. Lesley Sharpe and Jeremy Noakes (Oxford: Oxford University Press, 2017), 36–37.

12. See the discussion of Jewish oaths in medieval England in chapter 3 of the current volume.

13. In addition to the essay here, see Hasia Diner, *Roads Taken: The Great Jewish Migrations to the New World and the Peddlers Who Forged the Way* (New Haven: Yale University Press, 2015).

14. Petra Schulte, "Einleitung," in *Strategies of Writing: Studies on Text and Trust in the Middle Ages* (Turnhout, Belgium: Brepois, 2008), 3.

15. Warren I. Susman, "'Personality' and the Making of Twentieth-Century Culture," in *New Directions in American Intellectual History*, ed. John Higham and Paul K. Conkin (Baltimore: Johns Hopkins University Press, 1979), 212–26.

16. Anthony Giddens, *The Consequences of Modernity* (Stanford: Stanford University Press, 1990), 26.

17. David Ruderman, *Jewish Thought and Scientific Discovery in Early Modern Europe* (New Haven, CT: Yale University Press, 1995). Trusting a Jew in a particular setting with a particular occupation such as medicine, even in contemporary times, does not necessarily mean an absence of hostility toward Jews as a group. For an anecdotal example of this, see Anatole Broyard, "Doctor Talk to Me," *New York Times Magazine* (August 26, 1990).

Bibliography

Baron, Salo. *Social and Religious History of the Jews*. Vol. 11. New York: Columbia, 1967.
Birnbaum, Pierre, and Ira Katznelson, eds. *Paths of Emancipation: Jews, States, and Citizenship*. Princeton: Princeton University Press, 1995.
Broyard, Anatole. "Doctor Talk to Me." *The New York Times Magazine* (August 26, 1990). https://www.nytimes.com/1990/08/26/magazine/doctor-talk-to-me.html.
Cohen, Richard E., Jonathan Frankel, and Stefani Hoffman, eds. *Insiders and Outsiders: Dilemmas of East European Jewry*. Oxford: Littman, 2010.
De Vries, David. *Diamonds and War: State, Capital, and Labor in British-Ruled Palestine*. New York: Berghahn, 2010.
Diner, Hasia. *Roads Taken: The Great Jewish Migrations to the New World and the Peddlers Who Forged the Way*. New Haven: Yale University Press, 2015.
Endelman, Todd. *The Jews of Georgian England, 1714–1830*. Philadelphia: Jewish Publication Society of America, 1979.
Giddens, Anthony. *The Consequences of Modernity*. Stanford: Stanford University Press, 1990.
Hyman, Paula. *Gender and Assimilation in Modern Jewish History: The Roles and Representation of Women*. Seattle: University of Washington Press, 1995.
Kaufmann, Thomas. *Luther's Jews: A Journey into Anti-Semitism*. Translated by Lesley Sharpe and Jeremy Noakes. Oxford: Oxford University Press, 2017.
Luhmann, Niklas. *Trust and Power*. Translated by Christian Morgner and Michael King. Cambridge: Polity Press, 2017.
Reuveni, Gideon. "Prolegomena to an 'Economic Turn' in Jewish History." In *The Economy in Jewish History: New Perspectives on the Interrelationship Between Ethnicity and Economic Life*, edited by Gideon Reuveni and Sarah Wobick, 1–22. New York: Berghahn, 2010.
Ruderman, David. *Jewish Thought and Scientific Discovery in Early Modern Europe*. New Haven, CT: Yale University Press, 1995.
Schulte, Petra. "Einleitung." In *Strategies of Writing: Studies on Text and Trust in the Middle Ages*, edited by M. Mostert, D. I. V. Renswoude, and Petra Schulte, 1–12. Turnhout, Belgium: Brepois, 2008.
Sorkin, David. *The Transformation of German Jewry, 1780–1840*. New York: Oxford University Press, 1987.
Sosis, Richard. "Does Religion Promote Trust? The Role of Signaling, Reputation, and Punishment." *Interdisciplinary Journal of Research on Religion* 1 (2005): 1–30.
Stein, Sarah. *Plumes: Ostrich Feathers, Jews, and a Lost World of Global Commerce*. New Haven: Yale University Press, 2010.
Susman, Warren I. "'Personality' and the Making of Twentieth-Century Culture." In *New Directions in American Intellectual History*, edited by John Higham and Paul K. Conkin, 212–26. Baltimore: Johns Hopkins University Press, 1979.
Trivellato, Francesca. *The Familiarity of Strangers: The Sephardic Diaspora, Livorno, and Cross-Cultural Trade in the Early Modern Period*. New Haven: Yale University Press, 2009.
———. "Sephardic Merchants in the Early Modern Atlantic and Beyond: Toward a Comparative Historical Approach to Business Cooperation." In *Atlantic Diasporas: Jews, Conversos, and Crypto-Jews in the Age of Mercantilism, 1500–1800*, edited by Richard L. Kagan and Philip D. Morgan, 99–120. Baltimore: Johns Hopkins University Press, 2008.

NINA CAPUTO, Associate Professor in the Department of History at the University of Florida, is a scholar of medieval Jewish history and interfaith relations in medieval Europe. She is author of *Nahmanides in Medieval Catalonia: History, Community, Messianism* and *Debating Truth: The Barcelona Disputation of 1263, a Graphic History* (illustrated by Liz Clarke), and editor (with Andrea Sterk) of *Faithful Narratives: Historians, Religion, and the Challenge of Objectivity.*

MITCHELL B. HART is Professor of History and the Alexander Grass Chair in Jewish History at the University of Florida. He is editor (with Tony Michels) of *The Cambridge History of Modern Judaism, Volume 8: The Modern Period, 1815–2000.*

Section One
To Swear an Oath

1 Oaths, Vows, and Trust in the Bible

Robert S. Kawashima

WHAT DOES THE Bible have to say about oaths, vows, trust, and other related ideas and practices? As I pondered this question, it occurred to me that trust—trust in the speech of the Other—is the primitive notion, the basic or elementary concept, from which the others derive. Oaths and vows, that is, are derived notions in that they are ritual-linguistic technologies designed to instill and bolster a sense of trust in the Other's spoken word. And yet, for this very reason, they arise from and thus betray a certain lack of trust. One takes an oath or makes a vow only because without it, it is feared, one is less likely to keep one's word. Likewise, the giving of testimony is often accompanied by various rituals that are meant to reassure the intended audience of said testimony that the witness will not lie. The US legal system, for example, requires witnesses in its nominally secular courts of law to "swear," hand on Bible, "to tell," with God's help, "the truth, the whole truth, and nothing but the truth." In other words, a vestigial invocation of the deity, who apparently presides over truth telling, still constitutes a necessary component of the felicitous ritual oath, which is required to validate legally admissible testimony—all proceeding from a lack of trust.

According to this logic, the fullest demonstration of one's trustworthiness consists of keeping one's word without taking an oath—that is, without formally and explicitly invoking the threat of legal and/or divine sanctions. That Jewish apocalyptic figure known as Jesus of Nazareth, at least according to Matthew's Gospel, seemed to have some such ideal in mind when he admonished his audience, in the Sermon on the Mount, not to "swear" (*omosai*) but to simply say "yes" or "no" (5:33–37). In other words, all of one's declarations should be uniformly worthy of trust. Extracting from these preliminary remarks a general principle that will shape the analysis to follow, I would say that the conventions and institutions surrounding oaths and vows are attempts to translate the ideal of trust into forms better suited to the "real" world—a world, that is, in which mere mortals often prove to be unworthy of trust.

Oaths, vows, and trust thus all concern the proper use of language: namely, truth telling. It would behoove us, then, to consider how biblical tradition conceives of language as such. If the Bible does not offer us any actual expositions on the nature and function of language, it is worth noting the significance wisdom literature imputes to deceptive speech. To take one famous example, of seven things said to be "abominations" (*toʿavot*) to Yahweh, three have to do with language: a "lying [*shaqer*] tongue," a "false [*shaqer*] witness," and one who "sows discord among brothers," presumably through incendiary speech (Prov. 6:16–19; cf. Eccl. 5:3–5).[1] The story of the Tower of Babel (Gen. 11:1–9) provides us with a glimpse into something approximating the biblical view of language: language is that which makes collective existence possible. According to this etiology of the nations of the world, the human race originally spoke a "single language" (*safah ʾaḥat*). And thanks to this linguistic unity, to the originally universal dictionary of "singular words" (*devarim ʾaḥadim*), the human species originally constituted a "single people" (*ʿam ʾeḥad*) and was thus disturbingly powerful, powerful enough to attract the attention of God and his divine council: "Look, they are a single people, and they all have a single language; and this is only the beginning of what they will do, and nothing they devise to do will be impossible for them. Come, let us go down and there confuse their language, so that they will not understand one another" (11:6–7).[2] By "confusing" their single ur-language, that is, by shattering it into a plurality of distinct languages, Yahweh shattered the human family into a plurality of distinct nations, each united by its distinct language, each divided from the others by its distinct language—it being understood that national and linguistic boundaries naturally coincide. The "Table of Nations" in Genesis 10 seems to be premised on the same underlying idea, for it too presupposes the perfect coincidence between ethnic, linguistic, territorial, and national boundaries "by their families, their languages, their lands, their nations" (10:20, 31; see also 10:5). Given such a view of language, the individual whose word cannot be trusted—who breaks his oaths, perjures himself, and so forth—would necessarily isolate himself from the family of man, for his lying tongue would be just as confusing as truth spoken in a foreign language.

In fact, this biblical view of language derives from a very old tradition in the ancient Near East. Thus, in the Sumerian epic "Enmerkar and the Lord of Aratta," dating from the early second millennium BCE, the "spell of Nudimmud" evokes a time when "there will be no snake, no scorpion, . . . / And thus there will be neither fear nor trembling, / For man will then have no enemy. . . . / Yea, the whole world of well-ruled people, / Will be able to speak to Enlil in one language! . . . / For on that day, . . . / Shall Enki, for the debates between lords and princes and kings . . . . / Change the tongues in their mouth, as many as he once placed there, / And the speech of mankind shall be truly one!" (134–55).[3] Whether this passage is construed in the future tense, as Herman Vanstiphout does here, or in the past tense, as Thorkild Jacobsen does in his translation,[4] linguistic diversity is seen to weaken humankind. The fragmentation of language divides the human species into rival factions—hence the "debates" between political leaders. It is no coincidence that the diversity of animal species is linked in this passage to the diversity of human languages: just as the existence of "enemy" animal species keeps humanity in cosmic check by making postlapsarian nature a hostile environment—reminiscent of the "enmity" between the serpent and Eve, between its seed and her seed (Gen. 3:15)—so too the rivalry between nations diminishes humanity's cosmic stature by turning it against itself as its own worst enemy. Given such a view of language, the individual whose word cannot be trusted—who breaks his oaths, perjures himself, and so forth—would necessarily isolate himself from the family of man, for his lying tongue would set him up as an enemy of all other speaking beings, an interlocutor with whom all conversation would be as futile and meaningless as those "debates" endlessly taking place between the princes of this world. In other words, trust can only be sustained when people tell the truth. Without trustworthy speech, collective civilized life is simply impossible.

Ancient Greek tradition ascribes a similar importance to the oath. According to Hesiod, for example, Horkos, or Oath—that supernatural being who punishes those who dare to break their oaths—is one of the most ancient cosmic entities. In the *Theogony*, Hesiod identifies Oath as the offspring of Eris, or Strife (231), and in *Works and Days*, he maintains that the Erinyes, or Furies, assisted at Oath's birth (804).[5] In other words, Oath—and thus the underlying principle of trust—constitutes one of the primal cosmic forces, whose lineage is independent from and parallel to that of the gods—namely, that line of descent running from Heaven and Earth to the Titans (Kronos et al.) to the Olympians (Zeus and his cohort). What this means is that the antiquity and therefore authority of these primal cosmic forces rivals that of the gods themselves. Indeed, Zeus's regime, according to Hesiod once again, is founded in part on the river Styx, whom Zeus honors by making her the "great oath [*horkon*] of the gods" (*Theog* 399–400). Specifically, any Olympian god who "swears false" (*epiorkon*) on the waters of this primordial river suffers, in effect, a type of temporary bodily death:[6] "He lies without breathing for a full year, and never lays hands on ambrosia and nectar by way of food, but lies breathless and voiceless on his bed, wrapped in a malignant coma" (793, 795-98)—muteness being a fitting punishment for one who has abused the gift of speech. And even after he recovers from this coma, he is excluded from the company of the gods for nine years, a kind of temporary social death said to be even more onerous than the coma (801–3)—ostracism being a fitting punishment for one who has betrayed collective life with the corrosive effects of falsehood. The Olympian order, in other words, is founded, at least in part, on trust and true speech, on Zeus's ability to banish perjury from his realm.

Trust is also related to that cornerstone of civilization known as hospitality. For hospitality is none other than a discursive, even if unspoken, act of trust. To invite a stranger into one's home, or conversely, to accept an invitation to enter a stranger's home, is already, in effect, to give one's word to do no harm to the

Other. Insofar as this agreement could remain tacit, hospitality might even be said to epitomize the principle of trust—even if, as Émile Benveniste has pointed out, the bond between guest and host, at least in Homer's world, could be formalized in a solemn pact.[7] It is for this reason, I maintain, that hospitality is endowed with such an exalted ethical value in antiquity. It is surely no coincidence that, according to ancient Greek tradition, Zeus not only honors truth telling (the Styx), but also presides over the guest-host relationship. Conversely, the barbarism of the Cyclops consists, in large part, of his betrayal of this relationship—his attempt to devour Odysseus and his companions, who have entered his cave (*Odyssey* 9). Similarly in biblical tradition, the abomination of Sodom (Genesis 19)—that monitory example of wicked behavior—consists not, as is often thought, of some supposed sexual perversion, but rather, as Robert Alter (among others) has noted, the violation of the principle of hospitality (cf. Ezek. 16:49–50)—namely, the Sodomites' attempt to rape the men who have entered their city's gates.[8]

True hospitality, one should further note, is extended to a stranger as a stranger. In his philological analysis of *philos*—generally translated in relation to the semantic field of "friendship" and "love"—Benveniste argues that in ancient Indo-European societies, the concept of friendship was in fact "inseparable from a lively awareness of group and class membership," which is to say that it was "strongly permeated by values which are not personal but relational."[9] The key to understanding *philos*, he claims, is the connection in Homeric phraseology between *philos* (friend) and *xenos* (guest-stranger): "The notion of *phílos* expresses the behavior incumbent on a member of the community towards a *xénos*, the 'guest-stranger.'"[10] Friendship, in other words, amounts to the extension of kinship to those who are not kin. It is thus closely related to hospitality, which Jean-Claude Milner, distilling Benveniste's analysis of *philos*, succinctly defines as "treating as one's own he who is not, that is to say, affirming that he is a member of the same social group, precisely because he is not one, such is the strict relation of hospitality."[11] The same logic, I will argue, structures these values in biblical tradition as well.

Hospitality is thus a form of generosity, a form that is generous precisely because it is not technically owed. "In order to understand [the guest-host relationship] clearly," Benveniste explains, "we must envisage the situation of a *xénos*, of a 'guest,' who is visiting a country where, as a stranger, he is deprived of all rights, of all protection, of all means of existence."[12] In this regard, one should recall that the Greek term *xenia*, hospitality, is cognate with *xenos*, stranger, just as Zeus's epithet Xenios designates him as the protector of strangers—such as were Odysseus and his companions as they stood in supplication before the Cyclops. Conversely, it follows that to receive one's familiars or intimates—family members, for example, or friends, or comrades of one sort or another—is, in an important sense, merely to fulfill certain personal and even institutional obligations. To extend this principle back to the related concept of trust, the fullest expression of one's trustworthiness, the purest demonstration of the integrity of one's word, can only be offered to a stranger. In an important sense, then, one does not exactly "keep" one's "word" to one's parents, to take an obvious example. Rather, at least in biblical parlance, one merely "obeys" or "honors" them (see, e.g., Exod. 20:12; Deut. 21:18–21).

Oaths in the Bible

Having laid out this conceptual framework, let us turn to the form of oaths in the Bible.[13] The oath must first be defined in opposition to the simple declaration of one's intent to perform some act. Specifically, the oath is a speech-act, which as such has an illocutionary force above and beyond the declaration's merely locutionary sense. Linguistically speaking, Joab's warning to David provides us with what I take to be the paradigmatic form of the oath as such: "And now, arise, go out, and speak reassuringly to your servants. For I swear by Yahweh [*byhwh nishba'ti*] that if you do not go out, not a man will stay with you this night" (2 Sam. 19:8). God similarly declares, in response to Abraham's willingness to sacrifice his son Isaac, "By myself I swear [*bi nishba'ti*], says Yahweh, because you have done this thing and have not withheld your son, your only son, I will indeed bless you" (Gen. 22:16). The Hebrew perfect tense, which usually functions as a past tense, is best translated here with the English present tense, because it functions as a speech-act. There are in biblical Hebrew other present-tense forms—namely, the predicative participle and the imperfect tense—but these have a durative or progressive verbal aspect, whereas speech-acts, which are completed at the moment of speech, require the punctive or perfective aspect of the perfect tense. By the same logic, speech-acts in English require the simple present rather than the present progressive. For example, the officiant at a wedding says, "I now pronounce" rather than "I am now pronouncing"; the latter would be an infelicitous speech-act. To return to the Bible, it is in relation to the full form "I swear by Yahweh" that abbreviated oath forms should be parsed as grammatical "gapping." Thus, Saul's rash oath—"For by the life of Yahweh [*ḥay yhwh*], who saves Israel, even if it [the sin] is in my own son Jonathan, he will surely die" (1 Sam. 14:39)—presupposes the underlying speech-act "I swear."

One must also distinguish between the oath and the simple declaration in terms of the opposition of sacred to profane. The oath, by virtue of invoking the deity by name—or at least a human figure seen to represent the divine, as when Joseph swears "by the life [*ḥay*] of Pharaoh" (Gen. 42:15; see also 2 Sam. 15:21)—constitutes a sacred act of speech. Invoking the sacred simultaneously presupposes a curse—sometimes explicit, sometimes implicit—that is called down on the subject in the event that he breaks his oath. It's no coincidence, then, that Hebrew ʾ*alah* can mean either "oath" or "curse." To break such a speech-act pronounced in the name of God is a grave sin, one famously prohibited by the Ten Commandments: "Do not lift up [*tissaʾ*] the name of Yahweh your God for naught [*lashawʾ*]. For Yahweh will not acquit [*yenaqqeh*] one who lifts up his name for naught" (Exod. 20:7; Deut. 5:11). To "swear falsely" [*nishbaʿ lashaqer*] in God's name, the Priestly source explains in this regard, would be to "profane" (*ḥillel*) it (Lev. 19:12).[14]

The gravity of this sin becomes clear in the story of Jephthah's daughter in Judges 11. Jephthah makes a desperate and foolish vow (*neder*) to God on the eve of battle to the effect that, if he should defeat the Ammonites, he will offer up as a whole burnt offering whatever comes out of the door of his house upon his triumphant return. Tragically, it is none other than his daughter who comes out to greet him as he approaches his home. And yet, rather than break his vow, he chooses to perform this abominable sacrifice. As his unnamed daughter bravely exclaims: "My father, you have opened your mouth to Yahweh; do to me according to what has gone forth from your mouth [*yaẓaʾ mippikha*]" (Judg. 11:36). Saul faces a similar dilemma after foolishly placing his men, in the heat of battle, under an oath (*vayyoʾel*), cursing (*ʾarur*) "the man who eats food, until it is evening and I am avenged upon my enemies" (1 Sam. 14:24). Jonathan, his son, who is unaware of this oath-curse, unwittingly breaks it. When God's oracular silence makes it clear to Saul that someone has transgressed his solemn pronouncement and must be punished, he lays an oath on himself to execute the perpetrator, even if it is his own son (1 Sam 14:39). Once again, so sacred is the act of invoking God's name that it is only thanks to the intervention of the soldiers that Jonathan is "ransomed" (*vayyifdu*) from death (14:45). But partly as a result of breaking his oath, this story seems to imply, Saul will eventually lose the throne and his life.

In general, the breaking of an oath, insofar as it constitutes a transgression against the deity as opposed to a man, did not fall to human justice, but was instead relegated to a "danger belief," namely, the belief that the invisible hand of divine justice would punish such infractions against the sacred order.[15] Relevant here is that form of divine sanction referred to in biblical Hebrew as "bearing guilt" (*noseʾ ʿavon*), meaning the guilty party would die suddenly as the result of what we would now call an act of God. Consider Numbers 30, which lays out certain special provisions that apply to vows made by females to Yahweh.[16] Vows made by males, the law first establishes, must simply be fulfilled: "A man, when he makes a vow to Yahweh . . . shall not break his word. According to all that comes out of his mouth [*hayyoẓeʾ mippiv*] he shall do" (30:3; cf. Judg. 11:36). Vows made by girls and women, however, are subject to a type of preemptive power, which is invested in the female's father and, later, in her husband. While the father's veto power applies only to those vows his daughter makes while living in his house, the husband's power extends over her entire life, even over those vows she made "in her youth," while yet living in her father's house (Num. 30:4).

If the husband chooses to exercise this power immediately upon hearing of an oath, it is "annulled" (*hefer*) and God "forgives" (*yislaḥ*) her (30:9, 13). However, if he annuls it some time after hearing of it, "he will bear her guilt [*venasa' 'et-'avonah*]" (30:16). In other words, any man, woman, or child who breaks an oath is thought to be courting divine retribution, for the oath constituted a type of "fetter" (*'issar*) that "bound" (*'asar*) the speaking being to the numinous power of the deity whose name she or he dared to invoke (30:3, 4, 14). The one exception was an oath made by a daughter or wife, and subsequently vetoed by her father or husband, within a certain window of opportunity: in this case, there would be no adverse consequences. But if she were forced to break an oath by her husband outside of that grace period, he would "bear her guilt."

If broken oaths were God's concern and therefore left to divine justice, other crimes were relegated to danger beliefs, not because they were thought to fall outside of the realm of human justice, but because it was understood that human justice cannot reasonably be expected to mete out punishment in the absence of suitable evidence for identifying and convicting the perpetrator. In such cases, however, the mere possibility of pollution caused by the hypothetical crime still needed to be dealt with—see, for example, the ritual described in Deut. 21:1–9—and the all-seeing eye of God was ideally suited for prosecuting such undetected offenses. This would seem to be the function of the "Sotah Ritual" for the suspected adulteress described in Numbers 5.[17] Adultery, according to biblical law, was in fact a capital offense, but only when supported by incontrovertible evidence—ideally, being caught in flagrante delicto (Deut. 22:22), although other forms of evidence could apparently suffice, as the story of Judah and Tamar in Genesis 38 suggests. If a husband lacked such clear-cut evidence but nonetheless suspected that his wife had committed adultery, he could—and was perhaps even obliged to—bring his wife before the priest, who would force her to "swear" (*vehishbia'*) that she was innocent, as well as to drink "the bitter [*hammarim*] water that brings the curse [*ham'ararim*]" (Num. 5:19, 24). Not only did the woman swear her innocence in the name of Yahweh, but the curse itself, which invoked the name of God, was written onto a scroll and "washed" into the magic potion she was compelled to imbibe (5:23), thus potentially subjecting her to a twofold profanation of the sacred name. There were two possible outcomes: if she was guilty, she would suffer a certain physical malady as a "curse" (*'alah*) among her people (5:27); if she was innocent, she would "be acquitted" (*veniqqetah*) of this curse and eventually conceive a child (5:28). By design, then, the verdict might not be known for a number of years. In other words, this ritual was not designed to provide a jealous, vindictive husband with immediate satisfaction. Rather, it constituted a ritual ordeal, a merely symbolic ritual that subjected the suspected adulteress to the ordeal of facing the threat of divine sanction. The nebulous, unproven crime was effectively transmogrified into a concrete broken oath, for which sin the guilty wife should expect to "bear [*tissaʾ*] her guilt" (5:31). As a Priestly rite, it was probably meant first and foremost to deal with the potential pollution caused by a possible case of adultery, for which reason the law declares the man, in opposition to his wife, to be "acquitted [*veniqqah*] of guilt" (5:31). But it was also meant to assuage, or provide an outlet for, the husband's "spirit of jealousy" (5:14). In the absence of evidence proving the wife's guilt (5:13), the ritual assured both the husband and the priest that God would ultimately judge the case.

If the sanctity of God's name constituted, technically speaking, the primary victim of the broken oath, this did not mean that the human victim of this crime might not prosecute his own case against the perpetrator—although this strictly human dimension of the crime is not well attested in the Bible. In this regard, Genesis 21 comes to mind. Here, Abimelech, king of Gerar, proposes to Abraham that they enter into a covenant of mutual nonaggression. Abraham, just as he is about to "swear" (*nishbaʿ*) to do no harm to Abimelech, complains about the fact that some of the latter's servants have wrongly seized a well that he himself had dug (21:25)—that well that would eventually come to be known as *Beʾer Shevaʿ*, the "Well of Seven" and/or "Well of Swearing," or so this etiological tale would have us believe (21:30–31). To protect himself against future encroachments on his water rights, Abraham presents the king with seven (*shevaʿ*) ewe lambs, a gift that effectively adds a subclause to their "covenant" (*berit*), by making the king a "witness" (*ʿedah*) to the fact that the well in question does indeed belong to Abraham (Gen. 21:22–32). The logic of this story indicates that, should another dispute later arise over this well, Abraham would be able to appeal directly to Abimelech for justice out of respect for their covenant—quite apart from the punishment an offended deity might impose.

It is important to note that the covenant itself is a form of oath.[18] Thus, a *berit* is sometimes also referred to in terms of its founding "oath" (*ʾalah*) (e.g., Gen. 26:28 and Deut. 29:11), and at other times it is said to be sealed with "sworn" (*nishbaʿ*) oaths (e.g., Gen. 21:22–27). However, whereas the oaths and vows discussed thus far generally stipulate the performance of a one-time act (e.g., Jephthah sacrificing his daughter) or vouch for the veracity of a particular declaration (e.g., a wife being innocent of adultery) the covenant establishes a permanent relationship between parties. As a result, whatever stipulations it entails—its laws, judgments, or commandments—constitute ongoing obligations. This relationship was generally conceived of metaphorically in terms of kinship—hence the so-called loving-kindness or *ḥesed* enjoined on these two parties with respect to each other.[19] It is for this reason that the Davidic messiah, or anointed one, to take one particularly famous example, is declared by God to be his son, according to Ps. 2:7. This being the case, however, the covenant, ironically, represents a diminishment of the principle of pure trust. It is not just that the covenant, like all oaths, proceeds from a constitutive lack of trust. It is also that the much-vaunted idea of *ḥesed* is, in an important sense, the inverse image of that ideal of trust realized in the pure of act of hospitality. For hospitality, one recalls, is an act of generosity extended to a stranger as a stranger, whereas the covenant effectively makes kinship a precondition of *ḥesed*.

I have spoken thus far of oaths and vows as if they were the same thing.[20] In fact, there is an important distinction to be made. The oath is generally attached to a declaration whose veracity it is meant to ensure by invoking God; in this way, it seeks to establish trust between the speaker and his interlocutor. It may be true that in the covenant between Israel and God, God must fulfill a double role as both the second party and the presiding deity (see Heb. 6:13, commenting on Gen. 22:16), but the structure remains the same. The vow (*neder*), however, even if it is understood to entail an oath (Num. 30:11), is structured rather as a type of exchange of goods and/or services: if God grants his subject some favor, then the latter vows to offer in exchange some sort of sacrifice or tithe (Gen. 28:20–22; Judg. 11:30–31; Lev. 22:17–25; 27), or perhaps to perform some sort of devotional act such as the Nazirite vow (Num. 6). But since this dimension of the vow has more to do with a transaction between God and a devotee than with trust as such, I will set it aside here and will only include vows in my analysis, insofar as they constitute a species of oath pronounced in the name of God.

Trust in God

The concept of trust and its attendant notions thus turn out to be eminently biblical. A great deal of the Bible concerns itself with establishing and maintaining trust between Israel and God, with promises given and covenants made. Ever since Walther Eichrodt's *Theology of the Old Testament*, scholars have recognized the centrality of the covenant to biblical tradition: the law, the kingship of Yahweh, and numerous other biblical ideas all derive from Israel's covenant with God.[21] It was only with the discovery and analysis of covenant forms in other cultures of the ancient Near East that it became clear how unusual—possibly unique, even—is the biblical conceptualization of the covenant: specifically, that it could join a people to its deity, rather than one people to another. Thus, as recently as 2013, as highly informed a scholar as Michael D. Coogan could still maintain that "in the ancient Near East, the Israelites are the only group known to have characterized their relationship with a deity using the language of contract or treaty."[22] If the importance and distinctiveness of the biblical idea of the covenant thus goes without saying among at least some biblical scholars, what has not been adequately understood is its underlying significance.

What is crucial in this regard is not the possibility that the idea of a covenant between Israel and God might be unique—the future discovery of an ancient Near Eastern parallel would not affect my point. What is crucial, rather, is that a distinction can and should be drawn between two modes of religious thought: what I refer to as "mythical" and "historical" religions. Within mythical thought—which I define with reference to Mircea Eliade's ideas[23]—the relation between the divine and human worlds is established "in that time" (*in illo tempore*) and thus effectively built into the nontemporal and unchanging structure of the cosmos. Within the historical thought of biblical tradition, conversely, humankind begins in a state of alienation from God.[24] Yahweh and Israel, in particular, are, to begin with, strangers to each other. Their relationship must therefore be forged in and through time. And it is the function of the covenant to formalize this relationship. It is remarkable, for instance, that according to Joshua 24, Abraham and his father's house actually "served other gods" (24:2). What is equally surprising is that two of the Pentateuchal sources—namely, the so-called Elohist and Priestly sources—maintain that God had to reveal his true name to Moses and the children of Israel (Exod. 3:13–15; 6:2–3), which means that not even the venerable patriarchs of Genesis—Abraham, Isaac, and Jacob—knew God by name. And all of the prose sources agree that Israel constituted itself as a nation by voluntarily entering into a covenant with Yahweh. This voluntary oath amounted to a decision to ally oneself with this as opposed to that god: "Choose for yourselves whom you will serve" (Josh. 24:15). To fully appreciate the novelty of the biblical covenant and its attendant motifs, one need only recall Bruno Snell's observation regarding the Greeks' relationship to their gods: namely, that "they looked upon their gods as so natural and self-evident that they could not even conceive of other nations acknowledging a different faith or other gods."[25] Biblical tradition, meanwhile, had difficulty imagining even Israel's faith in its own God.

If, as I have already argued, the oath is a concession to human mistrust, it is the impressive achievement of the patriarchs—Abraham above all—to have trusted in and responded to God's call in the absence of an established relationship, centuries before the ultimate fulfillment of God's promises. Not without reason, Paul of Tarsus perceived in the portrayal of Abraham in Genesis 15 an exemplar of faith (Romans 4:2–3). But whereas Paul opposed "faith" (*pistis*) to "works" (*ergon*), Genesis 15 seems instead to oppose trust in its pure state to trust in its tainted form as a mere stipulation of a formal oath. It is crucial that, according to the Yahwist or J source, Abraham's trust comes first: "And Abram trusted [*vehe'emin*] in Yahweh," that is, trusted in God's simple declaration that Abraham would have numerous descendants. It is equally crucial that God, in response, "reckoned it to him as righteousness [*ẓedaqah*]" (15:6). Finally, one should not overlook the fact that it is only after Abraham's act of trust that God seals his covenant with Abraham: "In that day, Yahweh sealed a covenant with Abram, saying 'To your seed I give [*natatti*] this land'" (15:18). On the basis of ancient Near Eastern parallels, scholars have identified God's promissory covenant with

Abraham as a "royal grant," that is, an outright gift bestowed by a suzerain on a vassal in reward for services rendered, as opposed to obligatory covenants, which required the ongoing fealty of vassal to suzerain. In context, this particular land grant in Genesis would thus seem to constitute a reward for Abraham's demonstrated trust in God. If Abraham's "seed" will not actually possess the land for several centuries, the legal transfer of the land, according to the speech-act accompanying this covenant, takes place in Abraham's present: "I give," *natatti*, in the perfect tense.

Similarly, I do not think it a coincidence that Abraham finally receives the annunciation of Isaac's imminent birth while entertaining none other than God and his emissaries within his home (Gen. 18:1–15). It is important to note that the narrative gives no indication that Abraham recognized his guests: "And he raised his eyes and saw, and here were three men standing before him. And he saw them and ran toward them . . . and said, 'My lord [*'adonay*]'" (18:2–3)—"lord," that is, with a lowercase *l*.[26] The object of Abraham's perception is indicated by the indefinite noun phrase "three men," whom he addresses ambiguously as "my lord" or possibly "my lords"—*'adonay* is a plural form, but the rest of the sentence is addressed to a singular "you"—whereas in Genesis 15, Abraham, when he clearly knows that he is speaking to God, says rather, "my lord Yahweh [*'adonay yhwh*]" (15:2,8). Modern readers, who as a rule have little if any experience of true or pure hospitality—that is, hospitality extended to strangers—would do well to pause and consider Abraham's behavior here and the impact it may have had on God's opinion of him. "The Testament of Abraham," an apocalyptic text composed sometime around the turn of the era, understands the patriarch's virtue to be epitomized by his hospitality: "For he pitched his tent at the crossroads of the oak of Mamre and welcomed everyone . . . (all) on equal terms did the pious, entirely holy, righteous, and hospitable [*philoxenos*] Abraham welcome" (1:2–3, Recension A). God himself pronounces him "righteous in all goodness, (having been) hospitable [*philoxenos*] and loving until the end of his life" (1:5).[27] This ancient reader understood the significance of Abraham's reception of his guests better than his modern-day counterparts. The author of the Epistle to the Hebrews seems to have read this episode similarly: "Do not neglect to show hospitality [*philoxenias*] to strangers," he exhorts his audience, "for by doing that some have entertained [*xenisantes*] angels without knowing it" (13:2, NRSV). In fact, "some" might well refer to Abraham's nephew, Lot, as well, insofar as the latter earned his salvation from the judgment of the cities of the plain by virtue of the extravagant hospitality he lavished on the strangers he chanced on in the public square of Sodom and whom he all but forced to spend the night in his home (Gen. 19)—knowing all too well, I think it is implied, the treatment these men would likely receive outside overnight. Modern readers often condemn him for offering his virgin daughters to the mob that gathers at his door, but his ostensibly indecent proposal should really be understood as a sign of the importance Lot placed on hospitality and on his obligation to protect his guests.

In this way, both Abraham and Lot unwittingly played host to God and/or his emissaries. God, in response, rewarded both: Abraham finally begat Isaac and thus Israel; Lot begat Ammon and Moab. It is true that the denouement of Genesis 19 casts aspersions on these neighboring kinsfolk to the east, attributing their origin to an incestuous liaison between Lot and his two daughters. But it is also worth noting that, according to Deuteronomy 2, the sons of Lot have received their inheritance from none other than Yahweh himself. Lot, too, biblical tradition seems to admit, has sealed a covenant with God.

Trust in Man

If Abraham exhibits admirable trust in God, the trust he and the other patriarchs place in other men leaves much to be desired. As Abraham confesses to Abimelech, as he approached Gerar, he said to himself, "But surely there is no fear of God in this place" (Gen. 20:11). Within the context of Genesis, this is also to say that the patriarchs make better hosts than guests. Indeed, they consistently betray those who are good enough to receive them into their lands. And yet, in spite of their transgressions against the cardinal virtue of civilization, they continue to prosper, sometimes even at the expense of those whom they have betrayed.

Here we must recall Benveniste's analysis of hospitality and its relation to legal status: "We must envisage the situation of a *xénos*, of a 'guest,' who is visiting a country where, as a stranger, he is deprived of all rights, of all protection, of all means of existence."[28] This is precisely the situation that the patriarchs find themselves in throughout Genesis 12–50. As Abraham explains to Abimelech, "God made me wander from my father's house" in Mesopotamia (20:13). His subsequent life in Canaan, and briefly in Egypt, is consistently described by God, men, and author alike as a "sojourn" (*gur*) in foreign lands (12:10; 17:8; 20:1; 21:23, 34). Lot, similarly, after parting from his uncle's company and settling in Sodom, is said by the locals to be merely "sojourning" in their midst (19:9). What is more, biblical tradition insists that the ancestors did not "naturalize" as Canaanites. Abraham, as we have seen, refuses to let his son marry a local girl. Isaac and Rebekah, in turn, vexed by Esau's decision to marry Hittite women (26:34–35), send Jacob back to the "old country" to find a more suitable bride (28:1–5). As a result, Isaac (26:3; 35:27) and Jacob (28:4; 36:7; 37:1; 47:9), too, are mere "sojourners" in the land. It is only Jacob's sons—namely, the tribes of Israel—who will begin to intermarry with the natives.

"Sojourner" (*ger*), as well as the related word meaning "resident alien" (*toshav*), are technical terms for a foreigner who is not endowed with legal status vis-à-vis the land in which he is dwelling. This nonstatus within the local community makes him comparable to a servant or slave, hence the list found in the law of the sabbatical year: the sabbath of the land must provide not only for "you"—Israelites living on their inherited land—but also for "your male and female slaves, your paid servant, and the resident alien [*toshav*], who sojourn [*haggarim*] with you" (Lev. 25:6)—those without land. This is why Abraham, when he is in need of a burial site for his recently deceased wife, enters into negotiations with the sons of Heth to purchase a field from one of its citizens by declaring: "A sojourner and a resident alien [*ger vetoshav*] am I with you" (Gen. 23:4). This declaration not only explains his current need as a landless foreigner, it also establishes his legal status, which apparently needed to be registered as part of the sale of land.[29]

The patriarchs thus necessarily relate to the various Canaanite populations as mere landless foreigners. In several instances, they become guests, recipients of local hospitality. What is interesting is that they consistently betray the trust extended by their hosts. Let us briefly consider the so-called wife-sister stories, three episodes in which Abraham, and later Isaac, introduce their respective wives to the local populations as sisters, which is to say, as sexually available women: Abraham in Egypt (12:10–20), Abraham in Gerar (20:1–18), and Isaac in Gerar (26:1–33).[30] By lying about their wives' true identity, these two patriarchs recklessly expose their hosts to the crime of adultery. Indeed, Abraham twice allows Sarah to marry a foreign ruler: Pharaoh in Genesis 12 and Abimelech in Genesis 20. In Genesis 26, the mere possibility of this crime so angers Abimelech that he accuses Isaac of gross misconduct: "What is this you have done to us? One of the people could easily have lain with your wife, and you would have brought guilt upon us" (26:10). If Abraham's trust in Yahweh resulted in the sealing of a covenant between the two, it is the lack of trust exhibited by Abraham and Isaac that results in their covenants with Abimelech. First, the king of Gerar and his military adviser, remarking to Abraham that "God is with you in all that you do" (21:22), propose that a covenant be sealed between the two parties. Later, Abimelech and his staff similarly admit to Isaac that "Yahweh is with you," leading them, once again, to seek a covenant with the patriarch (26:28). These covenants constitute a type of boundary marker between Gerar and Israel. Indeed, part of the point of these two stories seems to be that the later inhabitants of Gerar, namely, the Philistines, are guilty of having violated these ancient oaths. Within the narrative setting of Genesis, however, these two covenants are actually defensive maneuvers on the part of Abimelech, who is not at all sure—quite understandably, I think—whether he can trust his sojourning neighbors.

Jacob gets similarly embroiled with the local population of the town of Shechem in Genesis 34. In this episode, he is effectively on the verge of "naturalizing" as a Shechemite: not only does he purchase a small plot of land from Hamor, the ruler of Shechem (33:19), he also considers marrying off his daughter Leah to Hamor's son, Shechem, the "prince of the land" (34:2). This couple's initial encounter, I should add, is not a rape in the modern sense of the word, but an improper seduction or elopement: Hamor "degraded her [*vay'anneha*]" (34:2)—or treated her "like a whore" (*kezonah*), as her brothers more colorfully put it (34:31)—insofar as he approached her directly, as if she were the type of girl who was simply there for the taking. What is more, Hamor's proposal goes well beyond this one marriage: he proposes that their peoples freely intermarry in general, and that Jacob's household "reside" (*teshevu*), trade, and acquire property (*vehe'aḥazu*) among them as well (34:10). Jacob and his household, for all intents and purposes, would have been transformed from landless sojourners into propertied citizens of Canaan. However, two of Jacob's sons, Simeon and Levi, trick and murder their hosts and would-be in-laws. Not coincidentally, their ruse involves a distinctive ethnic marker, namely, circumcision.

Given the sanctity of hospitality, one might have expected that these culprits would be punished by God for their barbaric acts. But in each case, they prosper instead. This blatant injustice is partly to be explained by the folkloric concept of the trickster: as aliens sojourning in foreign lands, the patriarchs needed to resort to trickery to survive. By the same logic, one should recall how Jael, according to the Song of Deborah (Judges 5), after apparently extending the hand of hospitality to Sisera, murders him in cold blood within her very home. And yet, the poem praises her for this treacherous act (5:24–27). To return to Genesis, the ultimate point of these stories of betrayal is, as I have argued elsewhere, that divine election results in blessing, even when it is not deserved.[31] As Isaac explains to Esau, regarding the blessing just stolen by his deceitful younger brother, "I have blessed him. Indeed, blessed he will be" (Gen. 27:33).

Conclusion

As a conciliatory gesture toward the rest of this volume, which will be decidedly post-biblical in focus, I would like to conclude by commenting briefly on the metaphorical dimension of the oath. I believe that this figurative dimension has contributed to certain significant developments in post-biblical Judaism.

The sacredness of the oath has, as one of its consequences, the fact that the subject of the oath is, in a sense, ritually polluted by virtue of making it: that is, just as one who touched certain sacred objects was rendered unclean and needed to be purified before returning to mundane existence—for example, those who manufactured and handled the "water for impurity" described in Numbers 19— so too one who invoked God's name was effectively tainted by coming into contact with its sacred power, at least until the taint was dissipated by the fulfillment of the oath. For this reason, as I noted earlier, the commandment against "lifting" the deity's name "for naught" warns that God will not "acquit" (*yenaqqeh*) one who does so (Exod. 20:7; Deut. 5:11). I would now add that the Hebrew verb *niqqah* is etymologically related to the idea of cleanness. Thus, in the Sotah Ritual, the wife would be "clean [*hinnaqi*] of this bitter cursing water" only if she was innocent (Num. 5:19), in which case the holy water would have no adverse effect on her. But if she was guilty, the pollution of adultery residing within her would react with the water's sacredness—in particular, the divine name that had been washed into the mixture—and thus bring down a curse on her: "And the man will be clean [*veniqqah*] of guilt, but this woman will bear her guilt" (5:31). One should similarly understand the terms of the oath that Abraham makes his servant swear in the name of Yahweh, namely, that he find a suitable wife for Isaac. The servant, Abraham stipulates, will be "clean" (*veniqqita*) of the oath, even without providing said wife, only if the woman he successfully finds should decline the offer of marriage (Gen. 24:8).

Insofar as the vow was structured as an exchange, it was thought to constitute a type of encumbrance on the subject. As we saw in Numbers 30, a vow made in God's name constituted a type of restrictive "fetter" (*'issar*) that "bound" (*'asar*) the subject until he or she fulfilled it. To fail to fulfill this vow resulted in the guilt of sin (*'avon*). By the same logic, in what I take to be the strictly secular act described in Prov. 6:1–5—pledging oneself as "surety for your neighbor" (*'aravta lere'ekha*)—one was similarly "snared" (*noqashta*) or "trapped" (*nilkadta*) by the "words of your mouth" (*'imrei-pikha*)—an echo of the "vow" (*neder*), which, according to one fixed phrase, "comes out of [one's] mouth" (*yoze' mippiv*). By the same logic, Deut. 23:22–24 represents one's vow to God as a debt that the subject must be careful to "pay" (*shallem*), lest it be counted as a "sin" (*het'*); likewise in Qohelet 5:3–5. The vow, in other words, has now become a monetary, rather than physical, encumbrance. And the "unpaid" vow, like the broken oath, was ultimately transformed into a sin with its attendant pollution.

I suspect that it is due to the figurative dimension of oaths and vows that, centuries after the destruction of the Second Temple in Jerusalem, Kol Nidrei— that ritual by which all vows were declared null and void—was instituted as part of the Yom Kippur service, whereas precursors to Kol Nidrei took place on Rosh Hashanah. Of course, on a general, commonsensical level, the relation between Kol Nidrei and the Day of Atonement is clear enough: to begin the new year with a clean slate, one needed to expunge any marks from one's existential ledger, and Yom Kippur constituted an auspicious day on which to undertake this spiritual cleansing. This connection between ritual and time, however, is also motivated on a specific, technical level. And these technical specificities are altogether biblical.

According to Leviticus 16, the high priest, on the Day of Atonement, would lay his hands on the so-called scapegoat, confess the sins of Israel on it, thereby transferring this burden onto the animal, and then send it into the wilderness: in this way, it would "bear [*venasa'*] all of the guilt [*'avonot*]" of the people to a place/entity named Azazel (16:8, 10, 21–22). In the same way, the wife guilty of adultery would "bear" (*tissa'*) the "guilt" (*'avon*) of her falsely sworn oath, just as Israel was commanded not to "lift" (*tissa'*) the deity's sacred name "for naught."

With the destruction of the temple and the cessation of animal sacrifice, all that was left to Judaism of the original Yom Kippur ritual was this confession, along with that practice vaguely referred to in Leviticus as "self-affliction" (23:27). Insofar as unfulfilled oaths were associated in the Bible with sin and impurity, the annulment thereof came to be associated with the purifying function of Yom Kippur. Indeed, one might even argue that it was a necessary component of atonement. The Day of Atonement was also associated in the Bible with the Jubilee Year described in Leviticus 25.³² On the tenth day of the seventh month of this most auspicious year, "liberty" was declared throughout the land: namely, debts were to be canceled—more precisely, amortized—so that mortgaged land would return to its owner and mortgaged people would return to their land and families. Insofar as unfulfilled vows came to be imagined in the Bible as debts to God, the annulment of vows also came to be associated with the cancellation of debts marked by the Jubilee Year and thus with the Day of Atonement.

Notes

1. See also Proverbs 12:5f, 17; 13:5; 14:5, 25; 17:7; 19:5, 9, 28; 21:28; 24:28; 25:18.
2. See also Psalm 55:10.
3. Herman L. J. Vanstiphout, trans., *Epics of Sumerian Kings: The Matter of Aratta* (Atlanta: Society of Biblical Literature, 2003), 65.
4. Thorkild Jacobsen, trans., *The Harps that Once . . .: Sumerian Poetry in Translation* (New Haven: Yale University Press, 1997), 275–319.
5. I cite the English translation by M. L. West: *Theogony and Works and Days* (New York: Oxford University Press, 1988).
6. Regarding the oath in Indo-European tradition, including the puzzling relation between *horkon* and *epiorkon*, see: Emile Benveniste, "The Oath in Greece," in *Indo-European Language and Society* (Coral Gables: University of Miami Press, 1973), 432–42; cited hereafter as *IELS*.
7. Benveniste, *IELS*, 278.
8. See Robert Alter, "Sodom as Nexus," in *The Book and the Text: The Bible and Literary Theory*, ed. Regina M. Schwartz (Oxford: Blackwell, 1990), 146–60.
9. Benveniste, *IELS*, 275, 277.
10. Benveniste, *IELS*, 278.
11. Milner, *Le triple du plaisir* (Lagrasse: Verdier, 1997), 25.
12. Benveniste, *IELS*, 278.
13. For a general overview, see Moshe Greenberg, Haim Hermann Cohn, and Menachem Elon, "Oath," in *Encyclopaedia Judaica*, ed. Michael Berenbaum and Fred Skolnik, 2nd ed. (Detroit: Macmillan Reference USA, 2007), 15:358–64.
14. Regarding the sources of the Pentateuch, see Richard Elliott Friedman, *Who Wrote the Bible?* (New York: HarperCollins, 1997).
15. For a succinct discussion of pollution in the Bible, including the danger beliefs surrounding it, see Tikva Frymer-Kensky, "Pollution, Purification, and Purgation in Biblical

Israel," in *The Word of the Lord Shall Go Forth: Essays in Honor of David Noel Freedman in Celebration of his Sixtieth Birthday*, ed. Carol L. Meyers and M. O'Connor (Winona Lake: Eisenbrauns, 1983), 399–414. Benveniste similarly argues that, in ancient Greece, the "punishment of perjury is not a human concern" (*IELS*, 442).

16. Regarding the intersection of gender and biblical law, see Robert S. Kawashima, "Gender: Hebrew Bible," in *The Oxford Encyclopedia of the Bible and Law*, ed. Brent Strawn (Oxford: Oxford University Press, 2015), 1:306–19.

17. See Tikva Frymer-Kensky, "The Strange Case of the Suspected Sotah (Numbers V 11–31)," *Vetus Testamentum* 34, no. 1 (1984): 11–26.

18. For a general overview, see Moshe Weinfeld, "Covenant," in *Encyclopaedia Judaica*, ed. Michael Berenbaum and Fred Skolnik, 2nd ed. (Detroit: Macmillan Reference USA, 2007), 5:249–53.

19. See Frank Moore Cross, *From Epic to Canon* (Baltimore: Johns Hopkins University Press, 1998), 3–21.

20. See Benveniste, *IELS*, 432–42 and 489–98.

21. Walther Eichrodt, *Theology of the Old Testament*, vol. 1 (Philadelphia: Westminster, 1961).

22. Michael D. Coogan, *The Old Testament: A Historical and Literary Introduction to the Hebrew Scriptures*, 3rd ed. (New York: Oxford University Press, 2013), 119.

23. See Mircea Eliade, *The Sacred and the Profane* (New York: Harcourt, Brace & World, 1959), and my interpretation of Eliade in "The Priestly Tent of Meeting and the Problem of Divine Transcendence: An 'Archaeology' of the Sacred," *Journal of Religion* 86, no. 2 (2006): 226–57.

24. See Robert S. Kawashima, "Covenant and Contingence: The Historical Encounter between God and Israel," in *Myth and Scripture: Contemporary Perspectives on Religion, Language, and Imagination*, ed. Dexter Callender (Atlanta: Scholars Press, 2014), 51–70.

25. Bruno Snell, *The Discovery of the Mind in Greek Philosophy and Literature* (Mineola, NY: Dover, 1982), 24.

26. Following a long-standing convention, English translations of the Bible generally render the divine name "Yahweh" (*yhwh*) as "LORD"—capital L, small capitals "ORD." Here, Abraham does not say "Yahweh," but "lord."

27. E. P. Sanders, trans., "The Testament of Abraham," in *The Old Testament Pseudepigrapha*, ed. James H. Charlesworth, 2 vols. (Garden City, NY: Doubleday, 1983–85), 1:871–902. The Testament here seems to allude to *Iliad* 6.14–15: "a man rich in substance and a friend [*philos*] to all humanity / since in his house by the wayside he entertained [*phileesken*] all comers" (Richmond Lattimore, trans., *The Iliad of Homer* [Chicago: University of Chicago Press, 1961]). See also "Apocalypse of Paul" 27, regarding the central position hospitality occupies within the conceptual realm of the virtues.

28. Benveniste, *IELS*, 278.

29. For more detailed analysis and further references, see Stephen C. Russell, "Abraham's Purchase of Ephron's Land in Anthropological Perspective," *Biblical Interpretation* 21, no. 2 (2013): 153–70.

30. The Middle Assyrian Laws confirm that the patriarchs are transgressing widespread norms of ethical behavior (MAL A ¶24); for further commentary on these three biblical passages, see also Robert S. Kawashima, "Literary Analysis," in *The Book of Genesis: Composition, Reception, and Interpretation*, ed. Craig A. Evans, Joel N. Lohr, and David L. Petersen (Leiden: Brill, 2012), 98–102.

31. Kawashima, "Literary Analysis," 98–102.
32. See Robert S. Kawashima, "The Jubilee Year and the Return of Cosmic Purity," *Catholic Biblical Quarterly* 65 (2003): 370–89.

Bibliography

Alter, Robert. "Sodom as Nexus." In *The Book and the Text: The Bible and Literary Theory*, edited by Regina M. Schwartz, 146–60. Oxford: Blackwell, 1990.

Benveniste, Emile. *Indo-European Language and Society*. Coral Gables, FL: University of Miami Press, 1973.

Coogan, Michael D. *The Old Testament: A Historical and Literary Introduction to the Hebrew Scriptures*. 3rd ed. New York: Oxford University Press, 2013.

Cross, Frank Moore. *From Epic to Canon: History and Literature in Ancient Israel*. Baltimore: Johns Hopkins University Press, 1998.

Duensing, Hugo, trans. "Apocalypse of Paul." In *Apocalyptic Literature: A Reader*, edited by Mitchell G. Reddish, 293–325. Peabody, MA; Hendrickson, 1995. Originally published in *New Testament Apocrypha*, vol. 2, edited by Wilhelm Schneemelcher. Rev. ed. Louisville: Westminster/John Knox, 1992.

Eichrodt, Walther. *Theology of the Old Testament*. 2 vols. Philadelphia: Westminster, 1961.

Eliade, Mircea. *The Sacred and the Profane: The Nature of Religion*. New York: Harcourt, Brace & World, 1959.

Friedman, Richard Elliott. *Who Wrote the Bible?* New York: HarperCollins, 1997.

Frymer-Kensky, Tikva. "Pollution, Purification, and Purgation in Biblical Israel." In *The Word of the Lord Shall Go Forth: Essays in Honor of David Noel Freedman in Celebration of his Sixtieth Birthday*, edited by Carol L. Meyers and M. O'Connor, 399–414. Winona Lake: Eisenbrauns, 1983.

———. "The Strange Case of the Suspected Sotah (Numbers V 11–31)." *Vetus Testamentum* 34, no. 1 (1984): 11–26.

Greenberg, Moshe, Haim Hermann Cohn, and Menachem Elon. "Oath." In *Encyclopaedia Judaica*, edited by Michael Berenbaum and Fred Skolnik, 15.358–64. 2nd ed. Detroit: Macmillan Reference USA, 2007.

Jacobsen, Thorkild, trans. *The Harps that Once. . .: Sumerian Poetry in Translation*. New Haven: Yale University Press, 1997.

Kawashima, Robert S. "Covenant and Contingence: The Historical Encounter between God and Israel." In *Myth and Scripture: Contemporary Perspectives on Religion, Language, and Imagination*, edited by Dexter Callender, 51–70. Atlanta: Scholars Press, 2014.

———. "Gender: Hebrew Bible." In *The Oxford Encyclopedia of the Bible and Law*, edited by Brent Strawn, 1:306–19. Oxford: Oxford University Press, 2015.

———. "The Jubilee Year and the Return of Cosmic Purity." *Catholic Biblical Quarterly* 65 (2003): 370–89.

———. "Literary Analysis." In *The Book of Genesis: Composition, Reception, and Interpretation*, edited by Craig Evans, Joel Lohr, and David Petersen, 83–104. Leiden: Brill, 2012.

———. "The Priestly Tent of Meeting and the Problem of Divine Transcendence: An 'Archaeology' of the Sacred." *Journal of Religion* 86 (2006): 226–57.

Lattimore, Richmond, trans. *The Iliad of Homer.* Chicago: University of Chicago Press, 1951.
Milner, Jean-Claude. *Le Triple du Plaisir.* Lagrasse: Verdier, 1997.
Roth, Martha T. *Law Collections from Mesopotamia and Asia Minor.* 2nd ed. Atlanta: Scholars Press, 1997.
Russell, Stephen C. "Abraham's Purchase of Ephron's Land in Anthropological Perspective." *Biblical Interpretation* 21, no. 2 (2013): 153–70.
Sanders, E. P., trans. "The Testament of Abraham." In *The Old Testament Pseudepigrapha*, edited by James H. Charlesworth, 1.871–902. 2 vols. Garden City, NY: Doubleday, 1983–85.
Snell, Bruno. *The Discovery of the Mind in Greek Philosophy and Literature.* New York: Dover, 1982.
Vanstiphout, Herman L. J., trans. *Epics of Sumerian Kings: The Matter of Aratta.* Atlanta: Society of Biblical Literature, 2003.
Weinfeld, Moshe. "Covenant." In *Encyclopaedia Judaica*, edited by Michael Berenbaum and Fred Skolnik, 5:249–53. 2nd ed. Detroit: Macmillan Reference USA, 2007.
West, M. L. *Theogony and Works and Days.* New York: Oxford University Press, 1988.

ROBERT S. KAWASHIMA holds a joint appointment in the Department of Religion and the Center for Jewish Studies at the University of Florida. He has written on various aspects of the Hebrew Bible—literary, linguistic, and legal—as well as on Homer and on literary theory. His first book, *Biblical Narrative and the Death of the Rhapsode* (IUP), was a finalist for the Koret Jewish Book Award.

2 "And in Most of Their Business Transactions They Rely on This"

Some Reflections on Jews and Oaths in the Commercial Arena in Medieval Europe

Ephraim Shoham-Steiner

JEWS AND CHRISTIANS in the European Middle Ages were opposing, competing, and at times mutually hostile groups.[1] Yet they were also close neighbors, business partners, and associates, especially in the tightly knit medieval urban environment. It was a laborious task, but almost a prime directive, to overcome ingrained hostility and mutual feelings of suspicion and build common trust on a level required to sustain daily life. However, building trust amid the feelings of tension nurtured over almost a millennium of religious competition, theological antagonism, ethnic hostility, and the innately unbalanced political, judicial, and legal status required a sincere effort.

In this chapter, I will focus on an internal Jewish debate about the use of oaths in the marketplace. In medieval Europe, most oaths sworn for commercial purposes involved invoking the name of the deity or a saint, or placing one's hand on a sacred object (a holy codex or a relic) as a means of validating the speech-act.[2] As participants in the marketplace, Jews also used oaths; not surprisingly, the invocation of the name of a deity or a saint by Jews elicited different responses among halakhists. The use of an oath represented a type of conceptual middle ground. Discussions of oath utterances do not reflect the ingrained fear of conversion, although the problem rabbis attributed to this speech-act was a confessional one. Rather, oaths represented the delicacy and fragility of commercial relationships between two individuals from two different religions. Thus the challenge at hand was forming the intricate network of interfaith relations and finding a religious comfort zone that would enable commerce and trade.[3] This very thin fabric demanded constant maintenance. In cases in which the trust was breached, what seemed to be the firm ties of the past quickly turned into the great and grave disappointment of present and the backdrop for harsh feelings and animosities in constructed memories and in literature designed to educate and admonish.[4]

The evidence I will discuss comes, for the most part, from internal Jewish sources, penned, compiled, preserved, and distributed in relatively closed circles by members of the male rabbinic learned elite of the Jewish communities. In the past, scholars took statements made by this rabbinic elite at face value and attributed the information gleaned from these sources such credence that modern readers were given the impression that it represented the thoughts, actions, mind-set, and mentality of the whole body of medieval Jewry. While this is partially true, we should read through the rabbinic sources against the grain. In my reading of these sources, I wish to present the rabbinic attitudes, the internal conversation among the individuals who constructed and consumed these texts, but in addition, I will suggest that a close examination reveals rabbinic anxieties regarding what seem to be other trends among medieval Jews, trends that some rabbis were attempting to curb or regulate. A close observation enables us to see through the rabbinic agenda and reconstruct what we may define as the *vox populi*, or better yet *voces aliae*, the suppressed voices of those individuals whose lives rabbis attempted to regulate, with oscillating levels of success. We will see how the attempt to be trustworthy and credible in the eyes of non-Jewish business associates prompted medieval European Jewish merchants and financiers to take steps that were deemed by some rabbis to be an erosion of Jewish core values. These trends were aimed at neutralizing the invocation of the name of foreign deities while swearing oaths in the marketplace, turning them in essence into a form of currency to enhance credibility. Thus, invoking the names of Christian saints, an act that seemed to some rabbis to be highly problematic, appears to have been registered very differently by other Jews in their quotidian mercantile exchange.[5]

As is clearly evident from both Jewish Hebrew and Christian Latin sources, Jews gave trust-based loans to their Christian neighbors. A short entry from the twelfth-century *Book of Remembrance (Sefer Zekhira* in Hebrew), a memoir compiled by Rabbi Ephraim ben Jacob of Bonn, illustrates this clearly.[6] This short composition is an amalgam of religious poetry (*piyyut*), a personal memoir, and a selection of historical anecdotes from various sources. Its main theme is the documentation of the persecutions of Jews during the twelfth century in northwestern Germany, northern France, and England.[7] After discussing the events of the Second Crusade in northern France (1146), Rabbi Ephraim concludes by praising the Almighty for the deliverance of French Jewry, who managed to emerge from the persecutions relatively unscathed:

> And in the other communities of *Zarfat* [northern France] we haven't heard of anyone who was killed or forced to baptize. Nevertheless, they did suffer financial losses. For the King of France has decreed: "Anyone who volunteered to go to Jerusalem, if he owed money to Jews his debt would be relinquished".

Indeed most of the loans provided by Jews in France are trust-based *(ba-amanah)*, thus they have lost a fortune.[8]

After having set aside the pressing life and death matters, Rabbi Ephraim turns in his account to the economic damage endured by the Jews in northern France. This short entry suggests that northern French Jewry suffered some serious financial loss during the Second Crusade. Relying on trust *(amana)* and royal protection as safeguards for their loans to non-Jews, northern French Jews had little or no form of value-based collateral.[9] The French royal decree, issued by King Louis VII with the intent of prompting knights into "taking the cross,"[10] stipulated that debts owed to Jewish financiers and creditors were either relinquished or suspended until the person who joined the Crusades returned safely from his endeavor. Thus those Jews whose debtors "took the cross" were hurt financially.[11]

This evidence of trust-based loans from the *Book of Remembrance* is corroborated by a slightly earlier source reflecting events that occurred in Cologne during the 1120s. In his autobiography *Opusculum de Conversione Sua*, the Jewish apostate Hermannus quondam Judaeus (literally, Herman who was once Judah, or a Jew) mentions that he lent a considerable sum of money, without collateral or guaranties, to Prince-Bishop Egbert of Münster.[12] Herman's immediate kin and fellow Jews admonished him for what they considered to be a foolish deed performed by an inexperienced teen and sent him to reside with the bishop in Münster in the winter of that year (possibly 1128) to serve as a constant reminder of the debt. Although the depiction of the Jewish reaction may have been a polemical insertion into the story, showing the Jews as greedy and money minded, it confirms that Jews were lending money to Christians, especially those with a high sociopolitical profile, in return for symbolic or little collateral.[13]

As is evident from the remainder of Herman's text, a bond of trust developed between the two individuals—the young Jewish representative of the Cologne-based merchant-banker Halevi family on the one hand and the wayfaring bishop, counselor to the emperor, on the other. This bridge over the religious divide and the bond of trust that was forged between the two grew to the point that it came to manifest one of the Jews' greatest and most ingrained fears in medieval Europe: the fear of conversion resulting from fraternizing and close association with Christians.

Commerce, Trade, and Faithfulness

From late antiquity, direct commercial contacts between Jews and non-Jews were viewed by rabbinic authorities as a potential minefield for the faithful. Rabbis feared that in these gray, unsupervised areas of interreligious contact, Jews would develop intimate relationships with non-Jews and eventually compromise their religious standing. However, these fears were overshadowed by a stronger rabbinic suspicion that certain acts and statements, such as swearing oaths and close social association, would bring Jews to acknowledge the potency of foreign deities. Fears of the first category are already manifested in the Hebrew Bible: "Lest thou make a covenant with the inhabitants of the land, and they go astray after their gods, and do sacrifice unto their gods, and they call thee, and thou eat of their sacrifice" (Ex. 34:15).

In light of this biblical command, rabbis attempted to curb, limit, and at times even altogether suppress potentially dangerous business liaisons between Jews and non-Jews. Rabbinic views on such matters were legally formulated in the tractate *Avodah Zarah* (literally, *Idol Worship*) of the Babylonian Talmud.[14] This tractate became a highly influential text among medieval European Jews in the twelfth century due to its attempt to regulate the social and business interactions between Jews and non-Jews.[15] For example, the rabbinic sages regulated days on which Jews must refrain from having any business dealings with non-Jews.[16] The rationale behind this concern was that the outcome of any business deal involving both Jew and non-Jew would prompt the non-Jewish partner to either thank his deity for the positive outcome or cause the gentile partner to beseech the deity in case of failure. Rabbis were also concerned about the possible use of products procured from Jews for idolatrous festivals and worship.[17]

With the growing Jewish population in medieval Europe, especially from the tenth century on, and exposure of Jews to the developing medieval Christian calendar of saint's days, rabbinic efforts to regulate business were rendered nearly obsolete. One had either to adhere to the rabbinic regulations of the Talmud at the risk of not being able to conduct proper business or ignore them altogether. The first commentary glosses known as *tosafot*, compiled in twelfth-century northern France on the Talmudic tractate *Avodah Zarah* (mentioned above) address this problem. Medieval rabbis made here a conscious attempt to reconcile the Talmudic dictum with the realities of medieval western European life in an effort to have their cake and eat it too. This attempt involved distinguishing between the idol-worshiping gentile population of antiquity and the gentile contemporaries of medieval European Jews. Some medieval rabbis argued that Christians were not performing "pure" blatant idol worship; if some of the practices resembled idol worship, it was simply because they pursued these habits as tradition in the form of ancestral custom *mos maiorum*.

Swearing Oaths in the Marketplace

In a revealing responsum attributed to the thirteenth-century German Jewish sage Rabbi Meir ben Baruch of Rothenberg (d. 1293), the author responds to "Rabbi Asher my teacher and kin" about a matter that greatly saddened him.

Rabbi Asher, who is mentioned as the recipient of the responsum, is Rabbi Meir's younger contemporary and student, Rabbi Asher ben Yehiel ("Rosh"), who resided in Cologne at the time.[18] It seems that several issues caused Rabbi Asher distress. One issue that appears in the following responsum concerns attempts made by Jewish merchants and businessmen in his immediate surroundings, probably his native Cologne, to gain their gentile business partners' trust by swearing what he thought were religiously objectionable oaths. The exact phrasing of Rabbi Asher's question did not survive, but it can be reconstructed from the answer Rabbi Meir supplied:

> And regarding what you wrote (to me) about those who "swear on the guilt of Samaria"[19] and in most of their business transactions they rely on this, and their livelihood depends on these depravities.[20] Indeed I share your grief over this matter and I have, time and again, chastised my adherents on this, crying out about it, in vain and to no avail. And I say about this time and again that it is over these matters that the properties of the house owners dwindle and collapse[21] and the debts go sour, indeed a measure for a measure, "in the pot that they cook they will be cooked."[22] Nevertheless I cannot protest for they claim they have a great man to rely on[23] [referring to Rabbi Jacob ben Meir, also called Tam[24]] who (they say) sanctioned this practice based on his claim that: "the Gentiles that live outside of the Land of Israel are not idol worshippers."[25] Furthermore, *for in our times all swear oaths invoking the names of the saints while they* [the non-Jews] *do not revere them as deities*. When they [the gentiles] do invoke the names of the saints they also mean to invoke Jesus, but they usually do not explicitly utter *his* name. And if you think that they do actually think about *him* while they swear the oath, these after all are matters of the heart and matters of the heart are not "real things."[26] Indeed, their thoughts [when uttering the names of the saints] were on the creator of the heavens (and earth).[27]
>
> Alas, on matters that are utterly forbidden where there is no way to allow any leniency they [my Jewish adherents] do not obey me let alone when, like in this case, they may rely and lean on this opinion they surely do not listen. And they do the deed wittingly and violate the dictum of Rabbi Samuel.[28] And how blind are they to think that by this they will actually prosper and gain, for they lose more than they gain. And he who suggested that I had ruled in favor of this practice had lied to you for on any matter where the great ones[29] disagree I always lean towards the more stringent side, unless this is a matter where the permit is simple and widespread in accordance with an older custom that may be relied on.[30]

The reader may wonder why I chose to cite this rather lengthy text in its entirety, as even in its original form, it is not very communicative and assumes much Talmudic knowledge in order to properly comprehend it. Due to its revealing nature, this correspondence allows a behind-the-scenes glance at the decision-making process among halakhists in matters of this sort. The responsum highlights Rabbi Asher and Rabbi Meir's strong objection to what became a widespread practice of Jewish merchants and creditors: swearing in the name of Christian saints.

Although this responsum is not dated, most clues point to the fact that it was probably written between 1270 and 1281.[31] During this period, Cologne was a hub of thriving commerce and financial activity, where Jews played an enormously important role in both trade and banking. Jewish traders resided in Cologne as early as the tenth century, and Jews from nearby regions flocked to the city for commerce, especially for its renowned triannual markets and fairs.[32] Several years prior to the suggested dating of this document, in 1266, the local archbishop granted the Cologne Jewry the exclusive rights to local moneylending and suppressed any competition. By so doing, the archbishop enhanced his income, taking a cut of the commission and interest while attempting to enhance his political leverage in the city. Archbishop Engelbert II von Falkenburg had the *Judenprivileg* he had drafted carved in stone and set first in the chapter of the Cologne Cathedral and then set on display on the cathedral's northern wall, where it remains to this day.[33] The exclusive status of Jews as the leading financiers was a source of great friction with the local businessmen and trade guilds.[34]

This economic privilege speaks volumes to the role of Jews in the Cologne economy in the mid-thirteenth century. It was during this time period that the local synagogue was renovated and beautified and an elaborate Gothic-style, lavishly decorated *bimah* (podium) carved in luxurious imported northern French limestone was installed. According to recent research, this was also the time when the famous Amsterdam Mahzor (called this due to its current location) was commissioned, produced, and used in the Cologne Jewish community (1270s).[35]

While the general objections raised in the responsum are abundantly clear, I would like to provide a close reading of the encoded rabbinic language of the text. The individuals criticized are described as swearing oaths "on the guilt of Samaria." Some light may be shed on this enigmatic expression from the words of Rabbi Eleazar ben Judah of Worms (1165–ca. 1240) in his early thirteenth-century commentary on the prayers for the Jewish festival of the New Year (*Rosh Hashanah*). Rabbi Eleazar, a perceptive observer of his life and times, and one of the adherents of the Ashkenazi Pietistic movement, makes the following comment on the phrase: "All knees will kneel to You and all tongues *will swear by Your name*."[36]

> And all tongues will swear by your name: and they will cease saying: "as your god lives Dan" and "as the way to Beersheba lives" for they will no longer "swear by the guilt of Samaria" but rather swear by Your name, and they will see and acknowledge that You are the only one.[37]

Alluding to the biblical verse from the prophecy of Amos, it seems that those who swore "by the guilt of Samaria" were Israelites invoking the name of a local deity. The classic interpreters of these verses associated the phrase "the guilt of Samaria" and the words "Dan and Be'ershevah" with the biblical Israelite worship of the calves (*agalim*) positioned by King Jerobam in the border towns of the northern Israelite kingdom, Dan in the north and Beersheba in the south (1 Kings 12:28–33).[38] The prophecy of Amos, who followed the Jehovian code of a single place of unified worship and a nonterritorial and nonfigurative deity, voiced criticism about worshiping the Israelite calves and invoking their names and place of worship in sworn oaths. Rabbi Eleazar used this reference as his point of departure when he voiced his hope that his Jewish contemporaries would also refrain from similar practices.

Rabbi Eleazar's comment on the prayer fits nicely with the critique expressed in the words of Rabbis Asher and Meir a generation and a half later. It seems that during the thirteenth century, it became more common among Jews to use the names of the Christian saints when swearing oaths in the commercial arena.

In his responsum, Rabbi Meir notes that those who act this way are said to tell their critics that their behavior was sanctioned by none other than the aforementioned Rabbi Jacob ben Meir, known as Rabbenu Tam. Furthermore, it seems that some Jews even said that Rabbi Meir himself had sanctioned this behavior, a claim that infuriated him and that he attempted to revoke in his responsum, lest his reputation be tarnished. To remove any shadow of doubt, Rabbi Meir provides a detailed answer, and although he made no explicit reference to the alleged authorization by Rabbi Jacob ben Meir to this practice, it likely refers to the gloss I will examine below.

Before we delve deeper into the details of the northern French twelfth-century gloss on the Talmud that Jews saw as enabling their invocation of the name of Christian saints in oaths, let us first go further back in time to the eleventh century, to Rabbi Jacob's maternal grandfather, Rabbi Shlomo ben Isaac ("Rashi," 1040–1105).[39]

In Exodus 23:13, we read the following: "And in all things that I have said to you beware; and make no mention of the name of other gods, neither let it be heard out of your mouth."[40] In his running commentary on the Pentateuch, Rashi comments:

> *Make no mention*: This means that one must not say to another 'Wait for me near such-and-such an idol' [church] or 'Stay with me on the festival of such and such an idol [saint's day].' It shall not be heard from a heathen through thine agency.[41] For consequently you will have brought it about that it has been mentioned through your agency.[42]

This idea is not Rashi's innovation. It comes from the Babylonian Talmud, tractate *Bekhorot* (2b), in which the Talmud quotes a statement by the father of the Talmudic sage Samuel: "One must not enter a partnership with a gentile, for it may end with a need for an oath, and the gentile will indeed swear the oath invoking the name of his deity, and it is about these matters that the Torah stipulated: 'It shall not be heard on your account' [literally, 'by your mouth'—*al pi'kha*]." It seems as if Rashi strictly adheres to the Talmudic precedent. However, in an anecdote found in a few sources that preserved Rashi's teachings, we hear of the following incident from his own life:

> Once a gentile owed an oath to our Master [Rashi] and he escorted the [gentile] debtor to the entrance of an idolatrous shrine [church] causing him to think he intended to make him swear an oath, but in his heart he [Rashi] had no such intention, for the sages have already said: "One should not strike a partnership with a gentile for there may be a situation where the gentile would want to swear an oath and he will wish to use the name of his idolatrous deity about which the Torah states: 'It should not be heard on your account'" (Sanhedrin 63b). Rather, he made it look as if he indeed wanted to cause the gentile to swear the oath. And they [the clerics at the church] brought out the rotting bones of their depravities [a relic] and the gentile put a coin on them in order to (dis)grace the idolatry.[43] At this point our Master believed[44] him and gave the gentile more time based on his oath. And from that time on, our Master had decided to restrict himself and refrain from negotiating great matters with non-Jews for there might be a chance the non-Jew would need to swear an oath, this in effect would cause the non-Jew to pledge money to his deity and thus an idolatrous worship will benefit directly on our master's account. Furthermore this behavior may suggest that the Jew actually acknowledges the idolatrous deity as effective and potent, for he brought someone to swear by it.[45]

This story, penned before 1096, discusses a business partnership between the northern French Jewish sage and a certain non-Jew. As Haym Soloveitchik has shown, Rashi and his family were in the viticulture crediting business, providing venture capital and high-risk loans to vineyard owners in the area of his hometown of Troyes in Champagne.[46] It seems from the text that Rashi only realized in hindsight that his behavior was a violation of the biblical commandment from Ex. 23:13.[47] The shrine of the saint and the reliquary it possessed were brought to serve as a guarantor for the loan, and by accepting this act of faith, Rashi inevitably attested to its validity. Later, Rashi identified the problem and vowed he would not fail in the future. Neither text is dated, but it stands to reason that Rashi made this strong claim in his biblical commentary based on his own life experiences recorded in his responsum. From Rashi's experience, it seems clear that Jewish moneylenders' acceptance of Christian oaths on holy relics certified a degree of trust.

The *tosfaot* (glosses) on the aforementioned Talmudic discussion restricting business partnerships with non-Jews record a debate between Rashi's grandchildren, Rabbi Samuel ben Meir ("Rashbam") and his younger brother, Rabbi Jacob ben Meir (Tam):

It is due to this dictum that Rabbi Samuel ben Meir forbade accepting an oath from a non-Jew based on an *a fortiori* claim (if striking a partnership which is a great matter is forbidden, a much lighter matter like accepting an oath is clearly forbidden). However Rabbi Jacob "Tam" allows this, for through this oath [uttered orally] the Jew may salvage assets from the non-Jews. Rabbi Jacob bases his claim on the Talmudic dictum from *Avodah Zarah* (6b) that a loan that is oral [involves no written deed] may be collected at any time (even in the days restricted by rabbinic law for commerce with non-Jews stipulated at the beginning of this tractate). His reasoning is that doing so is like salvaging assets from them and that is permitted . . . and Rabbi Jacob also supports his claim by saying: "In our time all the gentiles swear oaths invoking the names of their saints, and they do not consider the saints as deities. Although when they swear they invoke alongside the name of the saint the name of the heavens (and when they say so they actually mean "something else," i.e., Jesus) nevertheless this is not invoking the name of an idolatry for they really refer to the Lord creator of the heavens and earth. And although they summon together in this speech-act the Lord with another force and it is a Jew who caused them to swear these oaths in our business dealings with them, nevertheless it is not we [the Jews] who cause them to err and we [Jews] are not violating the prohibition of "placing a stumbling block before the blind" because the gentiles here are Noahides [sons of Noah] and although they are prohibited to worship idols they are not prohibited to share (believe that alongside the creator there are other powers that be). Besides, we are prohibited to "share" but not prohibited to cause others from performing speech acts that involve "multiplicity and participation."[48]

It is clear from the gloss that the editor of the *tosafot* on the Babylonian Talmud tractate *Sanhedrin* favored Rabbi Jacob's opinion, for he chose to present it in full after Rabbi Shmuel's and even elaborate on it.[49] It also seems clear that Rabbi Jacob realized that attempting to prevent his fellow Jews from the already widespread practice of asking non-Jews to swear oaths on relics and to invoke the names of saints was futile. Therefore, in an attempt to sanction the already widespread behavior, Rabbi Jacob provided a halakhic justification for the argument.[50] By the thirteenth century, Jewish merchants ignored the fine print of the rabbinic legal ruling and instead assumed a blanket sanctioning for all oaths. Basing themselves on the more lenient opinions of Rabbi Jacob Tam and Rabbi Isaac, and in an attempt to enhance non-Jewish business partners' trust, Jewish merchants and bankers were willing to swear oaths *themselves* using and invoking the Christian saints' names.[51] When these Jews were confronted on this matter by more stringent Jews, they replied that this practice was allowed by Rabbi Jacob Tam; some may have also added that they relied on Rabbi Meir of Rothenburg.

The elaborate discussions of Rabbi Jacob Tam and Rabbi Isaac "the Elder" of Dampierre in the twelfth century allow us to reevaluate the manner in which Jews were willing to understand the invocation of saints' names by non-Jews swearing oaths not as theological statements per se but in the less theologically charged and more businesslike fashion of a mercantile credibility enhancement mechanism. By exposing their thoughts and comments, even if they were recorded to sanction a dubious practice ex post facto, the leading halakhic masters brought the very concepts that could undermine the adherence to the Talmudic dictum to public knowledge, thus diffusing their negativity. It appears that in the eyes of those individuals operating in the commercial arena, it was not a giant leap to actually swear oaths for commercial matters using the names of Christian saints to instill a sense of trust and trustworthiness. For them, this was more a matter of creating a business conduit than a theological action. It may well be that the nature of the rift between Rabbis Asher and Meir and the people they were criticizing was not about idolatry or heresy but a more subtle theological issue: To what extent could an act of invoking a saint's name become a theologically neutral and merely economic tool? Could an oath made by a Jew invoking the names of Christian saints be understood by other Jews as a theologically hollow speech-act made for mercantile purposes alone, or was any invocation of a saint's name by a Jew a speech-act that was inherently so religio-theologically charged that it could not be considered solely on a utilitarian level?

It is not clear whether the practice criticized by Rabbis Asher and Meir was unique to Rabbi Asher's locale in Cologne or whether it was more widespread; the latter seems to be closer to reality. It appears that Jews in Cologne may have spearheaded a growing phenomenon throughout Germany and perhaps northern France as well, as they began using (or abusing, if we accept Rabbi Asher's critique) Rabbi Jacob's license to accept oaths made by non-Jews invoking the name of Christian saints and even swore oaths to their non-Jewish business partners in the same manner.

Interestingly, in his attack on this practice, Rabbi Meir warns that those who are believed to have embraced what he understands to be an erroneous custom might suffer divine retribution in the form of the failure of their business endeavors. We may thus wonder why the threatened retribution is not as severe as expected; although the practice of Jews swearing oaths and invoking the names of Christian saints is strongly criticized, terms like idolatry or heresy are not introduced into the discussion. This may be a result of the rabbinic acceptance that they were fighting a losing battle.

The story discussed earlier about Rashi and the gentile creditor allows us to formulate an understanding regarding the changing social atmosphere of those times. In the story, it was Rashi, the Jew, who needed to receive the oath from the Christian, and it was the Christian who went out of his way to please his Jewish debtor by going to a church and taking an oath involving relics. By the thirteenth century, matters had been reversed. Rabbis Asher and Meir were chastising Jewish merchants and businessmen who wittingly swore oaths invoking the names of Christian saints in an attempt to boost their trustworthiness in the eyes of their non-Jewish business partners. In many ways, this reversal of roles reflects the general paradigm shift in medieval Jewish history in northern Europe from the tenth and eleventh centuries to the thirteenth and especially the fourteenth century. The Jews began as a tolerated and even sought-after minority, at least in commercial matters. Their financial, credit, and commercial abilities were considered by lords and laymen alike as reason to seek their presence and engage in business with them. During this time, they had relatively little competition. By the thirteenth century, the situation had changed, and with the rise of the mercantile urban elite, Jews became yet another player in a more diverse economical game. The privilege granted to the Cologne Jews in 1266 illustrates this point vividly. The final clause in the stone-carved document prohibits the settlement in Cologne of the French Cahorsin bankers, explicitly to prevent competition with the Jews in the crediting business. The clause, probably included in the privilege at the behest of Jewish merchant bankers, exposes the fact that although the privilege of 1266 was an attempt to suppress the competition, they well understood that challenges to their monopoly would multiply.[52] It is no wonder that once their trade was no longer unique, Jews' legal and social standing constantly eroded during the thirteenth century until it was they who needed to boost their credibility among their Christian business partners.[53]

In the final lines of the responsum, Rabbi Meir comes to grips with the claim made by some of the Jewish merchants that it was he who sanctioned their practice of swearing oaths invoking the names of Christian saints. He vehemently denies this claim as false. Thus, another aspect of trust and trustworthiness is at play in this responsum: Rabbi Meir's own credibility among his rabbinic adherents and colleagues.[54] The language and imagery employed by Rabbi Meir is also worthy of attention. He writes that the Jews who swear oaths invoking the name of Christian saints are blinded by their belief that straying from the path might help them acquire wealth. The language and imagery of blindness applied here resonates with the Christian polemical imagery of the Jew as blind to the confessional Christian truth.[55] Rabbi Meir, in what seems like an intended twist, accuses Jews who turn a "blind eye" to their own religious behavioral code of blindness, stating that their attempt to earn the trust of their non-Jewish business partners and procure wealth blinds them to the real truth—that they lose more than they gain because they are compromising Jewish ideals.

Conclusion

We have surveyed some of the attitudes prevalent among Jews regarding the use of oaths in the commercial arena. Using medieval European rabbinic sources, we have seen how difficult it was for some Jews to reconcile the biblical verses as they were understood in the Talmud with the economical need to strengthen credibility, trustworthiness, and faith among their Christian business partners. Oaths, especially powerful ones, involved invoking the name of a deity or placing one's hand on an object that represented a metaphysical entity that would vouch for upholding a deal or a debt, such as a sacred codex or a relic of a saint. As we see, this was problematic for some Jews, such as the eleventh-century sage Rashi and some of his family members, including his grandson Rabbi Samuel ben Meir. The business environment of an eleventh-century marketplace in western Europe was still very much an oral environment, with few written deeds. In such an environment, the use of oaths to support one's credibility and trustworthiness was a frequent quotidian occurrence. Twelfth-century sources such as Rabbi Jacob Tam's gloss and his recorded disagreement with his older brother Rabbi Shmuel ben Meir disclose to us that attitudes were changing. By this time, it is clear that the more frequent and prevalent behavior involved Jews accepting oaths made by invoking the names of Christian saints on a daily basis. In the mind of Rabbi Jacob, probably adhering to a more popular trend or in an attempt to retain rabbinic relevance to a larger audience, the mercantile environment somewhat neutralized the religious nature of the invocation of the saint's name. It was still a powerful tool as it drew a supernatural power into the business dealing. In order to reconcile this, Rabbi Jacob was willing to view the saint not as drawing his power from the figure of Jesus but rather from the Almighty himself ("creator of the heavens"). This enabled him to sanction such behavior, which created an atmosphere where Jews felt more at ease with the practice of oath swearing. By the thirteenth century, we hear from Rabbi Asher and Rabbi Meir in Germany that Jews were already using the same oaths (invoking the names of Christian saints) as a common practice when dealing with Christians, to the point where they would swear such oaths themselves. This may be connected with the erosion of both the legal and commercial status of Jewish merchants, who were struggling to remain relevant in a more complex and economically advanced business environment. Unfortunately, the Jewish sources at our disposal are predominantly rabbinic. We have few sources that stem from the non-rabbinic commercial strata of Jewish society. The voice of the Jewish merchants and creditors themselves is either completely absent from the sources or mediated to us through rabbinic eyes and writing. At this point, we can only speculate about the merchants' actual practices, thoughts, and rationalizations.

Notes

1. This chapter is based on a talk delivered at the Oxford Center for Hebrew and Jewish Studies at Yarnton Manor in March 2014. I wish to thank the conference organizers and volume editors, Mitch Hart and Nina Caputo, for inviting me to the conference, and my fellow medievalists and early modernists Sara Lipton, Josh Teplitsky, and Rachel Fürst for

suggesting I look into this matter. I wish to thank my friend Dr. Jason Rogoff for reading this chapter and making some invaluable comments that helped me sharpen some of the claims made here. The research for this chapter was made possible by the generous aid of the Israel Science Foundation (ISF) and The Council for Higher Education Project: Israel Centers for Research Excellence (I-CORE), grant number 1754.

2. On the use of oaths in the medieval marketplace, see Ralph J. Hexter, *Equivocal Oaths and Ordeals in Medieval Literature* (Cambridge: Harvard University Press, 1975).

3. On this topic, see Ephraim Shoham-Steiner, ed., *Intricate Interfaith Networks: Quotidian Jewish-Christian Contacts in the Middle Ages* (Turnhout: Brepols, 2016).

4. A clear sense of this disappointment can be seen when reading through the following passage from the early thirteenth-century *Book of the Pious* (section 250 in the Parma edition): "'Whose mouth speaketh falsehood and their right hand is a right hand of lying' (Psalms 144:8). Once they [the Christian gentiles] decreed destruction [forced conversion, in Hebrew *Shemad*] on Israel [the Jews] to forcefully immerse them in their waters [baptism] and to cause the Jews to leave God the Lord of Israel so that we should be entrapped in the beliefs of the gentiles. And Israel [the Jews] were all engaged in fleeing from their localities. Many had lords and dignitaries who presented themselves as if they are amicable and friendly saying: 'Come to me and I shall protect you against your enemies.' They [the Jews] came to them but were nevertheless killed. That is why they said: a Jew shouldn't be intimate with a gentile." For the original Hebrew text, see Jehuda Wistinetzki, ed., *Das Buch der Frommen: nach der Rezension in Cod. De Rossi no. 1133 mit Einleitung und Registern von Jacob Freimann* [in Hebrew] (Frankfurt: Wahrman, 1924), 82.

5. The question of Jews and trust, trustworthiness, belief, and disbelief, especially regarding the legal and commercial relationship between Jews and Christians in medieval Europe, has been discussed before. It is closely associated with the more general and philosophical question of faith and trust, specifically within a network of relations crossing religious and what later in time developed into "confessional" boundaries. R. J. Zwi Werblowsky, "Faith Hope and Trust: A Study in the Concept of *Bittahon*," in *Papers of the Institute of Jewish Studies London*, ed. J. G. Weiss (Jerusalem: Magnes, 1964), 95–139. I wish to thank my friend Daniel Abrams for turning my attention to this somewhat forgotten paper by Zwi Werblowsky. On the Jew's oath, see Amnon Linder, "The Jewry Oath in Christian Europe," in *Jews in Early Christian Law: Byzantium and the Latin West, 6th–11th Centuries*, ed. J. Tolan et al. (Turnhout: Brepols, 2014), 311–59.

6. The memoir begins with the author's personal recollection of the events leading to the persecutions of the Second Crusade in 1146 and concludes with the events of 1196 in Speyer. Internal references in the text suggest that it was compiled as an addendum to the Hebrew chronicles that discuss the anti-Jewish riots and massacres of 1096 that were compiled during the 1140s–1150s in the Rhineland. Ephraim's text covers the next fifty years, from the fiftieth anniversary of the 1096 riots (1146) to the centennial anniversary (1196) of the 1096 events. Ephraim ben Jacob of Bonn, *Sefer Zehira Selichot ve'Quinot*, ed. A. Haberman (Jerusalem: Mosad Bialik, 1970). The modern detailed edition of the Hebrew chronicles about the 1096 events is Eva Haverkamp, *Hebräische Berichte über die Judenverfolgungen während des Ersten Kreuzzugs*, Hebraische Texte aus dem mittelalterlichen Deutschland Bd. 001 (Hannover: Monumenta Germaniae Historica, 2005).

7. The latter literally means "the islands of the sea," referring to the insular kingdom of England.

8. Shlomo Eidelberg, *The Jews and the Crusades: The Hebrew Chronicles of the First and the Second Crusades* (Madison: University of Wisconsin Press, 1977), 131. For a short introduction to the *Book of Remembrance*, see Eidelberg, *The Jews and the Crusades*, 117–20. For the Hebrew text of the quoted passage, see *Sefer Zekhira*, 27, rows 212–16.

9. On Jews in northern France in this time period, see Robert Chazan, *Medieval Jewry in Northern France: A Political and Social History* (Baltimore: Johns Hopkins University Press, 1973), 30–61; Emily Taitz, *The Jews of Medieval France: The Community of Champagne* (Westport, CT: Greenwood, 1994). On Jewish moneylending in a slightly later period, see William C. Jordan, *The French Monarchy and the Jews: From Philip Augustus to the Last Capetians* (Philadelphia: University of Pennsylvania Press, 1989), 3–90. See also Norman Golb, *The Jews in Medieval Normandy: A Social and Intellectual History* (Cambridge: Cambridge University Press, 1998), 217–52.

10. *Se croisier* in medieval French and *crux suscepit, crux accepit*, or *crucizo* in medieval Latin: namely, the vow to take the cross and join the Crusade.

11. Regardless of the question of whether this is indeed how matters had unfolded and how grave the losses, in the memory of the period, or at least in the attempt made by Rabbi Ephraim to shape that memory, this is how matters were recorded and remembered. Rabbi Ephraim was thought to be an important chronicler, especially among rabbinic circles, so much so that Rabbi Isaac ben Moses of Vienna ("Or Zaruah") attributed to him the fictitious story of the martyrdom of Rabbi Amnon of Mainz. On this, see I. G. Marcus, "A Pious Community and Doubt: *Qiddush ha-Shem* in Ashkenaz and the Story of Rabbi Amnon of Mainz," in *Essays on Hebrew Literature in Honor of Avraham Holtz*, ed. Zvia Ben-Yosef Ginor (New York: Jewish Theological Seminary of America, 2003), 21–46.

12. Jean-Claude Schmitt, *The Conversion of Herman the Jew: Autobiography, History, and Fiction in the Twelfth Century*, trans. A. J. Novikoff (Philadelphia: University of Pennsylvania Press, 2010), 204. On Herman and his autobiography, see also Aviad Kleinberg, "Hermanus Judaeus's Opusculum: In a Defense of Its Authenticity," *REJ* 151 (1992): 337–53. Herman's text has been discussed quite extensively over the past two decades. See Jeremy R. Cohen, "The Mentality of the Medieval Jewish Apostate: Peter Alfonsi, Hermann of Cologne, and Pablo Christiani," ed. Todd M. Endelman, *Jewish Apostasy in the Modern World* (New York: Holmes and Meyer, 1987), 20–47; K. F. Morrison, *Conversion and Text: The Cases of Augustine of Hippo, Herman-Judah, and Constantine Tsatsos* (Charlottesville: University of Virginia Press, 1992), 39–113; and most recently, Ryan Szpiech, *Conversion and Narrative: Reading and Religious Authority in Medieval Polemic* (Philadelphia: University of Pennsylvania Press, 2012), 60–91. The recipient of the loan, Ekbart or Egbert, bishop of Münster, was appointed to this diocese in 1127 and died in Cologne in January 1132.

13. In a later period, especially the thirteenth century, we can see more evidence of written deeds, especially for monetary and real estate transactions. Here too the mercantile communities in medieval Cologne may serve as a good example: see M. Stern and R. Hoeniger, eds., *Das Judenschrinesbuch der Laurenzpfarre zu Koln: Quellen zur Geschichte der Juden in Deutschland Band 1* (Berlin: Leonhard Simion, 1888). On the importance of written deeds in the monetary exchange between Jews and non-Jews in southern France, see J. Shatzmiller, *Shylock Reconsidered: Jews Moneylending and Medieval Society* (Berkeley: University of California Press, 1990). And for France, see A. Holtmann, "Jewish Moneylending as Reflected in Medieval Account Books: The Example form Vesoul," *The Jews of Europe in the Middle Ages: Tenth to Fifteenth Centuries* (Proceedings of the International

Symposium Held at Speyer, 20-25 October 2002), ed. C. Cluse (Turnhout: Brepols, 2004), 305–16. On the Anglo-Jewish starrs [from the Hebrew word *shtar* or *shtarot* (pl.)], see the nineteenth-century catalogue by M. D. Davis, *Hebrew Deeds of English Jews before 1290* (London, 1888), and Israel Abrams et al., eds., *Starrs and Jewish Charters: Preserved in the British Museum: with Illustrative Documents, Translations and Notes* (Cambridge: Cambridge University Press, 1930–32). More recently: Anne Causton, *Medieval Jewish Documents in Westminster Abbey* (London: Jewish Historical Society of England, 2007), and Judith Olszowy-Schlanger, "The Money Language: Latin and Hebrew in Jewish Legal Contracts from Medieval England," in *Studies in the History of Culture and Science: A Tribute to Gad Freudenthal*, ed. Resianne Fontaine et al. (Leiden: Brill, 2011), 23–50.

14. On this tractate and how it does not deal with idolatry but rather with the relationship between Jews and people considered by Jews to be idolaters, see Moshe Halbertal and Avishai Margalit, *Idolatry* (Cambridge, MA: Harvard University Press, 1992), 209–13.

15. On the predominance of the Babylonian Talmud as a source of Jewish legal thought and ruling among northern European Jews in the Middle Ages, see Talya Fishman, *Becoming the People of the Talmud* (Philadelphia: University of Pennsylvania Press, 2011), 91–154. See also the recent thought-provoking article by Haym Soloveitchik, "The Third Yeshiva of Bavel and the Cultural Origins of Ashkenaz: A Proposal," in *Collected Essays*, vol. 2, ed. Haym Soloveitchik (Oxford: Littman Library, 2014), 150–201. One of the issues discussed in this article is whether or not, and to what extent, tractate *Avodah Zarah* was part of the core curriculum in the Jewish academies in medieval Europe close to the time we first hear of a Jewish learned presence in this part of the world. See also Haym Soloveitchik, *Wine in Ashkenaz in the Middle Ages* [in Hebrew] (Jerusalem: Shazar, 2008), 157–90.

16. On this and other matters relating to the calendar and the keeping of time between Christians and Jews in medieval and early modern Europe, see Elisheva Carlebach, *Palaces of Time: Jewish Calendar and Culture in Early Modern Europe* (Cambridge, MA: Belknap, 2011).

17. On this and other matters behind this tractate in the Talmud, see Moshe Halbertal, "Coexisting with the Enemy: Jews and Pagans in the *Mishnah*," in *Tolerance and Intolerance in Early Judaism and Christianity*, ed. Graham N. Stanton and Guy Stroumsa (Cambridge: Cambridge University Press, 1998), 159–72.

18. The responsum can be found in the new comprehensive edition of Rabbi Meir's response; see Meir B. Baruch of Rothenburg, *Responsa*, ed. Ya'acov Frabstein [in (Hebrew] (Jerusalem: Machon Yerushalayim, 2015), 3:173–76 § 295–99 (formerly 1282–87) .The reference to Rabbi Asher appears in the opening remark found in § 295 and the responsum under consideration here appears in § 297. The original responsum contained answers to queries raised by Rabbi Asher on several matters. Later copiers and printers gave different numbers to each topic, but they are all part of one letter addressed by Rabbi Meir to Rabbi Asher and signed by Rabbi Meir at the end of § 299. On Meir of Rothenburg, see Irving A. Agus, *Rabbi Meir of Rothenburg: His Life and His Works as Sources for the Religious, Legal, and Social History of the Jews of Germany in the Thirteenth Century* (Philadelphia: Dropsie College for Hebrew and Cognate Learning, 1947); more recently: Ephraim Kanarfogel, "Preservation, Creativity, and Courage: The Life and Works of R. Meir of Rothenburg," *Jewish Book Annual* 50 (1992): 249–59; Simcha Emanuel, "Unpublished Responsa of R. Meir of Rothenburg as a Source for Jewish History," in *The Jews of Europe in the Middle Ages: Tenth to Fifteenth Centuries (Proceedings of the International Symposium Held at Speyer, 20–25 October 2002)*, ed. Christoph Cluse (Turnhout: Brepols, 2004), 283–93. More recently: Joseph I. Lifshitz, *Rabbi Meir of Rothenberg and the Foundation of Jewish Political Thought* (New York:

Cambridge University Press, 2015) 36–46. Asher studied with Meir and maintained constant contact with him for almost twenty years, although they lived in different localities in Germany. After Rabbi Meir was imprisoned for an unlicensed attempt to leave the German Reich (1286), Rabbi Asher played a facilitative role, along with others, in the attempts to free him from incarceration (1286–93). Later, after Meir's death in captivity, Rabbi Asher was active in the attempts to redeem his bodily remains from German imperial authorities. When these attempts failed and Rabbi Asher was himself in danger, he left Germany (1303) via France to Iberia, where he lived in Toledo until his death in 1327. See Alfred Freimann, *Ascher ben Jechiel: sein Leben und Wirken*, Jahrbuch der Jüdisch-Literarischen Gessellschaft band 12 (Frankfurt: David Droller, 1918).

19. A reference to the biblical verse in Amos 8:14: "Those who swear by the guilt of Samaria, saying: 'as your god lives Dan' and 'as the way to Beersheba lives' they shall fall to rise no more."

20. The Hebrew reads קדישים (*qudeshim*), which is a pun on the Hebrew word קדוש (*quadosh*), meaning saintly, but in this context, it is the pejorative קדש (*quadesh*), meaning a male cult prostitute (Deut. 23:18). The verse invoked here is from Job 36:14: "They die in their youth expire among the depraved (תמת בנער נפשם וחייתם בקדשים)." Rabbi Meir slightly altered the verse, writing וחייהם (their lives) instead of וחייתם (their livelihood or desire).

21. Rabbi Meir is invoking here the teaching of the Babylonian Talmud tractate *Baba Metziah* 71a: "All those who give loans with interest their businesses collapse." Through this allusion, it is clear that Rabbi Meir is referring to Jewish usurers who swear by the names of the saints as a means of enhancing their credibility.

22. Here Rabbi Meir alluded to a text in Babylonian Talmud tractate *Sota* 11a where the Talmud refers to the Egyptians who were drowned in the Red Sea. They are described as being "cooked" in the same cauldron they had attempted to "cook" the Israelites in. They had tried to drown the Israelites in the Nile, and they were eventually drowned. This also may be an allusion to baptism.

23. In the Hebrew phrasing, "They hang their claim on a high and vast tree (תולין באילן גדול)," referring to Rabbi Jacob ben Meir (Rabbenu Tam).

24. Rabbi Jacob ben Meir (~1100–71) of the northern French town of Ramerupot. See Avraham (Rami) Reiner, "Rabbenu Tam and his Contemporaries" [in Hebrew] (PhD diss., Jerusalem: Hebrew University, 2002). On Rabbi Jacob's attitude toward the business dealings in his time and his attempt to ease the way and lower the denominational hurdles for his fellow Jews, see S. Albeck, "Rabbenu Tam's Attitude to the Problems of his Time" [in Hebrew], *Zion* 19 (1954): 104–41. On the hegemony of Rabbi Jacob's school of learning and his powerful impact on rabbinic thought in northern France and Germany in the twelfth and thirteenth centuries, see Avraham (Rami) Reiner, "From Rabbenu Tam to Rabbi Isaac of Vienna: The Hegemony of the French Talmudic School in the Twelfth Century," in *The Jews of Europe in the Middle Ages: Tenth to Fifteenth Centuries (Proceedings of the International Symposium Held at Speyer, 20–25 October 2002)*, ed. Christoph Cluse (Turnhout: Brepols, 2004), 273–82.

25. See gloss (*tosafot*) on the Talmudic text in *Avodah Zarah* 2b text beginning with *Asur*. The glosses on tractate *Avodah Zarah* (that appear in the standard edition of the Babylonian Talmud [Rahm edition, Vilnius, 1881, hence forth BT]) were edited in northern France in the later years of the thirteenth century, probably in the circles of Rabbi Peretz of Corbeil. See Ephraim E. Urbach, *The Tosapists: Their History Writings and Methods* [in Hebrew] (Jerusalem: Mosad Bialik, 1980), 654–57.

26. דברים שבלב אינם דברים (lit: "thing that are in the heart are not real things"). The meaning of this legal construct is that in order to initiate a certain legal action, an intent ("inner thought") is not enough, and there is a need for a legal speech-act or actual deed to take place. On this concept of inner thoughts in Jewish legal thinking, see Itamar Warhaftig, "'Inner Thoughts' and Error in Halakha" [in Hebrew], *Dinei Israel: An Annual of Jewish Law and Israeli Family Law* 3 (1972):191–206.

27. "And although it is said that he who invokes the name of the heavens with any other entity should be severed from the face of the earth it seems odd that an Israelite will be prohibited to cause a non-Jew to invoke the name of the heavens and something else." This is the end of the quote from Rabbi Jacob ben Meir.

28. Referring to Rabbi Shmuel ben Meir, Rabbi Jacob's older brother. His opinion on the matter appears in the glosses (*tosafot*) on BT Sanhedrin 63b (for a translation and discussion of this source, see the following p. 16). The standard glosses (*tosafot*) on tractate Sanhedrin are an amalgam of the work of Rabbi Peretz of Corbeil and his students from the late thirteenth and early fourteenth centuries juxtaposed on the earlier glosses of the twelfth-century tosafists Rabbi Samson of Sans and his students. Se Urbach, vol. 2, 657–59 [in Hebrew]; Ephraim Kanarfogel, *The Intellectual History and Rabbinic Culture of Medieval Ashkenaz* (Detroit: Wayne State University Press, 2013), 28–29.

29. This statement probably refers to Rabbi Shmuel and Rabbi Jacob, the renowned twelfth-century tosafists.

30. The text was published in Hebrew in the 1960s by the late Isaac Ze'ev Kahana. See Rabbi Meir ben Baruch (Maharam) of Rothenburg, *Responsa Rulings and Customs: Collected, Annotated, and Arranged in the Order of the Shulchan Arukh* [in Hebrew], vol. 2, ed. Isaac Z. Kahana (Jerusalem: Mossad Harav Kook, 1960), 50–53 and 56–57.

31. We know of several questions that Rabbi Asher sent to his mentor Rabbi Meir. On this, see *Responsa of Rabbi Meir of Rothenburg and His Colleagues* [in Hebrew], ed. S. Emanuel vols. 1–2 (Jerusalem: The World Union of Jewish Studies, 2012), 149–63. In the collection of Rabbi Meir's responsa, edited by I. Z. Kahana, our responsum is prefaced by the one discussing the images in illuminated *Mahazorim* (communal festive prayer books, the Jewish equivalent of a Latin missal). See Rabbi Meir ben Baruch (Maharam) of Rothenburg, *Responsa Rulings and Customs: Collected, Annotated, and Arranged in the Order of the Shulchan Arukh* [in Hebrew], vol. 2, ed. Isaac Z. Kahana (Jerusalem: Mosad Harav Kook, 1960), 50–53, 56–57. Kahana identifies both our response and the one about the illuminated *Mahazorim* as letters addressed from Rabbi Meir to Rabbi Asher. Rabbi Asher was born in Cologne between 1245 and 1250. He studied with Rabbi Meir between 1265 and ca. 1270 and then returned to Cologne, where he resided until 1281. When Rabbi Meir's father, Rabbi Baruch, died in 1281, Meir returned from Rothenburg to Worms, where he was joined by Rabbi Asher in 1281 or 1282. Since the responsum is signed by Meir referring to his father as among the living, we can safely say it is from before 1281. Thus the time frame for a correspondence between the two can be narrowed down to 1270–81.

32. As Robert Chazan has noted in his analysis of the twelfth-century Jewish chronicles of the 1096 events, the Hebrew chroniclers, and especially Shlomo bar Shimon, drew from sources such as what he called "the deeds of the Jewish community of Cologne," where we find records of Jewish activity in the Cologne fairs from the early eleventh century. Robert Chazan, "The Deeds of the Jewish Community of Cologne," *Journal of Jewish Studies* 35 (1984): 185–95. See also Shlomo Eidelberg, *The Jews and the Crusaders* (Madison: University of

Wisconsin Press, 1977), 51–53. For the full Hebrew text of this chronicle, see Eva Haverkamp, *Hebräische Berichte über die Judenverfolgungen während des Ersten Kreuzzugs*, Hebraische Texte aus dem mittelalterlichen Deutschland Bd.001 (Hannover: Monumenta Germaniae Historica, 2005), 429–31.

33. On the privilege, see Joachim Oepen, "Das Judenprivileg im Kölner Dom," in *Der Kölner Dom und "die Juden": Kölner Dom Blatt: Jahrbuch des Zentral Dombau Vereins*, ed. Bernd Waker and Rolf Lauer (Koln: Verlag Kölner Dom 2008), 59–92. For an epigraphic analysis of the stone inscription, see Helga Giersiepen's article in the same collection: Helga Giersiepen, "'In Publico Aspectu Hominum': Ephigraphische Überlegungen zum Judenprivileg," Waker and Lauer, *Der Kölner Dom und "die Juden*," 93–112 On the possible connection between some of Rabbi Asher's questions to Rabbi Meir during this decade and the Cologne Judenprivileg, see Ephraim Shoham-Steiner, "The Writing on the Wall: A Mahzor, A Bimah and A Privilege; A Look at Social Processes in the 13th Century Jewish Community of Cologne," in *Visual and Material in Pre-Modern Jewish Culture*, ed. Katrin Kogman-Appel (Turnhout: Brepols, forthcoming 2020).

34. Adolf Kober, *Cologne*, trans. Solomon Grayzel. The Jewish Communities Series (Philadelphia: Jewish Publication Society of America, 1940), 22–25 and 105–6.

35. The Amsterdam Mahzor was most probably produced in the third quarter of the thirteenth century. Its beauty and the carefully executed illumination suggest it was designed for an affluent individual for communal use in a community following the Cologne rite. See Gabrielle Sed-Rajna, "The Decoration of the Amsterdam Mahzor," in *The Amsterdam Mahzor: History, Liturgy, Illumination* (Leiden: Brill, 1989) 56–70. For the Cologne rite, see Ezra Fleischer, "Prayer and Liturgical Poetry in the Great Amsterdam Mahzor," in the same volume, 39–42. On the synagogue renovation and the elaborate Bimah, see Sven Schütte and Marianne Gechter, eds., *Von der Ausgrabung zum Musem: Kölner Archäologie zwischen Rathaus und Praetorium—Ergebnisse und Materialen 2006-2012* (Stadt Köln: Köln, 2012), 110–41.

36. The phrase is from the medieval Hebrew prayer *Aleynu Leshabea'h*, the Jewish equivalent of the Latin "Te Deum Laudamus." On this prayer and its liturgical meaning, see Israel M. Ta-Shma, "Meqorah u'Mequoma shel Tfilat Aleynu Leshabe'ach: Seder Ha'ma'madot u'She'elat Siyyum Ha'Tfilah," in *The Frank Talmage Memorial Volume*, ed. Barry Walfish (Haifa: Haifa University Press, 1993) 85–98; and Israel J. Yuval, *Two Nations in Your Womb: Perceptions of Jews and Christian in Late Antiquity and the Middle Ages*, trans. Barbara Harshav and Jonathan Chipman (Berkeley: University of California Press, 2006), 190–204.

37. Rabbi Eleazar is alluding to the verse from the prophecy of Amos 8:14: "Those who swear by the guilt of Samaria, saying: 'as your god lives Dan' and 'as the way to Beersheba lives' they shall fall to rise no more." The reference in the book of Amos is to the temples of Dan and Be'ersheva that were the northern Israelite kingdom's temples dedicated to the God of Israel, where images of the calf were venerated as representations of the Lord. The prophet mocks those who invoke the name of the calf temples when they swear oaths. Interestingly, Rabbi Eleazar understands the practice of swearing the oaths in a similar manner to that in which Rabbi Asher and Rabbi Meir understand it. On Rabbi Eleazar's relation to the Ashkenazi Pietists, see Ivan G. Marcus, *Piety and Society: The Jewish Pietist of Medieval Germany* (Leiden: Brill, 1981), 109–29.

38. The calves symbolized the Israelite deity poised on the boundaries of the northern kingdom, thus demarcating the boundaries and magically protecting them.

39. On Rashi, see the new biography by Grossman. Avraham Grossman, *Rashi*, trans. Joel Linsider (Oxford: Litmman Library, 2012).

40. The original context of this dictum probably relates to the immediate context in scripture that goes on to discuss the agricultural festivals, the Feast of Unleavened Bread and the Feast of Sukkot. The verse stipulates that the names of other gods should not be mentioned, probably referring to invoking them in the context of the festivals. Some of the non-Israelite deities were closely associated with fertility, which was celebrated in these festivals, and the dictum is probably designed to prevent any form of syncretism of the Hebrew God with the Canaanite deities Ba'al, Ashera, etc.

41. In other words, "You shall make no business-partnership with a heathen through which it might happen that he will take an oath by the name of his god."

42. Rashi's commentary on this verse can be found in *Chumash with Targum Onkelos, Haphtaroth and Rashi's Commentary*, vol. 2, *Exodus*, trans. A. M. Silbermann and M. Rosenbaum (Jerusalem: Silbermann Family and Routledge, 1985), 125.

43. The text uses pejorative language when referring to objects held in reverence by Christians, such as relics referred to here as "the rotting bones of their depravities," and when the gentile honors the relics by placing a coin on the reliquary, the text refers to this act not as an act of honor but as an act of disgrace. The use of pejorative language when referring to Christian sacral objects, rituals, clerics, Jesus, Mary, and the saints is well known and well documented. Mordechai Breuer published a one-page appendix to his edition of the *Nizzahon Vetus* in which he listed thirty-three of these pejorative terms. See *Sefer Nizzahon Yashan: Sefer Vikkuah neged ha-Nozerim*, ed. Mordechai Breuer (Ramat-Gan: Bar-Ilan University Press, 1978), 194. On similar language in the twelfth century Hebrew chronicles of the 1096 events, see Anna Sapir Abulafia, "Invectives against Christianity in the Hebrew chronicles of the First Crusade," in *Christians and Jews in Dispute: Disputational Literature and the Rise of Anti-Judaism in the West (c. 1000–1150)* (Aldershot, VT: Ashgate, 1998). On cursing the Christians, see Yuval, *Two Nations in Your Womb*, 115–34, and additional bibliography in his notes. More recently on this topic: Ruth Langer, *Cursing the Christians?: A History of the Birkat Haminim* (New York: Oxford University Press, 2012).

44. There are two possible readings here. According to Elfenbein's edition, there are some sources that say that Rashi believed (ויאמן) the gentile after he swore the oath (ויאמן רבי), and there are some sources that state that Rashi withdrew then and there: וימאן

45. Israel S. Elfenbein, *Responsa Rashi (Solomon ben Isaac) ex codicibus librisque impressis congessit praefationem annotationnes indices adiecit* (New York: Shulsinger Bros., 1943), 23. Elfenbein correctly observed that this anecdote, which appears in a manuscript called *Isur ve'heter le'Rashi* in the Avraham Merzbacher (1812–85) collection of the Frankfurt Library, as well as a manuscript of the same name from the Jewish Theological Seminary library collection in New York and the *Book of Oreh*, were penned by the person Avraham Epstein called "Rashi's student and trusted secretary," Schmaia. See Avraham Epstein, "Schmaja: Der Schüler und Secretär Raschi's," *MGWJ* 41 (1897): 257–63 and 296–312. Our knowledge about R. Schmiah is far greater nowadays. There is no up-to-date summary of Shmaiah's biography and his role in preserving editing and glossing his master mentor's work, but one can consult Avraham Grossman and Uziel Fuchs's articles: Avraham Grossman, "Marginal Notes and Addenda of Rabbi Shemaiah and the Text of Rashi's Biblical Commentary" [in Hebrew], *Tarbiz* 60 (1990–91): 67–98; Uziel Fuchs, "Shnei Pirushim Hadashim al Masechet Tamid: Pirush Ashkenazi u'Pirush Rabbenu Shmaiah" [in

Hebrew], *Kobez Al Yad: Minora Manuscripta Hebraica* 15 (25) 2000: 95–141, especially 99–100 and the notes there.

46. Haym Soloveichik, "Can Halakhic Texts Talk History?" *AJS Review* 3 (1978): 153–96. This article was reprinted in: Haym Soloveichik, *Collected Essays*, vol. 1 (Oxford: Littman Library, 2013), 169–223.

47. I would suggest that the commentary on Ex. 23:13 was either written after the incident or that this bit was inserted and amended by Rashi in his already existing commentary on this verse post factum as a result of this incident. Rabbi Shmuel ben Meir ("Rashbam," 1085–1158), Rashi's grandson and close disciple, testifies in his running commentary of the Pentateuch (Gen. 37:2) that the aging master rewrote some of his commentaries on the Bible following their discussions and lamented the fact that he did not do so more frequently in accordance with the new natural understanding (as opposed to a more traditional homiletic approach) "that are newly taught of day by day." See Martin I. Lockshin, *Rabbi Samuel ben Meir's Commentary on Genesis: An Annotated Translation* (Lewiston-Lampeter-Queenston: Edwin Mellen, 1989), 241–42.

48. BT Sanhedrin 63b and the tosafist gloss there beginning with the word *Asur*. This text is also quoted in BT Bekhorot 2b and the tosafist gloss there beginning with the word "*Shemah*". On the matter of "multiplicity and participation" (*shituf*), see Jacob Katz, "Shlosha Mishpatim Apologetiyim Be'Gilgulehem" [in Hebrew], in *Halakhah and Kabbalah: Studies in the History of Jewish Religion in Various Faces and Social Relevance*, ed. Jacob Katz (Jerusalem: Magnes, 1986), 270–90, especially 278–79 and 289–90. On this, see Moshe Halbertal and Avishai Margalit, *Idolatry*, 111.

49. The editor of the glosses (*tosafot*) on tractate Sanhedrin of the BT is anonymous. Textual evidence in the glosses suggest, however, that it is likely that they were edited sometime during the end of the thirteenth century or the early fourteenth century in northern France by one of the students of the acclaimed tosafist and compiler of tosafot Rabbi Peretz ben Elijah of Corbeil (d. 1295): Benjamin Richler, "Manuscripts of the Tosafists on the Talmud" [in Hebrew], in *Ta-Shma: Studies in Judaica in Memory of Israel M. Ta-Shma*, vol. 2, ed. Avraham (Rami) Reiner et al. (Alon Shvut: Tevunot Press, 2011), 771–854, especially 815–33. Rabbi Peretz himself studied with French masters Rabbi Yehiel of Paris and Rabbi Samuel of Evreux, but he was also a close disciple of the German Jewish masters, such as Rabbi Meir of Rothenberg. See Urbach, *Ba'alei Ha-Tosafot*, vol. 2, 657; Kanarfogel, *The Intellectual History*, 37–110, especially 66–67. Recently: Shevach Shulman, "The Uniqueness of Rabbi Peretz ben Eliyahu as a Tosafist and as a *Posek*" [in Hebrew] (master's thesis, Ramat-Gan: Talmud Department, Bar-Ilan University, 2014). I thank my friend Judah Galinsky for turning my attention to Shulman's work.

50. Jacob Katz mentioned another twelfth-century northern French Jewish legal authority who had also elaborated on the subject: Rabbi Isaac ben Samuel of Dampierre (referred to more commonly by his acronym Ri "the Elder," d. 1189). In a quote of his found in the writings of the northern French exiled Rabbi Yerucham ben Meshulam (1290–1350), *Sefer Toldot Adam ve'Hava* (path 17, section 5), Rabbi Isaac writes, "There is another way to permit this practice (of causing a non-Jew to swear by invoking the name of the saints) for they [the Christians] swear the oaths invoking the names of their saints referring to the ones they call the 'evangelists.' They do not hold these saints in the same reverence as a deity. And although when they invoke the name of the heavens they refer to Jesus, in any case they do not mention any name of an idol. Furthermore when they invoke the saints their mind is set

on the creator of the heavens and the earth. Indeed they share the name of the almighty with 'another thing' [Jesus] but there is no prohibition to cause them to do so for the Noahides are not prohibited to 'share.'" The text here is so close to that of Rabbi Jacob ben Meir that I fear that Katz may have mistaken it for Rabbi Isaac's. In Rabbi Yerucham's text, the quote is attributed to Ri, but the Hebrew acronym for Ri and Rabbi Jacob (יעקב 'ר) could have been a scribal error. As is clear from Katz's notes, Ri was referring to oath formulations such as this one: *Per deum omnipotentem et per ista sacra quatuor evangelia*. This oath was usually performed while placing the hand over a copy of the holy scriptures. This oath formulation is mentioned during the reign of the Carolingian emperor Louis the Pious (778–840) in an oath dating back to 824; see Ferdinand Walter, *Corpus Iuris Germanici Antiqui*, vol. 2 (Raims, 1824), 368.

51. It stands to reason that the saints' names invoked were probably the local urban patron saints whose figures were well known and ever present in the medieval urban public sphere. A fine representation of these figures in an urban mercantile hub like Cologne is still visible at the Cologne Cathedral in a fifteenth-century retable by Stephan Lochner, The Altarpiece of the Patron Saints of Cologne, depicting St. Ursula her husband and the eleven thousand virgins, the Three Magi (whose relics are interred in the cathedral apsis) and St. Gereon alongside the Virgin Mary.

52. On the French Cahorsin moneylenders, see Noël Denholm-Young, "The Merchants of Cahors," *Medievalia et Humanistica* 4 (1946), 37–44. See also Kurt Grunwald, "Lombards, Cahorsins and Jews," *Journal of European Economic History* 4 (1975), 393–98, and more recently, Rowen W. Dorin, "Banishing Usury: The Expulsion of Foreign Moneylenders in Medieval Europe, 1200–1450" (unpublished Doctoral Dissertation, Harvard University, 2015), 17–18.

53. On the decline of social and legal status of Jews in western Europe, see Jeremy Cohen, *The Friars and the Jews: The Evolution of Medieval Anti-Judaism* (Ithaca: Cornell University Press, 1982). More recently: I. G. Marcus, "A Jewish-Christian Symbiosis: The Culture of Early Ashkenaz," in *The Cultures of the Jews: A New History*, vol. 2, ed. David Biale (New York: Schocken, 2002), 449–516. One of the finest overviews of this historical process appeared recently in the introduction to the Italian Jewish treatise *Sefer Malveh ve'Loveh* in the new edition by Robert Bonfil: *The Book of Moneylender and Borrower* [in Hebrew] (Jerusalem: Shazar, 2015), 44–76.

54. On the life of Meir of Rothenburg, see endnote 18 in this chapter. The matter of a rabbinic figure's stand among his rabbinic peers is age old and dates back to the Talmud: see Mishnah Tractate *Eduyot* 8:1; BT tractate *Shabbat* 60b; BT tractate *Avodah Zarah* 36a. In medieval literature, we find a famous comment accredited to Rabbi Jacob ben Judah Weil. While he officiated as rabbi in Augsburg (1429–38), Rabbi Jacob wrote about his fear of declaring that butter from a non-Jewish source is kosher: "I would permit this if I would not fear that my colleagues would mock me and refer to me as 'Jacob the permitter of forbidden things.'" (יעקב דשר איסורא) See Joseph ben Moses of Münster, *Sefer Lequet Yosher*, vol. 2: *Yoreh De'ah*, ed. Joel Catane et al. (Jerusalem: Machon Yerushalayim, 2013): hilkhot Yein Nesech section 5, 17.

55. On the blindness of Jews and the blindness of the figure of "Synagoga" (representing Jews' and Judaism's blindness to the confessional Christian truth in medieval Western art), see Moshe Barasch, *Blindness: The History of a Mental Image in Western Thought* (New York: Routledge, 2001); S. Lipton, "The Temple Is My Body: Gender, Carnality, and Synagoga in

the Bible Moralisée," in *Imagining the Self, Imagining the Other: Visual Representation and Jewish-Christian Dynamics in the Middle Ages and Early Modern Period*, ed. Eva Frojmovic (Leiden: Brill, 2002), 144–52; and more recently: Sara Lipton, "Unfeigned Witness: Jews, Matter, and Vision in Twelfth-Century Art," in *Judaism and Christian Art: Aesthetic Anxieties from the Catacombs to Colonialism*, ed. Herbert L. Kessler and David Nirenberg (Philadelphia: University of Pennsylvania Press, 2011), 45–74. Sara Lipton, *Dark Mirror: The Medieval Origins of Anti-Jewish Iconography* (New York: Metropolitan Books, 2014), 55–128. Nina Rowe, "Rethinking Ecclesia and Synagoga in the Thirteenth Century," in *Gothic Art & Thought in the Later Medieval Period: Essays in Honor of Willibald Sauerländer*, ed. Colum Hourihane (Princeton: Department of Art & Archaeology, Princeton University in association with Penn State University Press, 2011), 265–91.

Bibliography

Abrams, Israel, et al., eds. *Starrs and Jewish Charters: Preserved in the British Museum: with Illustrative Documents, Translations and Notes*. Cambridge: Cambridge University Press, 1930–32.

Agus, Irving A. *Rabbi Meir of Rothenburg: His Life and His Works as Sources for the Religious, Legal, and Social History of the Jews of Germany in the Thirteenth Century*. Philadelphia: Dropsie College for Hebrew and Cognate Learning, 1947.

Albeck, Shalom. "Rabbenu Tam's Attitude to the Problems of his Time." [In Hebrew.] *Zion* 19 (1954): 104–41.

Barasch, Moshe. *Blindness: The History of a Mental Image in Western Thought*. New York: Routledge, 2001.

Bonfil, Robert, ed. *The Book of Moneylender and Borrower*. [In Hebrew.] Jerusalem: Shazar, 2015.

Breuer, Mordechai, ed. *Sefer Nizzahon Yashan: Sefer Vikkuah neged ha-Nozerim*. Ramat-Gan: Bar-Ilan University Press, 1978.

Carlebach, Elisheva. *Palaces of Time: Jewish Calendar and Culture in Early Modern Europe*. Cambridge, MA: Belknap, 2011.

Catane, Joel, et al., eds. *Joseph ben Moses of Münster, Sefer Lequet Yosher*. Vol. 2, *Yoreh De'ah*. Jerusalem: Machon Yerushalayim, 2013.

Causton, Anne. *Medieval Jewish Documents in Westminster Abbey*. London: Jewish Historical Society of England, 2007.

Chazan, Robert. "The Deeds of the Jewish Community of Cologne." *Journal of Jewish Studies* 35 (1984): 185–95.

———. *Medieval Jewry in Northern France: A Political and Social History*. Baltimore: Johns Hopkins University Press, 1973.

Cohen, Jeremy. *The Friars and the Jews: The Evolution of Medieval Anti-Judaism*. Ithaca, NY: Cornell University Press, 1982.

———. "The Mentality of the Medieval Jewish Apostate: Peter Alfonsi, Hermann of Cologne, and Pablo Christiani," in *Jewish Apostasy in the Modern World*, edited by Todd M. Endelman, 20–47. New York: Holmes & Meyer, 1987.

Davis, Myer D, ed. *Sheṭarot: Hebrew Deeds of English Jews before 1290*. London: The Jewish Chronicle, 1888.

Eidelberg, Shlomo. *The Jews and the Crusades: The Hebrew Chronicles of the First and the Second Crusades.* Madison: University of Wisconsin Press, 1977.

Elfenbein, Israel S. *Responsa Rashi (Solomon ben Isaac) ex codicibus librisque impressis congessit praefationem annotationnes indices adiecit.* New York: Shulsinger Bros., 1943.

Emanuel, Simcha, ed. *Responsa of Rabbi Meir of Rothenburg and His Colleagues.* Vols. 1–2. [In Hebrew]. Jerusalem: The World Union of Jewish Studies, 2012.

———. "Unpublished Responsa of R. Meir of Rothenburg as a Source for Jewish History." In *The Jews of Europe in the Middle Ages: Tenth to Fifteenth Centuries (Proceedings of the International Symposium Held at Speyer, 20–25 October 2002),* edited by Christoph Cluse, 283–93. Turnhout: Brepols, 2004.

Epstein, Avraham. "Schmaja: Der Schüler und Secretär Raschi's." *MGWJ (Monatsschrift für Geschichte und Wissenschaft des Judentums)* 41 (1897): 257–63 and 296–312.

Fishman Taliya. *Becoming the People of the Talmud: Oral Torah as Written Tradition in Medieval Jewish Cultures.* Philadelphia: University of Pennsylvania Press, 2011.

Freimann, Alfred. *Ascher ben Jechiel: sein Leben und Wirken,* Jahrbuch der Jüdisch-Literarischen Gessellschaft band 12. Frankfurt: David Droller, 1918.

Fuchs, Uziel. "Shnei Pirushim Hadashim al Masechet Tamid: Pirush Ashkenazi u' Pirush Rabbenu Shmaiah." [In Hebrew.] *Kobez Al Yad: Minora Manuscripta Hebraica* 15 (25) (2000): 95–141.

Golb, Norman. *The Jews in Medieval Normandy: A Social and Intellectual History.* Cambridge: Cambridge University Press, 1998.

Grossman, Avraham. Joel Linsider, trans. *Rashi.* Oxford, England, and Portland, OR: Litmman Library, 2012.

———. "Marginal Notes and Addenda of Rabbi Shemaiah and the Text of Rashi's Biblical Commentary." [In Hebrew.] *Tarbiz* 60 (1990–91): 67–98.

Haberman, Avraham M., ed. *Ephraim ben Jacob of Bonn, Sefer Zehira Selichot ve'Quinot.* [In Hebrew.] Jerusalem: Mosad Bialik, 1970.

Halbertal, Moshe. "Coexisting with the Enemy: Jews and Pagans in the *Mishnah.*" In *Tolerance and Intolerance in Early Judaism and Christianity,* edited by Graham N. Stanton and Guy Stroumsa, 159–72. Cambridge: Cambridge University Press, 1998.

Halbertal, Moshe, and Avishai Margalit. *Idolatry.* Cambridge, MA: Harvard University Press, 1992.

Haverkamp, Eva. *Hebräische Berichte über die Judenverfolgungen während des Ersten Kreuzzugs.* Hebraische Texte aus dem mittelalterlichen Deutschland Bd.001. Hannover: Monumenta Germaniae Historica, 2005.

Hexter, Ralph J. *Equivocal Oaths and Ordeals in Medieval Literature.* Cambridge, MA: Harvard University Press, 1975.

Holtmann, A. "Jewish Moneylending as Reflected in Medieval Account Books: The Example form Vesoul." In *The Jews of Europe in the Middle Ages: Tenth to Fifteenth Centuries (Proceedings of the International Symposium Held at Speyer, 20–25 October 2002),* edited by C. Cluse, 305–16. Turnhout: Brepols, 2004.

Jordan, William C. *The French Monarchy and the Jews: From Philip Augustus to the Last Capetians.* Philadelphia: University of Pennsylvania Press, 1989.

Kahana, Isaac Z., ed. *Rabbi Meir ben Baruch (Maharam) of Rothenburg, Responsa Rulings and Customs: Collected Annotated and Arranged in the Order of the Shulchan Arukh.* 2 vols. [In Hebrew.] Jerusalem: Mossad Harav Kook, 1960.

Kanarfogel, Ephraim. *The Intellectual History and Rabbinic Culture of Medieval Ashkenaz.* Detroit: Wayne State University Press, 2013.

———. "Preservation, Creativity, and Courage: The Life and Works of R. Meir of Rothenburg." *Jewish Book Annual* 50 (1992): 249–59.

Katz, Jacob. *Halakhah and Kabbalah: Studies in the History of Jewish Religion in Various Faces and Social Relevance.* [In Hebrew.] Jerusalem: Magnes, 1986.

Kleinberg, Aviad. "Hermanus Judaeus's Opusculum: In a Defense of Its Authenticity." *Revue des Études Juives* 151 (1992): 337–53.

Kober, Adolf. *Cologne.* Translated by Solomon Grayzel. The Jewish Communities Series. Philadelphia: Jewish Publication Society of America, 1940.

Langer, Ruth. *Cursing the Christians?: A History of the Birkat Haminim.* New York: Oxford University Press, 2012.

Lifshitz, Joseph I. *Rabbi Meir of Rothenberg and the Foundation of Jewish Political Thought.* New York: Cambridge University Press, 2015.

Lipton, Sara. *Dark Mirror: The Medieval Origins of Anti-Jewish Iconography.* New York: Metropolitan Books, 2014.

———. "The Temple Is My Body: Gender, Carnality, and Synagoga in the Bible Moralisée." In *Imagining the Self, Imagining the Other: Visual Representation and Jewish-Christian Dynamics in the Middle Ages and Early Modern Period*, edited by Eva Frojmovic, 144–52. Leiden: Brill, 2002.

———. "Unfeigned Witness: Jews, Matter, and Vision in Twelfth-Century Art." In *Judaism and Christian Art: Aesthetic Anxieties from the Catacombs to Colonialism*, edited by Herbert L. Kessler and David Nirenberg, 45–74. Philadelphia: University of Pennsylvania Press, 2011.

Linder, Amnon. "The Jewry Oath in Christian Europe." In *Jews in Early Christian Law: Byzantium and the Latin West 6th–11th Centuries*, edited by J. Tolan et al., 311–59. Turnhout: Brepols, 2014.

Lockshin, Martin I. *Rabbi Samuel ben Meir's Commentary on Genesis: An Annotated Translation.* Lewiston-Lampeter-Queenston: Edwin Mellen, 1989.

Marcus, Ivan G. "A Jewish-Christian Symbiosis: The Culture of Early Ashkenaz." In *The Cultures of the Jews: A New History*, vol. 2, edited by David Biale, 449–516. New York: Schocken, 2002.

———. *Piety and Society: The Jewish Pietist of Medieval Germany.* Leiden: Brill, 1981.

———. "A Pious Community and Doubt: *Qiddush ha-Shem* in Ashkenaz and the Story of Rabbi Amnon of Mainz." In *Essays on Hebrew Literature in Honor of Avraham Holtz*, edited by Zvia Ben-Yosef Ginor, 21–46. New York: Jewish Theological Seminary of America, 2003.

Morrison, Karl. F. *Conversion and Text: The Cases of Augustine of Hippo, Herman-Judah, and Constantine Tsatsos.* Charlottesville: University of Virginia Press, 1992.

Olszowy-Schlanger, Judith. "The Money Language: Latin and Hebrew in Jewish Legal Contracts from Medieval England." In *Studies in the History of Culture and Science. A Tribute to Gad Freudenthal*, edited by Resianne Fontaine et al., 233–50. Leiden: Brill, 2011.

Reiner, Avraham. "From Rabbenu Tam to Rabbi Isaac of Vienna: The Hegemony of the French Talmudic School in the Twelfth Century." In *The Jews of Europe in the Middle Ages: Tenth to Fifteenth Centuries (Proceedings of the International Symposium*

Held at Speyer, 20–25 October 2002), edited by Christoph Cluse, 273–82. Turnhout: Brepols, 2004.

Richler, Benjamin. "Manuscripts of the Tosafists on the Talmud." [In Hebrew.] In *Ta-Shma: Studies in Judaica in Memory of Israel M. Ta-Shma*, vol. 2, edited by Avraham (Rami) Reiner et al., 771–854. Alon Shvut: Tevunot, 2011.

Rowe, Nina. "Rethinking Ecclesia and Synagoga in the Thirteenth Century." In *Gothic Art & Thought in the Later Medieval Period: Essays in Honor of Willibald Sauerländer*, edited by Colum Hourihane, 265–91. Princeton, NJ: Index of Christian Art, Princeton University in association with Penn State University Press, 2011.

Sapir Abulafia, Anna. *Christians and Jews in Dispute: Disputational Literature and the Rise of Anti-Judaism in the West (c. 1000–1150)*. Aldershot, VT: Ashgate, 1998.

Schmitt, Jean-Claude. *The Conversion of Herman the Jew: Autobiography, History, and Fiction in the Twelfth Century*. Translated by Alex. J. Novikoff. Philadelphia: University of Pennsylvania Press, 2010.

Schütte, Sven, and Marianne Gechter, eds. *Von der Ausgrabung zum Musem: Kölner Archäologie zwischen Rathaus und Praetorium: Ergebnisse und Materialen 2006–12*. Köln: Stadt Köln, 2012.

Sed-Rajna, Gabrielle. "The Decoration of the Amsterdam Mahzor." In *The Amsterdam Mahzor: History, Liturgy, Illumination*, edited by Albert van der Heide and Edward. van Voole, 56–70. Leiden: Brill, 1989.

Shatzmiller, Joseph. *Shylock Reconsidered: Jews, Moneylending, and Medieval Society*. Berkeley: University of California Press, 1990.

Shoham-Steiner, Ephraim, ed. *Intricate Interfaith Networks: Quotidian Jewish-Christian Contacts in the Middle Ages*. Turnhout: Brepols, 2016.

Shulman, Shevach. "The Uniqueness of Rabbi Peretz ben Eliyahu as a Tosafist and as a Posek." [In Hebrew.] Master's thesis, Ramat-Gan: Talmud Department, Bar-Ilan University, 2014.

Stern, Moritz. *Das Judenschrinesbuch der Laurenzpfarre zu Koln: Quellen zur Geschichte der Juden in Deutschland Band 1*. Edited by Robert Hoeniger. Berlin: Leonhard Simion, 1888.

Soloveitchik, Haym. "Can Halakhic Texts Talk History?" *AJS Review* 3 (1978): 153–96.

———. "The Third Yeshiva of Bavel and the Cultural Origins of Ashkenaz—A Proposal." In *Collected Essays*, vol. 2, edited by Haym Soloveitchik. Oxford, England, and Portland, OR: Littman Library, 2014.

———. *Wine in Ashkenaz in the Middle Ages*. [In Hebrew.] Jerusalem: Shazar, 2008.

Szpiech, Ryan. *Conversion and Narrative: Reading and Religious Authority in Medieval Polemic*. Philadelphia: University of Pennsylvania Press, 2012.

Taitz, Emily. *The Jews of Medieval France: The Community of Champagne*. Westport, CT: Greenwood, 1994.

Ta-Shma, Israel M. "Meqorah u'Mequoma shel Tfilat Aleynu Leshabe'ach: Seder Ha'ma'madot u'She'elat Siyyum Ha'Tfilah." In *The Frank Talmage Memorial Volume*, edited by Barry Walfish, 85–98. Haifa: Haifa University Press, 1993.

Urbach, Ephraim E. *The Tosapists: Their History Writings and Methods*. 2 vols. [In Hebrew]. Jerusalem: Mosad Bialik, 1980.

Walter, Ferdinand. *Corpus Iuris Germanici Antiqui*. Vol. 2. Berolini: Reimer, 1824.

Warhaftig, Itamar. "'Inner Thoughts' and Error in Halakha." [In Hebrew.] *Dinei Israel: An Annual of Jewish Law and Israeli Family Law* 3 (1972): 191–206.

Werblowsky, R. J. Zwi. "Faith, Hope, and Trust: A Study in the Concept of *Bittahon*." In *Papers of the Institute of Jewish Studies London*, edited by J. G. Weiss, 95–139. Jerusalem: Magnes, 1964.

Wistinetzki, Jehuda, ed. *Das Buch der Frommen: nach der Rezension in Cod. De Rossi no. 1133 mit Einleitung und Registern von Jacob Freimann*. Frankfurt: Wahrman, 1924.

Yuval, Israel J. *Two Nations in Your Womb: Perceptions of Jews and Christian in Late Antiquity and the Middle Ages*. Translated by Barbara Harshav and Jonathan Chipman. Berkeley: University of California Press, 2006.

EPHRAIM SHOHAM-STEINER teaches Medieval Jewish history at Ben-Gurion University of the Negev and is Director of the Center for the Study of Conversion (CSOC). He is author of *On the Margins of a Minority: Leprosy, Madness, and Disability among the Jews of Medieval Europe*. Among his other areas of interest are the medieval Jewish community in Cologne and Jewish Christian relations in medieval Europe.

3   The Oath of a Jew in the Thirteenth-Century English Legal Context

Joshua Curk

In Easter term[1] 1220, a Jewish man named Solomon Turbe was imprisoned at Gloucester Castle for "maliciously wounding" another Jew named Abraham Gabbay.[2] In an indication that this was in fact a legitimate charge, Abraham arranged four pledges for prosecution. However, prior to anybody appearing before the justices at the Exchequer of the Jews, Solomon's wife, Comitissa, was entered on the Plea Rolls as reporting that Solomon had died.[3] She alleged that Abraham, the man who had been assaulted by her late husband, had paid ten marks[4] to the guards in Gloucester castle to have Solomon thrown out of the castle window—it came out in later testimony that he had been seen falling "from the summit of the tower"—and that Solomon had died as a result. Comitissa then offered "to prove as Jewess against Jew, as the Court shall direct," and Abraham offered his defense as "Jew against Jewess."[5] This in itself was not unusual—the Exchequer of the Jews possessed and exercised jurisdiction over appeals of felony where either of the parties was Jewish, as well as jurisdiction over inquiry into the death of any Jew who might have been murdered.[6] The chief oddity in this case was that Comitissa, the widow bringing the charges, did not have to provide pledges for prosecution,[7] but Abraham, in accusing Solomon of assaulting him, did. The normative practice in cases involving a death, at least in London, was for the accuser to provide a gage or pledge in order for the charge to be pursued.[8]

The final wrinkle in the summary of the case is perhaps the most interesting for the purposes of this chapter: Solomon did not die immediately after falling or being thrown out of the tower; he lived long enough to be interrogated on two separate days, and crucially, he changed his version of the events leading to his fall. A "great number" of Jews and Christians of Gloucester questioned him on the Friday, at the sheriff's request. Solomon was asked how he came to fall, and in his response, he likened himself to King Saul—a thinly veiled reference to suicide. He had apparently thrown himself out the window in order that he might be saved (*salvus*). He was asked again whether or not somebody had caused his fall, and he again answered in the negative. At this point, his wife, Comitissa, arrived, causing Abraham to say repeatedly, "Flee hence, for 'tis by thy plot that I am slain."[9] On the Saturday, the sheriff sent the constable and the coroner to again question Solomon, at which point he appealed Abraham.[10] The verdict, given by four Jewish jurors, found that Solomon had fallen of his own accord and cleared Abraham of the charge.[11]

There did exist legislation that affected cases like this, and in this instance, the details of the case played out nearly exactly as provided for in the legislation: there was a potential murder where the victim, the defendant, and the accuser were all Jewish. The Jew who brought the charges, Comitissa, swore her oath on the Torah, as she was allowed to do under the terms of the charters that had been previously granted; the Crown's jurisdiction over Crown pleas was affirmed; and the Exchequer of the Jews' jurisdiction over inquiries into the death of a Jew who might have been murdered was exercised.[12] The denouement provides us with closure to the case: Comitissa alleged that she knew about Abraham's plot to kill her husband because Abraham, while being cured of the wounds caused by Solomon's assault, had spoken to the sheriff and caused her to be thrown into prison, where she was "so starved that she despaired of her life."[13] While in prison, she alleged that she had overheard Abraham conspiring with others for the death of her husband, offering ten marks to the two men contracted for the purpose. Notwithstanding the fact that ten marks was an astronomical sum to have in hand, let alone offer in a murder-for-hire plot, Abraham denied everything about the charge, and offered an alibi: he had been in Hereford on the day that Solomon fell to his death, and not Gloucester. Comitissa then charged that it was obvious that Abraham would pretend that he was not in Gloucester on that day "in order that none might hold him suspect of the murder."[14]

There are two salient points to take away from the case above concerning Comitissa: in the first instance, the legislation worked exactly as intended. In the second, and perhaps slightly more surprisingly, Comitissa's oath worked better than it ought to have. Her oath, presumably accompanying her offer to prove as "Jewess against Jew" and sworn on the Torah, was considered ample proof that her accusations were valid and seems to have negated the requirement for pledges to corroborate her accusation. There was no suspicion that what Comitissa had alleged was anything but the truth. Comitissa had blatantly lied, and yet the inherently present value of trust remained unassailed. Her extreme confidence that she would be trusted confirms that Jewish oaths were not only valuable forms of currency, but contained innate truth. Furthermore, Comitissa was not prosecuted after having had her ruse undone by Solomon's fantastic about-face. The case, in the end, seems to have been nothing more than a clumsy attempt at extortion, undone only by the dying man's conscience.

This case is illustrative of the difficulties in assessing both the purpose and the form of a Jewish oath in thirteenth-century England. It underscores issues not only with the theoretical application of a Jewish oath, but the practicalities of its use. Though the privilege of being trusted was not an exclusively Jewish entitlement at the time, there was an inherent trust built into a Jewish oath in medieval England—so much so that, certainly in the legal sphere, it appeared as though Jewish oaths were imbued with a level of gravitas not accorded to Christian oaths. This much is evident from the phrasing of the relevant parts of the 1275 legislation, where an attempt to correct this seeming lapse was made. But how did a Jew convey that his oath was trustworthy? For a Christian, the requirement to be a *probus et legalis* person was the unquestioned root of the ability to make an oath and have it trusted. For a Jew, on the other hand, this trust was precontracted. Though legislation at various points in the century changed the nature of the Jewish oath, it always assured the Jews of their right to make an oath along with implying an assured level of trust. Writing of a different context, Guido Kisch noted the need not only for a treatment of the law relating to Jewish oaths but also for a discussion of the form and wording of the Jewish oath.[15] To a lesser extent, this applies to English history, though recent research has certainly helped. However, as far as I am aware, no manuscript containing any form of a Jewish oath as it was practiced in England survives, forcing the focus of this essay toward the purpose of the oath rather than its arrangement. To this end, the following discussion seeks to shed light on several questions: What was the purpose of a Jewish oath in medieval England? What were the ways in which it was used? How did Jews work within the legislation regarding their oaths? These questions will be addressed by discussing several cases from the surviving evidence, and I argue that Jewish oaths in England were inherently flexible, despite legislation and convention designed to keep them static. Oaths for Jews in medieval England were a part of the very fabric of society, serving to keep that society not only together, but functional.

Trust was the abstract concept underlying a Jew's oath in medieval England. By making an oath, a medieval English Jew was doing two things: he was pronouncing for the record that his version of the truth as he understood it was a truthful narrative, and, implicitly, he added gravitas to the pronouncement. By asserting that his version of the truth was correct before the law, he was placing his own reputation on the line as a guarantee. Perjury was a very serious offense, and "failure in an oath, whatever the reason, seriously damaged a man's ability to live a normal life afterwards. It ruined his reputation and marked him out as one who could not be trusted."[16] There was no room for false oaths in medieval Anglo-Jewish society; were there suspicions for whatever reason, steps might be taken to remedy this temporary mistrust by having another Jew swear an oath regarding the veracity of the first Jew's oath.[17]

As a pertinent aside, the published sources referred to here are both the most germane to the topic and a plurality of the surviving evidence. With no exceptions, the primary sources in this essay were by-products of governmental administration in the thirteenth century. The most intensely cited are the Plea Rolls of the Exchequer of the Jews. These are the main records of the activities of the Exchequer of the Jews, which existed from the end of the twelfth century until the expulsion of the Jews from England in 1290. The rolls record a mixture of legal business and administrative activities, as documented by scribes who were likely in the employ of the Justices of the Jews, who heard pleas therein. The Charter Rolls "comprise grants and confirmations of liberties, privileges, offices, dignities, lands and pensions to corporations and individuals, civil and ecclesiastical."[18] They are similar to the Patent Rolls, with the chief difference being that the Patent Rolls contain a large number of judicial and administrative entries, and the issuance of a charter generally implied the presence of the king.[19] The *Rotuli de Oblatis et Finibus* recorded, generally, "the sums of money or other property, offered to the King by way of oblation or fine, for the enjoyment of honors, offices, lands, liberties, and privileges."[20] Fines composed a significant portion of royal revenue and are recorded in separate manuscripts, known as Fine Rolls. The *Curia Regis* Rolls, from the time periods in which they are used here, recorded litigation in the Court of Common Pleas and King's Bench, which sat at Westminster. Among many other things, the Pipe Rolls recorded a large portion of royal income, outstanding debts to the Crown, and royal expenses, and were recorded after annual audits at the Exchequer. The Close Rolls, produced in Chancery, enrolled the details of private "letters close" which were folded and sealed communications. They covered almost all aspects of political and administrative life, as well as details of the royal household and other nonpublic executive orders. Finally, the Calendar of Papal Registers records surviving papal bulls and letters that concern England, Scotland, and Wales, and renders them calendared in English. In the period of time covered in this essay, they were produced by papal scribes and subsequently sent to Britain.

In England, allowing the Jews to clear themselves on their oaths was considered a privilege. In this respect, the experience of the medieval Anglo-Jewry was comparable with continental Jews. There was an implicit trust in a Jew's oath by the thirteenth century. Where others, especially those who were reputed to be dishonest, had to exonerate themselves via other judicial methods,[21] Jews were distinctly privileged, for the vast majority of their collective stay in England, not only to swear oaths, but to have these oaths trusted. This was one of the few instances where it is apparent that the blanket judgments of an entire religion and its adherents that were so much a part of life in this period were occasionally beneficial to the Jews. The root cause of this overarching trust in the Jews as a people was an understanding that whatever else they might have been, they were not perjurious, and therefore were to be trusted in giving oaths. Christian observers likely knew that in a community as close-knit as that of the medieval Anglo-Jewry, the potential public shame of perjury was often sufficient to guard against any potential uttered falsehoods.

This trust had a lengthy evolution and was a direct result of the exemption of Jews from participation in ordeals. Jews were exempt from ordeals originally because the ordeal "was so indelibly Christian that it would be not only unfair but also, more important in Christian eyes, virtually meaningless to apply it to non-Christians."[22] This had been the case on the continent since at least the time of Charlemagne, where the oath had been the logical replacement for the ordeal.[23] The Jewish oath matured on the continent over the following centuries, and when Jews first arrived in England post-Conquest, the oath was undoubtedly brought with them. Ephraim ben Jacob, who was most familiar with the realities of Jewish life in twelfth-century England, wrote that the Christian proclivity of judgment by ordeal was bad law and custom by which the Jews could not live.[24]

Henry II's *Assize of Arms* of 1181, among other regulations, prohibited Jews from holding hauberks or coats of mail (*loricam vel aubergellum*). Alongside the traditional interpretation of this legislation as targeting Jewish pawnbrokers who might hold these defensive weapons in gage, this could very well be interpreted as an implied continuing repudiation of the ordeal for Jews and consequent requirement for compurgation by oath.[25] This prohibition on Jews holding weapons implied that the most confrontational version of the ordeal, the trial by battle—introduced to England by the Normans—was also banned, as a matter of course. The Jewish oath, then, had a lengthy genesis and accompanying pedigree by the thirteenth century, and despite the various changes in English legislation that affected Jewish oaths during this period, the fundamental character of the oath remained unchanged.

The earliest surviving legislation that regulated Jewish oaths in England dates to an 1190 charter of liberties that was granted to Isaac, son of Rabbi Josce, and to his children and men. This charter was a reissue—it had originally been issued to the Jews of England and Normandy by Henry II, and was also reissued later by John. Isaac was one of the wealthiest Jews in England at the time.[26] He owned houses in both Rouen[27] and London,[28] and was a lender of significant amounts to Henry II,[29] as well as to abbeys, both alone and in partnership with other Jews.[30] The charter was wide-ranging and covered many things, including two specific clauses concerned with oaths: in the first instance, that Isaac and his men might be judged by their Jewish peers in any quarrel arising with a Christian,[31] and in the second, in criminal cases, not only were these Jews to be allowed the privilege of being quit of any appeal lacking a witness—on their own oath—but also in the context of litigation, they were to be allowed to swear their oaths on the Torah.[32]

This charter was again reissued in April 1201, the first of two charters issued that day. Rather than being granted to a single Jew and his men, this reissue was addressed to all the Jews of England and Normandy. The king was paid for this reissue.[33] The second charter of the day was addressed only to the Jews of England.[34] Under this legislation, exclusive royal jurisdiction was reserved over Crown pleas involving Jews. These were rape, treasure trove, arson, assault, homicide, maiming, housebreaking, and theft. This legislation reaffirmed the Jewish privilege of having intracommunity disputes in all proceedings except for Crown pleas heard in Jewish courts and thus, obviously, according to Jewish law.

In 1275, the Statutes of the Jewry legislated Jewish oaths again, and implicitly revoked the 1190 and 1201 charters of privilege.[35] If a Jew lacked a warrantor, he was now to be disallowed from clearing himself on his own oath, as he had the privilege to do per the 1190 and 1201 charters. This clause of the statute was clear about the reasoning behind the change: the close of the clause stated that this had been done "so that he [the Jew] be not herein otherwise privileged than a Christian."[36] It was obvious for anyone who cared to see that Jewish oaths were considered to have a certain cachet that Christian oaths simply did not. The 1275 statutes also mandated that the Jews "shall neither plead nor be impleaded in any Court, nor be challenged or troubled in any Court, except in the Court of the King, whose Bond-men they are."[37] It had become clear, as the Jews' stay in England began to draw to a close, that their privileged position had become not only an awkward reminder of the freedoms of a bygone age but also a notice of the untenability of those freedoms in the evolved political and legal environment of the late thirteenth century.

In Comitissa's case, it was she as the Jewish plaintiff who had attempted to use the established legislative procedures in her favor, despite having no grounds to do so. It was not always thus, however. Evidence survives of a case from 1224 involving another alleged murder, but this time, the accused was a Jew and the victim was a Christian. The Jew, Bonevie Mutun, was accused of killing a Christian man named William, by Martin, the son of the dead William.[38] Bonevie held a remarkable sense of awareness of the relevant legislation: when he was asked whether he would like to clear himself of the charge by having the accusation heard by twelve Christians and twelve Jews, he answered that had no desire to put himself before any jury in express contradiction of King John's charter held by the Jews.[39] It does not seem likely that the court of King's Bench was unaware of recent legislation concerning Jews.[40] This raises an interesting point. Offering Bonevie a jury to hear the accusation might not only have been an example of the justice not acting entirely in good faith but by extension, an example of quotidian anti-Judaism in the aim of profiteering.[41] Justices were oath-bound to do "right justice to the best of their ability to rich and poor alike . . . and . . . they will execute all that is right and just in matters pertaining to the crown of the lord king."⁴² Similarly, the justices of the Jews in the Exchequer of the Jews swore an oath of faithful service to the king and not to the Jews themselves.⁴³ In neither of these oaths was there a stipulation regarding the treatment of Jews at law—perhaps more surprisingly so in the case of the justice of the Jews. Regardless, Henry de Bracton writes that following the oath of each justice, "let each of them be instructed to promote, to the best of his ability, the advantage of the lord king."⁴⁴ It does not seem a stretch to think that the justice hearing the case might have been angling for the escheat of Bonevie's goods and chattels to the profit of the king, which, in any event, happened at least partially.⁴⁵

Bonevie's response referred only to a charter given to the Jews by King John—but as above, there were two charters given by John. Bonevie's refusal to clear himself of the charge by putting himself in front of a mixed jury clearly refers to the first charter. That charter gave him the privilege to clear himself of a Crown plea by his own oath, as well as to be quit of any summons by anyone without testimony, also on his own oath.⁴⁶ Martin's accusation that Bonevie killed his father is clearly written as a complaint—something necessarily lacking what the judicial process might accept as valid testimony.⁴⁷ The second of the two charters was likely not what Bonevie had been referring to, because it guaranteed that any Crown pleas occurring among the Jews—and thus not involving Christians—and lacking an accuser might be investigated solely by Jews.⁴⁸ As Bonevie stood accused of killing a Christian, he was undoubtedly referring to the first of the two April 10, 1201, charters. Irrespective of Bonevie's knowledge of the law, an inquest by both Jews and Christians occurred, though not along the lines generally accepted: there were nineteen Christians making inquiry alongside the regular contingent of twelve Jews.⁴⁹ Unsurprisingly, the inquest was split along religious lines, with the Christians fairly positive of Bonevie's guilt and the Jews denying it. The case remained unresolved, with no judgment entered on the roll.⁵⁰ Despite this stalemate, it is fairly evident that trust not only in Bonevie but in the Jewish inquisitors as well was severely lacking. There was no admission of guilt and no pronouncement of such, but the epilogue to the case leaves no doubt that trust in the nonjudgment did not exist, nor did trust in the Jews' charters. Bonevie forfeited his house in the London parish of St. Michael Bassishaw,⁵¹ and the only trust remaining was intracommunal—the Jews of London paid 100*m*. for his release, presumably convinced of his innocence.⁵²

Even when the implicit trust in a Jew's word was seemingly absent, the issue was swiftly rectified via oath. In a case from Hilary term, 1220, a Jewish moneylender named David was accused of lending 20*s*. to Robert FitzHenry in return for interest of 10*d*. a week in interest; after David denied both this and having taken a gage for the loan, his own mother and wife, among others of his household, acknowledged under oath that they had made the said loan on gage and in the presence of the chirographers.⁵³ The oath was sacrosanct and used to rise above family ties—something that David was no doubt pained to discover. Intracommunal trust also could work in ways different than in Bonevie's case. Occasionally, the community might look inward for the resolution of a dispute, calling on those with intimate knowledge of the subjects to intervene. And if this knowledge was not considered intimate, it might still be more so than that of the justices of the Jews. In Michaelmas term, 1244, Manser of Huntingdon was attached to answer Peytevin of Bedford because he, Manser, as a chirographer, refused to allow three of Peytevin's chirographs to be placed in the chirograph chest.[54] Manser charged that the reason for this was that the chirographs had been made *sub poena*, and therefore he would not permit them to be deposited. Peytevin countered that there was a pre-existing dispute between them over a debt owed by Peytevin to Manser, and this was the real reason. They both agreed to put themselves on the oath of a third party—Master Moses—and each paid half a mark for it.[55] The rabbi was summoned, and under oath agreed with Peytevin—nothing apart from the previous dispute stood in the way of the chirograph deposit. There was a history between Peytevin and Manser: in Trinity term, 1244, Peytevin had appeared before the justices to make it known that "he holds Manasser of Huntingdon suspect, and craves that Manasser be not believed in aught that he may say touching him."[56] This is a fine example of a Jew attempting to poison the implicit trust in another Jew's potential oath by reason of a personal vendetta. Regardless, Manser was then in mercy, was removed from his office as chirographer, and the chirographs were dutifully placed in the chest. This resort to a single third party was hardly the norm; generally, when cases required third parties to pass judgment on a set of possible facts, the result was an inquest and not simply the word of a well-connected third-party Jew. This case is also not the only one illustrative of the flexibility of the oath: there was a degree of latitude in who took the oath, but rarely—if ever—in the oath itself. This transfer of trust only worked in a single direction; in *Manser v. Peytevin*, the oaths were still required, but the trust was temporarily transferred to the rabbi. In this way, personal vendettas could be rendered moot. The rabbi's oath had to be validated not only systematically, but on a personal level, by both Manser and Peytevin. Moreover, the justices hearing the case had to agree to this transfer of trust away from those intimately involved and its conveyance into the oath of the rabbi.

This transfer in trust was a part of the larger issue of flexibility in oaths, where the way in which the oath was taken and the people who swore the oath were transferable, but the trust inherently in the oath, proven by way of the oath's existence, was never commuted. Similar to the case involving Manser and Peytevin, the oath requirement was tweaked, in a manner of speaking, in a case involving the abbot of Kirkstead, tenant of the lands of Gilbert of Benniworth. Elias, son of Benedict, a Jew, had charged that the abbot owed a portion of a debt of 360*l*. by virtue of his tenancy of the lands of Gilbert of Benniworth, whose debt it was. The abbot produced a starr of acquittance,[57] allegedly written by Elias, absolving him of all debts owed by Gilbert of Benniworth. The problem was that this starr had been allegedly given to the abbot in 1223 (*istam acquietacionem fecit predictus El' predictis abbati et conventui die sancti Luce Evangeliste anno regis Henrico vij°*), and the current case dated to Easter term, 1278.[58] It was obvious to all concerned that a regular oath concerning the veracity of the starr was not at all useful, and the oath thus needed to be enhanced in some way. This was achieved simply by allowing for an understanding of the age of the starr to be inserted into the requirement for a trustworthy oath. Rather than only the usual necessity that oath makers be honest and lawful, a caveat was inserted noting that because the justices of the Jews were doubtful of the great age of the starr, the Jews called to act as jurors were to be not only lawful, but older (*Et quia justiciarii ob an-tiquum datum et confectionem predicti starri dubitabant . . . volentes plenius super hoc cerciorari veritatem in hac parte per xij legales et seniores judeos juratos quesiverunt*).[59] This was clearly acceptable to all parties; the way in which the scribe worded the plea also leads the reader to believe that this was not the first time that this legal workaround had been instituted, nor was this in any way a strange or unusual issue.

This flexibility in the protocol of the oath was also evident in Trinity term, 1280, in a case between Jornin, son of Abraham, a Jew, and Isaac of Southwark. Jornin gave the king one bezant[60] in order that Isaac might be made to swear on the five books of Moses (*Jorninus filius Abrahe dat Regi .j. bissancium ut Ysac de Suthwerke jurat super quinque libros Moysy quod*).[61] Isaac was present and immediately took his oath, and Jornin was then charged the bezant. A bezant seems to be a large amount to pay for an oath, though perhaps the reason for this offering may have been the increased severity that Jornin wished to have placed in trusting Isaac's oath. Jornin could afford the price he offered; the surviving records note his profit in many financial arrangements,[62] as well as the fact that he appears to have been not only accustomed to paying for what he wanted, but having had the means with which to do so.[63] The implication in the 1280 case was that the oath Jornin was seeking was not one of the normal variety, and he desired an oath of increased intensity—indicated not only by his offer of a bezant, but through the language used to describe the new oath. Swearing an oath on the five books of Moses might simply have been de rigueur, but more likely, Jornin's use of this terminology over the favored "Jewish roll" or "Jewish book" indicated the presence of a desire for increased trust. It is unclear whether this amounts to anything more than intensified rhetoric; it seems likely, however, that the significance of the proffered sum indicated that there was a physical difference in what was being used to confirm the oath. The difference may lie in swearing on a ḥumash as opposed to a Torah scroll, but there is no clear evidence either way. The lack of surviving evidence for this phraseology as denoting increased potency in England is not corroborated on the continent; in South Germany, a roughly contemporary Jewry oath also made reference to the five books of Moses (*alß helf dir gott und die funf bücher Moyses*),[64] though again in contrast to what the surviving evidence indicates in the English context, this oath was recited to the Jew who had to be sworn in and not by him. On the continent, there was also a distinction regularly made regarding what the swearing Jew was to take an oath on, which seems to be the opposite of what the surviving evidence indicates for England. Again in Germany, the *Meissener Rechtsbuch* indicated that the oath in most cases was to be taken on the book of Moses, but in a dispute over more than fifty marks, the oath was to be taken on the *Rodal*—the Torah scroll.[65]

As an English measuring stick, it is interesting to compare Jornin's case with that of another Jew, Meyrot, from Hilary term, 1278. Meyrot, a serjeant of the Jewry at York, was adjudged to be in mercy because he did not have a book of the Jewish law on which Jews could make their oaths (*Idem Meyrot quia serviens est judaismi Ebor' et non habuit librum legis judaice super quem judei potuerunt sacramentum facere in misericordia*).[66] For Christians, there exists the possibility that the Holy Gospels as such were not even required to make an oath; a thirteenth-century manuscript containing drawings of the evangelists and accompanying Gospel verses was possibly used in oath-making as a substitute for physical copies of the Gospels.[67]

That Jews in England were generally exempt from swearing an oath on anything other than the Torah is, according to the surviving evidence, a given. When the records noted that an oath was made by a Jew, the implication was that it was done on that which the Jews had been expressly privileged to swear. Conversely, when Christians made their oaths and these were recorded, on what exactly was sworn was usually left unsaid, though obviously this would be the Holy Gospels; from the 1230s onward, there are many examples that show a particular Christian or group of Christians swearing an oath on them.[68] Past the midpoint of the century, however, an increasing number of examples survive showing Christian oaths being made not on the Holy Gospels, but rather on the king's soul.[69] The reigning monarch's soul appears to have acquired a holy quality for oath-taking Christians, but there is no surviving evidence of this also being the case for Jews. Various kings were apparently not particularly bothered about the permanence of their own oaths, however. There is ample evidence of the personal oaths of thirteenth-century English kings being commuted or absolved completely. These absolutions, all made by the pope, involved forgiving the king of his obligations concerning oaths that might have infringed on royal power,[70] oaths pertaining to particular arranged marriages,[71] and at least once, in May 1255, the commutation of Henry III's oath to take the cross.[72] There also survive examples of Christians taking oaths on the king's soul after having touched the Holy Gospels—the soul of the reigning monarch seems to have reinforced the mettle of an oath made on the Holy Gospels.[73] Furthermore, in at least one instance, it was recorded that an oath on the king's soul might be taken "if need be"—the implication being that swearing an oath only on the Holy Gospels simply would not have sufficed for a situation of increased gravity.[74]

The most analogous incident where the oath of a Jew was amplified by referring to a facet of kingship occurred in 1252. Elias, son of Abraham, had been attached to answer a Christian man named Henry Trenchaunt for a debt of 12*l.*, according to a charter held in the Winchester chirograph chest. Henry claimed that he had a starr of acquittance; Elias claimed this to be fake, saying that the word "Wynton" had been substituted for "Wilton." Elias was so sure that the starr was a fake that he said he was "ready to prove this by Jews." The Jews appointed for the purpose came before the justices and said what they thought of the case's particulars "on the faith by which they are holden to the King, and upon their oath."[75] There is no indication why, at this point in the century, the Jewish oath had lost some of its former credence. Now, rather than an oath on the Torah being sufficient, the faith by which the Jews were holden to the king had assumed primacy of place, and the oath on the Torah had briefly assumed a quasi-secondary nature. Perhaps this unusual state of affairs did not extend beyond the judiciary, however. Later, in Trinity term, 1267, when Walter, a herdsman, was attached to answer a Jew named Isaac regarding unlawful detinue of gages, Walter put Isaac to his oath regarding the said chattels and their value, saying that if Isaac made his oath, he would satisfy him in respect to the chattels. The popular conception of a Jewish oath was, remarkably, in line with the royally mandated trust in the oath. Isaac was equal to the challenge, and "thereupon swears upon the Hebrew Book, that he delivered all the said chattels of the said value to the said Walter."[76] The Jewish oath had retained its value as a trust-inspiring verbal instrument. Walter was ordered to return to Isaac the chattels or their equal value and was placed in mercy; the bailiffs of the City of London were also mandated to distrain Walter by his lands and chattels, and Walter was given a day by which to return the chattels or their equal in coin.

The oath's significance in the trust relationships mentioned in this essay was as chief arbiter; it was the ultimate authority in Jewish disputes where competing narratives existed. In practice, the Jewish oath was a flexible instrument. It was perhaps not designed to be so, but the circumstances in which it was applied made it thus. The trust placed in the Jewish oath was also flexible. As a matter of course, it reflected what those who demanded the oath thought of it. It is possible that what Amnon Linder theorizes on a broad level, where "strong, centralized government (as in England) tended to skip all middle, mediating instances and deal directly with all its subjects," is, in England, precisely what caused Jewish oaths to be trusted in the first instance.[77] Paired with its later fluidity, these two causes are what imbued Jewish oaths with staying power. No doubt the formal nature of the oath, as well as its formal enforcement, also helped. Despite the oppressive legal environment of the thirteenth century, the oath continued not only to be used but to be trusted. Where we might expect the idea of trust to be more important than its actual practice, we see instead the opposite: there was never a decline in the expectation of trust in a Jewish oath, and this trust, despite being flexibly applied, was continually a stable entity.

Notes

1. Hilary, Easter, Trinity, and Michaelmas refer to the four main terms of administration in English government at the time, named after the four festivals of the Christian church. When discussing the legal and administrative business of the Exchequer of the Jews, more specific days cannot be quoted with any confidence—"what is recorded as taking place on a particular 'day' might, in reality, have occurred at any time within the succeeding week (and sometimes even later than that)." As in Paul Brand, ed., *Plea Rolls of the Exchequer of the Jews*, 6 (London: Jewish Historical Society of England, 2005), 4 (hereafter *PEJ* 6). See *PEJ* 6 for a detailed explanation of the dating conventions unique to each term.

2. J. M. Rigg, ed. *Calendar of the Plea Rolls of the Exchequer of the Jews*, 1 (London: Macmillan), 39. Hereafter *PEJ* 1.

3. *PEJ* 1:42.

4. A mark was a term of financial account. There were twelve pennies in a shilling and twenty shillings in a pound; a mark was equal to two-thirds of a pound.

5. *PEJ* 1:45.

6. *PEJ* 6:11.

7. Rigg discusses this briefly in his introduction to *PEJ* 1:x–xi.

8. A gage was an object, generally of significant value and liable to forfeiture, deposited as a guarantee of good faith; a pledge was a person or group of people who agreed to act as surety for another. Mary Bateson, ed., *Borough Customs*, vol. 1 (Selden Society vol. 18) (London: Quaritch, 1904), 23, 36.

9. *PEJ* 1:51.

10. An appeal was an accusation brought in court by one individual against another, generally of violence or of theft.

11. *PEJ* 1:51.

12. In *PEJ* 6:11, Brand writes that this jurisdiction was *ex officio*.

13. *PEJ* 1:50.

14. *PEJ* 1:50.

15. Guido Kisch, "Research in Medieval Legal History of the Jews," *Proceedings of the American Academy for Jewish Research* 6 (1934): 275.

16. Paul Hyams, "Faith, Fealty and Jewish 'Infideles' in Twelfth-Century England," in *Christians and Jews in Angevin England: the York Massacre of 1190, Narratives and Contexts*, ed. Sarah Rees Jones and Sethina Watson (Woodbridge: York Medieval, 2013), 139.

17. In 1220, it was found necessary to have a Jew, Elyas (his name is rendered "Hel," likely a diminutive for "Elyas"), swear on the Torah that another Jew, Benedict, would "on no account say aught but the truth upon oath"; see *PEJ* 1:44.

18. *Calendar of the Charter Rolls Preserved in the Public Record Office: Henry III, A.D. 1226–1257* (London, 1903), v.

19. *Calendar of the Charter Rolls Preserved in the Public Record Office: Henry III, A.D. 1226–1257* (London: His Majesty's Stationery Office, 1903), v.

20. Thomas Duffus Hardy, ed., *Rotuli de Oblatis et Finibus in Turri Londinensi asservati, tempore regis Johannis* (London, 1835), i.

21. Joseph Ziegler, "Reflections on the Jewry Oath in the Middle Ages," in *Christianity and Judaism: Papers Read at the 1991 Summer Meeting and the 1992 Winter Meeting of the Ecclesiastical History Society,* ed. Diana Wood, Studies in Church History, vol. 29 (Oxford: Blackwell, 1992), 213.

22. Robert Bartlett, *Trial by Fire and Water: The Medieval Judicial Ordeal* (Oxford: Clarendon, 1986), 54.

23. Shlomo Eidelberg, "Trial by Ordeal in Medieval Jewish History: Laws, Customs, and Attitudes," *Proceedings of the American Academy for Jewish Research* 46/47 (1979), 112.

24. Bartlett, *Trial by Fire and Water*, 54n64.

25. William Stubbs, ed., *Select Charters and Other Illustrations of English Constitutional History,* 9th ed., rev. H. W. C. Davis (Oxford: Clarendon, 1921), 183.

26. H. G. Richardson, *The English Jewry under Angevin Kings* (London: Methuen, 1960), 65.

27. Thomas Duffus Hardy, ed., *Rotuli Chartarum in Turri Londinensi asservati*, 1/1:105b (London: Eyre & Spottiswoode, 1837). Hereafter "*Rot. Chart.*"

28. Richardson, *The English Jewry under Angevin Kings*, 237. Richardson transcribes DL 36/1, f.87, no. 3, which is a charter of conveyance to Isaac.

29. Some of the larger sums, among examples in other years, can be found in *Pipe Roll 12 Henry II, 1165–66*, 19, 20, 78, 94, 96, 100, 114, and 115.

30. Richardson, *The English Jewry under Angevin Kings*, 44.

31. . . . *si Christianus habuerit querelam versus predictos Judeos, sit judicata per pares Judeorum.* See Thomas Rymer and Robert Sanderson, eds., *Foedera, Conventiones, Litterae, et Cujuscunque Generis Acta Publica,* 1/1 (London: G. Eyre and A. Strahan, 1816), 51. Hereafter "Rymer's *Foedera*, 1/1."

32. Rymer's *Foedera*, 1/1:51. *Et si ipsi appellati fuerint ab aliquo sine teste, de illo appellatu erunt quieti, solo sacramento super librum suum;* \& *de appellatu illarum rerum que ad coronam nostram pertinent, similiter erunt quieti, solo sacramento super rotulum ipsorum.* It remains to be seen if there is indeed an intentional difference in meaning in the changed verbiage between the first and second halves of this clause—namely, between swearing *super librum suum* and *super rotulum ipsorum.* See also discussion below.

33. *Rotuli de Oblatis et Finibus*, 133. For two later reissues of this charter, see *Cal. Charter Rolls, 1226–1257*, 357, and *Calendar of the Charter Rolls Preserved in the Public Record Office: Henry III–Edward I, A.D. 1257–1300* (London: His Majesty's Stationery Office, 1906), 164.

34. *Rot. Chart.*, 93b. This was a reissue of legislation issued by Richard on March 22, 1190, which referred back to a now-lost charter of Henry II.

35. Alexander Luders, ed., *The Statutes of the Realm*, vol. 1 (London: G. Eyre and A. Strahan, 1810), 221–21a.

36. Luders, *The Statutes of the Realm*, 1:221–21a. . . . *issi ke mes ne seit de ceo privilege autrement ke Crestien.*

37. Luders, *The Statutes of the Realm*, 1:221–21a. *E comaunde ke nul ne lor face mal ne damage ne tort, en lors cors ne en lor bens meobles ou nent meobles e kil ne pleydent ne seient enpleidez en nuly curt, ne chalangez ne travaillex en nuli curt fors en la curt le Rey ky serfs yl sunt.*

38. *Curia Regis Rolls, 1223–24*, no. 2644.

39. *Curia Regis Rolls, 1223–24*, no. 2644. . . . *dicit quod non vult ponere se super aliquam juratam contra libertatem suam quam ipsi Judei habent per cartam domini Johannis regis.*

40. The point is furthered by the fact that the *Curia Regis* Roll for Michaelmas term 8–9 Henry III, on which this case appeared, was made for the senior justice, Martin de Pateshull, a man one would rightfully assume was au fait with the various charters and legislative acts of the kingdom.

41. I use the term "anti-Judaism" here as defined by Gavin Langmuir, *Toward a Definition of Antisemitism* (Berkeley: University of California Press, 1996), 60, where "the pressure of popular anti-Judaism, the implementation of anti-Judaism, and anti-Judaism's long appeal to Christian self-interest combined to set in motion the process known as the self-fulfilling prophecy whereby a group already assumed to be inferior is forced by the majority to engage in conduct that seems further confirmation of the minority's inferiority."

42. Samuel E. Thorne, trans., *Bracton on the Laws and Customs of England*, vol. 2 (Cambridge, MA: Belknap, 1968), 309. Hereafter "*Bracton*, 2". As in Paul Brand, "Edward I and the Transformation of the English Judiciary," in *The Making of the Common Law*, ed. Paul Brand (London: Hambeldon, 1992), 149–50, this was the oath taken by justices in the General Eyre in the late 1220s or early 1230s, and it was not until 1290 that an oath for all royal justices and not simply justices in eyre had taken form.

43. *PEJ* 6:19. For an example later in the century seemingly showing not only the regularity of this oath but its requirement as well, see *Close Rolls, 1254–56*, 269, where having installed Adam de Greinville as Justice of the Jews, the king received from him *sacramentum fidelitatis regi debitum pretextu officii sui*.

44. *Bracton*, 2:309.

45. See discussion below.

46. *Rot. Chart.*, 93a.

47. *Curia Regis Rolls, 1223–24*, no. 2644. The plaint begins *Martinus filius Willelmi queritur quod Bonenie*. . . . The pleas far more commonly began with *optulit se*, or *petit versus*, or when the plaintiff was not actually pleading in person, *ponit loco suo* or *per attornatum suum petit versus*.

48. *Rot. Chart.*, 93b.

49. *Curia Regis Rolls, 1223–24*, no. 2644.

50. H. G. Richardson and G. O. Sayles, eds., *Select Cases of Procedure without Writ under Henry III* (Selden Society 60) (London: Quaritch, 1941), 5n1.

51. *Select Cases of Procedure without Writ*, 5n1, cites Thomas Duffus Hardy, ed., *Rotuli Litterarum Clausarum in Turri Londinensi asservati*, vol. 2 (London: Eyre & Spottiswoode, 1844), 7b (hereafter "*Rot. Lit. Claus.*, 2"), dating to November 15, 1224, where the house and appurtenances formerly belonging to Bonevie were given to Halengret and Semaine *Balistarius*; *Select Cases of Procedure without Writ*, 5n1, also notes *Rot. Lit. Claus.*, 2:194b, dating to July 28, 1227, where perhaps other property belonging to Bonevie, and described as *domos et terras qui fuerunt Bonevie Mutun Judei in Lond'* is given to Semaine *Balistarius* and a man named John de Gise. To the material cited in *Select Cases of Procedure without Writ* might be added *Cal. Fine Rolls, 1227–28*, no. 42, where the demand of the mayor and sheriff of London made by summons of the Exchequer to Semayne "by reason of the house and certain land formerly of Boneme Mutun in London, which he gave him" is to be placed in respite, and *Close Rolls, 1227–31*, 41, dating to April 19, 1228, where Semayne was to render a pair of gilded spurs annually for the house formerly belonging to Bonevie (*unum par calcarium deauratorum singulis annis*).

52. *Select Cases of Procedure without Writ*, 5n1, notes only that "it was presumably in connexion with this inquest that a fine of 100 marks was imposed on the Jews of London 'pro Bonevie Mutun.'" There was a related fine (*Cal. Fine Rolls, 1224–25*, no. 59) dating to January 15, 1225, where Bonevie was to be released from the Tower of London to Martin of Pateshull, and was to be delivered "to the Jews of London to keep, having accepted security from them that they will have him at the king's command whenever the king will wish and for rendering 100*m*. to the king, by which they made fine with him for having the same in custody." *Select Cases of Procedure without Writ*, 5n1, notes that the fine remained unpaid in Michaelmas term 1230 (see *Pipe Roll, 14 Henry III*, 100), and that the justices of the Jews were to make a writ for it (see *Memoranda Roll, 14 Henry III*, 31). There were six further audits before the debt was finally paid off; see E 372/76, m.16d (nothing paid in), E 372/77, m.12 (7*l*. paid in), E 372/78, m.7 (6*l*. 12*s*. paid in), E 372/79, m.17 (40*l*. 11*s*. 2*d*. paid in), E 372/80, m.8 (nothing paid in), and E 372/81, m.7 (10*l*. 12*s*. 6*d*. paid in, with the remaining 17*s*. 8*d*. paid in a further instalment).

53. *PEJ* 1:34. 10*d*. in interest per week on a 20*s*. loan works out to 216 percent per year. By 1233, legislation had capped the maximum rate of interest at 2*d*. in the pound per week. This legislation is printed in Richardson, *The English Jewry under Angevin Kings*, 294.

54. *PEJ* 1:106. At this point, each chirograph chest had four chirographers: two Jewish and two Christian, and, since 1194, it was law that Jewish debts be deposited as chirographs in the designated chests.

55. *PEJ* 1:106–7.

56. *PEJ* 1:76.

57. A starr was a Jewish deed or bond, generally of release of debt.

58. Sarah Cohen, ed., *Plea Rolls of the Exchequer of the Jews*, vol. 5 (London: Jewish Historical Society of England, 1992), no. 436. Hereafter *PEJ* 5.

59. *PEJ* 5, no. 436.

60. In this context, a bezant was a gold coin.

61. *PEJ* 6, no. 724.

62. Inter Alia: Hilary Jenkinson, ed., *Calendar of the Plea Rolls of the Exchequer of the Jews*, vol. 3 (Colchester: Spottiswoode, 1929), 139 (hereafter "*PEJ* 3"); H. G. Richardson, ed., *Calendar of the Plea Rolls of the Exchequer of the Jews*, vol. 4 (London: Jewish Historical Society of England, 1972), nos. 71, 324, and 475 (hereafter "*PEJ* 4"); *PEJ* 5, nos. 588, 690 (for a very interesting arrangement), 703, and 719; and *PEJ* 6, nos. 194, 485, 1201, and 1213.

63. *PEJ* 6, no. 107 (see also no. 99) where Jornin and another Jew, Hake of Canterbury, paid 1*m*. for the remission of a charge of assault, wounding, and maltreatment of Thomas de St. Michael; see also *PEJ* 4, 157, 160, 164, and 167, where Jornin paid for respite of tallage once, simple respite twice, and for having aid once.

64. Guido Kisch, "A Fourteenth-Century Jewry Oath of South Germany," *Speculum* 15, no. 3 (July 1940), 334.

65. Guido Kisch, "The Jewry-Law of the Medieval German Law-Books: Part I," *Proceedings of the American Academy for Jewish Research*, no. 7 (1935), 144.

66. *PEJ* 5, no. 294.

67. E 36/266.

68. Inter Alia: *Cal. Patent Rolls, 1232–47*, 244, 294; *Cal. Patent Rolls, 1247–58*, 288, 354, 562–3, 637; *Cal. Patent Rolls, 1258–66*, 14, 19, 38, 432, 654; *Cal. Close Rolls, 1272–79*, 50, 59, 66, 186, 563.

69. *Cal. Patent Rolls, 1232–47*, 59, 82, 84, 102, 135, 153, 232, 309, 319; *Cal. Patent Rolls, 1258–66*, 246, 258; *Cal. Patent Rolls, 1266–72*, 111, 130, 324, 582; this continued into the reign of Edward I. See *Cal. Close Rolls, 1279–88*, 370.

70. W. H. Bliss, ed., *Calendar of Papal Registers Relating to Great Britain and Ireland*, 1: 148 (London: Her Majesty's Stationery Office, 1893), hereafter "*Cal. Papal Registers*, 1", where in 1235 the king was unbound from an oath "not to revoke alienations contrary to that of his coronation" (see also SC 7/15/10); a 1262 absolution to the king and queen, as well as their sons Edward and Edmund, from observing statutes they had been compelled to take during the reforming period preceding the Second Barons' War (see SC 7/33/4); and a 1264 absolution of the king's oath to follow the provisions of Oxford (see *Cal. Papal Registers*, 1:403; see also SC 7/33/26, and Rymer's *Foedera*, 1/1:419).

71. *Cal. Papal Registers*, 1:153, dating to April 1236, freeing Henry III of his oath to marry Joan, daughter of the count of Ponthieu, on account of consanguinity (see also SC 7/15/13); SC 7/53/1, dating to the late 1250s, absolving Henry III of his oaths concerning the marriages of Margaret and Beatrice, his daughters; and *Cal. Papal Registers*, 1:579, dating to June 1298, absolving Edward I of his oath to wed his son Edward to one of Guy, count of Flanders' daughters in favor of Isabella, daughter of Philip IV of France (see also SC 7/7/19).

72. SC 7/3/43, where Henry was absolved of his oath to cross the sea after his vow of the cross had already been commuted.

73. *Cal. Patent Rolls, 1247–58*, 294, 296.

74. *Cal. Patent Rolls, 1266–72*, 730.

75. *PEJ*, 1:112.

76. *PEJ*, 1:144.

77. Amnon Linder, "The Jewry-Oath in Christian Europe," in *Jews in Early Christian Law: Byzantium and the Latin West, 6th–11th Centuries*, ed. J. V. Tolan, N. de Lange, L. Foschia, and C. Nemo-Pekelman (Turnhout: Brepols, 2014), 341.

Bibliography

Manuscript and Archival Sources

Records of the Exchequer—Pipe Office
E 372/76
E 372/77
E 372/78
E 372/79
E 372/80
E 372/81

Records of the Exchequer—Treasury of the Receipt—Miscellaneous Books
E 36/266

Special Collections—Papal Bulls
SC 7/3/43
SC 7/7/19

SC 7/15/10
SC 7/15/13
SC 7/33/4
SC 7/33/26
SC 7/53/1

Printed Primary Sources

Borough Customs. Vol. 1. Edited by Mary Bateson. Selden Society series, vol. 18. London: Quaritch, 1904.
Bracton on the Laws and Customs of England. Vol. 2. Translated by Samuel E. Thorne. Cambridge, MA: Belknap, 1968.
Calendar of the Charter Rolls Preserved in the Public Record Office: Henry III, A.D. 1226–1257. London: His Majesty's Stationery Office, 1903.
Calendar of the Charter Rolls Preserved in the Public Record Office: Henry III–Edward I, A.D. 1257–1300. London: His Majesty's Stationery Office, 1906.
Calendar of the Close Rolls Preserved in the Public Record Office, Edward I, A.D. 1272–1279. London: Her Majesty's Stationery Office, 1900.
Calendar of the Close Rolls Preserved in the Public Record Office, Edward I, A.D. 1279–1288. London: His Majesty's Stationery Office, 1902.
Calendar of the Fine Rolls of the Reign of Henry III: 1224–1234. Edited by Paul Dryburgh and Beth Hartland. Woodbridge: Boydell Press, 2008.
Calendar of Papal Registers Relating to Great Britain and Ireland. Vol. 1. Edited by W. H. Bliss. London: Her Majesty's Stationery Office, 1894.
Calendar of the Patent Rolls Preserved in the Public Record Office, Henry III, A.D. 1232–1247. London: His Majesty's Stationery Office, 1906.
Calendar of the Patent Rolls Preserved in the Public Record Office, Henry III, A.D. 1247–1258. London: His Majesty's Stationery Office, 1908.
Calendar of the Patent Rolls Preserved in the Public Record Office, Henry III, A.D. 1258–1266. London: His Majesty's Stationery Office, 1910.
Calendar of the Patent Rolls Preserved in the Public Record Office, Henry III, A.D. 1266–1272. London: His Majesty's Stationery Office, 1913.
Calendar of the Plea Rolls of the Exchequer of the Jews. Vol. 1. Edited by J. M. Rigg. London: Macmillan, 1905.
Calendar of the Plea Rolls of the Exchequer of the Jews. Vol. 3. Edited by Hilary Jenkinson. Colchester: Spottiswoode, 1929.
Calendar of the Plea Rolls of the Exchequer of the Jews. Vol. 4. Edited by H. G. Richardson. London: Jewish Historical Society of England, 1905.
Close Rolls, Henry III: 1227–1231. London: His Majesty's Stationery Office, 1902.
Close Rolls, Henry III: 1254–1256. London: His Majesty's Stationery Office, 1931.
Curia Regis Rolls of the Reign of Henry III Preserved in the Public Record Office: 7 to 9 Henry III. London: Her Majesty's Stationery Office, 1955.
Foedera, Conventiones, Litterae, et Cujuscunque Generis Acta Publica. Vol. 1, part 1. Edited by Thomas Rymer and Robert Sanderson. London: G. Eyre and A. Strahan, 1816.
The Great Roll of the Pipe for the Fourteenth Year of the Reign of King Henry the Third, A.D. Michaelmas 1230 (Pipe Roll 74). Pipe Roll Society, vol. 42, New Series vol. 4. Princeton, NJ: Princeton University Press, 1927.

The Great Roll of the Pipe for the Twelfth Year of the Reign of King Henry the Second, A.D. 1165–1166. Pipe Roll Society, vol. 9. London: Wyman & Sons, 1888.
The Memoranda Roll of the King's Remembrancer for Michaelmas 1230–Trinity 1231. Pipe Roll Society, vol. 49, New Series vol. 11. Princeton, NJ: Princeton University Press, 1933.
Plea Rolls of the Exchequer of the Jews. Vol. 5. Edited by Sarah Cohen. London: Jewish Historical Society of England, 1992.
Plea Rolls of the Exchequer of the Jews. Vol. 6. Edited by Paul Brand. London: Jewish Historical Society of England, 2005.
Rotuli Chartarum in Turri Londinensi asservati. Vol. 1, part 1. Edited by Thomas Duffus Hardy. London: Eyre & Spottiswoode, 1837.
Rotuli de Oblatis et Finibus in Turri Londinensi asservati, tempore regis Johannis. Edited by Thomas Duffus Hardy. London, 1835.
Rotuli Litterarum Clausarum in Turri Londinensi asservati. Vol. 2. Edited by Thomas Duffus Hardy. London: Eyre & Spottiswoode, 1844.
Select Cases of Procedure without Writ under Henry III. Edited by H. G. Richardson and G. O. Sayles. Selden Society series, vol. 60. London: Quaritch, 1941.
Select Charters and Other Illustrations of English Constitutional History. Edited by William Stubbs. 9th ed. Revised by H. W. C. Davis. Oxford: Clarendon, 1921.
The Statutes of the Realm. Vol. 1. Edited by Alexander Luders. London: G. Eyre and A. Strahan, 1810.

Printed Secondary Sources

Bartlett, Robert. *Trial by Fire and Water: The Medieval Judicial Ordeal.* Oxford: Clarendon, 1986.
Brand, Paul. "Edward I and the Transformation of the English Judiciary." In *The Making of the Common Law,* edited by Paul Brand, 135–68. London: Hambeldon, 1992.
Eidelberg, Shlomo. "Trial by Ordeal in Medieval Jewish History: Laws, Customs and Attitudes." *Proceedings of the American Academy for Jewish Research* 46/47 (1979): 105–20.
Hyams, Paul. "Faith, Fealty and Jewish 'Infideles' in Twelfth-Century England." In *Christians and Jews in Angevin England: The York Massacre of 1190, Narratives and Contexts,* edited by Sarah Rees Jones and Sethina Watson, 125–47. Woodbridge: York Medieval, 2013.
Kisch, Guido. "A Fourteenth-Century Jewry Oath of South Germany." *Speculum* 15, no. 3 (1940): 331–37.
———. "The Jewry-Law of the Medieval German Law-Books: Part I." *Proceedings of the American Academy for Jewish Research* 7 (1935): 61–145.
———. "Research in Medieval Legal History of the Jews." *Proceedings of the American Academy for Jewish Research* 6 (1934): 229–76.
Langmuir, Gavin. *Toward a Definition of Antisemitism.* Berkeley: University of California Press, 1996.
Linder, Amnon. "The Jewry-Oath in Christian Europe." In *Jews in Early Christian Law: Byzantium and the Latin West, 6th–11th Centuries,* edited by J. V. Tolan, N. de Lange, L. Foschia, and C. Nemo-Pekelman, 311–58. Turnhout: Brepols, 2014.
Richardson, H. G. *The English Jewry under Angevin Kings.* London: Methuen, 1960.
Ziegler, Joseph. "Reflections on the Jewry Oath in the Middle Ages." In *Christianity and Judaism: Papers Read at the 1991 Summer Meeting and the 1992 Winter Meeting of*

the Ecclesiastical History Society, edited by Diana Wood, 209–20. Studies in Church History, vol. 29. Oxford: Blackwell, 1992.

JOSHUA CURK received his doctorate from the University of Oxford in 2015. His research focuses on Jewish conversion to Christianity in medieval England and, more broadly, medieval English Jewish-Christian relations. He teaches high school history in Toronto.

4 What Is an Infidel?
Jewish Oaths and Jewish History in the Making of English Trust and Tolerance

Mitchell B. Hart

On the Oath of a Hindu

On December 4, 1739, the Court of Chancery in London heard the case *Ramkissenseat v. Barker, et al.*[1] In the history of jurisprudence, especially the development of rules of evidence, the case is known as *Omychund v. Barker*. It concerned the question of the validity of an oath sworn by an infidel. Omychund, the plaintiff, was a Hindu who lived in India and had done business with the father of the defendant. Barker Sr. worked for the East India Company in Patna, and Omychund had loaned Barker money. Barker's business venture was a success, but he refused to repay the loan and interest. When the Calcutta court agreed to take up the complaint against Barker, he fled India; he died en route to Europe. His son inherited not only his father's estate and debts but the suit brought against Barker Sr. by Omychund. As part of the initial court proceedings, testimony had to be taken. In order to testify in a court of law, the witnesses, including Ramkissenseat, would of course have had to take an oath. Ramkissenseat appealed to the court to have the oath translated and its Christian elements—"the words *corporeal* and upon the *holy evangelist*"—removed.[2] John Tracy Atkyns (who was also the advocate for the defendant) reports that the motion was supported by reference to a previous case in which "a Jew was ordered to be sworn to his answer upon the Pentateuch."[3]

Lord Hardwicke (Philip Yorke), the lord chancellor, ordered the phrase "upon the holy evangelist" removed from the oath that Ramkissenseat would take. The "general rule," according to the Lord Chancellor, was that

> all persons who believe in God, are capable of an oath; and what is universally understood by an oath, is *that the person who takes it, imprecates the vengeance of God upon him, if the oath he takes is false.* It was upon this principle that the judges were inclined to admit the *Jews* who believed a God, according to our notion of a God, to swear upon the Old Testament. And Lord *Hale* very justly

observes, it is a wise rule in the kingdom of *Spain*; that a heathen and idolator should be sworn upon what he thinks is the most sacred part of his religion. If a *Jew* should be indicted for perjury, and it is laid in the indictment that he swore *tactis sacro-sanctis Dei evangeliis*; yet according to *Hale* the word *evangeliis* in the indictment may be answered by the Old Testament, which is the *evangelium* of the Jews.[4]

In a recent essay on religious tolerance in England, Jacob Selwood asserts that "Jews are marginal to the legislative history of English religious toleration."[5] Certainly, Jews did not play the role that Catholics or dissenting Protestants did in the complex and protracted development of tolerance in England, yet their role may have been less marginal than Selwood imagines. As Lord Hardwicke's remarks cited above indicate, Jews could be invoked in cases in which no actual Jews were involved, but whose history in England could be deployed to advance the cause of religious tolerance of other groups.

The legal case was not settled in 1739. The court directed a commission to travel to East India to take the testimony of the plaintiff. It empowered an administrator to administer an oath "in the most solemn manner," and if the oath was "any other oath than the Christian, to certify in the court what was done of them."[6] The court took up the case, now *Omychund v. Barker*, again in 1744. Atkyns reports that in 1742, the commission in India administered an oath to Ramkissenseat and other witnesses "of the Gentoo [i.e., Hindu] religion according to their ceremonies."[7] The Calcutta court found for Omychund, the plaintiff. Barker challenged the decision on the grounds that an oath taken by an infidel (i.e., a Hindu) was invalid by definition according to the laws of England, as was any testimony offered.

What is the relationship between oaths and trust? How does an oath produce trust, and what sort of trust is this? The German historian Petra Schulte notes that "in relation to the intellectual history of the concept *fides*, the idea of trust during the entire medieval period was tightly bound up with the concept of Christian faith."[8] This belief in the inextricability between religion and reliability, between Christianity and trustworthiness, did not, of course, disappear in the early modern period. In many ways, it became even more intense and complicated, as reformation fractured Christianity and subsequent religious and civil wars gave even greater weight to the perceived nexus between religious orthodoxy, trust, and the validity of one's word. In England during the long eighteenth century, oaths came to play a crucial role in the perception that this nexus was secured and maintained.[9]

Recognizing this historical connection between Christianity, oaths, and trust in no way means that Christians naturally or unquestionably trusted one another or naively took one another at their word. Of course, Christians were also obliged to swear an oath in order to make their testimony legally binding and trustworthy. The point here is that Christian scripture and Christian ritual were assumed unproblematically to be able to produce this trust. Despite the still popular image of the eighteenth century as the century of antireligious skepticism and deistic rationality, the reality was that Christianity retained much of its intellectual and cultural force for most people—including elites—during this period.[10] Thus, it is not surprising that Christianity remained central to the formulation of oaths and the ability of an oath to produce at least an impression of reliability and trustworthiness.

Where, then, did this leave the so-called infidel or unbeliever? *Omychund v. Barker* presents us with evidence of a moment in which the leading lights of the eighteenth-century English judicial system sought to create or deny a space for the religious and legal tolerance of the non-Christian non-European. This essay offers a close reading of this court case—the record of which extends to over thirty pages—in order to highlight the ways in which Jews and Jewish history figured in the production of eighteenth-century British tolerance. It explores the numerous tensions and ironies in this process, as both advocates and opponents of the validity of the Hindu oath used the complex history of the Jews in England—from their settlement in the eleventh century to their expulsion in 1290, and their readmission in the seventeenth century—to argue their case.

To be sure, the proximate driving force in the case was more economic than philosophical, a product of a dispute over payment of debts. More generally, though, the court recognized that as trade and commerce continued to grow and extend beyond Britain's borders, commercial concerns demanded a working relationship with peoples of other religions and cultures. Thus, Hardwicke, the lord chancellor, began his initial remarks in *Ramkissenseat* by declaring his amazement that given the extensive nature of British dominion, no rule or method related to this question of the Hindu oath had yet emerged. In *Omychund*, the solicitor general, William Murray (Lord Mansfield), cast the import of the case as a matter of trust between different faith communities and courts, and ultimately a matter of the viability of contractual agreements. If Christians do not accept the oaths of heathens, he wondered, "what must the heathen courts then think of our proceedings? Will it not destroy all faith and confidence between the contracting parties? Is the case of the Turk or Jew swearing according to their religion different from the Indians swearing according to his?" (23).

Nonetheless, in taking up the question of the validity of the Hindu oath for an English court, those involved were compelled to interrogate and negotiate the boundaries of contemporary religious tolerance. Tolerance is more than the simple recognition of fundamental difference, and it is less than the acceptance of the idea that such differences are inconsequential or meaningless. Tolerance is not equality or egalitarianism. As Alexandra Walsham has written concerning early modern England, toleration "emphatically did not mean religious freedom.

Nor did it proceed from indifference or neutrality. To tolerate was not to recognize or to grant equal rights to a rival system of belief; it was to permit or license something of which one emphatically disapproved, to make a magnanimous concession to the adherents of an inherently false religion."[11] Neither side in *Omychund* sought to make either Hinduism or Judaism equal to Christianity. At the same time, what we see is a debate over the nature of Hinduism as "an inherently false religion," and just how magnanimous English law could be when it came to non-Christian testimony. In making their arguments, the judges and lawyers recovered and relied on the history of the legal tolerance of the Jew in Angevin England. This was, as we shall see, a complex negotiation.

Who Is an Infidel

The word of a Hindu was valid, it seems, either if the Hindu was not an infidel or if English law could be shown to accept the testimony of infidels in the past. Both of these approaches figure in the jurists' discussions. However, it is the latter argument, which hinged on the recovered history of the legal status of Jews in pre-expulsion England, that emerged as predominant.

Barker's advocate, Atkyns, argued that only an oath taken "upon the Evangelists" was valid in an English court, and invoked Henry de Bracton's phrase "*et hoec Sancta Dei evangelia*" together with the opinions of other legal authorities, all of whom defined a valid oath and testimony with reference to swearing on the Evangelists. "I appeal to your lordship's judgement, whether the people who are offered as witnesses, are capable of taking an oath, as the law of England conceives it" (16). Common sense would suggest that Atkyns, when referring to the Evangelists, meant the New Testament. However, as we shall see shortly, to strengthen his argument against the idea that a Hindu oath is valid, Atkyns would suggest a far more flexible and surprising definition of the term.

Atkyns's assertion that Hindus were incapable of taking a valid oath, and that therefore their testimony was worthless, went beyond the strictly legal question of what is a valid oath in an English court of law. The problem lay, ultimately, in the very nature of East Indians and their religion: "The most authentic histories of this part of the world [India] represent the natives as extremely ignorant, and particularly with regard to their notions of religion, absurd and ridiculous, and in their ideas of the Deity so gross, that it would be shocking even to mention. How then can they be said to perform such a ceremony with a sacred and religious mind, which the word *sacramentum* implies?" (16–17). For Atkyns, and no doubt many other Britons at the time, trust and reliability in the word or testimony of a Hindu could not be manufactured through the taking of an oath.

Thus, one component of the Barker defense strategy resided in the defamation of East Indians and Hinduism. Atkyns suggested that the Hindu religion was so "absurd and ridiculous" that it made any genuine spirituality or sacrality impossible. However, his argument relied not only on this sort of religious anthropology but also on legal precedent, and it is here that he reintroduced medieval English Jewry into the argument.

Anticipating the opposition, Atkyns cited the famous dictum of Lord Coke, the preeminent English jurist of the sixteenth century, together with the equally well-known rebuttal of Sir Matthew Hale. According to Hale, in his *The History of the Pleas of the Crown* (vol. 2),

> it is laid down by Ld. Coke (says Ld. Hale) that an infidel is not to be admitted as a witness; the consequence whereof would be that a Jew who only owns the Old Testament could not be a witness.
>
> But I take it that although the regular oath as it is allowed by the laws of England, is *tactis sacro-sanctis Dei evangeliis*; which supposeth a man to be a Christian; yet in cases of necessity, as in foreign contracts between merchant and merchant, which are many times transacted by Jewish brokers; the testimony of a Jew *tacto libro legis Mosaicæ*, is not to be rejected, and is used as I have been informed among all nations. (17)

Hale went on to note that many other countries had found a way to allow infidels to testify in courts of law, and that Spain had passed special laws related to the testimony of infidels. To invoke Spain as a model of progressive thinking and tolerance in seventeenth-century England, as Hale did, was a bold rhetorical move, Spain having been for two centuries one of England's major enemies, vying for naval and colonial power. He ended by asking his audience to consider how strange and problematic it would be if a murder in England were witnessed by only a Turk or a Jew, and neither of these two non-Christians could testify to what they saw because they could not be sworn in at court.

After quoting Hale at length, Atkyns offers his response, and it is here that we see the redefinition of "the Evangelists" mentioned above. Hale granted the wisdom of Lord Coke's opinion that an infidel cannot be a witness, but maintained that it does not follow that "therefore a Jew cannot be one." The Jew believes in God, just as the Christian does, he argued, "and the Old Testament is as much the *evangelium* to them, as the New is to us; and therefore widely different from the infidel, who has no notion of the true God."[12] The Jew, according to Atkyns, is therefore not an infidel, and thus the Jews cannot be used by the court to suggest that English law permits the testimony of an infidel.

The attorney general, Sir Dudley Rider, responded to Atkyns and argued the case for the validity of the Hindu oath. He invoked the Old Testament and pointed out that the biblical patriarchs "constantly considered the heathens capable of an oath" (Gen. 26:31, 31:53). He also wondered rhetorically about the difference between the Hindu ritual of touching the foot of a priest and the Christian practice of touching or kissing the scriptures while swearing an oath. Both "are no more than signs, and not material to the oath" (19). Rider then quickly returned to the Jews. What is an infidel? he asked. "Why, one who does not believe in the Christian religion. Then a Jew is an infidel, for the sense of *evangelium* has been perverted, and ought to be confined to the New Testament only; for it is used by our Saviour as good tidings, in opposition to the bondage the Jews then underwent, and was delivered to them first" (20).

Intolerance produced by tolerance, tolerance produced by intolerance, or both? If the Jews are not infidels, as Atkyns maintained, then their history in England was irrelevant in the case of *Omychund*. The historical fact that the Jewry oath was valid and the testimony of a Jew trusted could not be used to legitimize the oath and testimony of a Hindu. Judaism is thus raised to an equivalence, at least judicially, with Christianity in order to exclude Hinduism. On the other hand, to include the Hindu in the English legal system, Rider deflates Judaism through the Christian supercessionist argument—the bondage of Judaism (i.e., Jewish law) made irrelevant by the freedom of Christ—and returns the Jews to the category of infidel. The oath of a Hindu would be made valid in the eighteenth century because the oath of a Jew in the twelfth century was valid—but only if the Jew was an infidel in the eyes of the law.

Oaths and Jews

Eighteenth-century English men and women took oaths seriously; that is, they continued to see the taking of an oath as essential to the trustworthiness and reliability on which a well-ordered society depended. As Karen Macfarlane writes, "The importance of oaths in early modern English society can hardly be overestimated. The swearing of oaths was central to many civic and state rituals, from the swearing in of new constables to being allowed to vote."[13] And a belief in an afterlife, and the punishment of eternal hellfire in that afterlife—notions on which the validity of an oath was said to depend—remained vivid and potent, despite the eighteenth century's reputation for religious skepticism. According to Roy Porter, "amongst prominent laymen, Samuel Johnson upheld eternal hellfire and believed the 'quiver of Omnipotence' was 'stored with arrows.'" More generally, religion "was still a burning issue, if now only in a metaphorical sense."[14] As every commentator on the nature and history of the oath has remarked, the viability of the oath as a guarantor of truth-telling depended on a belief in God and the reality of eternal punishment—this is why atheists were the last group to be granted the right to testify in court and serve on juries. The philosopher John Locke, writing in the seventeenth century, advocated strongly for toleration, but, in Porter's words, "with limits: Papists should not be tolerated, because their beliefs were 'absolutely destructive of all governments except the Pope's'; nor should atheists, since any oaths they took would be in bad faith."[15]

Jews living in England in the middle of the eighteenth century were restrained from taking oaths related to matters of state because such oaths invariably contained the phrase "on the words of a true Christian." Oaths of loyalty to the monarch or of abjuration were not instituted to keep Jews from participating in English life. Such oaths were aimed at Catholics, and initially at Protestant Dissenters, or non-Anglicans. It bears emphasizing that compared to the concern evinced about the pope and the threat of papists—most immediately the Jacobite threat of a return of the Pretender—the concern with the Jews on the part of English jurists was minimal. William Hawkins's 1739 work, for example, is replete with laws related to papists, under the headings of treason, conspiracy, and all matters related to præmunire, or assertions of papal or foreign power and legal jurisdiction within England.[16]

As the advocates for reform of the laws governing oaths repeatedly pointed out, the Jews were not the primary targets of the oaths of loyalty but they nonetheless suffered on account of them. However, the oath taken by a Jew referred to by Lord Hardwicke, and before him Matthew Hale, was not one of the oaths of loyalty to the Protestant monarch and state that preoccupied thinkers and policy makers in the years after 1688 (and only ceased to be an issue in the nineteenth century). Rather, it was what is called the Jewry oath, the oath taken "in the Jewish manner" (*more judaico*).[17] When Jews were required to appear in secular, non-Jewish courts as either defendants or witnesses, a special Jewish oath was required. Its origins are obscure, in large part because copies of extant oaths do not come with either dates or places of composition. Scholars disagree on whether or not the Jewry oath was of Jewish or Christian origin. All agree, however, that the oath contained at least two essential components: a recognition of God as the creator of the universe and the articulation of the horrific punishments that awaited the perjurer in the afterlife.[18] Different versions of the oath, from different times and places, contained greater or lesser detail.

A Jewish oath was clearly part of the judicial system in England during the Angevin period.[19] In the charter granted by Richard I in March 1190 reaffirming the liberties granted the Jews by Henry II, there is the following: "And if they [the Jews] are appealed by any one without a witness let them be quits of that appeal on their own oath upon the book [of the Law] and let them quits from an appeal of those things which pertain to our crown on their own oath on their roll [of the Law]."[20] In *Omychund*, both sides invoked the history of the Jews and their participation in the medieval English legal system. There was ample evidence that Jews were able to take the Jewry oath, and that this then made the Jew reliable, at least within that particular context.

It is clear from Angevin law that Jews could testify in secular courts. As early as the reign of Richard I, and probably Henry I, the royal charter granting the Jews their privileges stated that "In a trial between Christian and Jew, each shall have two witnesses—one Jew, one Christian"; this law was renewed by King John in 1201 when he issued his charters of the Jews. Whether or not the special oath was required of the Jewish witness is unclear. Jews could also serve on juries. As Marianne Constable has shown, Jews were conceived as a separate and distinct community within medieval English law, and as such, they served on mixed juries. "Records from the Jewish Exchequer refer to at least four cases during 1278 involving a Christian and a Jew where mixed Christian/Jewish juries were used. The cases involved the unlawful detention of three books, rape, and the killing of a man in the Jewry. Several such records also remain for 1280."[21] A Jew could be convicted in an English court as a forger by the oath of another Jew. According to the Ordinances of the Jewry from 1194, Jews could also be lawyers: "All contracts between Jews and Christians shall be made in six or seven places, and before six officials, of whom two shall be lawyers that are Jews."[22]

Jews, then, were in no way excluded from participation in the medieval English legal system. Indeed, at times the Jews' inclusion appeared to be greater than that of some other groups, and produced resentment. For instance, clergy petitioned in a state paper addressed to Henry II around 1164 for privileges like those of Jews and Londoners:

> Behold, London is the chief seat of the kingdom of the English. If its citizens are accused, if they are summoned to the pleas of the crown, they answer in their own city, they are judged by their own laws: they do not purge themselves by the laws of battle, or the ordeal of water or red-hot iron, unless they choose these of their own accord, but there their oath is the end of all controversy.... So, too, for the Jews, by the proposed law their oath is the end of all lawsuits, whether civil or criminal. Would it not seem to thee unworthy, my lord the King, unless the clergy were granted a privilege which is indulged to lay citizens or Jews?[23]

This well-established participation of the Jew in medieval English justice became a crucial component of the debate in *Omychund*. Lord Coke's assertion that the Jew, qua infidel, was unqualified to testify appeared to be historically and legally untenable. Interestingly, as we've seen, Coke's notion of the Jew as infidel was invoked when it could be made to advance the case for Hindu inclusion. For example, in arguing on behalf of the plaintiff, the solicitor general at one point shifted the debate to the question of perjury. If a Jew can be indicted for perjury, "swearing as they do *tacto libro legis Mosaicae*," so too can Hindus. (A bit later on, the solicitor general would make the claim that in fact no Jew had been indicted for perjury, and Chief Justice Lee would correct him: "I have tried a *Jew* myself upon an indictment of perjury.")

Nonetheless, if a Jew could be indicted for perjury, this means that a Jew's oath, though not taken as a Christian, is valid. The solicitor general, too, made this case by reference to Lord Coke's dictum "that an infidel cannot be a witness." When Coke spoke of infidels, he meant Jews. "He always spoke of Jews as infidels," William Murray declared. And when he spoke of the oath, he meant a Christian oath, because in England in the sixteenth century, "they had no intercourse with Pagans" (22). Murray then made the argument that simply because a thing was not done in the past is no sound reason for not doing it in the present. If in the past there was no need to swear in pagans or infidels—that is, non-Christians—as witnesses, that did not mean that such a time had not arrived; it clearly had. More and more, England would have "commerce and intercourse" with pagans, and thus the need to rely on non-Christian testimony "will most frequently arise."

The solicitor general, like the other advocates for the validity of the oath and testimony of an Indian, employed a rhetorical strategy that relied on insisting that the Jew was in fact an infidel. If, as Lord Coke insisted, the Jew was an infidel, and nonetheless English history showed that the Jew had always been permitted to take a separate oath and participate in the English legal system, then the system could or must also abide the testimony of the Indian infidel. As proof of the validity of a Jewish oath in Angevin times, Murray cites a passage from John Selden: "Before the 18th of Edward the First, the person administering an oath to a Jew, said, 'if you don't speak the truth, every one of your sins and your parents' sins will come upon your head, and you will remain marked eternally by every curse found in the laws of Moses and in the prophets' (*veniant super caput tuum omnia peccata tua, & parentum tuorum, et omnes maledictions quæ in lege Mosaica et prophetarum inscriptæ sunt semper tecum maneant*). To which he answered, *Amen*" (22).

The Uses of the Jew in English Law

As the above passage demonstrates, the arguments put forth in *Omychund* regarding the nature of Hinduism, the status of Hindus, and therefore the reliability of the word of a Hindu in an English court in the eighteenth century depended in large part on the nature of Judaism, the status of Jews, and the word of a Jew in the twelfth or thirteenth century. What, if anything, made Jews and Hindus comparable, other than the fact that they were both non-Christians? What did or could the lawyers and justices know in the middle of the eighteenth century of the history and legal status of the Jews in medieval England? Or, to ask this another way, how was it possible that Coke's easily refuted opinion about Jews, oaths, and testimony was the object of discussion and debate, even if the majority of those present dismissed it in the end? It becomes clear, as the discussion unfolds, that these legal authorities had at their disposal a number of well-known studies that recounted the history of the Jews in England and offered detailed evidence of their legal status before the 1290 expulsion and after their return in the seventeenth century. At one point in the case, Thomas Madox's *History of the Exchequer*, published in 1711, is invoked, and so those involved obviously had access to Madox's extended discussion of the Jews' involvement in medieval England's economic and legal system. Madox makes clear that Jews were permitted "to have a Verdict or Declaration upon Oath according to the Custome of the Jews"; that is, Jews swore on the five books of Moses, with their hand resting on the book. As Madox shows, Jews were deeply embedded in and participants in the Angevin legal culture, as plaintiffs and defendants, witnesses, and members of mixed juries. Among many other royal privileges granted to the Jews, Madox notes that "if a plaint was moved between a Christian and a Jew, he who appealed the other should produce witnesses to deraigne his plaint, namely a lawful Christian and a lawful Jew; that if a Jew had a Writ concerning his plaint, such Writ should be his Witness; that if a Christian had a plaint against a Jew, the plaint should be tried by the Jews peers." In those cases where no witness could be found, Jews had the right "to be quitt of that appeal [accusation] by his single oath taken upon his Book."[24]

Omychund v. Barker was hardly the first time that Jews were used by English lawyers and jurists to work out the law's views on other aliens. Jonathan Bush has shown in great detail that sixteenth- and seventeenth-century British lawyers and jurists often invoked what Bush calls "the notional Jew." Such notional Jews "were unreal and irrelevant to actual English Jews," that is, to the Jews who began settling in England again in the latter part of the seventeenth century. Rather, the Jews who appeared in legal discussions "are best understood as part of Renaissance intellectual interests and rhetorical conventions. But because Jews were consistently portrayed as outsiders in political, religious, literary, and legal discussions, the figure of the Jew offered Renaissance lawyers a vehicle to make important practical legal points, albeit about non-Jews."[25] Bush's insight holds true for the eighteenth century as well. *Omychund* makes clear that for the judges and lawyers arguing about Hindus and Hinduism, medieval Jews were "good to think with."[26] The validity or invalidity of the contemporary Hindu oath was debated in large part with or through the case of the Jews in England nearly half a millennium before.

Hindus and Jews, Ethnography, Theology and History

The case for the validity of the oath of a Hindu did not, however, rest solely on proving that the Jew was an infidel whose word could be trusted. Advocates for the plaintiff also made the case in practical terms and on the basis of the nature of Hinduism itself. At one point, Murray, arguing for the plaintiff, responded to the objection that Hindus ought not to be admitted as witnesses because of the nature of Hinduism. Contrary to what their opponents say, he argued, Hindus in fact do believe in one God, and they believe themselves bound by the oath they take in the name of that God. "Look into books of travels, and you will find that heathens, especially Gentoos, believe in one God the creator of the world, though they may have subordinate deities, as the papists who worship saints." Among the references cited by the lawyers and justices in *Omychund*, the most significant was undoubtedly Bernard Picart and Jean Frederic Bernard's *Religious Ceremonies of the World*, a seven-volume comparative study of the religions of the world that had been translated into English in 1731. The authors of the authoritative study of the book have recently written, "No other work before then had ever attempted, in word and image, such a grand sweep of human religions. *Religious Ceremonies of the World* marked a major turning point in European attitudes toward religious belief and hence the sacred. It sowed the radical idea that religions could be compared on equal terms, and therefore that all religions were equally worthy of respect—and criticism."[27] Murray and Lee relied on this work more than once when making their argument for the validity of the Hindu oath.

If comparing religions of the world "is hardly surprising today, much less shocking," this was not always the case. "As late as the early eighteenth century, however, most Western writings about religion either laid out the true doctrine (that of the author) or focused on debunking the competitors." The various Protestant sects, Catholics, Jews, and Muslims all wrote either to defend themselves or denigrate the others. "The customs of the rest of the world's religions were lumped together as pagan idolatry."[28] Thus, we should not take for granted or fail to appreciate the boldness of the arguments put forth by Murray and the others in *Omychund*.[29]

While the lawyers and justices invoked a number of arguments for and against the validity of the Hindu oath, the Jews were never absent for long from the discussion. Responding to Murray's citation of *Religious Ceremonies* and the idea that Hindus, too, believed in one God and thus took their oaths in good faith, Chute, the main advocate for Barker, disputed this notion that Hinduism could claim an equality of sorts with Christianity and Judaism. Accepting the argument of the plaintiff, he declared, would seem to be insisting "there never was a false religion in the world" (25). Chute then proceeded to use the tolerance and inclusion of the Jews on the part of the English as a means to demonstrate the need to exclude the Hindus.

After the Restoration, Jews were "admitted to be sworn," that is, their oath was taken and their testimony accepted in an English court of law. This, according to Chute, was "no more than declaring what was the ancient law." Scripture tells us that the Jews were God's chosen; Christianity tells us that the Jews, because they may at some point be converted to the truth, must be given "superior credit" above all those who do not believe in the holy scriptures. This explains why Jews may take an oath that does not include the phrase "upon the faith of a Christian" (26–27). History and theology come together here to bring the Jews into the fold of noninfidels. Having established the theological underpinnings of the acceptance of the word of a Jew, the discussion turned to history.

The lord chancellor ruled that the case should be held over and a search made in the records for precedent regarding the indictment of Jews, and more generally the oath of Jews, or the Jewry oath. When the court reconvened on February 23, Lord Chief Baron took up the case for the validity of a Hindu's oath. Lord Coke's opinion, again, had to be refuted. If by "infidel" Lord Coke actually meant "atheist," then Hindus were not infidels. The "best testimonies"—Picart and Bernard's *Religious Ceremonies* and Joseph Pitton de Tournefort's *A Voyage into the Levant*—testify to the fact that Hindus believe in God, who is the creator of the world. Baron then turns from ethnography to history. Matthew Hale, as we know, rejected Coke's opinion on the Jews and oaths. The defendant's counsel also cited earlier legal authorities—Bracton, Briton, Fleta—to prove ostensibly that jurors or witnesses must be sworn on the Gospels. The historical record, however, shows us clearly that Jews were sworn, both before their expulsion in 1290 and after the Restoration. Madox's *History of the Exchequer* and Wilken's *Saxon Laws* both speak of Jews swearing oaths and testifying, and the latter refers to a sheriff's writ to appear (*venire fascias*) sent out to *sex legales homines* and *sex legales Judæos*—six qualified men and six qualified Jews. These are legal categories, not ontological judgments, suggesting that medieval English law made some invidious contrast between "Jews" and Christian "men." As remarked above, legally, Jews were a distinct community, with their own customs and laws. In matters involving legal disputes between a Jew and a Christian, the law recognized the Jewish community as a distinct corporate entity and made a place for Jewish participation and representation.

Lord Chief Baron appears to offer unequivocal evidence that Jews were understood to be acceptable as legal witnesses—especially, as Baron added, as witnesses when it came to cases of murder. If a reason for excluding a witness is that he does not believe in Jesus Christ, Baron concluded, then "I think the reason a very bad one, for the same reason would exclude Jews" (29).

When Lord Chief Justice Willes came to speak on behalf of the defendant, he, too, focused on the question of the Jews as infidels, arguing against Lord Coke and Serjeant Hawkins' interpretation of Coke. Interestingly, Willes claimed that he in fact had no objection to infidels being admitted as witnesses under certain circumstances. Like his fellow justices, Willes appears to argue that one may grant that Jews are infidels (i.e., non-Christians), but that did not prove Lord Coke's point that as a result of this they were excluded from participating in the English legal system. The historical record clearly shows this not to have been the case.

My Lord Coke is plainly of opinion, that Jews as well as Heathens were comprised under the same exclusion. Serjeant Hawkins in his *Pleas of the Crown*, though a very learned and painstaking man, is mistaken in his notion of Lord Coke's opinion; long before his time, and ever since the Jews returned to England, they have been constantly admitted as witnesses. The defendant's counsel are mistaken in their construction of Lord Coke, for he puts the Jews upon the footing with stigmatized and infamous persons: this notion, though advanced by so great a man, is contrary to religion, common sense, and common humanity; and I think the devils themselves, to whom he has delivered them, could not have suggested any thing worse. (30)

Willes, and all the other justices and lawyers, understood that an oath depended on an oath taker's belief in God and in God's ability and willingness to punish the liar or perjurer in the afterlife. Thus, Willes could repeat what others had said many times both before and after: the form of an oath "varies in countries according to different laws and constitutions, but the substance is the same in all" (32). In the end, it did not matter if the Hindu swore while touching the foot of the priest, or the Jew swore by putting his hand on the five books of Moses, or the Christian by swearing on the Gospels. What mattered, as the Lord Chancellor stated again, was that an individual believed "in God and His providence." In the end, the court found in favor of Omychund, affirming that a Hindu oath was indeed valid in an English court.

Omychund and English Toleration

Scholarly consensus has identified *Omychund v. Barker* as a major turning point in the history of law and religious tolerance. According to C. J. W. Allen, *Omychund* resolved the question of non-Christians and testimony in a court of law. After *Omychund*, "it was . . . regarded as an established rule that, in Phillips' words [*Treatise*, v. 1, 12], "not only Jews, but infidels of any country, believing in a God who enjoins truth and punishes falsehood, ought to be received as witnesses. . . . *Omychund v. Barker* also established that, although the substance of the oath must be the same in all cases, it was obviously necessary to allow persons to swear according to the particular ceremonies of their religion in such a manner as they considered binding on their conscience."[30] According to Paul Kaufman, *Omychund*'s take on oaths and religion became the norm for English and colonial American common law. "In 1744, *Omychund v. Barker* held that any religious person could testify after being sworn in the fashion most binding on her conscience. After *Omychund*, the common view was that 'not only Jews, but infidels of any country, believing in a God who enjoins truth and punishes falsehood, ought to be received as witnesses.' Since this development preceded the American Revolution, the colonies adopted this rule with the rest of the common law."[31]

More recently, Macfarlane has challenged this orthodoxy, at least as far as criminal cases are concerned: "There is no evidence that *Omychund v. Barker* had an immediate effect on the proceedings at the Old Bailey."[32] Macfarlane offers a host of examples to demonstrate her point that into the nineteenth century, English courtrooms, in criminal cases, continued to see an English Christian oath as "the most trustworthy." Both Jews and non-Christian blacks, for instance, were regularly interrogated as witnesses as to their religious beliefs before their oaths and testimony were admitted.

While *Omychund* certainly appears to have intended greater inclusion in the category of valid and reliable testimony, in the colonial context, the results were the opposite for a century after the ruling. Historian of English law and colonialism Reginald Goode has noted that colonial courts invoked the exclusionary rules of evidence set forth in *Omychund* "to bar the reception of testimony from prospective non-Christian Aboriginal witnesses."[33] This had the effect of making it far more difficult, even impossible, for courts to prosecute cases in which unsworn testimony figured. This was not remedied until 1853, and the passage of the (Colonies) Evidence Act. The act's preamble noted that "barbarous and uncivilized" people who "had no knowledge of God and of any religious belief" were "incapable of giving evidence on oath in any court of justice" within the British colonies. "The act enabled colonial legislatures to remedy this injustice by passing legislation to admit the unsworn testimony of non-Christian Aborigines and Indians."[34]

If the actual impact or influence of *Omychund* on the Anglo legal system was less absolute than many legal scholars suggest, many nonetheless believed that the case had produced an equivalence in oath taking and legal testimony, and thus suggested, in turn, a broadening or widening of the circle of tolerance. In England itself, *Omychund* was invoked repeatedly not only in legal works on the nature of evidence, but in public forums and discussions over oaths and religious tolerance. The case also figured in public debates over Jews and public office in the nineteenth century, in which the question of oaths figured prominently. For example, in a long letter to *The Standard* (London) in August 1833, Henry Vassall-Fox, Lord Holland, registered his "protest against the rejection of the bill for removing the civil disabilities of the Jews."[35] English Jews, Lord Holland maintained, who were "born in the allegiance of his Majesty," and thus ought not to suffer the deprivations or enjoy the special privileges that were part of the conditions under which they lived before their expulsion in 1290. He denied that Lord Coke's pronouncements about Jews had any force at present.

> It has, moreover, been declared, in the course of a solemn judgment in the Exchequer Chambers (*Omychund v. Barker*), by Chief Justice Wilkes, to be contrary to religion, sense, and humanity, and in that opinion not only the Solicitor General Murray, but the judges there present, including Chief Baron

Parker and Lord Chancellor Hardwicke, seem to have concurred. English Jews have been recognized and described as his Majesty's subjects in more than one statute; and by an act of 10 Geo. IV. cap. 4, they are authorized to exempt themselves from registering their real or personal property, by taking the oath of abjuration, without the words of "upon the true faith of a Christian."

Lord Holland's plea was taken up in other English newspapers and journals. On August 10, the editors of *The Lancaster Gazette and General Advertiser* endorsed "the very able Protest of Lord Holland, against the rejection of the Bill for removing the Civil Disabilities of the Jews." They quoted from Lord Holland's speech, including the invocation of Lord Mansfield and *Omychund v. Barker*, and then offered their own reasons for opposing those who supported the continuation of Jewish legal disabilities. "By universal admission," they argued, there is nothing in the religion of the Jews "which unfits them from discharging the duties of a good citizen."[36]

Omychund had some potential impact, then, on nineteenth-century debates about Jews and political oaths, those that had kept Jews from participating fully in English public life since the seventeenth century. However, as we've seen, these were not the oaths that the lawyers and justices who argued *Omychund* were interested in, and "the Jews" were those of the twelfth and thirteenth centuries and not those of the eighteenth and nineteenth.

Oaths and Trust

What sort of trust is produced by an oath? For an oath to produce trust in the testimony given, the oath taker must already in fact be trusted; those others present in the courtroom must be at least somewhat certain that the oath taker believes in God, or his or her own gods, and that this divinity can and will mete out punishments in the afterlife for perjury. This certainly seems to have been the case with the medieval Jewry oath, including the Jewry oath in Angevin England. The Jewry oath reveals something intriguing about the Christian approach to Judaism and Jews: by investing the Jewish oath with the power to impel Jews to tell the truth, and assuming that if the oath is administered correctly, it will indeed produce a truth-telling effect, Christian authorities signaled a belief, however implicit, in the nexus of Judaism, trust, and truth.

Even if they drew on an earlier rabbinic model, the Jewry oath was still by and large a product of Christian authorities, ecclesiastical and secular. Its power, these authorities believed, lay in the invocation of Jehovah, the imprecations taken from the Old Testament, and the administering of the oath by a rabbi in or in front of a synagogue, using a Torah. The inclusion of curses and punishments awaiting the perjurer suggests, of course, that lying is always a possibility, that trust in another's character only goes so far and then fear becomes necessary. But the threat of punishment in the case of perjury is hardly limited to the Jew; every judicial system takes account of the possibility of perjury. But the possibility of perjury implies the possibility of truth-telling. In the case of the Jew in Christian Europe, including medieval England, the Jewry oath, created by Christians, suggests that the Jew could tell the truth. If, as Christian popular imagery had it, the Jew was an inveterate liar, the oath would seem to make no sense.

If such a testimonial oath was capable of transforming an essentially untrustworthy, perfidious individual into someone whose word could now be taken on faith, then it seems clear that Christian authorities granted the efficacy of Judaism to produce truth and trust. *Omychund v. Barker* testifies to the ability of the historical and legal record of medieval English Jewry to produce tolerance not for eighteenth-century British Jews—the legal disabilities suffered by Anglo-Jewry would not disappear completely until the middle of the nineteenth century—but for Hindus and Hinduism. This was not complete acceptance, let alone a relativism that granted equality between Christianity, Judaism, and Hinduism. But it was a recognition that, as Lord Chief Justice Willes argued, "the form of oaths varies in countries according to different laws and constitutions, but the substance is the same in all."[37] And this, in turn, guaranteed that the word of an eighteenth-century Hindu, like that of a thirteenth-century Jew, could be trusted in a court of law.

Notes

1. *Ramkissenseat v. Barker, et. al.* December 4, 1739, in 1 *Atkyns* 18, English Reports 26, 13f.
2. *Atkyns* 18, p. 13.
3. I Vern. 263, Anon. Cited in Hale, *The History of the Pleas of the Crown*, part II, 279; 1 *Atkyns* 18, 14.
4. *Atkyns*, 14.
5. Jacob Selwood, "Present at the Creation: Diaspora, Hybridity and the Place of Jews in the History of English Toleration," in *Religious Tolerance in the Atlantic World: Early Modern and Contemporary Perspectives*, ed. Elaine Glaser (New York: Palgrave, 2014), 195.
6. *Ramkissenseat v. Barker*, 13.
7. Each witness, according to the report, touched with their hands "the foot of the brahmin or priest of the Gentoo religion." *Omychund v. Barker*, 1; *Atkyns* 22, 15.
8. Petra Schulte, "Einleitung," in *Strategies of Writing: Studies on Text and Trust in the Middle Ages*, ed. Petra Schulte, Marco Mostert, and Irene van Renswoude (Turnhout: Brepois, 2008), 3. My translation.
9. See Karen A. Macfarlane, "'Does He Know the Danger of an Oath?': Oaths, Religion, Ethnicity and the Advent of the Adversarial Criminal Trial in the Eighteenth Century," *Immigrants & Minorities* 31, no. 3 (2013): 317–45.
10. See Colin Kidd, *The Forging of Races: Race and Scripture in the Protestant Atlantic World, 1600–2000* (Cambridge: Cambridge University Press, 2006), chapter 4.

11. Alexandra Walsham, *Charitable Hatred: Tolerance and Intolerance in England, 1500–1700* (Manchester: Manchester University Press, 2006), 4.
12. This is why, Atkyns added, the testimony of Jews was admitted in *Robeley v. Langston* (2 Roll. 314). 1 *Atkyns* 8, 17.
13. Macfarlane, "'Does He Know the Danger of an Oath?,'" 318.
14. Roy Porter, *The Creation of the Modern World: The Untold Story of the British Enlightenment* (New York: W. W. Norton, 2000), 97.
15. Porter, *The Creation of the Modern World*, 106.
16. William Hawkins, *A Treatise of the Pleas of the Crown* (London, 1739), particularly chapter 19.
17. The designation *more judaico* is most familiar from its use in reference to the Jewry oath, but it was not limited to that. Guido Kisch noted that the phrase appeared in a text from the fourteenth century, the *Brünner Schöffenbuch*, and was used to describe the shape of a particular hat, a "real pointed hat 'of the Jewish manner.'" See Guido Kisch, "The 'Jewish Execution' in Medieval Germany," *Historia Judaica* 5, no. 2 (1943): 105n4.
18. Bertil Maler, "A propos de quelques formulaires médiévaux du 'sacramentum more judaico,'" *Stockholm Studies in Modern Philology* 5, no. 1 (1976): 120. Guido Kisch put the number of essential components at three, seeing the "solemn invocation of God" and the demonstration of God's omnipotence through biblical stories as two distinct elements. See Guido Kisch, *The Jews in Medieval Germany: A Study of Their Legal and Social Status* (Chicago: University of Chicago Press, 1949), 275. For a more recent overview of the Jewry oath, see Amnon Linder, "The Jewry Oath in Christian Europe," in *Jews in Early Christian Law: Byzantium and the Latin West, 6th–11th Centuries*, ed. John Tolan, Nicholas de Lange, Laurence Foschia, and Capuchin Nemo-Pekelman (Turnhout: Brepois, 2013), 311–59.
19. See Joseph Jacobs, "Notes on the Jews of England under the Angevin Kings," *The Jewish Quarterly Review* 4, no. 4 (July 1892): 637–38. And see the essay in this volume by Joshua Curk.
20. Joseph Jacobs, *The Jews of Angevin England: Documents and Records* (London: David Nutt, 1893), 135. The law was reaffirmed in the charters to the Jews by King John. It seems clear from the text that this and the other rights granted had already existed in the time of Henry I. See Jacobs, *The Jews of Angevin England*, 213–14.
21. Marianne Constable, *The Law of the Other: The Mixed Jury and Changing Conceptions of Citizenship, Law, and Knowledge* (Chicago: University of Chicago Press, 1994), 20.
22. Reproduced in Jacobs, "Notes on the Jews of England under the Angevin Kings," 641.
23. Quoted in Constable, *The Law of the Other*, 19.
24. Thomas Madox, *History and Antiquities of the Exchequer of the Kings of England* (London, 1711), 173–74.
25. Jonathan Bush, "'You're Gonna Miss Me When I'm Gone': Early Modern Common Law Discourse and the Case of the Jews," *Wisconsin Law Review*, no. 5 (1993): 1246.
26. On this idea as it applied to the function of Jews within the long history of Western Christendom, see David Nirenberg, *Anti-Judaism: The Western Tradition* (New York: W. W. Norton, 2013).
27. Lynn Hunt, Margaret C. Jacob, Wijnand Mijnhardt, *The Book That Changed Europe: Picart and Bernard's* Religious Ceremonies of the World (Cambridge: Harvard University Press, 2010), 1.

28. All quotations from Hunt, Jacob, and Mijnhardt, *The Book That Changed Europe*, 9.

29. For a much more comprehensive sense of how English writers used non-Christian religions largely, though not wholly, for propagandistic purposes (i.e., to reaffirm the superiority of Christianity), see David. A. Pailin, *Attitudes to Other Religions: Comparative Religion in Seventeenth- and Eighteenth-Century Britain* (Manchester: Manchester, 1984).

30. C. J. W. Allen, *The Law of Evidence in Victorian England* (Cambridge: Cambridge University Press, 1997), 51.

31. Paul Kaufman, "Disbelieving Nonbelievers: Atheism, Competence, and Credibility in the Turn of the Century American Courtroom," *Yale Journal of Law & the Humanities*, 15, no. 2 (2003): 403. The quote comes from Samuel March Phillips, *A Treatise on the Law of Evidence*, 8th ed. (London: Saunders and Benning, 1838), 12. See also Stephen Waddams, "Authority, Precedent, and Principle: The Nature and Authority of Precedent by Neil Duxbury," *The University of Toronto Law Journal* 59, no. 1 (Winter 2009): 128–29.

32. Macfarlane, "Does He Know the Danger of an Oath?," 329.

33. Reginald Good, "Regulating Indian and Chinese Civic Identities in British Columbia's 'Colonial Contact Zone,' 1858–1887," *Canadian Journal of Law and Society / Revue Canadienne Droit et Société* 26, no. 1 (2011): 70. See also Reginald Good, "Admissibility of Testimony from Non-Christian Indians in the Colonial Municipal Courts of Upper Canada/Canada West," *Windsor Yearbook of Access to Justice*, vol. 23 (2005): 55–94.

34. Good, "Regulating Indian," 71.

35. Henry Vassall-Fox, "Protest against the rejection of the bill for removing the civil disabilities of the Jews," *The Standard*, London, Monday, August 5, 1833, issue 1944. The letter also appeared in *The Morning Post* (London), on Wednesday, August 7, 1833.

36. *The Lancaster Gazette and General Advertiser*, Saturday, August 10, 1833, issue 1678. Omychund figured in other nineteenth-century public debates involving Jews and oaths. See, for instance, the newspaper reports and letters regarding the case of David Salomons, who was repeatedly prevented from taking his seat as an alderman in the City of London because he would not recite the required oath "on the faith of a Christian": "Report on Court of Exchequer, The Case of Mr. Alderman Salomons, M. P. Jewish Disabilities," *Daily News* (London), "Law Intelligence," January 27, 1852, issue 1772; also reported in *The Morning Post*, January 27, 1852; *The Era* (London), Sunday, Feb. 1, 1852, issue 697. See also the report on the court case *Salomons v. Miller* in *The Standard*, Thursday, May 12, 1853; also found in *The Derby Mercury* (Derby), Wednesday, May 18, 1853.

37. *Omychund v. Barker*, 30.

Bibliography

Allen, C. J. W. *The Law of Evidence in Victorian England*. Cambridge: Cambridge University Press, 1997.

Bush, Jonathan. "'You're Gonna Miss Me When I'm Gone': Early Modern Common Law Discourse and the Case of the Jews." *Wisconsin Law Review*, no. 5 (1993): 1225–85.

Constable, Marianne. *The Law of the Other: The Mixed Jury and Changing Conceptions of Citizenship, Law, and Knowledge*. Chicago: University of Chicago Press, 1994.

Good, Reginald. "Admissibility of Testimony from Non-Christian Indians in the Colonial Municipal Courts of Upper Canada/Canada West." *Windsor Yearbook of Access to Justice* 23 (2005): 55–94.

———. "Regulating Indian and Chinese Civic Identities in British Columbia's 'Colonial Contact Zone,' 1858–1887." *Canadian Journal of Law and Society/Revue Canadienne Droit et Société* 26, no. 1 (2011): 69–88.
Hale, Matthew. *The History of the Pleas of the Crown.* London: E. and R. Nutt, 1736.
Hawkins, William. *A Treatise of the Pleas of the Crown.* 3rd ed. London: E. Nutt, 1739.
Hunt, Lynn, Margaret C. Jacob, and Wijnand Mijnhardt. *The Book That Changed Europe: Picart and Bernard's Religious Ceremonies of the World.* Cambridge, MA: Harvard University Press, 2010.
Jacobs, Joseph. *The Jews of Angevin England: Documents and Records.* London: David Nutt, 1893.
———. "Notes on the Jews of England under the Angevin Kings." *The Jewish Quarterly Review* 4, no. 4 (1892): 628–55.
Kaufman, Paul. "Disbelieving Nonbelievers: Atheism, Competence, and Credibility in the Turn of the Century American Courtroom." *Yale Journal of Law & the Humanities* 15, no. 2 (2003): 395–433.
Kidd, Colin. *The Forging of Races: Race and Scripture in the Protestant Atlantic World, 1600–2000.* Cambridge: Cambridge University Press, 2006.
Kisch, Guido. "The 'Jewish Execution' in Medieval Germany." *Historia Judaica* 5, no. 2 (1943): 103–32.
———. *The Jews in Medieval Germany: A Study of Their Legal and Social Status.* Chicago: University of Chicago Press, 1949.
The Lancaster Gazette and General Advertiser, Saturday, August 10, 1833, issue 1678.
Linder, Amnon. "The Jewry Oath in Christian Europe." In *Jews in Early Christian Law: Byzantium and the Latin West, 6th–11th Centuries*, edited by John Tolan, Nicholas de Lange, Laurence Foschia, and Capuchin Nemo-Pekelman, 311–59. Turnhout: Brepois, 2013.
Macfarlane, Karen A. "'Does He Know the Danger of an Oath?': Oaths, Religion, Ethnicity and the Advent of the Adversarial Criminal Trial in the Eighteenth Century." *Immigrants & Minorities* 31, no. 3 (2013): 317–45.
Madox, Thomas. *The History and Antiquities of the Exchequer of the Kings of England.* London: John Matthews, 1711.
Maler, Bertil. "A propos de quelques formulaires médiévaux du 'sacrementum more judaico.'" *Stockholm Studies in Modern Philology* 5, no. 1 (1976).
Nirenberg, David. *Anti-Judaism: The Western Tradition.* New York: Norton, 2013.
Omychund v. Barker (Michaelmas term, 1744). 1 Atkyns 22. 26 English Reports.
Pailin, David. A. *Attitudes to Other Religions: Comparative Religion in Seventeenth- and Eighteenth-Century Britain.* Manchester: Manchester University Press, 1984.
Phillips, Samuel March. *A Treatise on the Law of Evidence.* 8th ed. London: Saunders and Benning, 1838.
Porter, Roy. *The Creation of the Modern World: The Untold Story of the British Enlightenment.* New York: W. W. Norton, 2000.
Ramkissenseat v. Barker, et al. (December 4, 1739). 1 Atkyns 18. 26 English Reports.
"Report on Court of Exchequer, The Case of Mr. Alderman Salomons, M. P. Jewish Disabilities," *Daily News* (London), January 27, 1852, issue 1772.
Schulte, Petra. "Einleitung." In *Strategies of Writing: Studies on Text and Trust in the Middle Ages*, edited by Petra Schulte, Marco Mostert, and Irene van Renswoude, 1–12. Turnhout: Brepois, 2008.

Selwood, Jacob. "Present at the Creation: Diaspora, Hybridity and the Place of Jews in the History of English Toleration." In *Religious Tolerance in the Atlantic World: Early Modern and Contemporary Perspectives*, edited by Eliane Glaser, 193–213. New York: Palgrave Macmillan, 2014.

Vassall-Fox, Henry, "Protest against the rejection of the bill for removing the civil disabilities of the Jews," *The Standard*, London, Monday, August 5, 1833, issue 1944.

Waddams, Stephen. "Authority, Precedent, and Principle: The Nature and Authority of Precedent by Neil Duxbury." *The University of Toronto Law Journal* 59, no. 1 (2009): 127–33.

Walsham, Alexandra. *Charitable Hatred: Tolerance and Intolerance in England, 1500–1700*. Manchester: Manchester University Press, 2006.

MITCHELL B. HART is Professor of History and the Alexander Grass Chair in Jewish History at the University of Florida. He is editor (with Tony Michels) of *The Cambridge History of Modern Judaism, volume 8: The Modern Period, 1815–2000*.

5 Trusting Adolphe Crémieux
Jews and Republicans in Nineteenth-Century France

Lisa Leff

THERE WAS NOTHING inevitable about the alliance that formed between Jews and republicans in nineteenth-century France. During the Revolution, the leaders of the first French republic had waged war on all religions, defrocking rabbis as they defrocked priests, seizing synagogues as they seized churches. Over the course of the nineteenth century, French republicans developed *laïcité*, a model of secularism in which religious expression is banned from the public sphere. As Joan Scott has put it, what distinguishes French *laïcité* from secularism *à l'américaine* is that the former centers on the "state's protection of individuals from the claims of religion" while the latter is about "the protection of religions from interference by the state."[1] One would assume that French Jewish leaders—leaders of *religious* institutions, after all—would have been as opposed as their Catholic counterparts to an ideology devoted to limiting their religion's public presence. And yet by the time the Third Republic was founded in 1870, official French Jewish institutions as well as individual members of the French Jewish elite had become trustworthy republicans. When and why did Jews in France become such staunch supporters of a political ideology that appeared to limit their freedom of public religious expression? Posed in reverse, the question is just as perplexing. What made republicans, who were rabidly anticlerical when it came to the Catholic Church, come to see Jews—not just as abstract individuals, but specifically as *Jews*—as some of their most trustworthy allies?

By the end of the nineteenth century, the alliance was clearly in place. Pierre Birnbaum has shown that by then, a remarkable number of French Jews began to pursue careers in state service, linking their fortunes to that of the republic itself.[2] Moreover, as French Jews began to participate in mainstream politics, they became known for their anticlerical views. Ari Joskowicz has shown that this was about more than self-defense against the *ultramontane* Catholic politicians seeking to strip Jews of their citizenship rights. Rather, it was an expression of Jews' abiding devotion to *laïcité*.[3] Indeed, the Jewish elite embraced this ideology well before it entered the mainstream. Already in the 1850s and 1860s, when republicans were in the opposition under the Second Empire and forced out of positions of influence, the main Paris-based French Jewish institutions had become bastions of republican ideology and democratic practice.[4]

The story of how Jews became trustworthy republicans is also the story of how this specifically French model of secularism was built. In the first half of the nineteenth century, when most French Jews were not yet assimilated enough to know much about the larger debates in French political culture, one member of the French Jewish elite, Adolphe Crémieux (1796–1883), presented himself as a central figure in both the emerging republican movement and Jewish communal institutions, and served as a bridge between the two worlds. Starting with his early legal cases and continuing into his career as a politician, Crémieux helped forge the French republican model of secularism. He argued time and again that equal rights for Jews was a cornerstone of the French Revolutionary tradition and that secularism, conceived as the protection of the individual from the claims of religion, was the best guarantee of Jews' rights.

To non-Jewish republicans, Crémieux was a worthy ally. Not only was he a savvy thinker and politician, but as a Jew, he became, paradoxically, a powerful symbol of the republican movement's secular agenda. Examining Crémieux's career thus provides a useful lens through which to see how Jews became trustworthy republicans, and republicans trustworthy philosemites.

Crémieux's career as a bridge between Jewish institutions and the republican left took shape in the 1820s, when he argued a set of landmark cases about the Jewish oath before the Nîmes Appeals Court. The cases involved a Jewish creditor who was attempting to collect a sum owed by the heirs of his debtor. The defendants claimed that the creditor had fabricated the agreement that he produced as evidence of the debt. For this reason, a lower court judge in Uzès ruled that the loan contract was not itself enough to support the plaintiff's claim; an oath was also needed, because the oath makes the testimony trustworthy because of its religious "solemnity." The judge further ordered the Jewish plaintiff to swear *more judaïco*. The Latin phrase means "in the manner of the Jews," and refers to a special oath Jews were supposed to swear in place of the traditional courtroom oath sworn by Catholic and Protestant subjects in that same court. The special Jewish oath, the judge maintained, was a protection of the plaintiff's rights rather than an attack on his religion, adding that "nothing prevents a judge from requiring a Catholic Christian to take the oath on the holy Gospel."[5] Here, the judge interpreted the Jewish oath as a means for guaranteeing freedom of conscience, the right of all citizens to worship as they pleased.[6]

Representing the creditor, Crémieux countered that the oath was a violation of his client's freedom of conscience, illegal under Restoration France's constitution, the Charter of 1814. He argued that the lower court in Uzès had misused the notions of religious equality and freedom in requiring the Jewish oath. In fact, the ruling compromised legal equality by creating "laws particular to each sect" in a country whose charter affirmed the unity of the nation under a common code of law. Crémieux interpreted Article 1 of the charter, which stated that "All Frenchmen are equal before the law," as meaning "the absence of all difference of any sort between individuals."[7]

For Crémieux, religious freedom was essentially the right to privacy. The law, he claimed, protects religious liberty by protecting its ministers, administrators, and buildings from attack. In contrast, individual believers are citizens, equal in that the law considers them all to be the same: they thus have no religion before the law. Were the law to recognize individual citizens' religion, it would be an attack on an individual's fundamental rights. This was because to find out what an individual citizen's religion was, the law would have to peer forcibly into the citizen's heart, and such an act was ultimately as impossible as it was illegal. Thus, Crémieux argued, the lower court had not protected religious liberty, but had rather violated it by undertaking what he called an "*inquisition into the religion of each citizen.*"[8] He won the case, and his success was lauded in both the Jewish world and in the legal profession, well known for its liberal leanings.

Well received as they would be among liberal jurists in the 1820s and '30s, Crémieux's arguments about the illegality of the Jewish oath had their origin in Jewish institutional circles. French rabbis and lay leaders from Eastern France had waged a campaign against the oath since the issue had first emerged in the aftermath of the Revolution. As in Nîmes, the Jewish oath had been introduced in Eastern France as a way of making Jews' testimonies credible before judges in the new secular state courts that were created under Napoleon. In post-Revolutionary French law, the Jewish oath represented a real anomaly. During the Revolution, Jews had been granted the status of citizens equal to their Catholic and Protestant neighbors, and enjoyed almost all of the same rights. This equal status appeared to be confirmed in Napoleon's Civil Code of 1804, which affirmed the equality of all citizens before the law.

Nevertheless, in this case, equality had not always meant swearing the same oaths in court. Instead, beginning in 1806, some French Jews were required to swear *more judaïco* in courts in Eastern France and in the neighboring German parts of the Empire. In these courts, Jews were required to swear while standing before a rabbi and an open Torah scroll, sometimes in a synagogue, sometimes in the courtroom. In some cases, the crucifix—a fixture in nineteenth-century French courtrooms—was veiled when the oath was taken.[9] Rabbis and Jewish lay leaders in early nineteenth-century Eastern France objected to using the oath because, they argued, it was a remnant of the legal disabilities they had left behind with their emancipation during the Revolution.

In fact, the Jewish oath had not really been an issue in the Revolutionary period. Rather, it was something of a novelty in Napoleonic-era French jurisprudence, borrowed from the German lands. In medieval Germany, gentile courts (and not Jewish authorities, it is important to note) required that Jewish witnesses, plaintiffs, and defendants use special oaths to assure that their testimonies could be trusted. In most cases, the formulations used in the oaths in German lands had been intentionally humiliating and intimidating. Jews pledged to speak truthfully, and guaranteed their word by imploring God to punish them harshly in case of perjury.[10] Before the Revolution, the only French province where Jews had been required to take a special oath was Alsace, where many German customs prevailed. Even there, it had never been imposed uniformly.[11] More importantly, the Jewish oath was outlawed everywhere in France in 1792, just one year after Alsatian Jews were made citizens and their separate courts dissolved. Throughout the Revolution, Jews testifying in court had simply said, "I swear," as did all other citizens.[12] The Napoleonic Code required all witnesses to swear to tell the truth in court, but did not specify the form the oath would take. An imperial decree of October 10, 1808, clarified the matter, requiring all witnesses to swear in court with one hand on a printed Bible.[13] Thus, even though nineteenth-century French Jews such as Crémieux would consistently speak of the oath as a throwback to the corporate disabilities of the past, in fact, it was largely a nineteenth-century phenomenon, reintroduced and diffused more widely than ever before in France.

Given this history, why was the Jewish oath introduced into courtrooms in wake of the French Revolution? The earliest cases suggest that it was part of a backlash against Jewish emancipation in Eastern France. Jewish-Christian tensions were exceptionally high in this region because many Jews there made their living as small-scale moneylenders to Christians. As one might expect, many of these tensions led to litigation. The first place where courts required the Jewish oath was Southern Alsace, where, in 1807, numerous pamphleteers were calling for Jews' expulsion from France because of their moneylending practices. In response, Napoleon had issued a temporary ban on Jewish moneylending in 1806, and by 1807, Christian debtors were beginning to appear in courts demanding that the loans they had contracted from Jews before 1806 be forgiven as well. In 1809, local Jewish leaders reported that the oath was being used to intimidate Jews so that they would not testify in civil cases, since Jews were not accustomed to taking oaths and were terrified of it.[14] Indeed, in at least one case, a Jewish defendant was willing to pay a six hundred-franc fine rather than submit to it.[15] It would be incorrect to say that all Jews opposed the oath, since some of the legal cases involved Jews suing their rabbis for refusing to administer the oath to them, thus making it impossible for them to testify. However, by the time of the Restoration (1814–30), Jewish leaders in Eastern France were united in their opposition to the oath and had organized a campaign against it.[16]

In these early cases, proponents of the oath framed their arguments as relating to the question of Jews' nationality. This is clear in the 1809 case before the Colmar Appeals Court, in which the judges held that Jews were in fact required to take the oath, reasoning, "The Jews of the Upper Rhine Department are of German origin, and thus the oath they must take must be made in the Synagogue, on a [Torah scroll]."[17] The decision thus represented a challenge to Jews' citizenship by depicting them as "Germans." Of course, Alsatian Jews were no more German than Protestant and Catholic residents of Alsace, which was annexed to France in 1648. Equally problematic in the framework of imperial law was the court's decision to deem "German custom" the appropriate usage for French citizens of "German origin." This created a legal category based on a group's descent, which was otherwise anomalous in Napoleonic jurisprudence, conflicting with the more generally individualistic framework of the code. From the moment it reappeared after the Revolution, then, the Jewish oath was justified with claims about Jews' special status as former "foreigners" still governed by provisions granted to them collectively before the Revolution.

Slightly different reasoning was provided by the Commercial Court in Mainz in the occupied Rhineland in November 1808. Here, the judges formulated for the first time what would later become the cornerstone of all arguments in favor of the oath, justifying it by relying on the principle of religious freedom. The Mainz judge saw the oath as a religious rather than a civil act. He argued that for a Jew to be bound by an oath, he would have to swear before a rabbi and on the Torah, which he holds sacred.[18] The judge invoked the principle of religious liberty to make his case, arguing that each witness must be "permitted" to swear according to his faith. His reasoning convinced the Minister of Justice, who accepted the Jewish oath as a protection of Jews' religious freedom.

Once the Empire gave way to the Restoration, judges beyond Alsace appear to have latched onto the idea that the Jewish oath represented a guarantee of religious freedom. By the 1820s, Jews even in comparatively tolerant southern France were being asked to swear it. For jurists in the period, the oath might have appeared to be a way to navigate the challenges of the Restoration's constitution, which had a somewhat paradoxical relationship to religion. On the one hand, Catholicism was declared to be the official state religion, as it had been under the Old Regime. At the same time, the Charter of 1814 guaranteed both freedom of conscience and equality of all citizens before the law. The oath provided jurists with a means to navigate this contradiction. On the one hand, judges could maintain their position that the oath was a religious rather than a secular or purely civil act, which appealed to their desire to reinstate Catholicism as the state religion. At the same time, prescribing a special form of the oath for Jews assured them that even in the Catholic courtroom, Jews' religious beliefs would not be violated.

Rabbis on both sides of the Rhine waged a campaign against the oath when it spread under the Restoration, and many of them refused to administer it when called to do so. For them, the question hinged on whether these new courts were truly open to all equally, or whether they were still Catholic courts that tolerated Jews, but only as foreigners who needed to swear according to their own formulae. The Paris-based national Jewish leadership was mobilized as well. In addition to numerous rabbis from Alsace, Lorraine, and the Rhineland, the French Chief Rabbi David Sinzheim and even the renowned Rabbi Ezekiel Landau from Prague wrote letters objecting to the oath. The cornerstone of these rabbis' arguments was the claim that Jews were religiously bound to tell the truth by swearing the ordinary oath on a printed Bible in the courtroom, as the Napoleonic Decree of October 1808 had specified. Nevertheless, in the reactionary climate of the 1820s on both sides of the Rhine, judges continued to require it, and with the approval of the Minister of Justice. Indeed, at this time, in spite of the numerous protests by rabbis and lay leaders, Jewish litigants and witnesses were required to swear it in new areas as well, including Bordeaux, Marseilles, and the former Papal States.[19]

In the debates over the Jewish oath in Napoleonic and Restoration France, two models of religious liberty collided. One would render Jews' testimony credible by using overtly religious formulations publicly; the other saw the imposition of those formulations as a violation of individual rights. For French Jews in this period, taking the Jewish oath was not a right to express their beliefs but rather a legal disability imposed on them, a humiliating and intimidating reminder that as Jews, their testimony was suspect.

Crémieux himself had been educated in the secular institutions established by Napoleon known, particularly in that era, for their liberal leanings. From the time of his youth, he had been an outspoken advocate of the Revolutionary tradition.[20] In his eyes, the spread of the Jewish oath beyond Eastern France in the 1820s was a worrisome sign of the growing conservatism of the regime. This was precisely the moment when political conservatives gained the upper hand in the Chamber of Deputies, and together with King Charles X, they openly challenged the Revolutionary commitment to religious equality and freedom. In this context, Crémieux's Nîmes Jewish oath cases provided an opportunity. Although he was certainly aware that the oath's widespread use was in fact a phenomenon of the nineteenth century, he depicted the *more judaïco* as a throwback to the legal disabilities of the Old Regime to connect his cause to the larger liberal struggle against Restoration reactionaries. A close examination of Crémieux's rhetoric in the Nîmes case shows how central building alliances with liberals was to his strategy in those cases. When he argued that the lower court had violated his clients' religious freedom with an "*inquisition* into the religion of each citizen," he associated the *more judaïco* with the Catholic Inquisition.[21] This was a clever tactic in the context of Nîmes, where the White Terror of 1815 (in which Catholics sought revenge for their suffering under the Revolutionary Terror against local Protestants) had been particularly brutal. By 1827, the Nîmes court was dominated by liberals. Crémieux's words resonated particularly well here, connecting the Jewish oath to the long history of Catholic violence against religious dissidents.

Crémieux won his cases in Nîmes. The Appeals Court held that the oath *more judaïco* was illegal because it compromised the equality of a certain class of citizens by placing them outside the law. Interestingly, on both sides, the lawyers and the judge all agreed that the oath was a religious rather than a civil act that brought an individual's religious conscience into the courtroom to guarantee truthful testimony. Yet for the court, a special Jewish oath was unnecessary "[because] the Jew, like any man except the Atheist, is religiously bound by the words, 'I swear;' since in speaking them, he takes God as a witness of the truth he affirms, and submits to all God's vengeance if he perjures himself."[22]

Crémieux's rhetoric in these cases resonated with liberals far beyond southern France, finding a receptive audience among lawyers at the Paris bar as well. The legal profession's most important nineteenth-century periodical, the *Gazette des Tribunaux*, celebrated Crémieux's victory, reporting that the pleadings had reached "the highest philosophical level," especially where he demonstrated that religious liberty was compromised when the state asked individual citizens what religion they professed. Crémieux's work especially impressed André Dupin (1783–1865), already one of the country's best-known lawyers, who would become a major political figure during and after the 1830 Revolution. Dupin came to Nîmes to support Crémieux in the second of the two cases in 1827. Soon after, he brought Crémieux to work with him in Paris on cases involving press censorship.[23] Once in the capital, Crémieux made other important connections. By 1830, he was able to take over the legal practice of Odilon Barrot, a liberal lawyer soon to enter politics, who had also been much impressed with his work in Nîmes.[24]

Even after establishing himself in Paris, Crémieux remained devoted to the cause of abolishing the Jewish oath. The context had changed somewhat; the liberals had come to power with the July Revolution of 1830, and Catholicism was proclaimed "the religion of the majority of Frenchmen" rather than the state religion. Helping to establish a new model of the relation between minority religions and the state seemed all the more important to the ambitious lawyer. In his 1839 case before the Saverne Appeals Court in Alsace, the facts were slightly different, involving a rabbi who refused to administer the oath rather than a plaintiff who refused to swear it. Nevertheless, Crémieux's arguments remained the same. He portrayed the oath as a violation of Jewish citizens' right to religious privacy rather than a protection of their religious freedom, as the oath's champions represented it. Two additional *more judaïco* cases would be argued in the 1840s: one before the Conseil d'Etat in 1844 and another before the Cour de Cassation in 1846. Though neither of these cases was argued by Crémieux, the arguments were again borrowed from the 1827 cases in Nîmes, and as in Nîmes, the oath was deemed contrary to the spirit of the French Constitution.

These cases from the 1830s and 1840s represented a victory for the Jewish lay leaders and rabbis who had long been campaigning against the oath. Though it would take decades before the oath fell from use completely, the cases paved the way for Jews to participate more fully in the French public sphere by making the courtroom a space where they felt equal, trustworthy simply as citizens. Through these legal cases, Jewish leaders and particularly Crémieux became agents in shaping how liberals conceived the neutral public sphere into which Jews were integrating.

But Crémieux's own agenda went beyond the Jews. He also sought to help shape a new model of public religious life for France. In these Jewish oath cases, Crémieux was one of the first to formulate the model of *laïcité* that republicans would later adopt, in which an individual's religious belief is deemed part of his private identity, inappropriate for public expression. And yet, for Crémieux as for later republicans, this did not mean that public space was entirely desacralized. Courts held that public space was a sacred space when it held that generic oaths were religious acts. This too foreshadows articulations of secularism by republicans later in the century. As historians Claude Nicolet, Mona Ozouf, and Pierre Rosanvallon have argued in their studies of republican ideology and practice, nineteenth-century republicans never depicted the public space as entirely free from all holiness. Rather, they sought to create a civic form of religiosity, complete with its own ministers, edifices, beliefs, symbols, and rituals, that would function as an alternative to Catholicism, and saw this new religiosity as superior because it applied to all people, not just to Catholics.[25]

As Crémieux began to make his way onto the national stage, his Jewishness became important in a new way. In fact, given his belief that an individual's religious faith was irrelevant in the public sphere, it is surprising how frequently he referred to his own Jewishness in the courtroom. An early example is instructive. In the 1827 Jewish oath case in Nîmes, where he had argued that an individual's religious belief is irrelevant to his credibility in court, he proclaimed:

> I am not arguing here for a trifle: my client's cause is that of all Jews; it is my cause. Yes, it's a Jew before you, fighting for his home and hearth, for his faith, for the most precious of all his freedoms. Why then am I without fear? Why then am I so full of hope? It's because I am arguing for what's right, and because you are my Judges![26]

Crémieux was building his career by portraying the French state as the liberator of the Jews. For this reason, the highly assimilated lawyer—one of the first French Jews to be educated in the prestigious Parisian Lycée Imperial and the secular French university in Aix-en-Provence—made his Jewishness an emblem of his *political* faith. Even as he argued that religious belief was irrelevant in the public sphere, his persona in the courtroom depended on brandishing his Jewishness as proof of his trustworthy support for the liberal cause.

For the rest of his career, Crémieux embodied a paradox when it came to being Jewish. On the one hand, his political position was that religion had no place in public, and yet on the other, the great orator touted his Jewishness as an emblem of his political commitments. Indeed, his initial election to the French Chamber of Deputies in 1842 was made possible by the publicity he received in the Damascus Affair, during which he had become well known beyond the legal profession as a Jewish defender of Jewish rights in the name of the universal liberal values of the French Revolution.

The Damascus Affair had begun in February 1840, when the Jews of Damascus were accused of colluding in the ritual murder of a European friar. In the investigation, Muslim and European Christian officials in Damascus, including the French consul, used torture to extract "confessions" from leading members of the Jewish community, and many died from their injuries. The French consul also sent stories about the events to the European press, inciting anti-Jewish prejudice back home. In response, Adolphe Crémieux, then vice president of the Central Consistory (the principal religious organization of French Jews), joined Sir Moses Montefiore of England on a trip to Egypt to advocate for the Damascus Jews before Mohammed Ali. Their work was successful: the accused were pardoned, and the two European Jews sent news reports home that defended the Jews, and just as importantly, Judaism, in the European press. Crémieux won over French liberal readers by portraying France as the defender of civilization, which for him necessarily included religious tolerance and equality. On his return to Paris, the lawyer and Jewish communal leader was greeted as a hero by the liberal press and the Jewish leadership alike.[27]

Liberals saw the case in terms larger than the defense of Jews: it was also a victory in their struggle to limit the influence of the Catholic Church in public affairs. In the Chamber of Deputies, liberals such as the antislavery activist François-André Isambert and the Jewish deputy Benoît Fould had criticized the French consul for his actions and his obvious prejudice. Crémieux looked at the case through a broader lens, using it to redefine French foreign policy as a secular mission to propagate French universalism rather than a Catholic one that merely propagated Catholicism. Crémieux linked his defense of the accused Jews of Damascus to the global propagation of the ideals of the French constitution, especially equality, religious tolerance, and abolition of torture in legal proceedings. For him, the French Revolution was incomplete until France made a change to its foreign policy. The Damascus Affair was an opportunity to define this new agenda by championing abroad, as at home, the ideals of freedom of conscience and the equality of Jews and Christians as individuals before the law. In his view, what had gone wrong in Damascus was that the Jews had been prosecuted simply for being Jewish. A civilized nation would make religion legally irrelevant. As Crémieux's colleagues on the Central Consistory put it:

> The Israelites of all countries, whose ancient and holy beliefs seem incriminated, are protesting with energy. Generous men outside of their faith have shared their indignation. In the English Parliament, in the French Chambers, voices have been raised in favor of the accused . . . a distinguished lawyer of the Paris bar, a member of our Consistory, and an Israelite, former Magistrate of the city of London, have just left to help the accused with counsel and devotion.
>
> France, the first country to abolish torture in criminal trials, does not want to perpetuate its use in the countries where it favors the progress of civilization. We do not ask any favors for the accused, in spite of what they have been through; we demand only an enlightened and regular justice, which does not use violence. If they are guilty, may they be left to the rigor of the country's law, if they are not, may their innocence be proclaimed. . . . Say a word, one single word, and the truth will be revealed, and we will thank you in the name of humanity, civilization and religion.[28]

And yet, as this quotation reveals, even as Crémieux sought to make Jewishness irrelevant to the law, he was simultaneously constructing a Jewish persona for himself. As in the *more judaïco* cases, this champion of secularism was portrayed as a Jew who had defended Judaism in the name of the civilized world.[29] In this sense, Crémieux's rhetorical strategy made religion quite relevant politically. And in this effort, he was not alone; some of his non-Jewish supporters on the left went much farther in depicting Crémieux as a sort of Jewish crusader for liberalism. One anonymous author explicitly wrote about Crémieux's trip to the East as a sacred mission for liberal legal principles in a poem published in the legal newspaper, the *Observateur des Tribunaux*:

> Crémieux, your mission is holy;
> It is worthy of you.
> Neither gold nor fear
> Has ever frightened or tempted you away from your faith.
>
> You don't sequester your faith away in the narrow sphere
> Of sects divided, nor of Hebrews rites;
> Your faith lives in these words, "All men are brothers;
> Let them be equal with one another!"
>
> Yes, since Judea, dispersed in the world,
> Is once again banned from this equality,

Run to Damascus; there, let your voice plant
Seeds, the fate of legality!

Go, unveil the error, and confound the imposture
Put the flame back in the hands of the innocent
Go tell Mohammed that torture
Puts the judge behind the executioner.[30]

Identifying Mohammed Ali of Egypt with the Prophet Mohammed, calling him an "impostor," and painting Crémieux's trip as a mission against "error" appealed directly to these liberal readers' ideas of a holy crusade. Yet though the mission Crémieux was undertaking was depicted as religious, it was certainly not identified as Christian; rather, it was a crusade of universally applicable legal principles.

Importantly, Crémieux is unmistakably Jewish in this poem. By using the term "banned" (*mise . . . au ban*), the author even alludes to the oppression Jews suffered under the Catholic Inquisition in much the way Crémieux himself had in his *more judaïco* cases in Nîmes. Crémieux's Jewishness was what made him trustworthy to republicans in the 1840s. As a Jew, he represented a voice of pure morality that speaks out against intolerance, greed, and oppression. As such, it served as a vehicle for this anonymous author to glorify French legal principles as a sacred crusade of Revolutionary principles by using terms that resembled and replaced the Catholic conception of France's mission.

Jewish leaders' willingness to take political stands publicly when it came to foreign policy was transformed by the Damascus Affair, and particularly by the support Crémieux had received from liberals for his mission to Egypt. In the midst of the events of 1840, the Jewish deputy, Benoît Fould, had initially hesitated to speak in the Chamber at the risk of seeming to represent particular "Jewish" interests. In stark contrast, once Crémieux himself was elected to the Chamber in 1842, he made frequent allusions to this event and to his Jewishness, even when it was not necessarily relevant.[31]

Reminding his fellow deputies of his Jewishness and his connection to the Damascus Affair provided Crémieux with a means to stress his political credibility before others similarly committed to the Revolutionary tradition of liberalism, and to anticlericalism in particular. One telling moment in this regard came on February 5, 1846, when members of the Chamber of Deputies were drafting a document supporting Polish nationhood. When Henri Monier de la Sizeranne proposed the wording "In the name of the rights of nations, in the name of Christian civilization and humanity," Crémieux objected, demanding that the document read simply *"civilisation tout court* (just civilization)." Murmurs broke out in the Chamber; one voice exclaimed, "It's an allusion to the persecution of the

Syrian Jews!" Monier de la Sizeranne responded with a clarification: "Since M. Crémieux . . . asks me why I insist on the words Christian civilization . . . I mean any civilization that takes the basic precepts of Christianity as its foundation and line of conduct, that is, which proclaims tolerance and freedom." Crémieux, long a supporter of the Polish nationalists, was not objecting to supporting their movement; rather, he was taking the opportunity to promote secularism, as conceived within the French Revolutionary tradition, in foreign policy.[32] Monier de la Sizeranne himself certainly understood this, gauging from his response. Crémieux's outburst pleased the increasingly acculturated Jewish reading public. Reporting on the matter in the French Jewish newspaper *L'Univers Israélite*, editor Simon Bloch commented, "The chamber did not adopt M. de la Sizeranne's version; the members probably thought that tolerance and freedom in France date back to our revolutions and not at all to the birth of the Gospel. Before '93, were our *rois très-Chrétiens* (good Christian kings) particularly tolerant toward Jews and Hugenots?"[33]

As in the Jewish oath cases, Jewish leaders' strategy with regard to French foreign policy was built on a paradox. On the one hand, they were calling for the French state to make religion irrelevant to foreign policy and simply pursue justice. In Damascus, this meant pursuing a "civilizing mission" that would defend a community wrongly accused because of prejudice, rather than a Catholic mission that would champion the rights of Christians. But on the other hand, Crémieux made publicizing and declaring his own Jewishness central when he articulated this agenda. Far from a fully neutral sphere in which religion was completely irrelevant, the public sphere as defined by the emerging French republican left was one in which Jewishness did appear as a voice of universal morality and modernity, identified as the fulfillment of the Revolutionary promise.

The Damascus Affair was a real turning point for Crémieux, and the publicity he received from his trip to Egypt made his political career possible. As such, it was also an important moment in the building of a coalition between members of the acculturated French Jewish elite and the political center left. When Crémieux was elected to the Chamber of Deputies in 1842, he sat with the members of the dynastic left such as Barrot, and in time, became a central figure in the republican movement as it was built in the 1840s. After taking part in the revolution of 1848, he was appointed Minister of Justice in the Second Republic, a post he would occupy again in the earliest phase of the Third Republic.

As republicanism coalesced as a political movement, it adopted the model of secularism that Crémieux and other Jewish leaders had articulated in the cases against the Jewish oath earlier in the century. By the 1840s, republican professors Jules Simon and Amédée Jacques built a campaign for secularism in education that championed religious privacy, arguing that the classroom was a public space that should be free from the teachings, confessions, practices, and iconography of particular religions. And like Crémieux's opponents in Nîmes, Simon and Jacques faced an opposition that sought to maintain a role for the Church in education by arguing for "freedom of education" as a form of religious liberty.

Crémieux's long life gave him much opportunity to work with allies like Simon and Jacques in creating this specifically French model of *laïcité*, in which religions are banned from the public sphere. This was not meant to impinge on an individual's religious belief. Indeed, as Minister of Justice in the Second Republic, it was Crémieux who penned the decree of March 10, 1848, guaranteeing freedom of worship. Rather, the goal was to remove religious expressions from public spaces. It is interesting to note that Léon Gambetta, another lawyer from the South remembered as an architect of the highly controversial Third Republican form of anticlericalism that overhauled primary school curricula, got his start in Paris working in Adolphe Crémieux's law office, and the two remained close for the rest of Crémieux's life.[34]

While none of this evidence should be read to suggest that Crémieux invented the French republican model of secularism, it is clear that he was among the first to articulate it and that he was involved, together with allies, in its broader development in nineteenth-century France. The coalition was important far beyond this one man. As other Jews made their way into politics, many also found themselves depicted as emblems of republicanism for similar reasons. In fact, the association between Jews and anticlericalism grew so strong that Crémieux's protégé, Gambetta, was regularly (and falsely) identified by antisemites as Jewish. By the 1880s, the association between Jews and a form of *laïcité* that sought to ban religion from public influence was firmly fixed. And yet paradoxically, Crémieux's own Jewishness was far from irrelevant to his career and the history of this alliance more broadly. In the eyes of liberals and republicans, what made this lawyer and politician trustworthy politically was the very fact of his Jewishness.

Notes

1. Joan Scott, *The Politics of the Veil* (Princeton, NJ: Princeton University Press, 2007), 15.
2. Pierre Birnbaum, *The Jews of the Republic: A Political History of State Jews from Gambetta to Vichy*, trans. Jane Marie Todd (Stanford: Stanford University Press, 1996).
3. Ari Joskowicz, *The Modernity of Others: Jewish Anti-Catholicism in Germany and France* (Stanford: Stanford University Press, 2014).
4. Philip Nord, *The Republican Moment: Struggles for Democracy in Nineteenth-Century France* (Cambridge, MA: Harvard University Press, 1995), 64–89.
5. Adolphe Crémieux, *Second plaidoyer sur cette question: Le Juif français doit-il être soumis à prêter le serment more judaïco?* (Nîmes: Gaude, 1827), 4–5.

6. For another discussion of this material on the Jewish oath, see Lisa Moses Leff, "The Jewish Oath and the Making of Secularism in Modern France," *Leo Baeck Institute Yearbook* 58, no. 1 (2013): 23–34.

7. Adolphe Crémieux, *Plaidoyer sur cette question: Le Juif français doit-il être soumis à prêter le serment more judaïco* (Nîmes: Gaude, 1827), *Plaidoyer*, 3, 6, 18–19.

8. Crémieux, *Second plaidoyer*, 23–27; Crémieux, *Plaidoyer*, 3.

9. As discussed in Crémieux, *Plaidoyer*.

10. Phyllis Cohen Albert, *The Jewish Oath in Nineteenth-Century France*, Spiegel Lectures in Modern Jewish History (Tel Aviv: Tel Aviv University Press, 1982), 31–32. Few other studies of the oath exist; those that do, such as the work of historian Guido Kisch, focus on the medieval period rather than the modern. The best overview is the article "The Jewish Oath," in the *Jewish Encyclopedia* of 1906, written by Gotthard Deutsch.

11. Albert, *Jewish Oath*, 32.

12. In a memorandum directing courts to drop this custom, the Minister of Justice depicted the oath *more judaïco* as contrary to the principles of equality and religious freedom. He explained: "The law does not distinguish between Jew and Christian, Protestant and Catholic, Conformist and Dissident." Letter from the Minister of Justice Marguerite-Louis François du Port-Dutertre to all Royal Tribunals and Commissariats, January 10, 1792, as cited in David Feuerwerker, *L'Emancipation des juifs en France, de l'Ancien Régime à la fin du Second Empire* (Paris: Albin Michel, 1976), 565–67.

13. Feuerwerker, *L'Emancipation*, 587.

14. Letter from the Upper Rhine Consistory to the Central Consistory of August 9, 1809, as cited in Feuerwerker, *L'Emancipation*, 575.

15. The defendant in the case was Emmanuel Dreyfus of Mulhouse, the court the Appeals Court in Colmar. As cited in Feuerwerker, *L'Emancipation*, 578–79.

16. Albert reasons that many of these lawsuits were likely initiated by Jewish creditors who needed to appear in court frequently to collect on the small sums they were owed and thus likely resented the campaign initiated by the communal leadership, which must have cost them dearly. See Albert, *Jewish Oath*, 9.

17. In this case, judges also relied on Old Regime legal precedent, referring to the *lettres patentes* of 1784, even though they were technically irrelevant to the case. From the *Journal de jurisprudence civile, commerciale et notariale et de la cour d'Appel séant à Colmar* 4, no. 8 (February 1809), art. 64e, as cited in Feuerwerker, *L'Emancipation*, 578.

18. Feuerwerker, *L'Emancipation*, 572.

19. On the spread of cases in Eastern France and Germany, see Feuerwerker, *L'Emancipation*, 576–87; on the cases in Southern France, see Albert, *Jewish Oath*, 9.

20. Two good biographies of Crémieux give good information on all periods of his life, including his school days. See Solomon Posener, *Adolphe Crémieux, 1796–1880*, 2 vols. (Paris: Félix Alcan, 1934); and Daniel Amson, *Adolphe Crémieux: l'oublié de la gloire* (Paris: Seuil, 1988).

21. Crémieux, *Second plaidoyer*, 23–27; Crémieux, *Plaidoyer*, 3.

22. Crémieux, *Second plaidoyer*, 32.

23. Crémieux, *Second plaidoyer*, 51–52, 61–62, 83.

24. Solomon Posener, *Adolphe Cremieux*, trans. Eugene Golob (Philadelphia: Jewish Publication Society, 1940), 52.

25. Claude Nicolet, *L'Idée républicaine: essai d'histoire critique* (Paris: Gallimard, 1982); Mona Ozouf, *Festivals and the French Revolution*, trans. Alan Sheridan (Cambridge,

MA: Harvard University Press, 1988); and Pierre Rosanvallon, *Le Sacre du citoyen* (Paris: Gallimard, 2001).

26. Crémieux, *Plaidoyer*, 31.

27. See *Le Temps*, the *Quotidienne*, the *Journal des Débats*, and the *Siècle*, throughout the spring and summer of 1840.

28. Central Consistory to the Minister of Foreign Affairs, July 20, 1840, in Central Archives for the History of the Jewish People (Jerusalem), HM 1058.

29. Jonathan Frankel, *The Damascus Affair: "Ritual Murder," Politics and the Jews in 1840* (New York: Cambridge University Press, 1997). See also Lisa Moses Leff, *Sacred Bonds of Solidarity: The Rise of Jewish Internationalism in Nineteenth-Century France* (Stanford: Stanford University Press, 2006), 120–6.

30. As excerpted in Eugène Roch, "Persécutions contre les Juifs de Damas, à la suite de la disparition du R. P. Thomas, religieux de l'ordre des Capucins, et de son domestique: recueil des documents," *L'observateur des Tribunaux: Journal des documents judiciaires* 1, nouvelle série de 1840 (1840): 92.

31. On Fould's hesitancy, see Roch, "Persécutions contre les Juifs de Damas," 83.

32. Crémieux was one of the founders of the Comité Polonais in 1831, along with other distinguished liberals such as Béranger, Odilon Barrot, Armand Carrel, Dupont de l'Eure, Victor Hugo, and Lafayette. See Posener, *Crémieux* (French), vol. 1, 117.

33. For an account of the entire incident with Bloch's commentary, see "Nouvelles divers," *UI* 3 (1845–46): 22.

34. Posener, *Cremieux* (English), 152, 206–07.

Bibliography

Albert, Phyllis Cohen. *The Jewish Oath in Nineteenth-Century France*. Spiegel Lectures in Modern Jewish History. Tel Aviv: Tel Aviv University Press, 1982.

Amson, Daniel. *Adolphe Crémieux: l'oublié de la gloire*. Paris: Seuil, 1988.

Birnbaum, Pierre. *The Jews of the Republic: A Political History of State Jews from Gambetta to Vichy*. Translated by Jane Marie Todd. Stanford: Stanford University Press, 1996.

Bloch, Simon. "Nouvelles divers." *L'Univers Israélite* 3 (1845–46): 22.

Central Consistory to the Minister of Foreign Affairs, July 20, 1840, in CAHJP HM 1058.

Crémieux, Adolphe. *Plaidoyer sur cette question: Le Juif français doit-il être soumis à prêter le serment more judaïco?* Nîmes: Gaude, 1827.

———. *Second plaidoyer sur cette question: Le Juif français doit-il être soumis à prêter le serment more judaïco?* Nîmes: Gaude, 1827.

Deutsch, Gotthard. "The Jewish Oath." In the *Jewish Encyclopedia*. New York: Funk and Wagnalls, 1906. http://jewishencyclopedia.com/articles/11640-oath-more-judaico, accessed online July 28, 2017.

Feuerwerker, David. *L'Emancipation des juifs en France, de l'Ancien Régime à la fin du Second Empire*. Paris: Albin Michel, 1976.

Frankel, Jonathan. *The Damascus Affair: "Ritual Murder," Politics and the Jews in 1840*. New York: Cambridge University Press, 1997.

Joskowicz, Ari. *The Modernity of Others: Jewish Anti-Catholicism in Germany and France*. Stanford: Stanford University Press, 2014.

Leff, Lisa Moses. "The Jewish Oath and the Making of Secularism in Modern France." *Leo Baeck Institute Yearbook* 58, no. 1 (2013): 23–34.

———. *Sacred Bonds of Solidarity: The Rise of Jewish Internationalism in Nineteenth-Century France*. Stanford: Stanford University Press, 2006.

Nicolet, Claude. *L'Idée républicaine: essai d'histoire critique*. Paris: Gallimard, 1982.

Nord, Philip. *The Republican Moment: Struggles for Democracy in Nineteenth-Century France*. Cambridge, MA: Harvard University Press, 1995.

Ozouf, Mona. *Festivals and the French Revolution*. Translated by Alan Sheridan. Cambridge, MA: Harvard University Press, 1988.

Posener, Solomon. *Adolphe Cremieux*. Translated by Eugene Golob. Philadelphia: Jewish Publication Society, 1940.

———. *Adolphe Crémieux, 1796–1880*. 2 vols. Paris: Félix Alcan, 1988.

Roch, Eugène. "Persécutions contre les Juifs de Damas, à la suite de la disparition du R. P. Thomas, religieux de l'ordre des Capucins, et de son domestique: recueil des documents." *L'observateur des Tribunaux: Journal des documents judiciaires* 1, nouvelle série de 1840 (1840): 92.

Rosanvallon, Pierre. *Le Sacre du citoyen*. Paris: Gallimard, 2001.

Scott, Joan. *The Politics of the Veil*. Princeton, NJ: Princeton University Press, 2007.

LISA LEFF is Professor of History at American University and Director of the Jack, Joseph and Morton Mandel Center for Advanced Holocaust Studies at the United States Holocaust Memorial Museum. Her research focuses on the Jews of modern France. Her book, *The Archive Thief*, won the Sami Rohr Prize for Jewish Literature from the Jewish Book Council and was a finalist for a National Jewish Book Award.

Section Two
The Business of Trust

6 "A Kind of Republic and Neutral Nation"

Commerce, Credit, and Conspiracy in Early Modern Europe

Joshua Teplitsky

T<small>RUST—AN ABSTRACT</small> concept—can come in many historical guises. Its conjoined twin, mistrust, can come in even more. Never entirely separable, the two are also not quite polar opposites, and the presence of one often reveals the existence of the other. In this essay, I would like to contribute to the discussion of trust in Jewish history in two parts. First, I will offer a broad consideration of the interplay between trust, distrust, and neutrality from the vantage point of the economic and political history of central European Jewry from the end of the Thirty Years' War in 1648 until the declaration of policies directed toward Jewish political and civil integration in the late eighteenth century, especially as that history was shaped by the Court Jews. I will explore the insights of modern theorists as well as contemporaries of the Court Jews who suggested that that Jews, as a diasporic people, were suitable bearers of trust but were simultaneously, for the same reasons, objects of mistrust. In the second part of the essay, I will examine a single literary specimen—a family megillah that tells the tale of deliverance from bogus accusations—to explore the mentalities of at least some Jews as highly conscious of the precariousness of neutrality as an element of trust. The two halves of the essay are united not just temporally but also in their shared themes of mobility and interconnectedness as elements that are both constituted by trust and generative of it, but can also be exploited for untrustworthy ends.

The Court Jew: Two Forms of Trust

Between 1650 and 1750, Jewish life in central Europe was shaped by the emergence of a new class of Jew: the Court Jew. By the close of the Thirty Years' War, debt and fighting had ravaged the traditional alliances between state activity and private capital. Yet the period following the desolation and expenditures of war saw a new constitutional stability for the territories of the Holy Roman Empire with the Peace of Westphalia in 1648, the end of a confessional conflict that had begun over a century earlier with the Reformation. This stability was, somewhat paradoxically, predicated on competition between various princes and electors, who had each achieved confessional unity within their domains. These territorial rulers promoted their stature through displays of material wealth and investment in standing armies, both of which were built by the state in partnership with private financiers, military suppliers, purveyors, and recruiters of mercenary fighters. This state-private partnership, rather than subordinating military activity to direct state control, enabled governments to extend their campaigns beyond their natural limits. The growth of military might and the centrality of military power to a state's prestige on the international stage brought with it an enhanced place for those private partners.[1]

Court Jews (*Hofjuden*) were a crucial ingredient in this historical development.[2] Hardly a single ascendant territory could be found without a Court Jew to privately finance the developments of states that—in an age before citizenship—had not yet developed the massive bureaucratic mechanisms to effectively tax their inhabitants. They operated as commissaries, provisioners of war materiel, and financiers. Court Jews furnished regimes with armaments, uniforms, and food, and supported refurbishment of fortresses. In the domestic affairs of the court, they provided furniture and linens, ornaments and jewels, and fine wines and spices. The Court Jew assumed the finances of the state, represented the state's debts to creditors, and extended his own credit to the state, which, in the Habsburg case, was always on shaky ground. As summed up pithily by Hannah Arendt: "behind the credit of every prince stood the credit of his *Hofjude*."[3]

The relationship between mercantile credit and personal reputation has a long history in early modern Europe. The extension of credit is fundamentally an expression of trust. Put simply by Bruce H. Mann, "people must conduct business on promises."[4] Before the emergence of impersonal credit scores and money markets, those promises were predicated on a reputation for trustworthiness. Credit mingles the material with the immaterial, monetary value with quality of reputation. In an emerging system of markets and commerce, personal relationships replace intimate knowledge of circumstances—trust can be a stand-in for personal expertise or intervention.[5]

A second form of trust contributed to the position of the Court Jew. The Court Jew's success was built not only on the reliance of sovereigns but on the trust of intraethnic and intrafamilial ties between Jews across distances. Familial interdependence and the bonds of trust it produced were an essential and salient feature of the mercantile conduct of Court Jews, as in other successful early modern enterprises.[6] Samuel Oppenheimer, the Court Jew to Emperor Leopold I, was linked to the major commercial centers of Europe through his sons-in-law and grandsons in Frankfurt am Main, to his brother in Heidelberg, to the Court

Jew Leffman Behrens in Hanover through marriage, and to the branches of the Gumperts family, which extended his reach into Italy, Amsterdam, and Cleves. A handful of families repeatedly occupied these prominent posts, maintaining them though a near-monopoly on the major contracts and commodities of the period. Glikl of Hameln, the Jewish female memoirist, was a relative of Leffman Behrens of Hanover through her husband's sister, and no fewer than three of her children were themselves married to Court Jews: her daughter Zipporah to Elias Gomperz of Cleves, Court Jew in Brandenburg; her son Zanvil to a niece of Samson Wertheimer (himself the successor to Samuel Oppenheim as Court Jew in Vienna); and her son Moses to the daughter of the Court factor (a similar term to Court Jew) in Bayreuth.[7]

Multinational ties allowed the Court Jews to marshal resources and transmit information efficiently and rapidly. Relatives in Frankfurt, Hanover, Heidelberg, Cleves, and Amsterdam circulated goods and information to each other across the German lands.[8] To fund the campaigns of Emperor Leopold, for example, Samuel Oppenheimer assembled munitions from Holland, wool from Bohemia, and spices from Hamburg, and arranged for the mass transport of arms and soldiers.[9] The Court Jews stood atop a pyramid of subcontractors and suppliers. Contemporary observers saw Jews as the quintessential networkers across borders; Anne-Robert-Jacques Turgot, the French physiocrat and advisor to Louis XIV, called them "a kind of republic and neutral nation for commerce among different states."[10]

Family ties made the actions of the Court Jew possible, but they did not guarantee his security, nor did they mean that all Jews involved in commercial relations with the state cooperated with and trusted one another. The world of the Court Jews was made up of divided and competing factions, each with their own patrons and clients, each jostling and elbowing to oust the others. The most prominent Court Jews carefully subcontracted work in a way that would ensure their individual superiority and the subordination of competitors.[11] The struggles between these leading Jewish families often contributed to the rise of new entrepreneurs and the fall of individual agents. Kinship did offer one basis for solidifying trust, but as common sense and historical knowledge demonstrate, even that could be easily unglued.[12]

The observation about a "neutral nation for commerce among different states" implies two forms of trust at work: the commerce across borders, which was achieved through family ties, and the willingness of states to rely on this network on account of its neutrality.[13] Perceived neutrality was of crucial importance. Jews were not the only people who operated in the context of wider networks; even noble families, with whom we tend to identify a deeply rooted sense of place, encompassed wide and stratified groups that preserved group interests. The additional component in the Jewish case, however, was structural.

In her 1946 article "Privileged Jews," and then in greater detail in the *Origins of Totalitarianism*, Hannah Arendt argued that the reasons for Court Jewish predominance were better sought in the economic circumstances of the age, which were closely tied to the structure of politics and society. She writes: "The decisive factor was that they were completely isolated from the population and had to give no consideration to any of the important classes in the country. It was their social independence that gave them the feeling of an independent political factor."[14] In other words, their trustworthiness was derived from their status as outsiders.[15]

This can be contrasted with the way we normally think of trust. Avner Offer has argued that "regard provides a powerful incentive for trust," meaning that reputation and personal investment are the hallmarks of good credit.[16] But Arendt draws our attention to the way that trust can sometimes be predicated not on familiarity but rather on strangeness, by focusing on the role of the Jew in the consolidation of the absolutist state, a state that was locked in a struggle with the historic privileges of the estates. Both to finance its costly campaigns against France to the west and the Ottomans to the east, and to assert its independent political might vis-à-vis the estates and cities within its domains, the Habsburg monarchy required financial support outside of the levers of power controlled by the nobility and members of the traditional estates. In the sixteenth century, the Habsburgs drew on loans from the Welsers and the Fuggers of Augsburg. The collapse of those houses, in part because of the extreme expenses of the Thirty Years' War, left a vacuum that Jews were prepared to fill. The Court Jew was thus a part of the gradual but steady aggrandizement of power by territorial rulers as they circumvented conventional political arrangements between ruler and nobility by taking recourse to new forms of commerce, a waystation on the path to consolidation of state centralization under absolutism. Jewish existence outside of the traditional modes of politics and economics made them the ideal—although not the sole—vehicles for achieving this end.[17]

Trust and Distrust in a Family Megillah from Prague

Early modern Jews understood the precariousness of neutrality, and some were prepared to turn fear into opportunity when politically expedient. Such opportunism occupies the core of a narrative of the imprisonment of Samuel Taussig (d. 1724), one of the wealthiest and most powerful Jews in Prague in the early eighteenth century. In 1703, just as Taussig was ascending to the leadership of this largest of Europe's urban communities, he was denounced, arrested, imprisoned, and—after the intervention of supporters—released when the charges against him were dropped. His dramatic arrest and miraculous deliverance were memorialized in a megillah, a commemorative scroll that preserved the memory of the affair so that it could be annually recounted and celebrated by his descendants as a day of deliverance in a form of personal Purim celebration.[18]

The genre of family megillah was a specialty of the Jewish denizens of Prague, a regular favorite for commemorating escapes from trauma, usually unjust arrest. In analyzing the family megillah as a genre, Rachel Greenblatt has shown that it possessed a number of significant features, among them the somewhat surprising fact that in contrast to the expected non-Jewish antagonist who wishes to persecute or annihilate the Jews—like Haman of the biblical tale—the enemy in these tales more often emerges from within the ranks of Jews themselves. According to Greenblatt, the family megillah was used as a device to perpetuate the memory of these conflicts with other Jews and to craft a careful message about righteousness and enmity. As a narrative record of a protagonist exonerated from false charges, it was a medium through which to deflect further condemnation.[19]

For the purposes of this discussion, I am interested less in the megillah as a genre that communicated memory or as a source of social history.[20] Rather, I would like to use it as an artifact of mentalités by focusing on the record of this denunciation to examine the fictive means by which its protagonists crafted a case that played on the anxieties that inhered in a Jewish politics that relied on transnationalism, and showed how reputations thereof could go awry, as a means of examining the implicit political precariousness of this system in the minds of contemporary Jews.[21] In the case of Taussig's arrest, bonds of international solidarity were transmuted from a value to a liability and a cause for serious suspicion. And yet, even as the megillah recounts anxiety over Jewish connectedness and the charges of disloyalty it might attract, its author cannot imagine any remedy but the court, and the Jews who had access to it, as a font of absolute power and arbiter of law.

The megillah's narrative opens in 1701, two years prior to the main drama of Taussig's arrest, at the time of the election of Prague's new Jewish leadership. The first years of the eighteenth century were dynamic ones for the Jews of Prague. Between 1701 and 1703, a Jewish community of conflict and competition gave way to a new order. A chief rabbi named David Oppenheim (nephew to the Court Jew Samuel Oppenheimer) was appointed, who, unlike his predecessors, would hold his tenure for over thirty years, and a new system for collective taxation was instituted, alongside which the customary elections of Jewish governors—formerly held triennially—was abolished in favor of a permanent ruling oligarchy.[22] At the helm of this oligarchy stood Samuel Taussig. Taussig belonged to a venerable Prague family—his father had overseen the leadership of the community only a decade prior—and he was among the chief architects of the new tax arrangement. In leading the consortium of men who were responsible for farming the taxes of the Jewish inhabitants of the city, Taussig was appointed as the *primas* of the Jewish community—the head of its civil administration.[23]

Following the establishment of this new leadership consortium, a Jew from the city by the name of Aaron Ries undertook to contest this election. Ries had tasted sour grapes not long before, when Taussig, now effectively the perpetual mayor of Jewish Prague, had Ries removed from his role as preacher, replacing him nepotistically with Barukh Taussig, Samuel's own son. On hearing the election results, Ries traveled to Berlin—which the megillah describes as his "fatherland"—where he prevailed on Frederick, Elector of Prussia, to recommend to Emperor Leopold in Vienna that a sixth governor be added to the customary five officeholders of Prague's Jewish Town.[24]

The leaders of Prague's Jewry responded to this electoral challenge by operating through the traditional channels of Jewish diplomacy, much as Ries had done: they dispatched delegates to Ries's power base in Berlin and to the imperial offices in Vienna. Like Vienna, Berlin was both a major center of territorial strength in the Holy Roman Empire and the home of a very young Jewish community: Vienna's Jews had been expelled in 1670 and restored not long thereafter; Berlin's small Jewish population had only been established a year later, in 1671.[25] It was the presence of Court Jews of high standing that had permitted the settlement of other Jews, and it was to the Court Jews that Prague's leaders turned to combat Ries's campaign against them. The Prague Jews met with success in their traditional intercessionary appeals. In Berlin, the Court Jew Esther Schulhoff—herself a native of Prague—took up the cudgel of the Prague Jews and convinced the elector to withdraw his support for Ries.

Ries was rebuffed, but this episode perpetuated an insult and personal vendetta he would continue to wage. Disgraced and fearing retribution, Ries quit Prague for Vienna, where he encountered another Jew by the name of Solomon Weisskopf who had similarly found himself on the losing side of a contest with Samuel Taussig and the Prague elders. Meeting by chance in a Viennese inn (at least according to the megillah's colorful telling), the two spurned men made common cause to exact revenge on their nemesis and conspired to denounce Samuel Taussig to the imperial authorities.

The collusion of these two individuals took place against a wider context of international conflict between the Habsburgs and the French under Louis XIV. By the autumn of 1702, the continent-wide War of the Spanish Succession was well into its second year. The war began as a contest over the Spanish throne between the Habsburg and Bourbon dynasties, but drew ever more parties into the conflict. Tensions were high and finances were low, and alliances could shift rapidly, as when the Bavarian elector, heretofore a faithful ally of Habsburg causes, joined the French side in 1702.[26]

It was against this backdrop that Ries and Weisskopf hatched their plan. They took their inspiration from news of the recent arrest of a Jew named Solomon ben Naftali Herz Levi. Levi, from French-controlled Metz, had been apprehended in Habsburg-allied Venice on charges of corresponding with the French king.[27] Recognizing the suggestive power of Jewish correspondence networks, the men sought to turn this situation to their own ends by falsifying a series of letters between Jews in French domains and Taussig, with the former allegedly beseeching Taussig to use his access to the court to intercede on behalf of their imprisoned coreligionist. They composed three letters, falsely claiming their authors as Lotharingian and Alsatian Jews, routed through Basel and addressed to Weisskopf. They then bound the three letters together with a superscript instructing Weisskopf to relay the bundle to Samuel Taussig that he might save the imprisoned man, thereby implicating Prague's leader in fraternizing with Jews across enemy lines.[28]

Their energies to have these forged letters "discovered" involved some convoluted trails. The packet of letters was first conveyed by a young Christian messenger to Weiskopf's at an inn by the name of Goldin Tobin House in Vienna's Leopoldstadt, where, it was hoped, they might be intercepted along the way. The proprietors of the inn, however, opened the letters themselves, whereupon they angrily returned them to the young courier, wishing to have nothing to do with Jewish letters, and the young man, in turn, brought them back to Ries and Weisskopf. Undeterred, the conspirators decided to embroil still other Christians in the plot, and they directed the packet to Count Trautmannsdorf, ambassador to Switzerland, at his home, presumably in Vienna. The count opened the packet and then gave the letters over to Weisskopf, to whom they were addressed. Sensing that he had a captive audience, Weisskopf read the letters aloud to the ambassador, hoping the latter might relay that information to his superiors.

The conspirators evinced an acute awareness of the various power players of the imperial court. Weisskopf also sent the letters along to Leopold, Count Lamberg. Although Lamberg was not an official minister or member of the war council, he was the favorite of Joseph, the crown prince and heir apparent to the Habsburg throne. As favorite, Lamberg's responsibilities included management of the stable and supplying women for the crown prince's amusement, acts of confidence by his patron.[29] Weisskopf understood that power in the system of the court had as much to do with personality and proximity as with function or institution.

The trap was set and ready to be sprung: in October 1703, Taussig arrived in Vienna as part of a delegation on behalf of the Jews of Prague to perform his role as leader of the newly appointed oligarchs of the community. His retinue was met with favor, and the delegation was handed an edict confirming the privileges of the Jews of the city for residence and commerce, as well as permitting some much-needed construction in the Jewish town. Taussig's presence in the city gave the conspirators the chance to drop their net. Abraham Reis approached Vienna's guard commander, the Marquis Ferdinand Marchese degli Obizzi, in feigned surprise that a traitor like Taussig could roam about so freely, prompting the commander to arrest the primas and lock him away, without any pretense of habeas corpus.[30] While Taussig was being arrested in Vienna, Weisskopf had stolen off to Prague to sow rumors at home of the leader's perfidy.

Here, we must pause to reflect on the underlying assumptions of the fabricated claim. The plot was cleverly subversive on a number of levels. Its plausibility stemmed from both the history of efforts Jews had made on behalf of other Jews and the dense network of communication between Jews of disparate locations. Jewish communication during this period was impressive. By this time, virtually every inhabitant of the German lands could reach a post office within a half-day's walk, thanks to the services of the famous Turn und Taxis firm.[31] But Jews also used more informal webs of communication, often sending letters and news with travelers who were passing through one town on the way to the next or visitors returning to a point of origin. A messenger from one rabbi to another would often come bearing a question and expect to quickly depart with its answer, often waiting for the respondent to pen it, who similarly felt pressure to compose his reply so as not to delay the messenger.[32] In fact, the swift pace of communication—a medium whose uses they were now casting aspersions on— was the only way Ries and Weisskopf could know of the affairs of Metz Jews in Venice. Communication by post could be used both to solidify bonds of trust and to expose allegedly untrustworthy dealings.

Just as importantly, the conspiring pair was alert to the importance of solidarity between Jews of competing states. Ries's attempts to join the ruling oligarchs of Prague had been foiled by exactly these means only a year prior when Prague's Jews sought intercession with the Court Jews of Vienna and Prague to direct their political affairs. The longest letter of the three forged messages explicitly invoked the phrase "all of the children of Israel are responsible to one another," a sentiment of shared peoplehood and mutual welfare.[33] The letters were compelling because, even in their forgery, they conveyed the thick ties of Jewish contact across vast space, noting debts between Jews in Prague and Basel, the regards of family members from Strasbourg to Vienna, and contacts between the wife of Alsace's chief rabbi, her widowed sister in Vienna, and Samuel Taussig in Prague—all messages that could easily have been lifted from the regular course of genuine epistolary correspondence of the age.

Finally, in casting aspersions on the contacts of Jews across the lines of the battlefield, the conspirators' plot took for granted the notion that Jews ought to conform somehow to political boundaries; that there is something suspicious in the act of correspondence between Jews across borders. The letters contain no talk of state secrets, and yet Weisskopf and the megillah's narrator understood that acting on behalf of a Jew of another polity, even corresponding with him, was suspect.

The megillah built drama around the content of the fallacious charges, but the story's continuation reveals that Jewish diplomacy was limited in its imagination to the tried and tested activation of Jewish networks of intercession. The agent of Taussig's redemption was a woman named Esther—like the biblical heroine of the archetypical Jewish intercessionary tale—whose trade in silver brought her into regular contact with nobles.[34] Learning of the arrest, Esther prevailed on the Marquis degli Obizzi to allow her to visit Taussig in his cell, which he permitted, provided they converse only in German, not in *loshn-koydesh* ("the Holy Tongue," i.e., Hebrew), "so that the guard would be able to understand them," thereby adding a dimension of the secrecy of Jewish language to the intrigue of Jewish networking.[35] Taussig tasked Esther with discovering the charge on which he was being detained, which she quickly learned was his alleged correspondence with France.

Access to influential men and women continued: Esther and associates approached Count Kinsky, the supreme chancellor of the Bohemian Chancellery (a largely ceremonial position), whom the text describes as a "wise and understanding man who well knows that we Jews do very little good for each other"—a remark thick with intracommunal polemic.[36] Esther further approached three widowed countesses, beseeching them to intercede with the emperor to gain an audience and a fair hearing for Taussig. Some of the nobles agreed to compose a recommendation to the emperor, but others cautiously warned her off the case, lest she become enmeshed and incriminated as well. At Taussig's instruction, Esther also communicated the details of his arrest via courier to the Jewish leadership in Prague, who expressed their despair at the fate that had befallen not only Taussig but "all Jews in all of Israel's diaspora."[37]

The megillah's formulation of this expression is telling. It appears clear that in the imaginations of the authors, and perhaps for the Jews they describe, the strategy for parrying accusations of transnational disloyalty was not a redoubling of efforts to prove local commitment. On the contrary, the Jews of Prague activated the selfsame devices for which Taussig was currently under fire by reaching out to multilateral contacts to apply pressure at specific points. As François Guesnet has shown in the case of efforts by Jews to forestall an expulsion from Prague in 1744, Jewish efforts at political mobilization tell us as much in their failures as they do in their successes.[38] Prague's Jews employed their networks across space, maintaining their familiar political practice that depended on transnational contact and lobbying.

Since the affair revolved around a small conspiracy, the leaders of Prague's Jewish community confronted Weisskopf and extracted a confession from him that he had fabricated the charges as a personal vendetta, arrogantly boasting that he had everyone in the palm of his hand "like clay in the hands of a potter"—a phrase that resonated with the liturgy of the High Holidays about the impotence of humans in the face of divine judgment.[39] Weisskopf demanded to be paid off to confess this truth to the authorities, but the representatives of the

Jews refused such demands without the express approval of their communal elders.

In the interim, the Prague elders learned of a man named Motl who knew of the conspiracy and, after interrogating him, discovered the letters in question. They in turn relayed them to Esther in Vienna, whereupon she showed them to people of influence who submitted a petition in support of Taussig to the emperor and Count Lamberg. When Lamberg recognized the truth of these words he arrested Weisskopf, imprisoning him in the guard tower.

Esther, the story's enduring heroine, prevailed on the imperial offices to empower a commission to try this case, charged with investigating the entire matter. After some difficulty in locating Weisskopf's coconspirator, Ries, it was discovered that he had burned his copies of the letters, but as luck would have it, a copy existed in Prague.[40] Taussig's advocates hurried to dispatch a courier to deliver a copy of the letters to a Count Herberstein, a member of one of the leading noble dynasties of the empire, to read, as he was "well acquainted with the writing and language of the Jews."[41] Even Herberstein's involvement, however, was not so easy to attain. He initially could not spare the time for what he considered such a trivial matter, but pressure from Prague's chief rabbi, David Oppenheim, on his in-law, the court Jew Samson Wertheimer, soon impressed on Herberstein the importance of his involvement.

Following the examination of both Taussig and Weisskopf by the imperial commission, Taussig was finally found innocent and released from prison on bail on January 27. In an inversion of fortunes, Weisskopf, the Haman of the story, was arrested in his place. To fully clear his name, Taussig's supporters called on another agent familiar with transnational arrangements to help them: Meir ben Yekutiel, the importer of etrogim, who, as a man who had to travel to procure this rare ritual fruit, was conversant in many languages. Meir visited Basel to determine if there was any truth to the claim that the letters originated there, and he found none, only falsehood. Finally, in June 1704, the emperor issued a decree absolving Taussig of all guilt and liability in this matter. Taussig declared a private Purim to be commemorated annually on the anniversary of his release, and the narrative draws to a close with wrongs righted and order restored.

Conclusion: The Paradox of Stability and Personal Precariousness

The dramatic, strange, and convoluted story of Taussig's arrest reveals the paradoxes at the heart of the position of the Court Jews. As interconnected insider-outsiders, the Court Jews and the multiple contacts they preserved engendered real opportunity, but also serious hazard. Taussig stood as an example of the charges that could be leveled as a result of innocent intervention on behalf of coreligionists, and yet his freedom was achieved through almost the same means, this time, however, within the borders of the German lands. In the political imagination of eighteenth-century Jews, the ties that bound them across space were still the most efficient and efficacious routes to securing a favorable outcome.

The positions of the Court Jews were thus both positions of power and precariousness, intimately bound up with the very operations of trust. Armed with the lessons of the court and aligned through marriage with many of the leading rabbinic figures of the period, the men and women of this class formed a ruling elite that created conditions for relative stability during this period. The Court Jews secured privileges for their retinues, relatives, and members of their orbit to gain the rights to trade, travel, and settle.[42] They averted expulsions, delayed the publication of anti-Jewish treatises, and funded the printing endeavors of new Jewish publishing houses. Court Jews represented Jewish interests in the halls of power, made significant contributions to building projects such as synagogues and study houses, and set the terms for the politics of communal leadership appointments.

Examples of the stellar rise and even more dramatic fall of Court Jews abound. The death of a patron could bring his Court Jew down with him. The sensational and infamous career of Jud Suess Oppenheimer—who rose to the level of financier and statesman in Heidelberg and, on the death of Heidelberg's duke, was publicly hanged—is only one such example.[43] Esther Schulhoff, who remained Court Jew to the elector in Brandenburg following the death of her husband, Jost Liebmann (also called Judah Berlin), similarly found herself under arrest, after the death of Frederick I in 1713, on charges of fraud and saddled with fine of 100,000 thaler.[44] Even living patrons could be fickle: Lefmann Behrens' grandsons, who inherited his estate and his role to the elector, found themselves under arrest in the mid-1720s.[45] And Samuel Oppenheimer, most famous of the Court Jews, had a career beset by arrests, mob violence, and courtly intrigue, involving his own arrest in 1683, his son's arrest in 1688, and the arrest of both in 1697.[46]

Whereas individual agents of the court rose and fell, a consensus prevailed—among noble rulers and Jewish constituents alike—that the institution of the Court Jews was worth preserving. An individual's career might be evanescent, but such was the cost of doing business. Contests between individuals sharpened the process of hierarchical power politics; they did not undermine the system.[47] Where one fell, another rose and assumed the same role. A Court Jew who fell from grace was not replaced by a Huguenot, an Anabaptist, or a local noble, nor did their utility immediately give way to rationalizing the system of taxation or the creation of a state bank, despite demands by some factions in court for precisely such a solution.[48]

Court Jews were thus both avenues to advancement and paths to destruction. The megillah that records this tale betrays the anxiety of its authors and audience, who were well aware of how plausibly and easily the activities of a "neutral nation" could be seen as inimical to the aims of the state. And yet, those same men and women of means were essential to resolving the affair. The couplet of networked efficiency and political outsider status meant that the Court Jew was a figure that both imperial office and Jewish subject had no choice but to trust. This fact was not lost on contemporaries: based on her reading of Glikl of Hameln, Natalie Zemon Davis has argued that "the Court Jews sometimes were seen by other children of Israel as a source of peril, not just of patronage and protection."[49] Glikl's opinion was forged in the experiences of her son's nearly being dragged down by Samuel Oppenheimer's creditors at the close of the seventeenth century. But an anxiety over the volatility of the Court Jews extended past the risks of a shaky business partner. The precariousness of Court Jewish life was certainly similar to other courtiers' fortunes, but it also had a particularly Jewish inflection, and contemporaries knew it.

This inflection provides the flip side of Arendt's observations about the unique place of the Jew as outsider. Jewish social and political independence was a decisive factor in establishing the value, utility, and trustworthiness of the Court Jew, but his supposed disinterest could also be turned to a distinctly Jewish weakness. The simple observation of "a kind of republic and neutral nation for commerce among different states" can be read in more than one way. Assuredly Jews conducted commerce among different states because they transcended circumscribed boundaries and borders, but a neutral nation and a separate republic could be a liability as well. Neutrality implies a lack of loyalty to *any* master or cause, an infinitely malleable and opportunistic cadre whose affiliations can never be fully assured, an accusation Jews would face at other times in the modern period. As the representation of Taussig's arrest and deliverance reveals, even Jews themselves were aware of the precarious position in which they found themselves and understood that connections across space and to the halls of power could be used both to forge bonds of trust and to show the very threats such transnational trust might pose to assessments of their loyalty and, as a result, to their own physical security.

Notes

1. Joachim Whaley, *Germany and the Holy Roman Empire, Volume II: The Peace of Westphalia to the Dissolution of the Reich, 1648–1806* (Oxford: Oxford University Press, 2012), 6–8; David Parrott, *The Business of War: Military Enterprise and Military Revolution in Early Modern Europe* (Cambridge: Cambridge University Press, 2012).

2. The Court Jew phenomenon was, by and large, limited to the political circumstances of central Europe. For the manifold activities of the Court Jews in the service of the state, see Selma Stern, *The Court Jew: A Contribution to the History of the Period of Absolutism*

in Central Europe (Philadelphia: Jewish Publication Society of America, 1950); Michael Graetz, "Court Jews in Economics and Politics," in *From Court Jews to the Rothschilds: Art, Patronage, and Power: 1600–1800*, ed. Vivian B. Mann, Richard I. Cohen, and Fritz Backhaus (Munich: Prestel, 1996), 27–43. For considerations of activities in the cities of northern Europe by Sephardic agents, rather than the central European Ashkenazim, see Jonathan I. Israel, *European Jewry in the Age of Mercantilism, 1550–1750*, 3rd ed., The Littman Library of Jewish Civilization (London: Littman Library of Jewish Civilization, 1998). On the Jews of eastern Europe, see Gershon David Hundert, "Was There an East European Analogue to Court Jews?," in *The Jews in Poland*, ed. Andrzej K. Paluch and Sławomir Kapralski (Kraków: Jagiellonian University, Research Center on Jewish History and Culture in Poland, 1992), 67–75.

3. Hannah Arendt, "Privileged Jews," *Jewish Social Studies* 8, no. 1 (1946): 11.

4. Bruce H. Mann, *Republic of Debtors: Bankruptcy in the Age of American Independence* (Cambridge, MA: Harvard University Press, 2002), 3.

5. The literature on credit and trust is vast. For some works on the subject, see Craig Muldrew, *The Economy of Obligation: The Culture of Credit and Social Relations in Early Modern England*, Early Modern History (New York: St. Martin's, 1998); Martha C. Howell, *Commerce before Capitalism in Europe, 1300–1600* (Cambridge: Cambridge University Press, 2010), 28; Clare Haru Crowston, *Credit, Fashion, Sex: Economies of Regard in Old Regime France* (Durham: Duke University Press, 2013), 6–7; Laurence Fontaine, *The Moral Economy: Poverty, Credit, and Trust in Early Modern Europe* (New York: Cambridge University Press, 2014).

6. Avner Offer, "Between the Gift and the Market: The Economy of Regard," *The Economic History Review* 50, no. 3 (1997): 458; Peter Mathias, "Risk, Credit, and Kinship in Early Modern Enterprise," in *The Early Modern Atlantic Economy*, ed. McCusker and Morgan (Cambridge: Cambridge University Press, 2001): 15-35.

7. Natalie Zemon Davis, "Riches and Dangers: Glikl Bas Judah Leib on Court Jews," in *From Court Jews to the Rothschilds: Art, Patronage, and Power 1600–1800*, ed. Vivian B. Mann, Richard I. Cohen, and Fritz Backhaus (Munich: Prestel, 1996), 49.

8. Stern, *Court Jew*, 18–19; 27–28.

9. Israel, *European Jewry in the Age of Mercantilism*; Stern, *Court Jew*; Mordechai Breuer, "Part 1: The Early Modern Period," in *German-Jewish History in Modern Times, Volume 1: Tradition and Enlightenment, 1600–1780*, ed. Michael A. Meyer, et al. (New York: Columbia University Press, 1996), 104–26; Friedrich Battenberg, "Die Jüdische Wirtschaftselite Der Hoffaktoren Und Residenten Im Zeitalter Des Merkantilismus—Ein Europaweites System?," *Aschkenas* 9, no. 1 (2009): 31–66.

10. Roger Clément, *La Condition Des Juifs De Metz Sous L'ancien Regime* (Paris: Jouve, 1903), 117.

11. Stern, *Court Jew*, 30. See, for example, the rivalry between the Court Jewish houses in Frankfurt, the Drach, and Kann. Stern, *Court Jew*, 188–94; Graetz, "Court Jews in Economics and Politics," 35.

12. In her influential study of the Sephardic trading families centered on the port city of Livorno, Francesca Trivellato has demonstrated that trust cannot be taken for granted as necessarily existing between members of a shared ethnic group. Francesca Trivellato, *The Familiarity of Strangers: The Sephardic Diaspora, Livorno, and Cross-Cultural Trade in the Early Modern Period* (New Haven: Yale University Press, 2009).

13. For a treatment of other early modern (Jewish) thinkers' valuation of Jewish diaspora existence as essential to their political neutrality and economic utility, and therefore a rationale for their toleration, see Jonathan Karp, *The Politics of Jewish Commerce: Economic Thought and Emancipation in Europe, 1638–1848* (Cambridge: Cambridge University Press, 2008), 12–42.

14. Arendt, "Privileged Jews," 11.

15. Arendt, "Privileged Jews," 12. Arendt was not the only one to apprehend the Court Jews in this manner. Selma Stern similarly explained their utility in terms of the unwillingness of others and the outsider status of the Jew, and the war contractor in particular, as "an object of great mistrust." Stern, *Court Jew*, 18.

16. Offer, "Between the Gift and the Market," 454.

17. They were not the exclusive agents in this process: Johann Joachim Becher (1635–82) offers an example of a non-noble natural philosopher and court physician who worked to make commerce—that unproductive and suspect occupation—acceptable to the courts of the Holy Roman Empire. Pamela H. Smith, *The Business of Alchemy: Science and Culture in the Holy Roman Empire* (Princeton, NJ: Princeton University Press, 1994). Nor was the merit of Jewish detachment unique to the German lands. The Sephardic-Converso traders of the Atlantic, Mediterranean, and Indian Oceans were similarly a stateless diaspora that were able, on this account, to move fluidly across national borders and even between Christendom and the Ottoman and Mughal Empires. Jonathan I. Israel, "Jews and Crypto-Jews in the Atlantic World Systems, 1500–1800," in *Atlantic Diasporas: Jews, Conversos, and Crypto-Jews in the Age of Mercantilism, 1500–1800*, ed. Richard L. Kagan and Philip D. Morgan (Baltimore: Johns Hopkins University Press, 2009).

18. The megillah has been published both in the original Yiddish and in German translation. It is likely to have been composed by Hayyim Taussig, a relative of the protagonist, sometime before 1720. *Megillat Shmuel*. vol. 15, Kobez Al Jad (Berlin: Mekize Nirdamim, 1899); S. H. Lieben, "Megillath Samuel," *Jahrbuch der Gesellschaft für Geschichte der Juden in der Čechoslovakischen Republik* 9 (1938): 307–42.

19. Rachel L. Greenblatt, *To Tell Their Children: Jewish Communal Memory in Early Modern Prague* (Stanford: Stanford University Press, 2014), 83–107.

20. Readers interested in the facts of this episode can consult the careful reconstruction in Alexandr Putík, "The Prague Jewish Community in the Late 17th and Early 18th Centuries," *Judaica Bohemiae* 35 (2000): 82–84; 94–98.

21. In this approach, I am following the methods laid out in Natalie Zemon Davis, *Fiction in the Archives: Pardon Tales and Their Tellers in Sixteenth-Century France* (Stanford, CA: Stanford University Press, 1987): 3–4.

22. Gerson Wolf, "Zur Geschichte Des Jüdischen Gemeinwesens in Prag," *Allgemeine Zeitung des Judenthums* 27, no. 17 (April 21, 1863): 255. In one fell swoop, Prague politics were radically altered and an oligarchy recognized both de facto and de jure by imperial law. A patriciate of this sort was in force in a number of Jewish locales. In Frankfurt am Main, Jewish affairs were dominated by "the Ten." Israel Halpern, "Mahloket Al Breirat he-Kahal be-Frankfurt de-Main ve-Hedeha be-Folin u-be-Vihem," in *Yehudim ve-Yahadut be-Mizrah-Europah* (Jerusalem: Magnes Press, 1969). On the chief rabbi, David Oppenheim, see Joshua Teplitsky, *Prince of the Press: How One Collector Built History's Most Enduring and Remarkable Jewish Library* (New Haven, CT : Yale University Press, 2019). On the many tensions of the Prague Jewish community, see the examples in Tobias Jakobovits, "Das Prager und Böhmische Landesrabbinat ende des Siebzehnten und Anfang des Achtzehnten Jahrhunderts," *Jahrbuch der Gesellschaft für Geschichte der Juden in der Čechoslovakischen*

Republik 5 (1933): 79–136; Putík, "The Prague Jewish Community in the Late 17th and Early 18th Centuries," 65–95.

23. See Wolf, "Zur Geschichte Des Jüdischen Gemeinwesens in Prag"; Reuven Ha-yisraeli, "Toldot Kehilat Prag Be-Shanim 1680–1730 Le-or Ha-'Kopiar' Shel R' David Oppenheim" (master's thesis, Tel-Aviv University, 1965), 119, 143–46; Alexandr Putík, "Prague Jews and Judah Hasid: A Study on the Social, Political and Religious History of the Late Seventeenth and Early Eighteenth Centuries, Part III," *Judaica Bohemiae* 41, no. 1 (2011): 35–37.

24. *Megillat Shmuel*, 6. On the episode, see Putík, "The Prague Jewish Community in the Late 17th and Early 18th Centuries," 87–88.

25. On Berlin's Jews, see Steven M. Lowenstein, *The Berlin Jewish Community: Enlightenment, Family, and Crisis, 1770–1830* (New York: Oxford University Press, 1994), 10–22. For a short overview on Vienna, see John P. Spielman, *The City & the Crown: Vienna and the Imperial Court, 1600–1740* (West Lafayette, IN: Purdue University Press, 1993), 123–35.

26. Charles W. Ingrao, *The Habsburg Monarchy, 1618–1815*, 2nd ed. (Cambridge, England, and New York: Cambridge University Press, 2000), 110.

27. The empire's west was a volatile region. It changed hands repeatedly over the course of the decades straddling the turn of the century. This was not solely the product of military conquest: to ameliorate the crushing debt of their overlords, residents of the region more than once transferred (or threatened to transfer) their allegiance to a different lord. Claudia Ulbrich, *Shulamit and Margarete: Power, Gender, and Religion in a Rural Society in Eighteenth-Century Europe* (Boston: Brill Academic, 2004), 110, 132.

28. *Megillat Shmuel*, 8.

29. Ingrao, *Habsburg Monarchy*, 124.

30. *Megillat Shmuel*, 12–13.

31. For a survey of the history of the European postal service in early modern Europe, see Harm Von Seggern, "Die Entstehung Des Postwesens in Mitteleuropa—Eine 'Kommunikationsrevolution'?," *Francia* 34, no. 2 (2007): 195–216; Wolfgang Behringer, "Core and Periphery: The Holy Roman Empire as a Communication(s) Universe," in *The Holy Roman Empire 1405–1806*, edited by R. J. W. Evans, Michael Schaich, and Peter H. Wilson (Oxford: Oxford University Press, 2011), 347–58.

32. Yedidya Alter Dinari, *Hakhme Ashkenaz be-Shilhe Yeme ha-Benayim: Darkhehem ve--Kitvehem ba-Halakhah* (Jerusalem: Mosad Byalik, 1984), 231. See also a letter of Moses Hagiz to the judges of Mantua, 1732, published in *Kovetz Beit Aharon ve-Yisrael*, 12:6 (72), 7, in which he explains that although he had no intention of replying to a letter, the messenger pressured him to compose a few lines so that he could depart. In this case, messengers were not passive carriers; they could also affect the content of the writing.

33. Derived originally from the Babylonian Talmud, Tractate Shevuot 39a, to refer to a legal system in which Jews could fulfil religious precepts on behalf of other Jews, by the nineteenth century it would be further enlarged and secularised to refer to mutual aid.

34. On Esther as paradigm, see François Guesnet, "Die Politik Der 'Fürsprache': Vormoderne Jüdische Interessenvertretung," in *Synchrone Welten; Zeitenräume Jüdischer Geschichte*, ed. Dan Diner (Göttingen: Vandenhoeck & Ruprecht, 2005), 69–72.

35. See the comparable situation during the imprisonment of the grandsons of Leffman Behrens in Isaak Marcus Jost, "Eine Familien-Megillah, Aus Der Ersten Hälfte Des 18. Jarhhunderts," *Jahrbuch für die Geschichte der Juden und des Judenthums* 6, no. 1 (1861): 69.

On the long history of charges of secrecy as the province of Jews in Christian Europe, see Elisheva Carlebach, "Attribution of Secrecy and Perceptions of Jewry," *Jewish Social Studies* 2, no. 3 (1996): 115–36. See also Daniel Jütte, *The Age of Secrecy: Jews, Christians, and the Economy of Secrets, 1400–1800* (New Haven, CT: Yale University Press, 2015).

36. *Megillat Shmuel*, 16.
37. *Megillat Shmuel*, 17.
38. François Guesnet, "Textures of Intercession—Rescue Efforts for the Jews of Prague, 1744/1748," *Jahrbuch des Simon-Dubnow-Instituts* 4 (2005): 355–75.
39. *Megillat Shmuel*, 18.
40. How or why these letters were produced in multiple copies remains a curious fact of the tale, but one that is not out of step with the production of letters in early modern Europe.
41. *Megillat Shmuel*, 23.
42. Court Jews also represented income disparity. In their unprecedented accumulation of wealth, they loomed high above the communities in which they lived and served. Lowenstein, *Berlin Jewish Community*, 18. On the income disparity between the Jews of Prague, see Alexandr Putík, "Prague Jews and Judah Hasid: A Study on the Social, Political and Religious History of the Late Seventeenth and Early Eighteenth Centuries, Part I," *Judaica Bohemiae* 38 (2002): 84–85.
43. For this complex affair, see Yair Mintzker, *The Many Deaths of Jew Suss: The Notorious Trial and Execution of an Eighteenth-Century Court Jew* (Princeton, NJ: Princeton University Press, 2017).
44. Stern, *Court Jew*, 52–55; Deborah Hertz, "The Despised Queen of Berlin Jewry, or the Life and Times of Esther Liebmann," in *From Court Jews to the Rothschilds: Art, Patronage, and Power: 1600–1800*, ed. Vivian B. Mann, Richard I. Cohen, and Fritz Backhaus (Munich: Prestel-Verlag, 1996).
45. For an eighteenth-century account of their fall, see Jost, "Eine Familien-Megillah, Aus Der Ersten Hälfte Des 18. Jarhhunderts," *Jahrbuch für die Geschichte der Juden und des Judenthums* 6, no. 1 (1861): 40–82.
46. Max Grunwald, *Samuel Oppenheimer und sein Kreis (ein Kapitel aus der Finanzgeschichte Österreichs)* (Vienna: W. Braunmüller, 1913); Graetz, "Court Jews in Economics and Politics"; Chava Turniansky, ed. *Glikl: Zikhronot, 1691–1719* (Jerusalem: Merkaz Zalman Shazar le-toldot Yisrael: Merkaz Dinur le-heker toldot Yisrael, ha-Universitah ha-Ivrit, 2006), 482–87; Davis, "Riches and Dangers," 51.
47. For an essay into stability as inhering in institutions even as individual members' careers varied, see the now-classic J. H. Plumb, *The Origins of Political Stability, England, 1675–1725* (Boston: Houghton Mifflin, 1967).
48. Attempts at creating a bank were mooted in 1703 following Oppenheimer's death. His death had demonstrated the bad credit of the state, though, propped up only by his own fancy work. This meant zero confidence for the state bank's credit, and it was therefore unable to attract investors. Charles W. Ingrao, *In Quest and Crisis: Emperor Joseph I and the Habsburg Monarchy* (West Lafayette, IN: Purdue University Press, 1979), 12–13. On attempts to establish a bank in the Habsburg monarchy in the first decade of the century, see Brigitte Holl, *Hofkammerpräsident Gundaker Thomas Graf Starhemberg und die österreichische Finanzpolitik der Barockzeit (1703–1715)*, (Vienna: Verlag der Österreichischen Akademie der Wissenschaften, 1976).
49. Davis, "Riches and Dangers," 46.

Bibliography

Arendt, Hannah. "Privileged Jews." *Jewish Social Studies* 8, no. 1 (1946): 3–30.
Battenberg, Friedrich. "Die jüdische Wirtschaftselite der Hoffaktoren und Residenten im Zeitalter des Merkantilismus—ein europaweites System?" *Aschkenas* 9, no. 1 (2009): 31–66.
Behringer, Wolfgang. "Core and Periphery: The Holy Roman Empire as a Communication(s) Universe." In *The Holy Roman Empire 1405–1806*, edited by R. J. W. Evans, Michael Schaich, and Peter H. Wilson, 347–58. Oxford: Oxford University Press, 2011.
Breuer, Mordechai. "Part 1: The Early Modern Period." In *German-Jewish History in Modern Times, Volume 1: Tradition and Enlightenment, 1600–1780*, edited by Michael A. Meyer, Michael Brenner, Mordechai Breuer and Michael Graetz, 79–260. New York: Columbia University Press, 1996.
Carlebach, Elisheva. "Attribution of Secrecy and Perceptions of Jewry." *Jewish Social Studies* 2, no. 3 (1996): 115–36.
Chazan, Robert. *Reassessing Jewish Life in Medieval Europe*. New York: Cambridge University Press, 2010.
Clément, Roger. *La condition des Juifs de Metz sous l'Ancien Regime*. Paris: Jouve, 1903.
Crowston, Clare Haru. *Credit, Fashion, Sex: Economies of Regard in Old Regime France*. Durham and London: Duke University Press, 2013.
Davis, Natalie Zemon. "Riches and Dangers: Glikl Bas Judah Leib on Court Jews." In *From Court Jews to the Rothschilds: Art, Patronage, and Power 1600–1800*, edited by Vivian B. Mann, Richard I. Cohen and Fritz Backhaus, 45–57. Munich: Prestel, 1996.
Davis, Natalie Zemon. *Fiction in the Archives: Pardon Tales and Their Tellers in Sixteenth-Century France*. The Harry Camp Lectures at Stanford University. Stanford, CA: Stanford University Press, 1987.
Dinari, Yedidya Alter. *Hakhme Ashkenaz be-Shilhe Yeme ha-Benayim: Darkhehem ve-Kitvehem ba-Halakhah*. Jerusalem: Mosad Byaliḳ, 1984.
Fontaine, Laurence. *The Moral Economy: Poverty, Credit, and Trust in Early Modern Europe*. New York: Cambridge University Press, 2014.
Graetz, Michael. "Court Jews in Economics and Politics." In *From Court Jews to the Rothschilds: Art, Patronage, and Power: 1600–1800*, edited by Vivian B. Mann, Richard I. Cohen and Fritz Backhaus, 27–43. Munich: Prestel, 1996.
Greenblatt, Rachel L. *To Tell Their Children: Jewish Communal Memory in Early Modern Prague*. Stanford: Stanford University Press, 2014.
Grunwald, Max. *Samuel Oppenheimer und sein Kreis (ein Kapitel aus der Finanzgeschichte Österreichs)*. Vienna: W. Braunmüller, 1913.
Guesnet, François. "Die Politik der 'Fürsprache': vormoderne jüdische Interessenvertretung." In *Synchrone Welten; Zeiträume jüdischer Geschichte*, edited by Dan Diner, 67–92. Göttingen: Vandenhoeck & Ruprecht, 2005.
———. "Textures of Intercession—Rescue Efforts for the Jews of Prague, 1744/1748." In *Jahrbuch des Simon-Dubnow-Instituts*, vol. 4, edited by Dan Diner, 355–75. Göttingen: Vandenhock & Ruprecht, 2005.
Ha-yisraeli, Reuven. "Toldot Kehilat Prag Be-Shanim 1680–1730 Le-or Ha-'Kopiar' Shel R' David Oppenheim." Master's thesis, Tel Aviv University, 1965.
Halpern, Israel. "Mahloket Al Breirat He-Kahal be-Frankfurt de-Main ve-Hedeha be-Folin v-be-Vihem." In *Yehudim ve-Yahadut be-Mizrah-Europah*, 108–35. Jerusalem: Magnes Press, 1969.

Hertz, Deborah. "The Despised Queen of Berlin Jewry, or the Life and Times of Esther Liebmann." In *From Court Jews to the Rothschilds: Art, Patronage, and Power: 1600–1800*, edited by Vivian B. Mann, Richard I. Cohen and Fritz Backhaus, 67–77. Munich: Prestel-Verlag, 1996.

Holl, Brigitte. *Hofkammerpräsident Gundaker Thomas Graf Starhemberg und die österreichische Finanzpolitik der Barockzeit (1703–1715)*. Vienna: Verlag der Österreichischen Akademie der Wissenschaften, 1976.

Howell, Martha C. *Commerce before Capitalism in Europe, 1300–1600*. Cambridge: Cambridge University Press, 2010.

Hundert, Gershon David. "Was There an East European Analogue to Court Jews?" In *The Jews in Poland*, edited by Andrzej K. Paluch and Sławomir Kapralski, 67–75. Kraków: Jagiellonian University, Research Center on Jewish History and Culture in Poland, 1992.

Ingrao, Charles W. *The Habsburg Monarchy, 1618–1815*. 2nd ed. Cambridge: Cambridge University Press, 2000.

———. *In Quest and Crisis: Emperor Joseph I and the Habsburg Monarchy*. West Lafayette, IN: Purdue University Press, 1979.

Israel, Jonathan I. *European Jewry in the Age of Mercantilism, 1550–1750*. The Littman Library of Jewish Civilization. 3rd ed. London: Littman Library of Jewish Civilization, 1998.

———. "Jews and Crypto-Jews in the Atlantic World Systems, 1500–1800." In *Atlantic Diasporas: Jews, Conversos, and Crypto-Jews in the Age of Mercantilism, 1500–1800*, edited by Richard L. Kagan and Philip D. Morgan, 3–17. Baltimore: Johns Hopkins University Press, 2009.

Jakobovits, Tobias. "Das Prager und Böhmische Landesrabbinat ende des Siebzehnten und Anfang des Achtzehnten Jahrhunderts." *Jahrbuch der Gesellschaft für Geschichte der Juden in der Čechoslovakischen Republik* 5 (1933): 79–136.

Jost, Isaak Marcus. "Eine familien-Megillah, aus der ersten hälfte des 18. Jarhhunderts." *Jahrbuch für die Geschichte der Juden und des Judenthums* 6, no. 1 (1861): 40–82.

Jütte, Daniel. *The Age of Secrecy: Jews, Christians, and the Economy of Secrets, 1400–1800*. New Haven: Yale University Press, 2015.

Karp, Jonathan. *The Politics of Jewish Commerce: Economic Thought and Emancipation in Europe, 1638–1848*. Cambridge: Cambridge University Press, 2008.

Lieben, S. H.. "Megillath Samuel." *Jahrbuch der Gesellschaft für Geschichte der Juden in der Čechoslovakischen Republik* 9 (1938): 307–42.

Lowenstein, Steven M. *The Berlin Jewish Community: Enlightenment, Family, and Crisis, 1770–1830*. Studies in Jewish History. New York: Oxford University Press, 1994.

Mann, Bruce H. *Republic of Debtors: Bankruptcy in the Age of American Independence*. Cambridge, MA: Harvard University Press, 2002.

Mathias, Peter. "Risk, Credit and Kinship in Early Modern Enterprise," in *The Early Modern Atlantic Economy*, edited by John J. McCusker and Kenneth Morgan, 15–35. Cambridge: Cambridge University Press, 2001.

Megillat Shmuel. Edited by Aron Freimann. *Kobez Al Jad*, vol. 15. Berlin: Mekize Nirdamim, 1899.

Mintzker, Yair. *The Many Deaths of Jew Suss: The Notorious Trial and Execution of an Eighteenth-Century Court Jew*. Princeton, NJ: Princeton University Press, 2017.

Muldrew, Craig. *The Economy of Obligation: The Culture of Credit and Social Relations in Early Modern England*. Early Modern History. New York: St. Martin's, 1998.

Offer, Avner. "Between the Gift and the Market: The Economy of Regard." *The Economic History Review* 50, no. 3 (1997): 450–76.
Parrott, David. *The Business of War: Military Enterprise and Military Revolution in Early Modern Europe*. Cambridge: Cambridge University Press, 2012.
Plumb, J. H. *The Origins of Political Stability, England, 1675–1725*. Boston: Houghton Mifflin, 1967.
Putík, Alexandr. "The Prague Jewish Community in the Late 17th and Early 18th Centuries." *Judaica Bohemiae* 35 (2000): 4–140.
———. "Prague Jews and Judah Hasid: A Study on the Social, Political and Religious History of the Late Seventeenth and Early Eighteenth Centuries, Part I." *Judaica Bohemiae* 38 (2002): 72–105.
———. "Prague Jews and Judah Hasid: A Study on the Social, Political and Religious History of the Late Seventeenth and Early Eighteenth Centuries, Part III." *Judaica Bohemiae* 41, no. 1 (2011): 33–72.
Ruderman, David B. *Early Modern Jewry: A New Cultural History*. Princeton, NJ: Princeton University Press, 2010.
Seggern, Harm von. "Die Entstehung des Postwesens in Mitteleuropa—Eine 'Kommunikationsrevolution'?," *Francia* 34, no. 2 (2007): 195–216.
Smith, Pamela H. *The Business of Alchemy: Science and Culture in the Holy Roman Empire*. Princeton, NJ: Princeton University Press, 1994.
Spielman, John P. *The City & the Crown: Vienna and the Imperial Court, 1600–1740*. West Lafayette, IN: Purdue University Press, 1993.
Stern, Selma. *The Court Jew: A Contribution to the History of the Period of Absolutism in Central Europe*. Philadelphia: Jewish Publication Society of America, 1950.
Teplitsky, Joshua. *Prince of the Press: How One Collector Built History's Most Enduring and Remarkable Jewish Library*. New Haven, CT: Yale University Press, 2019.
Trivellato, Francesca. *The Familiarity of Strangers: The Sephardic Diaspora, Livorno, and Cross-Cultural Trade in the Early Modern Period*. New Haven: Yale University Press, 2009.
Turniansky, Chava, ed. 2006. *Glikl: Zikhronot, 1691–1719*. Jerusalem: Merkaz Zalman Shazar le-toldot Yisrael, 2006.
Ulbrich, Claudia. *Shulamit and Margarete: Power, Gender, and Religion in a Rural Society in Eighteenth-Century Europe*. Boston: Brill Academic, 2004.
Whaley, Joachim. *Germany and the Holy Roman Empire, Volume II: The Peace of Westphalia to the Dissolution of the Reich, 1648–1806*. Oxford: Oxford University Press, 2012.
Wolf, Gerson. "Zur Geschichte des jüdischen Gemeinwesens in Prag." *Allgemeine Zeitung des Judenthums* 27, no. 17 (April 21, 1863): 255–57.

JOSHUA TEPLITSKY is Assistant Professor in the Department of History at Stony Brook University. His research centers on the history of the Jews of central Europe during the early modern period, and his larger scholarly interests include Christian-Jewish relations, the history of political cultures, and the history of the book. He is author of *Prince of the Press: How One Collector Built History's Most Enduring and Remarkable Jewish Library* (New Haven, CT: Yale University Press, 2019).

7 Jewish Peddlers and Non-Jewish Customers in the New World

Between Profit and Trust

Hasia Diner

FROM THE LATTER part of the eighteenth century through the 1920s, one-third of world Jewry engaged in a great migration, a phenomenon that saw millions of Jews leaving the homes of their birth and embarking on journeys on a global scale. While many migrated within central and eastern Europe, the Ottoman Empire, and North Africa, mostly going from rural communities and small towns to large cities, most crossed one or more national borders, and many got on ships that took them across an ocean or two in search of new homes.

They found their new homes in a big new world, places that previously had had no or few Jews. Most of these places opened up to them in the context of the age of European colonial expansion, as white people, under the aegis of their various nations, discovered parts of the world abounding in a range of natural resources that could be extracted, refined, and sold for profit. Some Jewish immigrants of this great age also headed for regions of the Old World, which, with the commercialization of agriculture, experienced new and dramatic infusions of cash into their countryside. This money then found its way into the hands and pockets of families who previously had lived at the subsistence level, in cashless circumstances.

Economically driven, the great Jewish migration of the modern era involved about four million Jews who left places they perceived held few or no economic opportunities and opted for places pulsating with possibilities for making a living. Many, with the proportion varying depending on time and place, opted for on-the-road peddling, calculating that as an occupation, it offered the quickest and surest launch on the path toward personal and familial stability. Familiar to them as an ordinary and ubiquitous element in the Jewish economy, they decided that it provided a reasonable, if not excellent, way to establish themselves in radically new settings. Not that all Jewish immigrants to the New World peddled, but so many did that it shaped their lives in these destinations, and even those who did not peddle had contact with peddlers in community, family, and business settings.

Without understating the difficulties of the occupation, the physical rigors, and the dangers—both human and environmental—they faced, most New World peddlers succeeded well enough to engage in this relatively unpleasant occupation for only a limited period of time, and from it, nearly all moved on to more stable and less arduous business ventures. Their children did not follow them onto the road. Only newly arrived Jewish immigrants peddled in North, Central, or South America, southern Africa, the Antipodes, Scandinavia, or the British Isles, and the fact of its temporariness bore witness to the almost global success experienced by those who spent time selling from the road.

Place mattered relatively little, and a fairly common and productive pattern developed around the peddler's new world. They tended to work on a weekly cycle, getting their goods from some Jewish wholesaler headquartered in a village, town, or city. Typically, the peddlers set out on the road with a pack, bag, box, or wagonload, on Sunday or Monday morning, and ranged around a fixed territory, their *medineh*, as most referred to it, one assigned, even if informally, by the wholesaler who provided the goods for sale. The peddler plied this route all week, going from house to house, farmstead to farmstead, mining camp to mining camp, and returning on Friday to his home base, some smaller or larger Jewish enclave. The peddlers spent the weekend resting, engaging with other Jews, and of equal importance, on Saturday night, paying their creditors for the previous week's goods, then filled up their packs and headed out for another week on the road.

The weekend part of the peddling operation took place in an almost exclusively Jewish context. Jewish peddlers got their goods from Jewish shopkeepers, who got their goods from Jewish wholesalers, who in turn relied on the owners of Jewish peddler warehouses, individuals with connections to more substantial Jewish distributors in the big cities of whatever land this operation took place in. The distributors, whether large or small, received many of their goods from Jewish manufacturers and indeed from Jewish importers.

But at the other end of the operation, the peddlers, who rightly can be considered the foot soldiers of this highly integrated Jewish economy and the shock troops of the great migration, sold exclusively to non-Jews. In the places they went to, all New World (or what we might want to label the Jewish New World) regions and countries, Jewish peddlers functioned as the sellers of goods, bringing consumer items for personal consumption to farmers, plantation workers, loggers, miners, the dwellers of textile and other kinds of mill towns, and the women and men who did the basic work of these societies. The newly arrived Jewish immigrant peddlers knocked on the doors of these people's homes, introduced themselves, and invited the women, the typical customers, to look into their bags.

As peddlers sold on the installment plan, taking small payments from each customer, they visited the same homes every week, taking the amount owed for goods already purchased, hoping to entice the customers into buying yet another item or two. Around the world, regardless of country or continent, they sold a particular kind of good, never necessities like food or fuel, but rather consumer goods that represented to the customers' new, cosmopolitan, and higher levels of consumption, including needles, thread, buttons, lace, ribbons, eyeglasses, dress patterns, pictures and picture frames, watches, jewelry, towels, sheets, blankets, and the like. For the customers with whom the Jewish immigrant peddlers engaged, these items fell into the category of luxuries that made life more pleasant.[1]

Jews came as peddlers to places where women and men did not have to buy such goods. They did not, in actuality, need tablecloths, new clothes, curtains, and the other items of this sort, which did not spell the difference between survival and desperation.[2] Likewise, the customers had other options as to where to shop. Local stores dotted the countryside, often, although not always, owned and operated by individuals who represented the same racial, ethnic, religious, and linguistic group identities as the customers, merchants who at first blush would seem to be the logical ones to whom the peddlers' desired customers would go. In the work camp and plantation settings, employers frequently maintained stores for the workers and their families, allowing them to purchase goods against their paychecks.

Additionally, others peddled in these regions. In the United States in the early and mid-nineteenth century, the Yankee peddler made his way across the country.[3] Before and after the Civil War, Irish and German men could be found on the roads selling house to house, and by the end of the nineteenth century, Syrian peddlers, mostly Christians from Lebanon, showed up in nearly all the places that Jewish peddlers went.[4]

In part because the customers had some choice, though it varied by time and region, the millions of Jewish peddlers who fanned out around the world had to instill trust in their potential customers. For one, as Jews, non-Christians who had migrated to Christian-dominated lands, they had to, by means of their actions, dispel inherited anti-Jewish imagery from the Christian Bible, which permeated Christian theology. Even if customers had never met a Jew before in the flesh, they had encountered them in the narratives of the life and, more importantly, the death of Jesus. The Jewish newcomer peddlers had to show, by their business dealings and their personal interactions, customer by customer, that they embodied virtue, honesty, and reliability rather than avarice, cunning, and deceitfulness.

Trust had to flourish between the customers and the peddlers, and this necessity functioned as a two-way street, binding them to each other. Both parties had a stake in the transaction, and each had to convince the other of their honesty, reliability, and fine qualities.[5] Surely, trust constitutes a *desideratum* of all commercial relationships, and in that peddling did not differ from more conventional forms of commerce, namely shopkeeping, deriving an income from a stationary store to which customers come in, buy, and hopefully return for some future purchase. Clearly, in every exchange of money for goods and services, the seller has to convince the buyer to buy, and must therefore stand by his products. He can sell shoddy or defective products only once. After that, the customer can, with impunity, take her pounds, pesos, or dollars elsewhere. She can tell her neighbors to avoid this store or that. Likewise, the store owner who acts disrespectfully to the customers runs the risk that the women and men in whose hands his livelihood lies will avoid doing business with him. Those who come to buy have to trust that they will be treated well and will get the goods they want at a price they can afford.

The need for trust holds on the other side of the relationship as well, although with fewer consequences. The seller has to assume the reliability of the money handed over in exchange for the goods. The currency has to enjoy the backing of the state, checks should not bounce, and more recently, credit cards should not be rejected. The merchant has to trust that the customers who come into the store will behave according to set norms, and will not steal or destroy the merchandise. When the commerce involves a shopkeeper and a customer, the consumer has a greater need, in the final analysis, to trust the seller than the other way around.

But with peddlers, a different kind of balance of trust had to develop, and if the roles had not completely reversed in terms of who needed to trust whom more, the peddler had a much greater stake in convincing the customer to trust her than the store keeper did. The customer had a greater modicum of power in her dealings with the peddler than she had when she crossed the threshold of a stationary shop. Notably, unlike any other form of commerce, peddling took place not in public but in the intimacy of private spaces, which in turn made the relationship between the merchant and the consumer more fraught than other, shop-based transactions. Because it took place away from the supervising eye of the public, it required that a more highly articulated trust develop between the two parties, with the seller to a degree more dependent on the goodwill of the buyer than the other way around.

In this worldwide drama of Jewish migration, facilitated in a large degree by peddling, every sale mattered. No home was too far off the beaten path, no customer too poor, to not be a potential purchaser of some item or another. If the peddler kept his prices down to the lowest possible level and sold to the largest number of women, then he could manage to fulfill the goals of his migration: namely, establishing a new home in a new place. The immigrant peddlers, who used their earnings to send money back home to help out their families and to eventually bring over brothers, sisters, and other relatives, as well as wives and children, operated by one small transaction after another. They made constant but miniscule profits by selling goods at slightly higher prices than what the goods, supplied by the Jewish wholesalers, had cost them, and their profits grew as they made more and more sales.

At its simplest level, the peddlers, as immigrants to a new place, as aliens to a local culture, had to make it clear by their business actions that what they sold had value. They could not sell subpar goods at too-high prices. If they did, the customers could retaliate in two ways, and each would severely chip away at the peddlers' operations. The customer could merely not pay the money she owed the peddler. While the peddler could go to the local authorities to try to force the woman to pay the balance due on the goods, the local authorities saw the peddlers as outsiders whom they barely tolerated, and little in the sources indicates that they came to the aid of the peddlers in trying to get money from local residents. Peddlers just had to write the items off as a loss. Equally powerful, the purchaser of a blanket that tore immediately, or a mirror that tarnished, or glasses that did not aid vision would never buy from that peddler again. If she did not trust him or his goods, she could easily refuse to answer the door when he knocked or slam it in his face, sending him off without a sale. The peddler knew this, and nearly all testimony offered by customers from around the world sang the praises of the Jewish peddlers as honest sellers of goods that satisfied the customers' standards.[6]

To make their necessary many small-scale sales, the peddlers, day by day and week by week, needed not only to go off to wherever customers could be found, but they also had to make sure that they would do nothing to frighten likely customers, women who might logically be skeptical about opening their doors to strangers. The women had to trust that if they let the peddlers into their homes, they would not be subjecting themselves to any kind of personal harm, whether sexual or otherwise.[7] Notably, peddling took place during the daytime, when the men would be at work and the women, standing face to face with these foreigners, outsiders who barely spoke the local language, had to be able to feel confident that nothing adverse would happen to them.

Beyond the concern of the peddlers to build up trust among the women so that they could sell something from their jumble of goods, they understood that they must do nothing to raise the suspicions of the men, in most cases the husbands of those women who had just spent some of the family's hard-earned money on a handkerchief, a necktie, or a pair of suspenders. The peddler realized that if word got out in a local community that he had behaved inappropriately, particularly by breaching gender etiquette, he could be hounded out, either by people refusing to let him into their homes or even not paying him for goods they had previously purchased, or by being driven out of town. It is not hard to imagine some combination of armed local police and vigilantes, riding horses, pursuing a peddler, and expelling him because of real or rumored inappropriate behavior. After all, the peddler *was* a stranger in every sense of the word, and as a stranger, he raised suspicion among some powerful forces around him.

But peddler-female customer relationships, born of the commercial transaction, involved another way in which trust functioned. Since women opened the door, invited in the peddler, looked in his sack, and made their decisions—to buy or not to buy—on their own, they defined themselves, in highly patriarchal societies, as empowered to make financial decisions.[8] Women often, as described in their memoirs and other autobiographical fragments, decided to not tell their husbands that they had purchased a locket or a brooch from an itinerant Jew. They squirreled these trifles away, wearing them when they wanted, but also pawning them when they needed. She who had usurped a degree of power from her husband in essence engaged in a conspiracy with the peddler, and she had to trust that he, the immigrant Jew, would never betray her secret and tell her husband that she had spent the money he had earned and that he had not given her permission to waste on such useless objects.

The peddlers had every reason to behave in such ways as to instill trust in local people. They no doubt realized that elements of the local power structure might in fact be quite happy to see these outsider peripatetic merchants fail. The peddlers challenged the hegemony of the local merchants. They came into the women's homes, sold to them at lower prices, and brought the goods directly into their domestic spaces. Local shopkeepers generally despised the Jewish immigrant peddlers and at times, in places around the world, enlisted religious and government authorities to wage campaigns against them. Sometimes the shopkeepers did so by recruiting their political representatives to raise the fees for peddler licenses or to try to restrict peddler licenses to citizens, a move that obviously would have cut out all Jewish peddlers, since only new immigrants made a living in this manner. Jewish citizens did not peddle.

By and large, those campaigns failed, and they did so largely because the peddlers had forged bonds of trust among the female customers and usually even among their husbands, proving themselves to be reliable, safe, and decent men who had not violated accepted norms of behavior. Even in extreme cases where anti-peddler action escalated into major national events, as in Limerick, Ireland, in the first decade of the twentieth century when a Redemptorist priest, Father Creagh, launched a two-year campaign against the Jewish "weekly men," the women stood by their peddlers, defying their husbands and the priests.[9] In doing so, they demonstrated how deeply they trusted the Jewish immigrants, nearly all of whom had come from Lithuania, to deal fairly. This and other, less well-recorded confrontations around the New World showed the importance of trust and the wisdom of the peddlers in cultivating it as a business strategy.

The issue of trust became even more complicated in places like the American South in the decades after the end of slavery, places where racial cleavages dominated public life. Immigrant Jewish peddlers flocked to this region after the Civil War and sold to both white and African American customers. They entered both sets of homes and had to accommodate both sets of customers, each with very different and obviously unequal rights and power in local society. The Jewish peddlers recognized the need and managed to satisfy both groups.

On the one hand, they went into African American homes and showed, through their behavior, that they could be trusted to act differently than other white men. They removed their hats in respect and referred to their customers not by their first names or by the ubiquitously used (by whites) "girl," but by "ma'am" and "Mrs." They allowed black women to try on clothes, something they could never do in the shops in town.[10] In this scenario, the Jewish peddler acted toward the customer, a woman who in public had no power or rights, as though she had the upper hand. And she did. She did not have to let the peddler in, and she did not have to buy from him. Eager to cultivate in her a willingness to purchase eyeglasses or pictures and picture frames, he inspired in her the goodwill that fostered trust. She knew that when he came into her home, he would not reenact the humiliation that dominated her public life.

On the other hand, the Jewish peddlers had to prove to local white residents of the region that despite their dealings with African Americans in their homes, they would do nothing in public to upset the racial status quo. The Jewish peddlers, all immigrants, all newcomers who functioned outside of the Christian communal structure, had to be able to show that even if they did conduct such business, they did so without any ulterior motive to disturb the prevailing racial order. The peddlers needed white women to also buy from them, and they also needed the local authorities to protect them and allow them to stay, do their business, and succeed.

Even earlier, in the days of slavery, Jewish peddlers came onto plantations in the South. They sold to the slave owners, who welcomed their arrival, in some cases so avidly that they actually kept a special room ready for the peddler so that when he finished his business, he could sleep comfortably for the night. Reluctantly, the slave owners allowed the peddlers to sell goods to the slaves. Slaves could earn small bits of money by growing garden vegetables and also by renting themselves out (or being rented out) to other white farmers in the area. Slaves could keep some of their earnings, and with that money, they availed themselves of the peddlers' presence to spruce up their quarters, choose their own clothes, and the like. Writers for magazines that slave owners read warned their readers that these Jews could be abolitionists in peddlers' clothing.[11] To do his business, the peddler had to convince the skeptical white planters that in fact they carried mirrors and clothing and glasses and not antislavery tracts or ideas. The owners had to trust that the peddlers purveyed consumer goods and not subversive thoughts.

In mining camps, mill towns, and post-emancipation plantations on multiple continents that depended on semiservice labor, the peddlers also had to foster trust among two contradictory and oppositional groups. On the one hand, they had to convince the customers that they did not represent employer interests. The customers had to feel confident that the man who came into their home and offered various consumer goods was not also spying on the family for the owners who sought to regulate the behavior of the workforce. These workers had to trust that what they said and did in front of the peddler would not filter back to the employer who held so much power over them. On the other hand, the employers had to trust that in their forays into the workers' abodes, the peddlers did not do anything to spread radical thinking, socialism in particular, which could upset the profoundly unequal relationship between the large laboring population and the employers who hoped to keep the workers in their place.[12]

Peddlers had yet another economic incentive to forge positive bonds with their customers. Peddlers who had moved up from selling by foot with the pack on their back to the horse and wagon stage amplified their business operations by loading up their wagons with scrap, such as old bones, rags, paper, feathers, and tin, to sell to jobbers, junkyard dealers, or manufacturers. In many places, they also filled up their wagons, as they emptied them out of consumer goods, with herbs and feathers found in the countryside.[13] For these activities, they enlisted their female customers to collect for them, paying the women with either cash or goods. Either way, to gather up the detritus of the countryside that they could then turn into cash, the peddlers needed to convince local women to enter into informal partnerships for and with them. This too required not only that they learn how to communicate with the customers, but that the customers trust them and believe that the time they put into collecting would in fact pay off. The women who spent time in the outdoors scavenging for bits and pieces of tin had to have confidence that the peddlers would pay them, whether in money or goods, for their efforts.[14] By acting as partners with the peddlers, the women heightened the bonds of trust with these strange, foreign men who earned a living so differently than did the men in their own communities.

From a business perspective, the peddlers also needed to cultivate trust among customers because many—and the number cannot be calculated with anything approaching accuracy—of the peddlers decided that when they had saved enough money, they would settle down as shopkeepers in some town situated in the regions where they had peddled. In the hinterlands of these regions, peddlers had met women and men in their homes every week. They had crossed people's thresholds, sold them goods, and gotten to know them and their children, and when the time came to give up their ambulatory life and become local merchants, the peddlers—now about to be former peddlers—cashed in, as it were, on the trust they had built up during their peddling days. Rather than developing a transitory relationship, peddlers hoped that when they opened stores, their former customers would continue to buy from them.

This desire transcended business. The peddlers hoped that in these towns where they would settle with wives and children, the women and men who had trusted them in their homes would provide a comfortable space for the creation and sustaining of Jewish community life, which would become part of the civic landscape.

But during his peddling days, the peddler had other but equally compelling reasons to build up trust with his customers. For peddling to work, immigrant Jewish peddlers needed places to sleep for the night.[15] True, the peddler could sleep on the bare ground, in a field, an empty lot, or the forest. If he had graduated to going by wagon, he could stretch out in the back, on top of his goods. But ideally, he would sleep in a bed in the home of the last customer of the day, comfortable and not exposed to the elements. The peddlers also welcomed the opportunity to eat in their customers' home.[16] While eating at their customers' tables involved numerous pitfalls, given the Jewish dietary restrictions that some, and probably many, followed, peddlers still relished those foodstuffs that their customers might give them and that they, the Jews, defined as kosher, or acceptable. After a day on the road, whether by foot or by wagon, the peddler, even a strict observer of *kashrut*, happily ate, if offered them, bread, fruit, milk, and eggs cooked in their shells, considering eating these foods inside a house, at a table, to be more pleasant than eating while sitting on the hard ground and consuming what few and by necessity dry items he had carried with him.[17]

Because peddlers had to satisfy these quotidian and practical needs nightly, securing a place to sleep, wash up, and eat, it became imperative for them to behave in such a way as to win the trust of their customers. The customer had every right and reason to refuse the customer a place to lodge or food to eat, and the peddlers knew this. They made a point of dressing with dignity, almost always wearing a suit and hat. When they entered a home, they tipped their hat and bowed to the woman who responded to their knock, and regardless of whether the woman was an African American in the Jim Crow South or a Native American on a plantation, the peddler knew that to make a sale and to get a glass of cold water and hopefully a bed at the end of an arduous day, he had to convey to his customer and potential host that he posed no danger to them.

Evidence of this can be drawn from around the world, and one place can easily stand for any other. For a paper this brief, examples have had to be jettisoned in favor of the larger, global picture, but one example might be useful to demonstrate how some customers viewed the Jewish peddlers.

Maine in the mid-nineteenth century can provide such a case study, and the material has been drawn from an unlikely and, as such, possibly objective source: R. G. Dun, a credit rating agency, which canvassed people all over the United States and Canada about the businessmen in their midst, wanting to gauge their trustworthiness. To assess the reputations of local merchants, the Dun reporters went around and asked about each one, noting in their ledger books what had been said about this one and that one. The Dun reporters, in their voluminous commentary on local businesses, never hesitated to remark if the subject of their inquiry happened to be a Jew, and by and large, in their estimation, that word did not carry a particularly positive connotation. The reporters for Dun seemed to have felt comfortable using pejorative language when it came to commenting on Jews, pointing out their flaws whenever they wanted, and attributing those flaws to the fact of their Jewishness. Dun did not like the Jews in part because Jews avoided local banks and other formal credit sources when they needed money. Since Jewish merchants operated within the relatively closed realm of the Jewish community, they made their business transactions impenetrable to Dun, a network of reporters who sought exactly that kind of information.

Yet even taking R. G. Dun's negative reaction to Jews into consideration, its agents commented often and regularly in their distinctive and terse notations, full of idiosyncratic abbreviations, that local people, in this case in Maine, had little negative to say about the Jews, and that indeed most people with whom they transacted business respected the Jewish immigrants and considered them trustworthy businessmen, the peddlers in particular. Mayer Waterman, a peddler in Kittery as of October 1847, an anonymous reporter remarked, "has no visible property in this town except a horse and wagon and a load of DG [dry goods] . . . never heard a word angst [against] his char [character], is unmarred, said by some to be rich. Strictly temperate"—this last not a minor comment in the state that passed the nation's most stringent anti-alcohol law just a few years later in 1851. A year later, the reporter found Waterman "still peddling—respected by many. Has no R. E. [real estate] no other visppy [visible property] except horse, wagon and stock. Yet is said to be rich. A very quiet gentlemanly man." As to Solomon Silverman of Blue Hill, Hancock County, the Dun investigator offered that he "is an honest man . . . is attentive to his bus [business] and always on the move . . . Gets his in NY . . . has no attachable ppy beyond the contents of his cart . . . Diligent in his peddling." Finally, locals considered Lewis Bloomberg of Waterville in 1883 to be "a man of gdhbts [good habits]. Indu [industrious]. Hon [honest], for the past 2 yers [years] has driven a peddlers cart." The operative words here, "good character," "gentlemanly," "good habits," "respected by many," and "never heard a word against," counted for much with the credit bureau.[18] Drawn from local gossip and acquired by asking around, these words reflected popular views about specific people who made their way through the countryside, selling from house to house. At least as far as the people of rural Maine, or at least these towns, saw it, there was little negative and much positive to say about the Jewish peddlers, the immigrant men who had come from abroad and whom the locals got to know over the course of their time on the road.

It became the peddler's project to present himself in the most positive and attractive way, as friendly, clean, and probably most importantly, as the honest bearer of quality goods at a price the customers defined as fair and just. The peddlers' quest for trust was a matter of utmost importance and something that most seem to have accomplished regardless of time or place during the great Jewish migration.

Since trust always goes two ways, the Jewish peddler had to also trust his customers, and indeed, without that trust, he might never have ventured into the South African Transvaal, the mining camps of Australia, the iron ore mines of Michigan's Upper Peninsula, Ireland's midlands, or the rubber plantations up and down the Amazon. He had to know, with a degree of confidence, that going out into these strange places, relatively uncharted regions from a Jewish perspective, that the women and men he would encounter would not only buy from him but would not cause him harm.

Scholars have long recognized that as a human activity, all migration involves a not inconsiderable amount of risk taking. They have posited that the mere act of leaving familiar homes, however limited the economic options there, and setting out for new ones requires a willingness on the part of the migrant to hazard unforeseen dangers, whether physical or psychological. Emigrants had no way to know what crises they would face during the crossing itself or what unknowns awaited them at their destination. The migrant had to believe that the benefits of the new place would outweigh the perils of the move.

In this vein, the immigrant Jewish peddlers resembled all other immigrants, at all times and in all places. But for the peddler, this calculus became particularly acute. Unlike his fellow Jewish immigrant, particularly from the latter half of the nineteenth century onward, who mostly came to the United States and mostly remained in New York City, working in the nearly all-Jewish garment industry, the millions who chose places other than the United States—South Africa, Latin America, and Australia, for example—as well as those who did not tarry in New York but spread out over the rest of the continent as peddlers, took different and greater risks. Those who took to the roads as peddlers put themselves in circumstances where they spent five days out of seven with no relatives, friends, or other Jews to protect them or to provide the emotional support that comes with familiarity.

They also knew well, whether through informal conversation or the Jewish press, that wherever Jewish peddlers had gone, some had gotten robbed, assaulted, and even murdered.[19] They made easy targets for armed ruffians, who functioned all over the Jews' new world. So for their own safety, the Jewish peddlers had to learn to trust the women and men of the regions where they operated. They had to believe that if someone robbed them on the road, local authorities would aid in recovering their goods; that if someone assaulted them, the guilty parties would be brought to justice. Episodes from around the world—various parts of the United States, Scotland, Wales, Ireland, Australia, and South Africa—show that the peddlers, having won the trust of their customers, could in fact rely on them and their neighbors, to do those things.

Peddler murders took place with enough regularity and got reported often enough in the Jewish press to be part of the common knowledge that the peddlers took with them. Notably, even though local merchants did not like the peddlers and considered them formidable economic competitors, when Jewish peddlers fell victim to murderers, local law enforcement authorities went to great lengths to investigate, seeking out the suspects, bringing them to trial, and, if they were found guilty, meting out punishment, including execution.[20] While these trials and executions did not help peddlers per se, the fact that they took place must have confirmed to the peddlers that despite their status as immigrant Jewish outsiders in a community, they could trust the local people to treat them with enough care and respect to make their time there bearable.

The need for the peddlers to trust their customers took multiple other forms. The peddlers likewise realized on a more daily level the importance of trusting their customers, and here the issue of sleeping in the customer's house can be particularly illustrative. The Jewish immigrant peddler, in his halting English, Spanish, Mayan, French, Dutch, Afrikaans, Cherokee, Ute, Swedish, Gaelic, or whatever other language his customers spoke, had to ask directly if he might lodge for the night in the home of his last customer of the day. Since he had his weekly circuit and tended to go to the same house on the same day of the week, he understood the need to scout out the best prospects, to figure out who among his customers might be the nicest, most congenial, and provide the safest setting.

After all, for a man who carried cash and goods to sleep in a stranger's home involved a real challenge. He could be murdered in his sleep. Someone could rummage through his pack and steal from him the jewelry, watches, and other items that were his very lifeline. The prospect that someone could take his money while he slept also did not seem illogical or paranoid. When peddlers, in their memoirs, revealed the fear they felt as they lay down in the homes of people in the countryside, they describe a situation full of danger.[21] They reveal how vulnerable they felt having literally put their lives into someone else's hands.

But since this kind of arrangement underlay the system, the peddlers had to assume not only the customers' basic goodness, but that if the circumstances arose, the Christians in whose home they slept would protect them. This assumption reflected the kind of trust that the peddlers had developed in their New World customers, bearing witness to the kinds of relationships that had developed.

Peddler testimony, regardless of where they had migrated, tells of customers reaching out to the peddlers who stayed in their homes, making them comfortable, and engaging with them one on one in as sociable a manner as people who barely speak each other's language can. Peddlers in autobiographies, memoirs, and family histories—all, obviously, sources to be treated with skepticism—recalled friendly conversations after dinner with their customers. They wrote about evenings spent with the host family, reading the Bible together, as the customers, particularly Protestants, expressed joy at having one of the people of Israel in their home. South African narratives, gleaned from Jewish peddler encounters with Afrikaner farmers, described how the husband of the family asked the Jewish immigrant *smous*, the term for peddler, to read from the Old Testament, presumably because as a Jew, he gave the text greater authenticity. Other peddler memoirs described how peddlers offered some free merchandise to customers in exchange for lessons in the language of the land. Often, as peddlers recalled it, when they tried to pay the family for the food and lodging, the husband or wife refused, claiming that they considered helping the peddler to be a matter of Christian duty and neighborliness. Either way, almost no peddler accounts recount how their hosts tried to convert the Jews to Christianity but rather how respectfully they asked about Jewish practices.[22]

Such amity, while no doubt exaggerated in the memoirs, reflected the trust that evolved between peddlers and their customers and that the peddlers depended on to make the risks of the journey into the hinterlands worthwhile. Those risks had to be worthwhile for their own safety but also from an economic perspective, which had brought them in the first place to northern Maine, New Zealand, Manitoba, the mining towns of Wales, or the Jamaican sugar plantations. They went to places where they could make a living, and they had to trust the local people to whom they sold that they would be able to do so.

They sold on the installment plan. This meant that a peddler left an item, be it a blanket, a set of towels, a garment, or a watch, with a customer who had put down only a small fraction of what he charged for it. He had no choice but to trust his customer, to believe that when he came back the next week, she would be there and would pay the next bit. He had to consider that she would not either depart with her item or, over the course of the intervening week, decide that she would not pay. While it is not possible to tally up all the sales made globally by the peddlers and to then compute how many customers failed to pay in full, the ultimate success of nearly all the peddlers—the fact that nearly all moved up to becoming stationary shopkeepers—indicated that most customers at most times paid, or paid enough to propel the peddlers off the road and into other, more sedentary occupations.

The trust that they must have had that the customers would pay and that they, the itinerant Jewish merchants, would cross the thresholds of these strangers' homes and not be harmed bore witness to the level of trust they harbored. Conversely, the fact that women on multiple continents, in many nations and countless regions, opened their doors and let these men, usually speakers of some strange language, the bearers of an alien religion, into their homes also involves a deep reservoir of trust. That they let these Jewish men, with packs on their backs, into their homes at hours when their husbands were not present also speaks volumes about the trust that underlay this particular commercial transaction.

If the peddlers and their customers are to be believed, little hatred, antagonism, or suspicion marred the exchange of goods for money. Rather, wherever the peddlers went, regardless of continent, country, region, and time, trust flourished between the two essentially equal players in this home-centered business undertaking. Both wanted something out of it. The peddler wanted to make a sale, and the customer wanted some material item, and both had to trust the other, and they did. No wall of mistrust separated the Jews and the non-Jews, the sellers and the buyers. In the main, they respected the differences that existed between them but did not consider those differences to be more meaningful than the mutual dependence they had on each other. The world the peddlers and their customers made together constituted a new chapter in Jewish history, one that made the New World so very different than the Old.

Notes

1. The literature on the history of consumption is enormous and cannot be succinctly cited. See John Brewer and Roy Porter, eds., *Consumption and the World of Goods* (New York: Routledge, 1993), 1. Much of this literature goes back to the work of Fernand Braudel and such works as *Capitalism and Material Life, 1400–1800* (New York: Harper and Row, 1967); Neil McKendrick, John Brewer, and J. H. Plumb, eds., *The Birth of Consumer Society* (Bloomington: Indiana University Press, 1982); Peter Stearns, *Consumerism in World History: The Global Transformation of Desire* (New York: Routledge; 2006); Martin Daunton and Matthew Hilton, *The Politics of Consumption: Material Culture and Citizenship in Europe and America* (Oxford: Berg, 2001); and Susan Strasser, Charles McGovern, and Matthias Judt, eds., *Getting and Spending: European and American Consumer Societies in the Twentieth Century* (New York: Cambridge University Press, 1998).

2. On the material level of rural Americans through much of the nineteenth century, see David Danborn, *Born in the Country: A History of Rural America* (Baltimore: Johns Hopkins University Press, 1995).

3. The literature on Yankee peddling is fairly robust, and enough material exists to be able to compare Yankee peddlers' experiences with those of Jews. See "The Persistent Fringe of House to House Selling in American History," *Bulletin of the Business Historical Society* 9, no. 2 (1935): 24–28; Fred Mitchell Jones, *Middlemen in the Domestic Trade of the United States, 1800–1860* (Urbana: University of Illinois Press, 1937); Thomas D. Clark, *The Rampaging Frontier: Manners and Humors of the Pioneer Days in the South and the Middle West* (Bloomington: Indiana University Press, 1939), 301–20; Lewis E. Atherton, "The Pioneer Merchant in Mid-America," *University of Missouri Studies: A Quarterly of Research* 14, no. 2 (1939): 7–37; Richardson Wright, *Hawkers and Walkers in Early America*

(Philadelphia: Lippincott: 1927); Theodore F. Marburg, "Manufacturer's Drummer, 1852, with Comments in Western and Southern Markets," *Bulletin of the Business Historical Society* 22, no. 3 (1948): 106–14; Lee M. Freedman, "The Drummer in Early American Merchandise Distribution," *Bulletin of the Business Historical Society* 21, no. 2 (1947): 39–44; Lewis E. Atherton, "Itinerant Merchandising in the Ante-Bellum South," *Bulletin of the Business Historical Society* 19, no. 2 (1945): 35–59; J. R. Dolan, *The Yankee Peddlers of Early America* (New York: Clarkson N. Potter, 1964); Penrose Scull, *From Peddlers to Merchant Princes: A History of Selling in America* (Chicago: Follett, 1967); Paul J. Uselding, "Peddling in the Antebellum Economy: Precursors of Mass-Marketing or a Start in Life?" *American Journal of Economics and Sociology* 34, no. 1 (1975): 55–67; David Jaffee, "Peddlers of Progress and the Transformation of the Rural North, 1760–1860," *Journal of American History* 78, no. 2 (1991): 511–35; and Joseph T. Rainer, "The Honorable Fraternity of Moving Merchants: Yankee Peddlers in the Old South, 1800–1860," unpublished PhD dissertation, College of William and Mary, 2000.

4. The literature on Arab peddling in Latin America and the United States is extensive, and some makes the comparison between Arab and Jewish peddlers. Notably, literature on Jewish peddlers makes no attempt to compare or link their subjects with other immigrant peddlers. See Philip K. Hitti, *The Syrians in America* (Piscataway, NJ: Gorgias, 2005); Stewart G. McHenry, "The Syrian Movement into Upstate New York," *Ethnicity* 6, no. 4 (1979): 327–45; Afif I. Tannous, "Acculturation of an Arab-Syrian Community in the Deep South," *American Sociological Review* 8, no. 3 (June, 1943): 264–71; Albert Harouni and Nadim Shehadi, *The Lebanese in the World: A Century of Emigration* (London: Center for Lebanese Studies in Association with I. B. Tauris, 1992); Aaron D. Jesch, "A Peddler's Progress: Assimilation and Americanization in Kearney, Nebraska, 1890–1924," unpublished PhD dissertation, University of Nebraska, 2008; Oswaldo Truzzi, "The Right Place at the Right Time: Syrians and Lebanese in Brazil and the United States: A Comparative Approach," *Journal of American Ethnic History* 16, no. 2 (1997): 3–34; Adele L. Younis, *The Coming of the Arabic-Speaking People to the United States* (New York: Center for Migration Studies, 1995); Louise Fawcett, "Arabs and Jews in the Development of the Colombian Caribbean, 1850–1950," *Boletin Cultural y Biubliografico* 35 (1998), 57–79; William Sherman, Paul Whitney, and John Guerrorro, *Prairie Peddlers* (Bismarck: University of North Dakota Press, 2002); Philip M. Kayal and Joseph Kayal, *The Syrian-Lebanese in America: A Study in Religion and Assimilation* (Boston: Twayne, 1975); Alixa Naff, *Becoming American: The Early Arab Immigrant Experience* (Carbondale: Southern Illinois University, 1985); Eric J. Hooglund, ed., *Crossing the Waters: Arabic-Speaking Immigrants to the United States Before 1940* (Washington, DC: Smithsonian Institution, 1987); and John Tofik Karam, "A Cultural Politics of Entrepreneurship in Nation-Making: Phoenicians, Turks, and the Arab Commercial Essence in Brazil," *Journal of Latin American Anthropology* 9, no. 2 (2004): 319–51.

5. Jane Tai Landa, *Trust, Ethnicity, and Identity: Beyond the New Institutional Economics of Ethnic Trading Networks, Contract Law, and Gift-Exchange* (Ann Arbor: University of Michigan Press, 2001).

6. See, for example, R. G. Dun's investigation into Solomon Silverman in Maine in *R.G. Dun and Company Collection*, Maine, Vol. 3, 3, 57; Vol. 4, 512.

7. While sexual relations between peddlers and female customers might well have taken place, accounts of sexual assault are found mainly in popular literature of the time; see, for example, Baila Shargel and Harold L. Drimmer, *The Jews of Westchester: A Social History* (Fleischmanns, NY: Purple Mountain, 1994), 35–36.

8. On women and pawning see Melanie Tebbutt, *Making Ends Meet: Pawnbroking and Working-Class Credit* (New York: St. Martin's Press, 1983); and Wendy Woloson, *In Hock: Pawning in America from Independence through the Great Depression* (Chicago: University of Chicago Press, 2009).

9. *American Jewish Yearbook: 5665 (1904-1905)* (Philadelphia: Jewish Publication Society of America, 1905), 19-24.

10. Melissa Walker and James C. Cobb, eds. *The New Encyclopedia of Southern Culture*, vol. 2, *Agriculture and Industry* (Chapel Hill: University of North Carolina Press, 2008), 50-51.

11. For more on slave owners' attitudes toward peddlers and fears of abolitionist leanings, see Bertram Korn, *Jews and Negro Slavery in the Old South, 1789-1865* (Elkins Park, PA: Reform Congregation Keneseth Israel, 1961), 63. Korn originally presented the published material in 1961 in a speech to the American Jewish Historical Society.

12. For examples of Jewish peddling in industrial areas to workers, see Dario Euraque, "The Arab-Jewish Economic Presence in San Pedro Sula, the Industrial Capital of Honduras: Formative Years, 1880s-1930," *Immigrants and Minorities* 16, nos. 1-2 (1997): 94-124, especially 95-96; and Barbara Weinstein, *The Amazon Rubber Boom: 1850-1920* (Stanford: Stanford University Press, 1983), 51.

13. On Jews and scrap, see Jonathan Z. Pollack, "Success from Scrap and Second-Hand Goods: Jewish Businessmen in the Midwest, 1890-1930," in *Chosen Capital: The Jewish Encounter with American Capitalism*, Rebecca Kobrin, ed. (New Brunswick, NJ: Rutgers University Press, 2012), 93-112. See also Devera S. Stocker, Bess Alper Dutsch, and Naomi Buchhalter Floch, "History of the Traverse City Jewish Community: Part Two," *Michigan Jewish History* 20, no. 1 (January, 1980): 4-19.

14. "Benzely, Mrs. Marion," 1982, 54-C, Upper Midwest Jewish Archives.

15. Abram Vossen Goodman, "A Jewish Peddler's Diary, 1842-1843," *American Jewish Archives* 3, no. 3 (1951): 81-111, especially 96 and 98; Abraham Kohn, "Diary of his Life in Chicago, Ill. and New England, 1842-1845," American Jewish Archives, Small Collections, 6384.

16. Louis Schmier, "For Him the 'Schwartzers' Couldn't Do Enough: A Jewish Peddler and His Black Customers Look at Each Other," in Maurianne Adams and John Bracey, eds., *Strangers and Neighbors: Relations between Blacks and Jews in the United States* (Amherst: University of Massachusetts Press, 1999), 223-36, especially 228.

17. M. L. Marks, *Jews among Indians: Tales of Adventure and Conflict in the Old West* (Chicago: Benison Books, 1992), 53; Abraham Peck, "That Other 'Peculiar Institution'": Jews and Judaism in the Nineteenth Century South," *Modern Judaism* 7, no. 1 (1987): 99-114, especially 106.

18. R. G. Dun and Company Collection, Maine, vol. 3:3, 57; vol. 4:512.

19. Rudolf Glanz, *Jew and Mormon: Historic Group Relations and Religious Outlook* (New York: Waldron, 1963), 163-64; Alfred R. Schumann, *No Peddlers Allowed* (Appleton, WI: C. C. Nelson, 1948).

20. See, for example, *Particulars of the Murder of Nathan Adler on the Night of November Sixth, 1849, Venice, Cayuga County, N.Y., Including the Whole Testimony Taken by the Coroner and the Inquisition and Arrest of the Three Bahams* (Auburn, NY: Finn and Rockwell, 1850); see also Richard Brown, "Nathan Adler Stops at the Bahams," *New York Folklore Quarterly* 24, no. 1 (1968): 27-43; "Transcript of Irving M. Engel Oral Memoir, New York, N.Y., 1969-1970," Small Collections 3213, American Jewish Archives.

21. "Memoir," Isaac Frank, Small Collections, SC-14538, American Jewish Archives, 15.

22. For examples, see Schmier, "For Him the 'Schwartzers' Couldn't Do Enough," 223–36, especially 228; quoted in Korn, *Jews and Negro Slavery*, 68; Peck, "That Other 'Peculiar Institution,'" 106; and Casper (Kasirel) Sober, *The Story of My Life, 1876–1956*, 37, unpublished memoir in possession of the author. My thanks to Dara Pefit for sharing this with me; Abe Schapera, "The Jews of Namaqualand," *Jewish Affairs* 35, no. 12 (December, 1980): 23–29 (24).

Bibliography

Archival Sources and Oral Histories

"Benzely, Mrs. Marion." 1982, 54-C. Upper Midwest Jewish Archives. University of Minnesota Libraries.

Frank, Isaac. "Memoir." Small Collections, SC-14538. American Jewish Archives, 15. Hebrew Union College–Jewish Institute of Religion, Cincinnati.

Kohn, Abraham. "Diary of his Life in Chicago, Ill. and New England, 1842–1845." Small Collections, 6384. American Jewish Archives. Hebrew Union College–Jewish Institute of Religion, Cincinnati.

Particulars of the Murder of Nathan Adler on the Night of November Sixth, 1849, Venice, Cayuga County, N.Y., Including the Whole Testimony Taken by the Coroner and the Inquisition and Arrest of the Three Bahams. Auburn, NY: Finn and Rockwell, 1850.

R. G. Dun and Company Collection, Maine. Vol. 3, 3, 57; Vol. 4, 512. Baker Library, Harvard Business School.

Sober, Casper (Kasirel). *The Story of My Life, 1876–1956*, 37. Unpublished memoir.

"Transcript of Irving M. Engel Oral Memoir, New York, N.Y., 1969–1970." Small Collections 3213. American Jewish Archives. Hebrew Union College–Jewish Institute of Religion, Cincinnati.

Published Primary and Secondary Sources

American Jewish Yearbook: 5665 (1904–1905). Philadelphia: Jewish Publication Society of America, 1905.

Atherton, Lewis E. "Itinerant Merchandising in the Ante-Bellum South." *Bulletin of the Business Historical Society* 19, no. 2 (1945): 35–59.

———. "The Pioneer Merchant in Mid-America." *University of Missouri Studies: A Quarterly of Research* 14, no. 2 (1939): 7–37.

Braudel, Fernand. *Capitalism and Material Life, 1400–1800*. New York: Harper and Row, 1967.

Brewer, John, and Roy Porter, eds. *Consumption and the World of Goods*. New York: Routledge, 1993.

Brown, Richard. "Nathan Adler Stops at the Bahams." *New York Folklore Quarterly* 24, no. 1 (1968): 27–43.

Clark, Thomas D. *The Rampaging Frontier: Manners and Humors of the Pioneer Days in the South and the Middle West*. Bloomington: Indiana University Press, 1939.

Danborn, David. *Born in the Country: A History of Rural America*. Baltimore: Johns Hopkins University Press, 1995.

Daunton, Martin, and Matthew Hilton. *The Politics of Consumption: Material Culture and Citizenship in Europe and America.* Oxford: Berg, 2001.
Dolan, J. R. *The Yankee Peddlers of Early America.* New York: Clarkson N. Potter, 1964.
Euraque, Darío. "The Arab-Jewish Economic Presence in San Pedro Sula, the Industrial Capital of Honduras: Formative Years, 1880s-1930." *Immigrants and Minorities* 16, nos. 1-2 (1997): 94-124.
Fawcett, Louise. "Arabs and Jews in the Development of the Colombian Caribbean, 1850-1950." *Boletin Cultural y Biubliografico* 35 (1998): 57-79.
Freedman, Lee M. "The Drummer in Early American Merchandise Distribution." *Bulletin of the Business Historical Society* 21, no. 2 (1947): 39-44.
Glanz, Rudolf. *Jew and Mormon: Historic Group Relations and Religious Outlook.* New York, Waldron, 1963.
Goodman, Abram Vossen, "A Jewish Peddler's Diary, 1842-1843." *American Jewish Archives* 3, no. 3 (1951): 81-111.
Harouni, Albert, and Nadim Shehadi. *The Lebanese in the World: A Century of Emigration.* London: Center for Lebanese Studies in Association with I. B. Tauris, 1992.
Hitti, Philip K. *The Syrians in America.* Piscataway, NJ: Gorgias, 2005.
Hooglund, Eric J., ed. *Crossing the Waters: Arabic-Speaking Immigrants to the United States before 1940.* Washington, DC: Smithsonian Institution, 1987.
Jaffee, David. "Peddlers of Progress and the Transformation of the Rural North, 1760-1860." *Journal of American History* 78, 2 (1951): 511-35.
Jesch, Aaron D. "A Peddler's Progress: Assimilation and Americanization in Kearney, Nebraska, 1890-1924." Unpublished PhD dissertation. University of Nebraska, 2008.
Jones, Fred Mitchell. *Middlemen in the Domestic Trade of the United States, 1800-1860.* Urbana: University of Illinois Press, 1937.
Karam, John Tofik. "A Cultural Politics of Entrepreneurship in Nation-Making: Phoenicians, Turks, and the Arab Commercial Essence in Brazil." *Journal of Latin American Anthropology* 9, no. 2 (2004): 319-51.
Kayal, Philip M., and Joseph Kayal. *The Syrian-Lebanese in America: A Study in Religion and Assimilation.* Boston: Twayne, 1975.
Korn, Bertram. *Jews and Negro Slavery in the Old South, 1789-1865.* Elkins Park, PA: Reform Congregation Keneseth Israel, 1961.
Landa, Jane Tai. *Trust, Ethnicity, and Identity: Beyond the New Institutional Economics of Ethnic Trading Networks, Contract Law, and Gift-Exchange.* Ann Arbor: University of Michigan Press, 2001.
Marburg, Theodore F. "Manufacturer's Drummer, 1852, with Comments in Western and Southern Markets." *Bulletin of the Business Historical Society* 22, no. 3 (1948): 106-14.
McHenry, Stewart G. "The Syrian Movement into Upstate New York." *Ethnicity* 6, no. 4 (1979): 327-45.
Marks, M. L. *Jews among Indians: Tales of Adventure and Conflict in the Old West.* Chicago: Benison, 1992.
McKendrick, Neil, John Brewer, and J. H. Plumb, eds. *The Birth of Consumer Society: The Commercialization of Eighteenth-Century England.* Bloomington: Indiana University Press, 1982.
Naff, Alixa. *Becoming American: The Early Arab Immigrant Experience.* Carbondale: Southern Illinois University, 1985.

Peck, Abraham. "That Other 'Peculiar Institution'": Jews and Judaism in the Nineteenth Century South." *Modern Judaism* 7, no. 1 (1987): 99–114.

"The Persistent Fringe of House to House Selling in American History." *Bulletin of the Business Historical Society* 9, no. 2 (1935): 24–28.

Pollack, Jonathan Z. "Success from Scrap and Second-Hand Goods: Jewish Businessmen in the Midwest, 1890–1930." In *Chosen Capital: The Jewish Encounter with American Capitalism*, edited by Rebecca Kobrin, 93–112. New Brunswick, NJ: Rutgers University Press, 2012.

Rainer, Joseph T. "The Honorable Fraternity of Moving Merchants: Yankee Peddlers in the Old South, 1800–1860." Unpublished PhD dissertation. College of William and Mary, 2000.

Schmier, Louis. "For Him the 'Schwartzers' Couldn't Do Enough: A Jewish Peddler and His Black Customers Look at Each Other." In *Strangers and Neighbors: Relations between Blacks and Jews in the United States*, edited by Maurianne Adams and John Bracey, 223–36. Amherst: University of Massachusetts Press, 1999.

Schumann, Alfred R. *No Peddlers Allowed*. Appleton, WI: C. C. Nelson, 1948.

Scull, Penrose. *From Peddlers to Merchant Princes: A History of Selling in America*. Chicago: Follett, 1967.

Schapera, Abe. "The Jews of Namaqualand." *Jewish Affairs* 35, no. 12 (1980): 23–29.

Shargel, Baila, and Harold L. Drimmer. *The Jews of Westchester: A Social History*, Fleischmanns, NY: Purple Mountain, 1994.

Sherman, William, Paul Whitney, and John Guerrorro. *Prairie Peddlers*. Bismarck: University of North Dakota Press, 2002.

Stearns, Peter. *Consumerism in World History: The Global Transformation of Desire*. New York: Routledge, 2006.

Stocker, Devera S., Bess Alper Dutsch, and Naomi Buchhalter Floch. "History of the Traverse City Jewish Community: Part Two." *Michigan Jewish History* 20, no. 1 (1980): 4–19.

Strasser, Susan, Charles McGovern, and Matthias Judt, eds. *Getting and Spending: European and American Consumer Societies in the Twentieth Century*. New York: Cambridge University Press, 1998.

Tannous, Afif I. "Acculturation of an Arab-Syrian Community in the Deep South." *American Sociological Review* 8, no. 3 (1943): 264–71.

Tebbutt, Melanie. *Making Ends Meet: Pawnbroking and Working-Class Credit*. New York: St. Martin's, 1983.

Truzzi, Oswaldo. "The Right Place at the Right Time: Syrians and Lebanese in Brazil and the United States: A Comparative Approach." *Journal of American Ethnic History* 16, no. 2 (1997): 3–34.

Uselding, Paul J. "Peddling in the Antebellum Economy: Precursors of Mass-Marketing or a Start in Life?" *American Journal of Economics and Sociology* 34, no. 1 (1975): 55–67.

Walker, Melissa, and James C. Cobb, eds. *The New Encyclopedia of Southern Culture*. Vol. 2, *Agriculture and Industry*. Chapel Hill: University of North Carolina Press, 2008.

Weinstein, Barbara. *The Amazon Rubber Boom: 1850–1920*. Stanford: Stanford University Press, 1983.

Woloson, Wendy. *In Hock: Pawning in America from Independence through the Great Depression*. Chicago: University of Chicago Press, 2009.

Wright, Richardson. *Hawkers and Walkers in Early America*. Philadelphia: Lippincott, 1927.

Younis, Adele L. *The Coming of the Arabic-Speaking People to the United States*. New York: Center for Migration Studies, 1995.

HASIA DINER is Paul and Sylvia Steinberg Professor of American Jewish History and Director of the Goldstein-Goren Center for American Jewish History at New York University. She is author of *Roads Taken: The Great Jewish Migration to the New World and the Peddlers Who Forged the Way* in addition to several other books in the field of American Jewish history, American immigration history, and the history of American women.

8 Belonging and Trustworthiness

Jewish Businessmen in the Public Rhetoric around the "Trustworthy Businessman" in Post-World War I Germany

Stefanie Fischer

IN POST-WORLD WAR I Germany, state authorities tightened the licensing process in the livestock business in order to solve a trust crisis among cattle traders, farmers, and meat consumers.[1] Like all markets, the German livestock market in the interwar period was built on complex trust relationships between consumers, producers, and distributors. At the center of this market cycle were long-established middlemen, mainly cattle traders who channeled goods from producers to the market. The cattle-dealing business had been a predominantly Jewish domain in the German provinces from the beginning of Jewish settlement and remained so until its destruction during the Nazi era.[2] The strong Jewish presence in the cattle trade was a result of historical trade restrictions prohibiting Jews from owning land, thus confining them to trade until the eve of the emancipation in the nineteenth century. In Bavaria, these historical trade restrictions were lifted only in 1871. This prevented the emancipation and consequently the urbanization of the Jews longer than was the case in Prussia. As a result, in 1933 Bavaria, a large percentage of the Jewish population still lived in rural areas and most of them made their living in the cattle-dealing business.

The cattle trade was a risky business, governed by rituals that followed specific, long-established rules. Deals were sealed with a handshake, not a paper contract. The lack of written documentation created a precarious situation that was rendered even more insecure by the uncertain nature of the livestock. There was no reliable or objective data available for each cow; the buyer had to trust the word of the salesman. In this risky business sector, respecting traditional business culture and traditions—such as trust in verbal agreements and the rejection of written sales contracts—was a crucial prerequisite for a successful business built on mutual trust.[3] Traditionally, trust was built into cattle dealing through repeated personal business relations. Often, the business partners had known each other for many years; sometimes, their families had done business together for generations.

Sociologists call this kind of trust "process-based trust." Often, it can function as a guarantee for reliability, stability, and thus economic success. However, such process-based trust can be ruptured in the face of changing business conditions, including increasing cultural diversity among business partners, or an increase in immigrants during times of economic strife. Such was the case in the cattle-dealing sector in Germany following World War I, when trust in the meat sector in general—and the cattle-dealing business in particular—was severely shaken. The trust crisis became urgent as war veterans who failed to find jobs in their trained professions were pushed into the trade sector. These so-called wild cattle traders operated in the market with no professional experience in cattle dealing.[4] The numbers of new cattle dealers were alarming: before 1914, there were 6,000 cattle traders in Bavaria; after the war, the number had increased by one-third, to 9,716.[5] Increasing numbers sought a living in the cattle-dealing business, and in 1922, as many as 16,000 businessmen applied for a trade license that would grant them the right to deal in livestock.[6] A lurid 1922 article in the *Münchner Augsburger Abendzeitung* (*Munich-Augsburg Evening News*) argued that among those who applied for a trade license were thousands of butchers, war veterans, and bankrupt farmers.[7] The increasing number of traders, the author explained, resulted in intense competition among them. Each of these cattle traders aimed to make a decent living, each had high allowances for housing and shipping costs, and state fees and taxes also put a strain on the price of meat. Consequently, since each trader had to offer customers the best prices for their livestock, meat prices skyrocketed. As a result, large parts of the population were no longer able to afford meat.[8] During the war, more pigs were slaughtered than raised, so cows, normally kept as productive livestock, were also slaughtered for food.[9] The resulting livestock shortage and extremely high meat prices put enormous strain on consumers' budgets, as well as on the relationship between customers and meat suppliers.

The new cattle dealers were widely accused of respecting neither the long-established business culture nor its traditions.[10] For example, a merchant was considered respectful and trustworthy if he agreed to buy an animal for a certain amount of money, came back later to pick up the cow, and then paid for it. However, a merchant was seen as untrustworthy if he confirmed the purchase of an animal, but never returned to pay for and pick up the cattle because he had made a better deal with another farmer.[11] The first farmer then was left with his unsold livestock, and eventually felt betrayed because he had trusted the merchant to return and pay for the contracted cow. Such practices ruptured the trust relationships between farmers and cattle traders. The old cattle-dealing business, in which traders and farmers built up trust through repeated interactions, relied on personal conflict management. A crisis of trust emerged as the high number of new cattle traders fostered an alienation of business partners.

Both critics and representatives of the cattle-dealing business sought to restore trust by supplementing process-based trust with institution-based trust.[12] Sociologists define trust as institution based when a third party, such as a state office, guarantees the trustworthiness of an actor based on a defined set of standards. Business partners then put their trust in a state-authorized license rather than in their own social exchanges and experiences. For example, the farmer who was no longer able to trust the (new) cattle trader based on his own social experience would rather trust a license from a state institution that certified the trader as "trustworthy."[13] In this particular case, the Bavarian state and district governments instructed the state office for livestock trade to restore trust in the cattle-dealing business through a tighter licensing process. This bureaucratic process institutionalized the bureaucratic category of "trustworthy businessman"—*der reelle Kaufmann*—to fortify trust in the meat sector in general and the cattle-dealing business in particular. This move was especially significant in a business sector that was stigmatized as Jewish and thus untrustworthy.

Still, the implementation of institution-based trust is highly problematic: trust is naturally based on social experiences between actors. A third party, such as a public authority, cannot artificially produce trust between anonymous business partners. A crucial prerequisite for the production of trust is the expectation of care taking.[14] As this is generally missing between institutions and individuals, public authorities substitute trustworthiness with reliability.[15] In other words, to be licensed as a "trustworthy businessman," each cattle trader had to prove his reliability to the public authorities.[16] Consequently, the livestock trade office (*Landesamt für Viehverkehr*) checked the reliability of each cattle trader based on a set of standards. Only those whom the public authorities testified to be reliable were finally granted a trade license certifying their trustworthiness. This bureaucratization signaled a radical change in how trust was built up between business partners in the cattle-dealing business.

In this essay, I examine how the state attempted to regulate business relations by introducing the category of the "trustworthy businessman" as a conferrable and measurable quality. How did the livestock trade office define this category? How did cattle traders themselves—Jewish and non-Jewish alike—respond to the trust crisis? How did antisemitism impact the implementation of trust in this trading sector, and how did it affect Jewish and non-Jewish traders? To answer these questions, I will examine different actors—cattle traders, state authorities, associations of cattle dealers, and farmers—as well as the rhetoric used in public discussions. I have limited my analysis here to the German state of Bavaria from the first postwar years until after the 1923 inflationary peak. Since the trust crisis was not limited to Bavaria, the argument I make here about the bureaucratic category of the "trustworthy businessman" has ramifications for the German Reich in general.

Negotiating Trustworthiness

In looking at how the livestock trade office, cattle trader associations, and farmers negotiated the standards for "trustworthiness," it becomes clear that the state authorities built on process-based trust, which was produced between traders and farmers in repeated daily interactions, in the process of implementing institution-based trust.

Immediately after the end of World War I, the livestock trade office began issuing a number of regulations to officially fight "wild" and "untrustworthy" cattle traders and to vehemently support trustworthy traders. The office argued that particularly the new traders did not respect the business culture and traditions and were fundamentally untrustworthy.[19] Thus, they could not be called reliable or granted trade licenses.[20] This effort took aim at particular types of traders. The office promoted cattle businesses that had been registered before 1910—before the economy was hit by crisis and war. Those traders were called "old trustworthy merchants" (*alte reelle Händler*) and were the principal qualifiers of the certification of "trustworthy businessmen."[21] In addition, the law declared full-time traders more reliable than part-time traders. The majority of part-time traders were Christian pub owners and butchers,[22] rather than well-established medium-sized businesses, most of which were run by Jews, who were not affected by this new legislation.[23]

In addition, state authorities argued that peddlers who did not own retail stores, yet traded in the streets rather than in public markets, were also unreliable. Included in this category were schmoozers, who were cattle traders with low business volume, or who prepared transactions for medium-sized merchants.[24] In general, schmoozers did not own retail stores and would sell their animals in the streets or directly from a farmer's barn.[25] For example, the district government of the Upper Palatinate argued in a letter to all Bavarian district governments in 1921: "A cattle dealer who has no barn does not deserve to be called a merchant . . . he is a schmoozer and he presents a threat to public safety; schmoozers have to be eliminated if we want the cattle-dealing business ever to become trustworthy. We must do this, now or never."[26] In contrast, merchants who owned retail stores (*Ladengeschäfte*) were considered trustworthy. State authorities argued that cattle traders had to apply for a trading license (*Gewerbelegitimationskarte*), whereas peddlers or schmoozers who did not meet the criteria for a merchant instead had to apply for a peddling license (*Wanderlegitimationskarte*).[27]

In general, commercial law defined a merchant (*Kaufmann*) as a person who purchased or sold goods or commodities for profit. In contrast, peddlers were seen as hucksters, and by definition were merchants of a lesser degree.[28]

Thus, public authorities fervently fought peddling and bargaining, which were considered untrustworthy, and above all, antiquated. Instead, they endorsed the concept of a "modern" retail store with fixed prices. Trade under state control, such as trade in the cattle markets or by licensed merchants, was considered reliable, whereas trade on farms, in the peasant's barn, or on the streets was not endorsed. Ostensibly, public safety concerns drove this sort of regulation. Trade outside the urban markets came with the risk of spreading animal diseases, and possibly tax evasion. In short, such trading was beyond the control of state authorities or regulators who could mediate or supervise transactions.[29]

In another crucial piece of legislation, the advisory body of the Bavarian State Office for Livestock Trade prohibited the combination of horse and cattle trade in 1921. State bureaucrats argued that the combination of two "such profitable businesses" would privilege the traders who carried out both, while discriminating against those who focused on only one trade sector.[30] The state perceived expanding and joint businesses as a threat to the economy, and labeled owners of joint businesses as untrustworthy insofar as they functionally controlled a larger share of the market. In some towns, such as Ansbach, horse and cattle traders who were affected by this new legislation jointly protested against it in 1921; nevertheless, their action was dismissed by the livestock trade office.[31]

In general, this new regulation mostly affected Jewish enterprises, because it was particularly common within Jewish families for brothers or in-laws to work together to combine the trade of productive animals, such as horses and cattle.[32] For example, brothers Samson and Siegmund Wurzinger were from the small town of Rothenburg ob der Tauber. The Wurzinger brothers had practiced horse and cattle trade for many years. After the livestock trade office prohibited the combination of horse and cattle trade, the Wurzinger brothers separated. From that point on, Samson Wurzinger operated individually as a cattle trader, while his brother Siegmund independently ran the horse trade. Only one year later, Samson was accused of closing a horse deal in the name of his brother Siegmund, and the district government promptly confiscated Siegmund's trade license for three months.[33]

The category of "trustworthy businessman" was used by cattle trader associations, the farmers' association, and state authorities alike to ameliorate the trust crisis in the meat sector. The German cattle dealer association, founded in 1900, counted many Jewish businessmen among its members. In fact, one of its first chairmen was Jewish merchant Hermann Daniel, who chaired the federal organization from c. 1910 to 1916. The association was divided into several state and district associations, and beginning in 1909, the federal association published a monthly business journal covering the most recent developments in the field, *Allgemeine Viehhandels-Zeitung*.[34] Professional associations could also lobby for their group in political committees, as could the corporate lawyer for the Association of Bavarian Cattle Traders, M. Gramminger. He supported the Bavarian state government and its governing bodies in mitigating the trust crisis after World War I. The cattle trader associations used the same vocabulary as the government, calling for the elimination of untrustworthy, "wild" cattle traders from their association.[35] In 1919, the Association of Bavarian Cattle Traders called for purging the business of untrustworthy elements (*Säuberung von unreellen Elementen*).[36] However, unlike influential state bureaucrats, such as Deputy Assistant Undersecretary Johann Attinger in the Bavarian Ministry for Agriculture, who blamed the cattle traders alone for the trust crisis in the meat sector, cattle trader associations vehemently promoted an inclusionary policy instead. This meant that they emphasized the positive agency of cattle traders, and also shed light on the bias of state authorities in the licensing process. For example, in 1924, the cattle trader associations criticized the blatant prejudices of many courts when it came to lawsuits in the cattle business.[37] Four years earlier in 1920, the Bavarian State Office for Livestock Trade argued that a merchant may not be labeled unreliable based on assumptions alone, but that his (un)reliability had to be demonstrably proven. The legislation further insisted that "speculations and rumors are insufficient." Rather, any accusations and punishable acts first had to be reviewed and verified.[38] Indeed, distrust resulting from prejudices, assumptions, and rumors put additional strain on the licensing process. The corporate lawyer for the Association of Bavarian Cattle Traders, M. Gramminger, also pointed out the bias of state authorities in the licensing process. He strongly condemned the heavy-handed practices of state agencies issuing trade licenses. Such practices resulted in an extremely high surplus of cattle traders in this business. Furthermore, he complained about the state agencies' practice of issuing trade licenses based on social criteria rather than on the applicants' educational background. This policy privileged war veterans regardless of their education or professional background.[39] Gramminger called for a rethinking of the entire licensing process. He suggested issuing trade licenses based on applicants' professional experience rather than their social background. According to Gramminger, cattle traders who had no formal education in their field and no reputation in the business community were not to be seen as trustworthy.[40] Ultimately, the state office for livestock trade supported Gramminger's idea of promoting applicants with a professional background as "trustworthy businessmen." Only those who were able to present evidence of formal education in the livestock business were allowed to call themselves "trustworthy businessmen."[41]

In general, official accreditation and formal education are crucial for the production of trust in any profession.[42] Anthony Giddens argues that it is not a lack of power that results in the erosion of trust but a lack of information. Applied to the cattle-dealing business, this suggests that a lack of information about the background of the cattle trader weakens the production of trust.[43] Giddens's insight helps to explain efforts on the part of the state and the trade associations to professionalize cattle traders by implementing institution-based trust. By imposing external business norms and methods of certification, the state both defined what information was important and controlled its circulation. Thus, the policies of both the State Office for Livestock Trade and the Association of Bavarian Cattle Traders promoted a process of professionalization in the cattle-dealing business.

Biographies of the younger generation of Jewish cattle traders (born between 1900 and 1926) suggest that this policy supported a development that had already begun. While the older generation of Jewish cattle traders (born between 1870 and 1900) was still trained by their fathers in how to manage a business, testimonies from the younger generation attest that many of them had received additional formal commercial training before inheriting their fathers' businesses in the interwar period. Since there were no specialized schools for cattle dealing in the 1920s, they usually went to regular business schools.[44] For example, the second-generation cattle trader Karl Freising (b. 1900) from the small town of Roth graduated from middle school, and then completed commercial training in a Jewish business in Treuchtlingen, twenty-four miles south of Roth. After his graduation from business school, he took over his father's cattle-dealing business back in his hometown of Roth in 1918.[45] This kind of advanced education enabled the younger generation to build up a business that was fully reliant on modern business practices, including streamlined record keeping and expanded territories of business. Thus, the younger generation met all the defined criteria for professional merchants and hence trustworthy businessmen.

Cattle dealers' endeavors to meet all the criteria for the bureaucratic classification as trustworthy businessmen were also evident in the fact that they named their businesses "firms" rather than "trading businesses." In particular, medium-sized businesses consciously called themselves "cattle-dealing firms," such as "Firm Max Aal & Son" or "Bermann & Oppenheimer Firm, Wholesaler of Cattle, Hops and Real Estate." The terms "firm," "company," or even "enterprise" signaled that these businesses conformed to modern standards and were thus fundamentally distinct from peddling, which was considered an antiquated, shady, and untrustworthy occupation.

Hence, cattle traders and cattle trader associations, as well as state authorities, responded to the trust crisis by calling for a modernization and professionalization of the business. This discussion and rebranding was part of a general debate about the need to modernize the business world, which had its beginnings at the end of the nineteenth century and was accompanied by new technologies that promoted rationalization and modernization.[46] For example, merchants who used to travel by bike or on foot were now able to ride a motorbike or drive a car, and thus could conduct business over much greater distances than before. With the expansion of the railway system, goods could be shipped from one place to another within a few days. In addition, refrigerators enabled merchants to transport meat over much greater distances from slaughterhouses to consumers. Similarly, the invention of the telephone provided merchants with new means of communication with customers and business partners. As a consequence of these new technological inventions, business became more efficient, but also more anonymous. This development deeply cut into the traditional business culture of cattle dealing, resulting both in an alienation of business partners and in increased competition among traders. There was little opportunity for the farmer and the cattle trader to build personal and long-lasting relationships. Consequently, attempts by the state offices to make the cattle-dealing business more reliable were also intended to counter the image created by the rituals and verbal elements of traditional cattle dealing, elements that marked it as a "non-modern" business. Thus, the formal category of the trustworthy businessman was introduced to professionalize and modernize the cattle trade, a business sector in which strangers would be able to interact.[47] In other words, the "modern" version of cattle trading was meant to allow impersonal, anonymous, and formal business relationships, rather than the more informal and personal relationships that drove the traditional model of cattle dealing.

Despite all these modernization efforts, the State Office for Livestock Trade still relied on process-based trust in its efforts to solve the ongoing trust crisis. The concept of the trustworthy businessman strongly promoted a culture of established personal contacts in a changing world that had become more anonymous. The trust crisis between cattle traders, farmers, and consumers was ameliorated by relying on the daily interactions between traders and farmers that had proven to be a guarantee for stability and success. Thus, the crisis in the meat business was addressed by only partially modernizing the business.

Antisemitic Accusations in the Debate around the "Trustworthy Businessman"

Regardless of the fact that the majority of all cattle traders were non-Jews, the business as a whole was labeled a "Jewish business." Jews as a group, but also the entire cattle-dealing business, were stigmatized as untrustworthy and shady, aiming to exploit farmers. Particularly in times of economic crisis, the trust relationship between the cattle traders, farmers, and consumers was shaken by distrust that was exacerbated by antisemitic stereotypes.

The public debate around the trustworthy businessman was intensified by antisemitic agitators, who branded Jewish businessmen as usurers, smugglers, and profiteers, and blamed them for ruining the postwar economy. At the height of the meat crisis, right-wing conservatives and antisemites accused Jewish businessmen of intentionally causing high meat prices and called for their exclusion from the business.[48] Johann Attinger, deputy assistant undersecretary for the Bavarian Ministry for Agriculture, mentioned in a 1920 report that such accusations were made at meetings of farmers associations during World War I, where members clamored for the elimination of Jewish cattle dealing.[49]

Individual non-Jewish cattle traders were also among those who put the blame for the disastrous situation solely on Jewish cattle traders. One of them was Nazi cattle trader Johann Müller from the Bavarian village of Altenmuhr. He accused his Jewish colleagues of hoarding fatstock in their barns rather than distributing it to urban slaughterhouses at the peak of the hyperinflation in the fall of 1923. Consequently, the State Office for Usury Affairs (*Landeswucherabwehrstelle*) sent Detective Weigel to investigate the matter. Detective Weigel's investigation proved the Nazi cattle trader wrong. He reported that the business records of the Jewish cattle dealers were in "painful" order, and that they held only productive livestock and no fatstock in their barns. Moreover, Weigel revealed that the Nazi cattle trader himself kept slaughter animals, namely sheep, on his farm.[50]

Even though these antisemitic accusations were part of public debate and rhetoric, in practice, the bureaucratic category of the trustworthy businessman did not differentiate between Jewish and non-Jewish businessmen. The characteristics of a trustworthy businessman were negotiated between various actors, among them state authorities, the Association of Bavarian Cattle Traders (many of their members were Jewish merchants), and farmers associations. All of them agreed on the fact that a trustworthy businessman had to be well acquainted with the business culture and well established in the rural community, and that he needed to run a retail business. In particular, the traditional medium-sized businesses, which personally interacted with farmers and channeled the farmers' goods to urban markets, fulfilled all these criteria.

As empirical research has shown, the majority of medium-sized cattle-dealing businesses were, in fact, run by Jewish families and were located in small towns.[51] Most of them had been engaged in business before the war, continuing a long family tradition, and had known the business culture and the farmers in their *medineh*, the Yiddish term for a business district, for generations: these businesses were marked by continuity and thus reliability.[52] These well-established businesses had produced process-based trust within the business community, laying the foundation for institution-based trust.

In contrast, schmoozers and new traders—primarily non-Jewish war veterans, bankrupt farmers, butchers, and innkeepers—did not enjoy institution-based trust from the livestock trade office. These new cattle traders had no experience in the field, and they did not know the unwritten laws of the business. The schmoozers, on the other side, were simply financially impotent and considered antiquated and untrustworthy. Neither group had generated process-based trust and thus, the livestock trade office considered them unreliable and pushed them out of the cattle-dealing business through state regulation.

On the whole, the well-established medium-sized cattle-dealing businesses enjoyed the full trust of the Bavarian State Office for Livestock Trade, and consequently, that of farmers and meat consumers. To put it somewhat differently: they enjoyed full institution-based trust.[53] With this conservative policy, which favored tradition and old structures, the livestock trade office built on process-based trust in the process of developing institution-based trust. This process-based trust was produced between cattle traders and farmers simply through doing business with one another. The degree to which antisemitism impacted these trust relationships remains an open question, considering that most of the traders were Jewish and were publicly accused of exploiting farmers. According to the sociologist Lynne Zucker, gender, age, and religion may be obstacles in the trust-building process, but do not function as a hindrance to it either. In other words, even if farmers had antisemitic resentments, these did not prevent them from building up a trust relationship with "their individual cattle trader"[54] through social experiences and business transactions. Both cattle traders and farmers were equally responsible for the production and preservation of this trust relationship. Even so-called untrustworthy business methods—such as the *Viehhändlersprache*, or "cow dealer speak," consisting mainly of Yiddish and Hebrew words and often blamed as being an argot used to fix prices clandestinely without farmers' understanding—did not function as exclusionary, but rather were inclusive. Both farmers and cattle traders, Jews and non-Jews, used these business practices. Therefore, this long-established business culture incorporated everyone who participated in the cattle trade into a trust community. Prejudices in the social and/or religious background of a business partner could produce distrust and hamper the trust-building process; however, daily interaction ultimately functioned as the strongest element in its development. Hence, farmers and cattle traders cooperated in a trust relationship as accepted, though not always equal, business partners.

Still, when the concept of the "trustworthy businessman" was publicly debated, contemporary academics such as Houston Stewart Chamberlain, Max Weber, and Werner Sombart offered their "scholarly" interpretations of "the Jews as a pariah people."[55] They all argued, albeit slightly differently, that "the

Jewish trader" was unmodern and presented a threat to the economy and the modern nation state. In other words, the category of the trustworthy businessman stigmatized all so-called Jewish business characteristics[56] as untrustworthy, including peddling, *schmoozing*, and retailing in the streets. According to Weber and Sombart, Jews were "a religious group associated with trade, not entrepreneurship."[57] This approach was also reflected in the bureaucratic category of the trustworthy businessman, which was not only introduced to restore trust in the business, but also to modernize the "unmodern" and "Jewish" cattle trade.

Such antisemitic accusations that Jews were untrustworthy, greedy, shrewd, and dishonest businessmen prompted members of the Jewish community to react.[58] In 1903, Rabbi Max Grunwald of Hamburg responded to Houston Stewart Chamberlain's allegations in an essay on "the honor of the Jews in the world of business" (*kaufmännische Ehre bei den Juden*).[59] Rabbi Grunwald argued that according to history, usury and capitalism were deeply anchored in "Aryan" Roman trade traditions. The Jews, on the other hand, safeguarded their truthfulness, despite the fact that they were only respected if they had money. The penniless Jew was never regarded as trustworthy.[60]

The debate around Jewish businessmen ethics is part of a general debate about business practices in Germany that had its beginnings even before the war. This is portrayed in Oswald Bauer's monograph on "the honorable businessman" (*Der ehrbare Kaufmann*), first published in 1906, with a second edition after World War I in 1919. Bauer claimed that the entire "business sector (*Kaufmannstand*) had become a sanctuary for those who did not qualify for a 'higher' profession," meaning a more academic and bourgeois profession. He also argued that this development had harmed the entire business community.[61] Bauer explained that a trustworthy businessman had to be well-educated, diligent, and considerate, have good business practices (*Geschäftsgewandtheit*), and, above all, demonstrate a solid character. If he met all of these standards, he might even be called an "educated merchant" (*gebildeter Kaufmann*).[62] Bauer emphasized that a noble businessman or merchant had good manners and enjoyed a good reputation. He also came from a well-established, prosperous family, because the newly wealthy tended to show off their affluence.

In Bauer's view, young German businessmen suffered from a lack of recognition of their profession. Bauer complained that, unlike their English counterparts, German businessmen were harmed by German society's obsession with academic titles and military ranks. Unlike these celebrated academics or military personnel who won promotions and recognition, businessmen simply remained businessmen for their entire careers. This lack of respect is reflected in the unpublished autobiography of Aron Liebeck, a Jewish bookkeeper from Königsberg, East Prussia. Liebeck, the son of a provincial trader and then a well-established businessman and citizen of Königsberg, repeatedly emphasized his personal integrity and honesty—portraying himself as a "trustworthy, honest businessman" in his 1928 autobiography.[63] As Stefanie Schüler-Springorum has pointed out, unlike Jewish academics, lawyers, or doctors, Jewish businessmen experienced different conflicts in the "the great Jewish drama of modernity."[64] Jews in bourgeois professions were seen as those who had successfully emancipated themselves, while Jews in trade were criticized for having remained in occupational patterns that resulted from pre-emancipatory, meaning unmodern, times.

During the time of emancipation, it was argued that the Jews' moral degeneration resulted from their preoccupation with trade. Therefore, the famous advocate of emancipation David Friedländer, who came from a Jewish business family in Königsberg, affirmed Jewish commercial integrity to the Prussian Emperor Frederick William III in 1817.[65] Friedländer not only argued for the civic improvement of the Jews in general, but also envisioned a "modernized Judaism" and "advocated through commerce a real, constitutive function for Jewish social existence."[66] Friedländer accepted that "in practice, the merchant must be prepared like a warrior, since doing business is tantamount to participating in a Hobbesian war of all against all." He recognized that the humblest form of Jewish traders, the hawkers and peddlers [Kleinhändler] who must live by their wits, may never be receptive to the moral reconstitution he proposed. Still, he affirmed that commerce would be impossible if bereft of honesty. If anyone, it is the businessman who must be convinced of the dignity of human beings.[67]

According to Friedländer, the acceptance of Jews as equal business partners would result in their integration into bourgeois society as they finally became citizens and belonged to a nation-state. Being trustworthy also meant being loyal to the state; reciprocally, being labeled as untrustworthy excluded businessmen from the much-desired German people's community (Volksgemeinschaft). If a state authority labeled businessmen as trustworthy, it lent credence to the notion that they belonged to the nation-state. As historian Robin Judd has shown, other social and religious groups within German society were also considered untrustworthy and thus excluded from the people's community. Catholics, for example, were seen as "untrustworthy, sexually brutal, and offensive to the liberal vision of the modern vision"[68]: like Jews, they were seen as a threat to the modern nation-state.

Conclusion

The trust Jewish businessmen put in the bureaucratic category of the trustworthy businessman is reflected in files from the late 1930s. When the Nazis tried to push Jews out of the cattle-dealing business, Jewish cattle traders persuasively argued to the authorities that they met all the criteria of trustworthy businessmen. For example, an attorney named Landenberger claimed in a defense letter to the district government of the city of Weissenburg that the Jewish cattle trader firm Bermann & Oppenheimer had been operating for half a century and had credibly proven itself to meet all the criteria of a solid and trustworthy business. Landenberger further testified that the firm enjoyed an excellent reputation and the full trust of farmers from the district and beyond.[69] He sent his defense letter to the district authorities on September 10, 1935; at that point, Jews still enjoyed full civil rights in Germany. Only five days later, the racist Nuremberg laws were passed, classifying German Jews as state subjects, without full civil rights. Sources like this letter indicate that the concept of the trustworthy businessman was introduced as a bureaucratic category after World War I, when antisemitism was a part of public debate but had not yet created distrust between cattle traders and farmers. Until the Nazis defined the trustworthy businessman in racial terms, it had functioned as a regulatory measurement in a modern business world. It became an integral and widely accepted category in the business culture in which Jews and non-Jews participated equally.

The Nazis declared that Jewish businessmen were intrinsically untrustworthy. From 1933 onward, Jewish cattle traders were first attacked and then slowly deprived of their trading licenses.[70] Nevertheless, the concept of the trustworthy businessman did not lose its social significance after World War II. This continuation is demonstrated in letters to the West German reconciliation office in which former neighbors and customers of Jewish cattle traders testified that their former business partners and neighbors were indeed trustworthy. For example, sixty-six-year-old butcher and farmer Heinrich Eder testified to the reconciliation office in 1959 that the Jewish Behr family, which had operated a cattle-dealing business in the village of Mönchsroth for several generations, were indeed *reelle Kaufleute*, or "trustworthy businessmen."[71] The concept of trustworthy businessmen had thus expanded from a bureaucratic category into a social category that defined who belonged to the business community.

This essay has demonstrated the high significance of Jews in rural trade in the German countryside. Numerous studies have highlighted the long tradition of exclusion of Jews from German society, as well as antisemitism in German culture and society. However, the present study has revealed that by including social aspects such as trust rather than purely focusing on economic data, the complexities of Jewish/non-Jewish relations within economic and social exchange are brought to light. Process-based and institution-based trust, as well as antisemitism, often existed in parallel. In other words, Jews were a crucial and accepted part of rural business culture: they were trusted business partners, despite the fact that the stereotypical Jew was widely stigmatized as utterly untrustworthy. The sharing of long-established business rituals that included all participating parties created a trust community beyond religious and social boundaries. Prejudices directed at the social or religious background of a business contact might hamper the trust-production process, but daily interactions generally functioned as a stronger element than bias in the formation and continuation of trust-based relationships among individuals and institutions.

Notes

1. See *Niederschrift zur Neuregelung des Vieh- und Fleischverkehrs in Bayern*, November 21, 1919, Bavarian State Archives (BayHStA), MWi 8073. The licensing process was not new; it had been introduced in 1916 when the economy was under state control (*Zwangswirtschaft*). See Margot Grünberg, *Der deutsche Viehhandel* (Postberg: Bottrop i.W., 1932), 64–67.

2. Monika Richarz, "Emancipation and Continuity. German Jews in the Rural Economy," in *Revolution and Evolution: 1848 in German-Jewish History*, ed. Werner E.-E. Mosse et al., vol. 39 in Schriftenreihe wissenschaftlicher Abhandlungen des Leo Baeck Instituts (Tübingen: Mohr, 1981), 95–116; and Robert Uri Kaufmann, *Jüdische und christliche Viehhändler in der Schweiz 1780–1930* (Zürich: Chronos, 1988).

3. Monika Richarz, "Viehhandel und Landjuden im 19. Jahrhundert. Eine symbiotische Wirtschaftsbeziehung in Südwestdeutschland," in *Menora: Jahrbuch für deutsch-jüdische Geschichte*, ed. Julius H. Schoeps (Munich: Philo, 1990), 66–88; and Stefanie Fischer, *Ökonomisches Vertrauen und antisemitische Gewalt: Jüdische Viehhändler in Mittelfranken, 1919–1939*, vol. 42 in Hamburger Beiträge zur Geschichte der deutschen Juden (Göttingen: Wallstein, 2014), 94–138.

4. Grünberg, *Viehhandel*, 9.

5. Excerpt from *Münchner Augsburger Abendzeitung* [Munich Augsburg Evening News], February 28, 1922, No. 88, State Archives Nuremberg (StAN), Rep. 270, IV, Regierung K.d.I, Abg. 1968, Titel IX, No. 402.

6. Excerpt from *Münchner Augsburger Abendzeitung* [Munich Augsburg Evening News], February 28, 1922.

7. Excerpt from *Münchner Augsburger Abendzeitung* [Munich Augsburg Evening News], February 28, 1922.

8. George Frederick Warren, *Die Erzeugungs- und Absatzverhältnisse der deutschen Vieh- und Milchwirtschaft* (Berlin: Verlagsbuchhandlung Paul Parey, 1929), 28–29.

9. Alfred Rudolph, *Der Absatz von Vieh in der Landwirtschaft: Freier Handel, Zwangswirtschaft oder gemeinsamer Vertrieb?*, unpublished diss. (Landwirtschaftliche Hochschule, Berlin, 1923); Grünberg, *Viehhandel*, 60.

10. Excerpt from *Münchner Augsburger Abendzeitung* [Munich Augsburg Evening News], February 28, 1922, No. 88, StAN, Rep. 270, IV, Regierung K.d.I, Abg. 1968, Titel IX, No. 402.

11. Bavarian Cattle Dealer Association to the State Ministry of Agriculture, January 31, 1927, BayHStA, MWi 8074.

12. See also Lynne Zucker, "Production of Trust: Institutional Sources of Economic Structure, 1840–1920," *Research in Organizational Behavior* 8 (1986): 53; Luhmann has also referred to the meaning of trust in order to diminish social complexity; see Niklas Luhmann, *Vertrauen: Ein Mechanismus der Reduktion sozialer Komplexität*, 4th ed. (Stuttgart: Lucius & Lucius, 2000), 27–37. The licensing process was not new at all; it had been already introduced in the year 1916 when the economy was under state control (*Zwangswirtschaft*). See Grünberg, *Viehhandel*, 64–67.

13. Zucker, "Trust," 53.

14. Ute Frevert, "Vertrauen—eine historische Spurensuche," in *Vertrauen: Historische Annäherungen*, ed. Ute Frevert (Göttingen: Vandenhoeck, 2003), 7–66, especially 56.

15. In philosophical thought, trust does not equal reliability; however, reliability is crucial in the trust production process. For example, a person who has been testified to be reliable can be trusted more easily. Other than trust, reliability is not bound to moral norms and therefore applies for bureaucratic processes. See Annette Baier, *Reflections on How We Live* (Oxford: Oxford University Press, 2010), Oxford Scholarship Online, 2015. doi: 10.1093/acprof:osobl/9780199570362.001.0001; see chapter "Demoralization, Trust, and Virtues," 173–275.

16. Cattle dealing was a predominantly male business; however, there were also some women who dealt livestock. Most of them were widows or wives of cattle traders who worked part-time in this profession. See Fischer, *Ökonomisches Vertrauen und antisemitische Gewalt*, 78–81.

17. Falk Wiesemann, "Einleitung: Zur Geschichte der jüdischen Gemeinden seit 1813," in *Die jüdischen Gemeinden in Bayern, 1918–1945: Geschichte und Zerstörung*, ed. Baruch Z. Ophir and Falk Wiesemann (Munich: Oldenbourg, 1979), 13–29; Stefan Schwarz, *Die Juden in Bayern im Wandel der Zeiten*, Geschichte und Staat 241/243 (Munich: Olzog, 1980); Michael Brenner and Daniela F. Eisenstein, eds., *Die Juden in Franken*, vol. 5 in Studien zur jüdischen Geschichte und Kultur in Bayern (Munich: Oldenbourg, 2012).

18. The number of Jews in the cattle-dealing business was 37 percent above the number of Jews in any other so-called Jewish profession; for example, the number of Jews in the law sector was "only" 13 percent in Bavaria in the 1920s. See Fischer, *Ökonomisches Vertrauen und antisemitische Gewalt*, 33.

19. Council of Bavarian Agriculture to the State Ministry of Agriculture, Munich, August 4, 1919, BayHStA MWi 8073.

20. Bavarian State Ministry for Agriculture to the district governments, Munich, December 28, 1921, StAN, Rep. 270, IV, Regierung K.d.I, Abg. 1968, Titel IX, No. 402.

21. State office for livestock trade, excerpt from the decree (*Rundschreiben*) V2 to all district governments, October 20, 1920, BayHStA, MWi 8073.

22. See Fischer, *Ökonomisches Vertrauen und antisemitische Gewalt*, 37.

23. State Ministry of Agriculture to all district governments, Munich, December 28, 1921, StAN, Rep. 270, IV, Regierung K.d.I, Abg. 1968, Titel IX, No. 402; see also Fischer, *Ökonomisches Vertrauen und antisemitische Gewalt*, 31–45.

24. The Yiddish term "schmoozer" stems from the Hebrew word שמועות (Shmuot) meaning rumor; the verb "to schmooze" also refers to palaver and flattery. In this context, schmoozer means a small-scale salesman or middleman who acts as an agent between a farmer and a well-to-do cattle dealer. Among the schmoozers were Jewish and non-Jewish businessmen alike; all of them scouted potential business partners for a medium-sized cattle dealer. The term schmoozer is still used among German farmers today; see Fischer, *Ökonomisches Vertrauen und antisemitische Gewalt*, 47; see also Susanne Bennewitz, "All Talk or Business as Usual? Brokerage and Schmoozing in a Swiss Urban Society in the Early Nineteenth Century," in Gideon Reuveni and Sarah Wobick-Segev, eds., *The Economy in Jewish History: New Perspectives on the Interrelationship between Ethnicity and Economic Life* (New York: Berghahn, 2011), 79–93.

25. State Office for Livestock Trade decree (*Rundschreiben*) V 19 to all district governments, Munich, July 27, 1922, StAN, Rep. 270, IV, Regierung K.d.I, Abg. 1968, Titel IX, No. 402.

26. District government of the Upper Palatinate, Department for Domestic Affairs, to all district governments, June 30, 1921, p. 3, StAN, Rep. 270, IV, Regierung K.d.I, Abg. 1968, Titel

IX, No. 402. [German original: "Ein Viehhändler, der keinen Handelsviehstall hat, verdient den Namen Händler nicht; er ist nach meinen Begriffen ein Viehschmußer, und mit dieser gemeingefährlichen Gattung von sog. Händlern muß endlich einmal aufgeräumt werden, wenn andere das Viehhandelsgewerbe auf eine reele [sic] Grundlage gestellt werden soll. Jetzt oder nie ist der Zeitpunkt gekommen das zu tun."]

27. Expressed by the district government of the Upper Palatinate and of the city of Regensburg in a letter to all district governments, June 30, 1921, StAN, Rep. 270, IV, Regierung K.d.I, Abg. 1968, Titel IX, No. 402.

28. Oswald Bauer, *Der ehrbare Kaufmann und sein Ansehen*, 2nd ed. (Stuttgart: Union, 1919), 13.

29. District government of the Upper Palatinate, domestic affairs, to all district governments, June 30, 1921, StAN, Rep. 270, IV, Regierung K.d.I, Abg. 1968, Titel IX, No. 402.

30. State Ministry of Agriculture to all district governments, Munich, December 28, 1921, StAN, Rep. 270, IV, Regierung K.d.I, Abg. 1968, Titel IX, No. 402.

31. Minutes of the city council of Ansbach, June 19, 1921, Municipal Archives of Ansbach, ABc R 12/22.

32. See Fischer, *Ökonomisches Vertrauen und antisemitische Gewalt*, 69–71. Though the sources do not indicate any clear antisemitic motivations behind this legislation, it is plausible that the legislation was driven by the antisemitic accusation that Jewish horse traders sold horses to the French army during World War I.

33. See the Wurzinger case, correspondence between the State Office for Livestock Trade and the city council of Rothenburg o/T, 1922–24, Municipal Archives of Rothenburg o/T, Box 976.

34. See August Skalweit, *Die Viehhandelsverbände in der deutschen Kriegswirtschaft* (Berlin: Hobbing, 1917), 1–7.

35. German Cattle Dealer Association, Bavarian section, to the State Ministry of Trade, Commerce, and Industry, Munich, April 4, 1919; the North-west German Cattle Dealer Association shared this opinion in a letter to the Reich Minister for Food and Agriculture, July 4, 1922; see also the draft of a decree on the abolition of war-related economic regulations in the public meat sector, c. August 18, 1920. All can be found in BayHStA, MWi 8073.

36. Excerpt from the report "Neuregelung des Vieh- und Fleischverkehrs in Bayern," November 21, 1919, BayHStA, MWi 8073.

37. The Bavarian Cattle Dealer Association complained to the Bavarian Ministry of Justice that the courts were biased against cattle dealers; association further argued that the courts would often make snap judgments without any solid proof: May 15, 1924, BayHStA, MWi 8073.

38. Taken from the decree (*Rundschreiben*) V2 issued by the State Office for Livestock Trade, October 20, 1920, BayHStA, MWi 8073.

39. Dr. Gramminger, cited in an article by the *Münchner Neueste Nachrichten* [Munich's Latest News], No. 161, April 15, 1923; the German Meat Association, Cologne-Kalk, also criticized this practice in a letter to the Chamber of Crafts, Munich, July 13, 1925; both sources in BayHStA, MWi 8073; see also *Was bringt uns die völlige Wiederherstellung der Gewerbefreiheit?*, in ed. Bund der Viehhändler Deutschlands, Allgemeine Viehhandels-Zeitung. Wochenschrift für Viehverkehr, Viehverwertung, Viehhaltung; offizielles Organ des Deutschen Viehhandels-Bundes und aller Viehhandels-Verbände im Bundesgebiet, vol. 32, Garmisch-Partenkirchen 1925, supplement.

40. See Martin Hartmann, "Einleitung," in *Vertrauen. Die Grundlagen sozialen Zusammenhalts* ed. Martin Hartmann; Claus Offe (Frankfurt am Main: Campus, 2001), 15.

41. Excerpt taken from a meeting of the Bavarian Cattle Dealer Association in 1929, BayHStA, MWi 7819; members of the Jewish community also supported the idea of vocational training for the Jewish youth; see Wilhelm Cohn, *Die Berufswahl der jüdischen Jugend*, vol. 8 in Nürnberger-Fürther Israelitisches Gemeindeblatt (1927), H. 1, 1.

42. Zucker, "Trust," 94.

43. Anthony Giddens, *The Consequences of Modernity* (Cambridge, UK: Polity, 1991), 1–54, especially 33.

44. Fischer, *Ökonomisches Vertrauen und antisemitische Gewalt*, 88–91.

45. Statutory declaration of Karl Freising, New York, to the Bavarian Reconciliation Office, June 11, 1958, BayHStA, BEG 35235, K-1379.

46. In any profession, the process of professionalization is accompanied by social as well as political debates; see Wiebke Lisner, *"Hüterinnen der Nation": Hebammen im Nationalsozialismus*, vol. 50 in Reihe Geschichte und Geschlechter (Frankfurt: Campus-Verlag, 2006), 12.

47. Hasia Diner has also emphasized the relevance of personal relationships in Jewish-non-Jewish business encounters; see Hasia Diner, *Roads Taken: The Great Jewish Migrations to the New World and the Peddlers Who Forged the Way* (New Haven: Yale University Press, 2015), 203–5.

48. Minutes from the seventeenth meeting of the Bavarian Farmers' Association, Munich, July 12, 1923, BayHStA, MWi 8073; see also Helmut Walser Smith. "The Discourse of Usury: Relations between Christians and Jews in the German Countryside, 1880–1914," *Central European History* 32, no. 3 (1999): 255–76.

49. Dr. Attinger, "Die Bayerische Viehverwertung," *Süddeutsche Landwirtschaftliche Tierzucht* 18, 1920, BayHStA, MWi 8073; see also Elke Kimmel, *Methoden antisemitischer Propaganda im Ersten Weltkrieg: Die Presse des Bundes der Landwirte* 38 (Berlin: Metropol-Verlag, 2001), 164. Calls for cattle markets to exclude Jews were first raised by the antisemite Otto Böckel in the German state of Hesse in the 1890s. However, these so-called judenfreie cattle markets failed in the same decade, as they were avoided by farmers. See David Peal, "Antisemitism by Other Means? The Rural Cooperative Movement in Late Nineteenth-Century Germany," *Leo-Baeck Institute Year Book* 32, no. 1 (1987): 135–53; Jacob Toury, "Antisemitismus auf dem Lande: Der Fall Hessen 1881–1895," in *Jüdisches Leben auf dem Lande: Studien zur deutsch-jüdischen Geschichte*, ed. Reinhard Rürup and Monika Richarz, vol. 56 in Schriftenreihe wissenschaftlicher Abhandlungen des Leo-Baeck-Instituts (Tübingen: Mohr Siebeck, 1997), 173–88.

50. Detective Weigel to the Bavarian State Office for Usury Affairs, Nuremberg, September 10, 1923, StAN, Bayerische Landeswucherabwehrstelle, Zweigstelle Nürnberg, No. 64.

51. See Fischer, *Ökonomisches Vertrauen und antisemitische Gewalt*, 51–68.

52. Fischer, *Ökonomisches Vertrauen und antisemitische Gewalt*, 51–68.

53. Needless to say, medium-sized businesses included Christian cattle traders as well. Still, Christian traders dominated the small-scale as well as the wholesale business. See Fischer, *Ökonomisches Vertrauen und antisemitische Gewalt*, 51–68.

54. See also Diner, *Roads Taken*, 5; and Jonathan D. Sarna, "The 'Mythical Jew' and the 'Jew Next Door' in Nineteenth-Century America," in *Anti-Semitism in American History*, ed. David A. Gerber (Urbana: University of Illinois Press, 1986), 57–77.

55. Before Weber published the first version of *The Protestant Ethic* in 1905, Werner Sombart published his monumental works *Modern Capitalism* in 1902 and *The German Economy in the Nineteenth Century* in 1903.

56. See Werner Sombart, *Die Juden und das Wirtschaftsleben* (Leipzig: Duncker & Humblot, 1911), 147.

57. Jack M. Barbalet, *Weber, Passion and Profits: The Protestant Ethic and the Spirit of Capitalism in Context* (New York: Cambridge University Press, 2008), 183; Max Weber's *The Protestant Ethic and the Spirit of Capitalism* was first published in 1905 as two articles in the *Archiv für Sozialwissenschaft und Sozialpolitik*; in 1920, a revised version appeared in *Gesammelte Aufsätze zur Religionssoziologie*. See Jack M. Barbalet, "Max Weber and Judaism: An Insight into the Methodology of *The Protestant Ethic and the Spirit of Capitalism*" in: *Max Weber Studies* 6.1 (2006): 51–67, 1.

58. See also Gerald Tulchinsky, "'Said to be a very Honest Jew': The R.G. Dun Credit Reports and Jewish Business Activity in Mid-19th Century Montreal," *Urban History Review* 18 (1990): 200.

59. Max Grunwald, "Die kaufmännische Ehre bei den Juden: Vortrag von Rabbiner Dr. Max Grunwald aus Hamburg," *Im deutschen Reich: Zeitschrift des Centralvereins Deutscher Staatsbürger Jüdischen Glaubens* 2 (1903). Max Grunwald responded in his essay to Houston Steward Chamberlain's accusations against the Jews in his racist monograph *Die Grundlagen des 19. Jahrhunderts* (Munich: Bruckmann, 1899); *The Foundations of the Nineteenth Century* (Munich: Bruckmann, 1911).

60. Max Grunwald, "Die kaufmännische Ehre bei den Juden," 129–49, especially 142.

61. Bauer, *Der ehrbare Kaufmann*, 7; see also Grünberg, *Viehhandel*, 9. Unfortunately, there is no additional biographical information about Bauer available beyond the fact that he wrote this book.

62. Bauer, *Kaufmann*, 11.

63. See Stefanie Schüler-Springorum, "A Soft Hero: Male Jewish Identity in Imperial Germany through the Autobiography of Aron Liebeck," in *Jewish Masculinities: German Jews, Gender, and History*, ed. Benjamin M. Baader, Sharon Gillerman and Paul F. Lerner (Bloomington: Indiana University Press, 2012), 90–113, especially 104.

64. Schüler-Springorum, "A Soft Hero," 107.

65. Martin L. Davies, "The Business of Tolerance: David Friedländer (1750–1834) and the Civic Constitution of German-Jewish Existence," in *Religion and Politics in Britain and Germany*, ed. Richard Bonney, Franz Bosbach, and Thomas Brockmann (München: Saur, 2001) 53; see also Uta Lohmann, *David Friedländer: Reformpolitik im Zeichen von Aufklärung und Emanzipation: Kontexte des preussischen Judenedikts vom 11. März 1812* (Hannover: Wehrhan, 2013). I am grateful to Kathrin Wittler for drawing my attention to this article.

66. Davies, "Tolerance," 54.

67. Davies, "Tolerance," 58–60.

68. Robin Judd, *Contested Rituals: Circumcision, Kosher Butchering, and Jewish Political Life in Germany, 1843–1933* (Ithaca, NY: Cornell University Press, 2007), 73; see also Tulchinsky "'Honest Jew'": 207.

69. Defense letter by Attorney Landenberger to the district government of Weissenburg, Nuremberg, September 10, 1935, State Archives of Upper Bavaria, StAnW 3277.

70. Stefanie Fischer, "Economic Trust in the 'Racial State': A Case Study from the German Countryside," in *The Holocaust and European Societies: Social Processes and Social Dynamics*, ed. Frank Bajohr and Andrea Löw (New York: Palgrave and Macmillan, 2016), 47–67.

71. Testimony of Heinrich Eder, sixty-six years old, butcher and farmer, to the district court of Dinkelsbühl, Dinkelsbühl, July 28, 1959, Reconciliation File Behr, Hermann, May 17, 1954, BayHStA, BEG 8187; K-1109.

Bibliography

Archival Sources

Bavarian State Archives (BayHStA)

Papers from the Bavarian Reconciliation Office. Various individual cases. BEG 35235, K-1379; BEG 8187; K-1109
Papers from the State Ministry of Economic Affairs. BayHStA, MWi 7819; MWi 8074; MWi 8073.

Municipal Archives of Ansbach

Various papers regarding cattle dealing and "Jewish affairs." ABc R 12/22.

Municipal Archives of Rothenburg o/T

Various papers regarding butchering and cattle dealing. Box 976.

State Archives Munich (StAM)

Office of the district attorney, case of Bernhard Bermann, StAnW 3277.

State Archives Nuremberg (StAN)

Papers from the regional government of Central Franconia, department for domestic affairs. Rep. 270, IV, Regierung K.d.I, Abg. 1968, Titel IX, No. 402.
Papers from the State Office for Usury Affairs, regional office in Nuremberg. No. 64.

Published Sources

Baier, Annette. *Reflections on How We Live*. Oxford: Oxford University Press; 2010. Oxford Scholarship Online, 2015. doi: 10.1093/acprof:osobl/9780199570362.001.0001
Barbalet, Jack M. "Max Weber and Judaism: An Insight into the Methodology of *The Protestant Ethic and the Spirit of Capitalism*." In *Max Weber Studies* 6.1 (2006): 51–67.
———. *Weber, Passion and Profits: The Protestant Ethic and the Spirit of Capitalism in Context*. New York: Cambridge University Press, 2008.
Bauer, Oswald. *Der ehrbare Kaufmann und sein Ansehen*. 2nd ed. Stuttgart: Union, 1919.
Bennewitz, Susanne. "All Talk or Business as Usual? Brokerage and Schmoozing in a Swiss Urban Society in the Early Nineteenth Century." In *The Economy in Jewish History: New Perspectives on the Interrelationship between Ethnicity and Economic Life*, edited by Gideon Reuveni and Sarah Wobick-Segev, 79–93. New York: Berghahn, 2011.
Brenner, Michael, and Daniela F. Eisenstein, eds. *Die Juden in Franken*. Volume 5 in Studien zur jüdischen Geschichte und Kultur in Bayern. Munich: Oldenbourg, 2012.
Cohn, Wilhelm. *Die Berufswahl der jüdischen Jugend*. Volume 8 in Nürnberger-Fürther Israelitisches Gemeindeblatt (1927), H. 1, 1.
Davies, Martin L. "The Business of Tolerance: David Friedländer (1750–1834) and the Civic Constitution of German-Jewish Existence." In *Religion and Politics in Britain and Germany*, edited by Richard Bonney, Franz Bosbach, and Thomas Brockmann, 51–62. Munich: Saur, 2001.

Diner, Hasia. *Roads Taken: The Great Jewish Migrations to the New World and the Peddlers Who Forged the Way*. New Haven: Yale University Press, 2016.

Fischer, Stefanie. "Economic Trust in the 'Racial State': A Case Study from the German Countryside." In *The Holocaust and European Societies: Social Processes and Social Dynamics*, edited by Frank Bajohr and Andrea Löw, 47–67. New York: Palgrave and Macmillan, 2016.

———. *Ökonomisches Vertrauen und antisemitische Gewalt: Jüdische Viehhändler in Mittelfranken, 1919–1939*. Volume 42 in Hamburger Beiträge zur Geschichte der deutschen Juden. Göttingen: Wallstein, 2014.

Frevert, Ute. "Vertrauen—eine historische Spurensuche." In *Vertrauen: Historische Annäherungen*, edited by Ute Frevert, 7–66. Göttingen: Vandenhoeck, 2003.

Giddens, Anthony. *The Consequences of Modernity*. Cambridge, UK: Polity, 1990.

Grünberg, Margot. *Der deutsche Viehhandel*. Postberg: Bottrop i.W., 1932.

Grunwald, Max. *Die Grundlagen des 19. Jahrhunderts*. Munich: Bruckmann, 1899.

———. "Die kaufmännische Ehre bei den Juden: Vortrag von Rabbiner Dr. Max Grunwald aus Hamburg." *Im deutschen Reich: Zeitschrift des Centralvereins Deutscher Staatsbürger Jüdischen Glaubens* 2 (1903): 129–49.

———. *The Foundations of the Nineteenth Century*. Munich: Bruckmann, 1911.

Hartmann, Martin. "Einleitung." In *Vertrauen. Die Grundlagen sozialen Zusammenhalts*, edited by Martin Hartmann and Claus Offe. Frankfurt: Campus, 2001.

Judd, Robin. *Contested Rituals: Circumcision, Kosher Butchering, and Jewish Political Life in Germany, 1843–1933*. Ithaca, NY: Cornell University Press, 2007.

Kaufmann, Robert Uri. *Jüdische und christliche Viehhändler in der Schweiz 1780–1930*. Zürich: Chronos, 1988.

Kimmel, Elke. *Methoden antisemitischer Propaganda im Ersten Weltkrieg: Die Presse des Bundes der Landwirte*. Vol. 38. Berlin: Metropol, 2001.

Lisner, Wiebke. *"Hüterinnen der Nation": Hebammen im Nationalsozialismus*. Volume 50 in Reihe Geschichte und Geschlechter. Frankfurt: Campus, 2006.

Lohmann, Uta. *David Friedländer: Reformpolitik im Zeichen von Aufklärung und Emanzipation: Kontexte des preussischen Judenedikts vom 11. März 1812*. Hannover: Wehrhan, 2013.

Luhmann, Niklas. *Vertrauen: Ein Mechanismus der Reduktion sozialer Komplexität*. 4th ed. Stuttgart: Lucius & Lucius, 2000.

Peal, David. "Antisemitism by Other Means? The Rural Cooperative Movement in Late Nineteenth-Century Germany." *Leo-Baeck Institute Year Book* 32, no. 1 (1987): 135–53.

Richarz, Monika. "Emancipation and Continuity: German Jews in the Rural Economy." In *Revolution and Evolution: 1848 in German-Jewish History*, edited by Werner E. Mosse, Arnold Paucker, and Reinhard Rürup, 95–116. Volume 39 in Schriftenreihe wissenschaftlicher Abhandlungen des Leo Baeck Instituts. Tübingen: Mohr, 1981.

———. "Viehhandel und Landjuden im 19. Jahrhundert. Eine symbiotische Wirtschaftsbeziehung in Südwestdeutschland." In *Menora: Jahrbuch für deutsch-jüdische Geschichte*, edited by Julius H. Schoeps, 66–88. Munich: Philo, 1990.

Rudolph, Alfred. "Der Absatz von Vieh in der Landwirtschaft: Freier Handel, Zwangswirtschaft oder gemeinsamer Vertrieb?" Unpublished diss., Landwirtschaftliche Hochschule [agricultural university], Berlin, 1923.

Sarna, Jonathan D. "The 'Mythical Jew' and the 'Jew Next Door' in Nineteenth-Century America." In *Anti-Semitism in American History*, edited by David A. Gerber, 57–77. Urbana: University of Illinois Press, 1986.

Schüler-Springorum, Stefanie. "A Soft Hero: Male Jewish Identity in Imperial Germany through the Autobiography of Aron Liebeck." In *Jewish Masculinities: German Jews, Gender, and History*, edited by Benjamin M. Baader, Sharon Gillerman, and Paul F. Lerner, 90–113. Bloomington: Indiana University Press, 2012.

Schwarz, Stefan. *Die Juden in Bayern im Wandel der Zeiten*. Geschichte und Staat 241/243. Munich: Olzog, 1980.

Skalweit, August. *Die Viehhandelsverbände in der deutschen Kriegswirtschaft*. Berlin: Hobbing, 1917.

Smith, Helmut Walser. "The Discourse of Usury: Relations between Christians and Jews in the German Countryside, 1880–1914." *Central European History* 32, no. 3 (1999): 255–76.

Toury, Jacob. "Antisemitismus auf dem Lande: Der Fall Hessen 1881–1895." In *Jüdisches Leben auf dem Lande: Studien zur deutsch-jüdischen Geschichte*, edited by Reinhard Rürup and Monika Richarz, 173–88. Volume 56 in Schriftenreihe wissenschaftlicher Abhandlungen des Leo-Baeck-Instituts. Tübingen: Mohr Siebeck, 1997.

Tulchinsky, Gerald. "'Said to Be a Very Honest Jew': The R.G. Dun Credit Reports and Jewish Business Activity in Mid-19th Century Montreal." *Urban History Review* 18 (1990): 200–209

Warren, George Frederick. *Die Erzeugungs- und Absatzverhältnisse der deutschen Vieh- und Milchwirtschaft*. Berlin: Verlagsbuchhandlung Paul Parey, 1929.

Was bringt uns die völlige Wiederherstellung der Gewerbefreiheit?. In ed. Bund der Viehhändler Deutschlands, Allgemeine Viehhandels-Zeitung. Wochenschrift für Viehverkehr, Viehverwertung, Viehhaltung. Vol. 32, Garmisch-Partenkirchen 1925, supplement.

Wiesemann, Falk."Einleitung: Zur Geschichte der jüdischen Gemeinden seit 1813." In *Die jüdischen Gemeinden in Bayern, 1918–1945: Geschichte und Zerstörung*, edited by Baruch Z. Ophir and Falk Wiesemann, 13–29. Munich: Oldenbourg, 1979.

Zucker, Lynne. "Production of Trust: Institutional Sources of Economic Structure, 1840–1920." *Research in Organizational Behavior* 8 (1986): 53–111.

STEFANIE FISCHER is a junior faculty member (wissenschaftliche Mitarbeiterin) at the Technical University Berlin / Center for Research on Antisemitism, specializing in the study of European Jewish history, especially Jewish economic history. Her book *Ökonomisches Vertrauen und antisemitische Gewalt: Jüdische Viehhändler in Mittelfranken* won the 2012 Fraenkel Prize from the Wiener Library in London and the Irma Rosenberg Prize from Vienna University.

Section Three
Intimacy of Trust

9 The Voice of a Jew? Petrus Alfonsi's *Dialogi contra Iudaeos* and the Question of True Conversion

Nina Caputo

IN 1106, IN the recently conquered town of Huesca on the frontier of the Crown of Aragon, a Jewish man by the name of Moses converted to Christianity. At the time of his baptism, he adopted the name Petrus Alfonsi: Petrus to honor the apostle, on whose feast day he was baptized, and Alfonsi to honor his godfather, Alfonso I, the Battler, of King Aragon.[1] This event in itself might have been of little consequence. Since scant evidence remains about the conversion of Jews to Christianity during this important phase of the Christian conquest of Muslim territories in Iberia, it is difficult to know whether many Jews converted, and if they did, under what circumstances.[2] Hence, it is not surprising that no records pertaining to Moses's background or position in the Jewish community remain. But the fact of his conversion is well known, because shortly after his baptism, he penned a carefully crafted anti-Jewish polemical tract that calls attention to this fact. Petrus Alfonsi's *Dialogi contra Iudaeos* circulated widely and had attracted a relatively sizable (in medieval terms) readership already before the end of the twelfth century. It remains extant today in nearly 80 medieval texts, a substantial number of which are complete copies, but several fragments and redactions remain as well.[3] We also know that this text had an impact on subsequent polemical writing. Echoes of the author's appeal to and denigration of rabbinic evidence can be heard in several later disputations and polemical works.[4]

The processes of converting and of writing about one's conversion are necessarily intertwined with essential issues of trust. Socially and institutionally, the voluntary convert must trust that the community to which she intends to convert would accept and integrate her. Such considerations would have been of particular consequence, one can imagine, in a premodern context, when severing ties from one's family and religious community had significant social, economic, and legal consequences that were officially, if not practically, irreversible. However, the mechanics of trust are notoriously difficult to pin down. The sort of trust that comes into play in relation to conversion is structurally analogous to notions of faith or conviction—faith that God will accept the gesture of conversion with pleasure and then reward it; faith that the newfound religious conviction will endure the trials of daily life; faith that the rewards of converting will eventually outweigh the temporary drawbacks.[5]

The Jewish convert to Christianity was an ambivalent figure in the Middle Ages. Embodying the possibility of a utopic time when all would share one faith, while directly challenging well-established social and cultural boundaries, the convert occupied an awkward space in medieval culture. Petrus Alfonsi's mode of self-representation in the opening pages of the *Dialogi* gives a hint of this. Like many texts of this period, this work includes a distinct introductory section, or *proemium*, in which the author addresses the reader directly and explains the structure of the work. Drawing attention to his former position as a Jew poised between Muslim and Christian intellectual spheres, Alfonsi presents his conversion to Christianity as the product of a thoughtful process; however, since he never articulates what impelled him to accept baptism, the decision process is not entirely self-evident.[6]

The opening passages of the work provide a double frame-narrative that introduces and then helps ground the *Dialogi* as an authoritative and trustworthy account of the practical, theological, and philosophical merits of Christianity. But more important, perhaps, is the work the author does to establish his credentials as an expert in Jewish law and interpretation, philosophical reasoning, and the basic tenets of Islam. His authority and authenticity as a mediator between these related but very different theological systems emerges directly from his ability to set the scene. Carefully deployed storytelling tools supply Alfonsi's characters texture and dimension. Through a conversation between Petrus and Moses, Alfonsi provides his reader with crucial information about his education, his community of origin, and his intellectual leanings. Though this text is not technically a conversion account, the frame narratives help invest the author of this work with an aura of trustworthiness as an authoritative source for information about Judaism, Islam, and philosophy precisely because he had renounced Judaism and resisted the draw of Islam in favor of Christianity.

Setting the Scene

To demonstrate that his conversion was authentic, Alfonsi opens with a fairly conventional statement of creed, proclaiming his acceptance of the Trinity, the virgin birth, the Jews' responsibility for the crucifixion, and finally the resurrection. Having internalized these truths, he states, he attained "so exalted a degree of this faith, by the impulse of divine mercy, [that] I took off the cloak of falsehood and was stripped bare of the tunic of iniquity and was baptized." He continues: "At the moment of baptism, in addition to those things that were already mentioned, I believed in the blessed apostles and the holy Catholic Church."[7] But while he self-consciously directs his readers' attention to the fact of his conversion, he makes absolutely no effort to examine—or even mention—any internal spiritual struggles or doubts that may have led him to reject Judaism and embrace Christianity. Nor does he make any claims about the possibility that this work might be used to encourage the conversion of others. Rather, he focuses the reader's attention on the minor drama between the two characters.

Affirming that he was absolutely changed with his recognition of the Christian truth, he goes on to explain what impelled the composition of his book. Members of the Jewish community, he claims, accused him of having left the fold due to a failure of his learning or a desire for "worldly honor" or gain. Therefore, he wrote the *Dialogi* as a rejoinder to his critics:

> I have composed this little book so that all may know my intention and hear my argument, in which I set forth the destruction of the belief of all the other nations, after which I concluded that the Christian law is superior to all others. Moreover, last, I have set down all the objections of any adversary of the Christian law and, having set them down, have destroyed them with reason and authority according to my understanding.[8]

Alfonsi staged the *Dialogi* as a debate between a Jew named Moses and a Christian named Petrus. He notes that the configuration of names is no coincidence: "I have arranged the entire book as a dialogue, so that the reader's mind may more quickly achieve an understanding. To defend the arguments of the Christians, I have used the name that I now have as a Christian, whereas in the arguments of the adversary refuting them, I have used the name Moses, which I had before baptism."[9] Alfonsi's decision to write the fictional disputants essentially as his own alter egos reinforces the reader's expectation that his dramatic evolution might also play out in this dialogue. So, while he reflects on the theological differences between Judaism and Christianity, his method of signaling his spiritual change is narratological and dramatic rather than contemplative or meditative.

Having accounted for his credentials, Alfonsi uses the remainder of the *proemium* to provide an outline of the structure of the book and its arguments—the first four chapters demonstrating the fallacy of Judaism, the fifth "destroying the law of the Saracens," and each of the final six dealing with central Christian theological doctrines. Constructing this text as a dialogue between Jew and Christian enabled Alfonsi to formulate a précis of the essential Christian doctrines that he found most compelling. On a practical level, the *proemium* also serves as a justification for making accessible to a Christian audience a polemical tract that animated Jewish arguments and interpretations. This effort to position himself as an expert in Jewish learning early in the text establishes his credibility as a reliable mediator in and reporter of the fundamental differences between Judaism and Christianity. He gives no indication that he endured spiritual hardship or anxiety about leaving his family and accustomed practices. Rather, as we have seen, Alfonsi states that his anxiety resulted from an expression of distrust in the sincerity of and motives for his conversion by members of the Jewish community. But it bears noting that this text was written in Latin, clearly for a Christian audience, whose support and acceptance he seems to take for granted. So Alfonsi used the opportunity of composing this text to defend his commitment to his new faith, and his introductory remarks allowed him to confront and assuage his readers' possible doubts about his conversion and conviction.

Trust and Conversion

Much of the philosophical literature on trust stresses the social necessity of maintaining a patina of trust in the social sphere in order for society to function productively. Scholars writing in this field also emphasize that trust is mostly invisible, unspoken except in unusual or "nonroutine" circumstances.[10] Conversion from one faith to another in the Middle Ages was a nonroutine circumstance—socially, psychologically, and practically. While trust remains unspoken in matters of conversion, distrust finds clear and frequent expression. I could supply multiple examples of Christian distrust of Jewish converts, but one will suffice here. Writing during the first quarter of the twelfth century, Guibert of Nogent asked, "If a Jew undergoes baptism with a mind bent on financial gain, as so often happens, surely he does not receive remission for his sins?"[11] In the context of Guibert's text, this example of the false convert is a bit gratuitous. Guibert inserts it in the context of a discussion of the efficacy of divine sacrament when administered by a malfeasant priest to show that even divine mercy has limits. But it helps illustrate, as does the case of Petrus Alfonsi, that the counter forces of trust and distrust were directly instrumental in shaping the way that medieval conversion and converts were perceived in their chosen religious communities and in the communities they left behind.

Built into the Christian theology was an ethical imperative to receive and accept those who submitted themselves to Christianity. And this ethical position depended on an unspoken trust that those who voluntarily received baptism did so because they had fully embraced Christian doctrine. The convert's small role in bringing about the ideal of a united and religiously homogenous Christendom came into direct conflict with an active distrust of converts' intentions and convictions. The delicate balance between trust and distrust, between faith and doubt, had direct consequences in the way converts presented themselves and in the way they were received by the members of their newfound faith.[12] Reading Petrus Alfonsi's text through the analytical frame of trust helps bring into sharper relief the author's efforts to certify his standing first as a convert, one who had traversed a great religious, linguistic, and intellectual divide between Judaism, Christianity, and Islam, and then as a Christian, whose interpretation of doctrine and philosophy is both authentic and trustworthy.

Issues of trust are integral both to the work of medieval conversion and to methods modern scholars employ when interpreting conversion historically. What and how we know about individual religious conversion in the Middle Ages, from our assessments of converts' motives to the way we read and interpret medieval statements about conversion, is fundamentally shaped by our assumptions about and expectations of conversion documents. Petrus Alfonsi's differentiation between areas of Jewish and Christian expertise self-consciously and explicitly demands that his reader trust that the fragmentation reflected a complete sublimation of Judaism on the part of the author.

The Construction of a Medieval Convert

Modern interpreters approach medieval conversion with trepidation. Since medieval treatments of this issue are, by definition, politically and culturally charged, their credibility is not always without question. The nature of religious conversion itself, both as a phenomenon and as a narrative or literary construct, poses a considerable challenge to any effort to examine conversion historically. According to Karl Morrison, moderns distinguish between the text and the event, while medievals conflated the two.[13] This difference of perception of what merits attention renders medieval conversion accounts nearly opaque to the modern analytical eye. People entered the Christian faith beginning in the earliest days of Christianity under a wide variety of different circumstances, ranging from a deeply personal dramatic internal transformation to compulsory mass conversion. Sometimes their experiences were captured in texts that do not necessarily meet modern standards of trustworthiness. For many modern readers, any hint that a conversion account may have been written with a motive other than a compulsion to provide true testimony impinges on the veracity of the conversion as a whole. Contemporary analytical impulses among historians and scholars of religion to seek rational explanations for actions—cause and effect—threatens to distort expectations of how conversion finds expression. The difficulty of satisfactorily defining conversion raises the question of whether it is possible at all to make medieval conversion as a phenomenon transparent or even approachable through critical and especially historical study.

Medieval converts (and preachers) had at their disposal a highly developed lexicon of words and tropes for describing the inner transformations of the newly converted, whether within Christianity or to Christianity. As Morrison has noted:

> By the twelfth century, conversion had been established as a paradigm for individual and collective life. The expansion of and consolidation of European society, the development of critical, systematic methods in sacred doctrine (which is also to say, in logic) and the flowering of monastic institutions and

ascetic theology demanded that ways of understanding the paradigm set forth in the New Testament be reappraised in the light of Christianity's long and continuing experience of conversion.[14]

The drive to represent converts in literary form found a corollary in church-sponsored missionary campaigns intended to offer sinning Christians, heretics, and infidels the opportunity to find the truth of Jesus Christ. Indeed, there had emerged a small subgenre of literature in which the problem of conversion or converts figured fairly clearly, including a handful of conversion narratives in which the authors figured as exemplars. As a general rule, medieval Christian conversion accounts map a laborious process, whether as a result of personal anguish or external impediments, in which the subject sought a more complete and pure means of serving God. Conversion was realized in the identification and actualization of an improved form of devotion, whether by accepting baptism, for those turning to Christianity from outside, or by embracing a religious or monastic life for those within the faith. Personal conversion experiences, such as those described by Guibert of Nogent or Hermannus quondam Judaeos, for example, reflect on the crisis of faith that brought the converts to submit to a life dedicated to religion and serving (the Christian) God.[15] Preachers implored their flocks to retreat from their state of perpetual sin and turn to prayer and dedicated service of God. But this message came intertwined with the presumption—expressed clearly and persistently—that the abandonment of sin brought with it the real danger that the penitent might revert to the same behavior she or he had forsworn.[16]

Conversion (along with anxiety about backsliding) emerged as a prominent theme in twelfth-century literature that could be deployed, depending on the context, for multiple purposes. These include its use as a metaphor for universal redemption or legitimation of military or political action, as an idealized form of behavior that others were encouraged to follow, or as a narrative or confession serving personal spiritual needs. The twelfth-century aesthetic favored a dramatic, tension-filled internal spiritual struggle between good and evil.[17] Indeed, conversion accounts were typically formulated as edifying texts for communities of believers. Petrus Alfonsi's rather matter-of-fact treatment of his own conversion in *Dialogi contra iudaeos* as an event worthy of only passing interest marks it as a text of a different order.

The double frame-narrative that at the beginning of the *Dialogi contra iudaeos* provides information that the author believed was crucial for understanding the polemical disputation that follows. The first of these frames introduces the author and his authorial intentions, while the second sets the dramatic scene. The latter of the two, which opens the body of the book, reintroduces the Jewish disputant Moses as "a most perfect friend . . . who had been my companion and fellow student from the very earliest age."[18] Why would Alfonsi go to the lengths of adding these dramatic details, especially as they seem to duplicate or at least complicate information he had presented in the prologue when he explained that Moses had been his name before his conversion?

The double narrative-frame does important work for the author. It provides an opportunity to present an apparently neutral justification for his composition of this polemical work. In addition, it enables Alfonsi to establish his own credentials as a master of rabbinics, philosophy, and Christian doctrine. He cleverly disaggregates his confident, self-referential authorial voice, presented in the initial frame-narrative in the prologue, from the characters' voices that come to life in the second frame-narrative. Alfonsi goes on to explain some of the decisions he took as author of his *Dialogi*. This approach makes a significant stylistic impact. As the author, who takes credit for setting the dramatic scene, identifying and shaping the characters, and molding the structure of the debate, Alfonsi positions himself as a visible and powerful stage manager. But he also integrates himself—or different versions of himself—into the text as the animating force behind both characters and, of course, behind the author. Alfonsi's attention to the process of constructing a book and his effort to establish his own authority as an interpreter of text who could skillfully deploy prooftexts give his polemic a distinctive flavor.

Alfonsi's self-representation in the *Dialogi* provides an important opportunity for raising questions about perceptions and understandings of conversion, medieval self-representation, and our modern responses to and conceptions of medieval religious identity. How might the knowledge that a convert wrote the *Dialogi* have shaped the way that medieval readers understood it? Did this add to the cultural and interpretive authority or currency and thus appeal of the work? Or, to formulate this question more broadly, how might we describe or understand the cultural significance and resonance of the convert in medieval Christianity? Because Alfonsi's authorial voice is both assertive and audible, this text provides an important resource for addressing questions of medieval self-representation, interfaith relations, and the political and social significance allotted to converts during the High Middle Ages. I would suggest that Alfonsi's creation of a literary representation of the convert navigated the uncertain waters connecting a vexingly unrealized goal of a universal Christendom and the political and social realities of complicated interfaith relations.

The Voice of a Jew?

The conversion of Jews to Christianity held special symbolic and theological resonance for Christians. As David Berger has observed, "the fundamental theory governing Jewish status in early medieval Europe was marked by tension and ambivalence—a result of the contradiction between the theoretical goals of a universal Christian mission and an argument for toleration that came close to discouraging Jewish conversion."[19] The successful conversion of gentiles was understood as an indication of divine satisfaction with the secular and ecclesiastic institutions of Christianity. Similarly, the punishment of the Jews, as demonstrated by the destruction of the Temple and the prolonged subsequent dispersion, was understood as an expression of divine displeasure with the Jews' willful blindness to the truth of Christianity. Demoted from their place as God's chosen but preserved in the Christian era as adherents to the first revelation and witnesses to the life and death of Jesus, Jews occupied a distinctive place in the Christian story of redemption. The conversion of a remnant of Jews at the end of days would herald the final judgment, and any conversion before that point would speed the time to redemption. The twelfth century saw an increase in Christian polemicizing against Judaism, both written and oral. By the thirteenth century, the church (sporadically) implemented compulsory sermons, forced disputations, and increasing regulations in an effort to persuade Jews to convert to Christianity. Each Jewish convert, most especially if he was a member of the intellectual elite, was viewed as a tremendous victory for Christianity. Indeed, Alfonsi himself seems to acknowledge this belief by drawing his reader's attention to both his royal sponsor and his exceptional Jewish learning.

Alfonsi's conversion from Judaism is crucial to the drama and logic of this text, though he refrains from idealizing either the path by which he came to his new faith or any sense of triumph for having arrived there. Various narrative or compositional devises alert his reader that his own life experiences rendered him a uniquely trustworthy mediator between Christian and Jewish arguments. Individually and by virtue of being layered, one on top of the other, the frame narratives complicate the reader's experience of this text. The first frame narrative, in the *proemium*, in which Alfonsi introduces the fact of his conversion and his purpose in writing a polemical dialogue, explicitly draws the reader's attention to the textual and literary nature of the work. For example, he declares early on that "I have composed this little book," and again in the following paragraph, he says: "I have arranged the entire book as a dialogue, so that the reader's mind may more quickly achieve an understanding . . . I have divided the book under twelve headings [*tituli*], so that the reader may find whatever he desires in them more quickly."[20]

Until this point, Alfonsi's opening passage accords in many ways with traditional twelfth-century academic prologues: it introduces the author and his credentials, situates the work in a relative time, and outlines the contents, which suggests that he likely intended this as a didactic rather than an edifying book.[21] But Alfonsi almost immediately shepherds the reader into a carefully constructed fictional world in which the subjects of the dialogue, the two friends, Petrus and Moses, engage in a relatively fast-paced, emotionally charged discussion about the most pressing issues of theology. This layer of introduction is, indeed, directly in keeping with the genre of disputation prologues, such as the introductions to Gilbert Crispin's and Peter Abelard's disputations. Both of these authors of disputations set their debates in intimate settings so that the reader is made to eavesdrop on a private conversation. In Gilbert's text, the scene is a monastery in which a Jewish businessman who frequently visits initiates a theological discussion; in Abelard's text, the disputation is set in a dream sequence.[22]

Questions of authorship and authority emerge in various registers as a critical concern for Alfonsi and the characters he depicts. The second frame-narrative (where Moses approaches his dear, long-absent friend) and indeed the dynamic quality of the debate, produce an air of realism that the reader is happy to embrace. And yet both characters repeatedly break the fourth wall by forthrightly drawing attention to the fact that they are characters in a book. In one of many instances scattered throughout this text, early in the first chapter, or *titulus*, Moses suggests that Petrus, as author of the text, should adopt a clear organizing strategy: "If it seems good to you, let us assign individual headings to individual issues, so that once each has been delimited we may advance in an orderly manner from one argument of the debate to another."[23] So, how does this device and the tension it produces shape the trajectory of the argument plotted out in the text? What impact does this have on Petrus Alfonsi's authorial voice in relationship to the voices attributed to his characters?

The creative (and one might also suggest, emotional) engagement and activity of the author is apparent at every level in the construction of this work, and most explicitly in the interplay between the author and his characters. Alfonsi's *Dialogi* is by no means the only medieval work in which an author draws attention to himself as author; nor is it the only fictionalized polemic in which the author identifies himself as a character. It is distinctive, though, insofar as the author deliberately draws attention to the fact that each of the voices in the text represents alternative versions of himself.[24] The result is that Alfonsi seems to relinquish or at least diminish his own authorial control of the text as a rhetorical stratagem. In the frame narrative and in the structure of the fictional debate, Alfonsi represents the polemical text as a reply to direct Jewish challenges. His ascription of responsibility to the Jews for making this composition necessary occurs both explicitly—in Alfonsi's claim that Jews doubted the sincerity of his conversion—and implicitly, through the structure of the disputation itself. While he presents the Jewish character as a representation of fundamentally flawed interpretation, Alfonsi's pointed bestowal of his birth name on the Jewish character also seems to suggest that that mode of thinking and reasoning remained animated in him.

By splitting his voice in this way, Alfonsi places his reader in the unusual and possibly uncomfortable position of recognizing that Moses, Petrus, and their narrative animator shared an educational framework, the same experience of social and religious alienation, a single view of the world, and similar didactic functions in the text itself. But more importantly, his claim of identity with both characters—both of whom he mobilized to demonstrate the truth of Christianity—seems at some level to suggest that conversion is not an absolutely transformative process. It also trains attention on the mechanics of writing about conversion and the medieval inclination toward writing as part of the process of conversion.

The frame narratives that open his text clearly and explicitly articulate a conceptualization of conversion. Conversion, he seems to be asserting, neither dulled his understanding of Jewish traditions and literature nor clouded his apprehension of Christian theology or doctrine. Rather, it provided him the tools to carve out a unique domain of expertise within Christian philosophy. For Alfonsi, the very fact that he was born and educated in a Jewish community within an Arabic speaking Muslim land established his authority as a uniquely perceptive interpreter of Jewish texts as well as an expert in things Muslim. Thus, by representing himself as a rare and precious creature, he marked conversion and converts as invaluable to Christianity in more than the traditional theological sense. Instead, he, as a Christian convert, brought clarity of thought produced by a deep, if not native, understanding of other theological or religious doctrines, a level of expertise those born Christian could not attain.

Once again, this is apparent in the structure of the text. In each chapter, Moses is the first to speak, making it incumbent on Petrus to argue in defense of Christianity. Still, control over the terms of argument and sources of authority always remains securely in the Christian disputant's hands. Petrus, not surprisingly, has the last word in each exchange. The fact that the religious disputation revolves around significant theological principles related to the purpose of suffering in history, the function of religious law and prayer, redemption, and the nature of God and his relationship with man establishes that each argument delineated by Moses serves as a referendum on the relative morality and worth (or lack thereof) of Jews and Judaism. And as Alfonsi's audience would expect, at each turn, the Jewish character uses faulty logic, misguided readings of scripture, and resorts to assumptions about the nature of God and his involvement in human history that, from a Christian perspective, are silly at best and dangerous at worst.[25] Petrus resorts to abusive, derisive statements about Jews and Judaism, yet Moses addresses Petrus with respect, even admiration.

In only a small number of cases are the arguments attributed to Moses rooted in any recognizable biblical authority. When Moses's arguments build on prooftexts, their application is inevitably revealed by Petrus to be deeply problematic. Two examples from the text should suffice to illustrate this point. The first appears in the second chapter, which includes a debate about why the second exile of the Jews stretched on for such an excruciatingly long period of time, Petrus asserts that the Jews' ignorance about why they were forced into exile in the first place (or their willful refusal to accept the explanation advanced by Christians) necessarily obscured the reason for the duration of this exile. In response, Moses cites biblical prooftexts that explain the Babylonian exile and then applies these examples to make sense of the second exile. This argument, which includes passages quoted from Exodus and Lamentations, lays claim to Jewish chosenness as an immutable quality that passed from generation to generation, along with periods of punishment when circumstances warranted. The convert Petrus responds to this argument by dismissing the Jewish interpretation of the sources as self-contradictory, irrational, and inadequate. While Moses initially accepts Petrus's terms, saying "What you say is sound and produces a reasonable and just understanding for the wise,"[26] in the end, he reiterates his understanding—or, misunderstanding, as the Christian author claimed—of the biblical texts on which the argument was based.

Again, in the chapter on Islam, which, ironically, is where Alfonsi's Moses speaks with the greatest relative authority and self-confidence, Moses questions Petrus about his motives in converting to Christianity, rather than Islam:

> I wonder why, when you abandoned your paternal faith, you chose the faith of the Christians rather than the faith of the Saracens, with whom you were always associated and were raised . . . you read [their] books, and you understand the language . . . Indeed [their] law is generous. It contains many commands concerning the pleasures of this present life, by which divine love is shown to have been greatest toward them.[27]

Moses's statement about the appeal of Islam, in keeping with the stereotype of Jewish carnality, focuses on rewards and acts that serve human pleasures, rather than the human spirit or God. Nevertheless, the Jewish character maps out a relatively well-informed sketch of Muslim belief and practice, one that transcends crass stereotypes of paganism and idolatry typical in most medieval Christian characterizations. However, as Leor Halevi has pointed out, Alfonsi places this relatively accurate depiction of the "Law of Muhammad" in Moses's mouth so that Petrus can systematically debunk the Jew's representation—once again—as misguided and thoroughly carnal.[28] Remarkably, the corrective offered by Petrus camouflages any firsthand knowledge of or experience with Islam that Alfonsi himself acquired during his lifetime as a Jew in al-Andalus, only to replace it with a textual reiteration of hackneyed Christian inventions.

Read together, these two examples reflect a distinctive relationship with textual authority. In both cases, Petrus eschews any interpretation according to the literal sense of the text. But his approach is not strictly in accordance with typical Christian readings either. Throughout much of the book, Alfonsi presents Petrus as countering Moses's interpretations and arguments with historical data or rationalism (in fact, he is rather pedantic in his presentation of philosophical reason, especially in the first chapter of the work). What is known to have occurred in history—the march of events as recognized by commonly held consensus—stands on its own without need for external authority. As such, Moses's arguments that the second exile can be understood through traditional exegetical practices that measure recent events against similar events in the past—in this case, applying the prooftexts related to the Babylonian exile to make sense of the second exile—are deemed thoroughly without reason. The same process of evaluation applies in the consideration of Islam. Moses focuses on the human experience of Muslim practices rooted in a relatively responsible rendering of textual authority, which Petrus counters with a presentation of "historical" facts about Mohammad (i.e., that he was overly sexualized, his moral corruption was born out in military struggles and losses, etc.).[29] Here too, the Christian disputant gives preference to evidence derived from the Christian understanding of history and tradition over scriptural authority.

The mode of exchange Alfonsi imposes on his two fictional disputants reflects a distinctive understanding of traditional modes of authority. Emerging from the terms and methods of engagement assigned to the two disputants is a dismissal of more than the theological and practical bearings of Judaism. Through the process of acknowledging the convert's wisdom and being subjected to humiliation, the Jewish disputant rapidly demonstrates that contrary to Christian expectation, he—and by extension, his community as well—has collectively relinquished control of the biblical sources. And it is well known that Alfonsi introduced evidence based on the Talmud, and particularly the aggadic portions of Talmud, mastery of which he also attributed not to Moses, but to Petrus, the convert.

The Voice of a Convert?

Given Alfonsi's status as a convert and his self-identification with Moses, one might be justified in expecting that rational debate in the *Dialogi* would, by the end of the debate, convince Moses that Christianity is correct and just, and Judaism thoroughly misguided. However, at the conclusion of the disputation, when Petrus and Moses part company, neither one of them has been persuaded of the truth of the other's claims. Though Moses repeatedly concedes that Petrus's reason and method of argument is superior to his own, he remains convinced that his own sources of authority and interpretation are superior. He departs still confident in the truth of Judaism:

> Moses: Certainly, God gave a great deal of his wisdom to you and illuminated you with great reasoning power [*ratio*] that I am unable to vanquish. Instead you have confounded my objections with reason.
> Petrus: . . . If you believe what we believe and have yourself baptized, you will enjoy the same illumination of the Holy Spirit, so that you will recognize what

things are true and repudiate those that are false. Now, then, since I have pity upon you, I implore God's mercy to illuminate you with the fullness of his Spirit and to give you a better end than beginning. Amen.[30]

It is the objective of many Christian polemical works to show that Jews are unable or unwilling to accept the truth. Consequently, Jewish characters in medieval Christian polemical tracts rarely come to recognize the truth of Christianity.[31] But by putting an autobiographical stamp on the frame narratives, Alfonsi complicates the issue. As the frame narrative tells us, Petrus Alfonsi himself successfully transcended this stereotype; however, his fictional Jewish alter ego in this text has acquired significant information about Judaism, Islam, and even Christianity, but he lacks the rationality and intellectual discipline necessary to internalize the convert's arguments (even as he characterizes them as compelling). But while this somewhat surprising turn helps solidify the Christian credentials of the Christian disputant, it has the disconcerting consequence of suggesting that perhaps the author's conversion did not result in his full and total transformation. The fictional stage, set by the frame narrative, makes it difficult to tell.

I raise this issue not to challenge the fact or sincerity of Petrus Alfonsi's conversion, but to pose the question of how this text was read and how it is read today. The complexly interconnected personal voices, the dramatic frame in which he set the dialogue, the use of prooftexts, and the effort to establish interpretive authority all hint at a stance that appears a bit defensive to the modern eye, but perhaps not so to the medieval eye. The manuscript tradition of this work may provide a clue. Almost all of the nearly 80 copies conform to one of two recensions and show little deviation from the sources. While a handful of texts excerpt specific arguments, only a small number of these compromise the form and/or content of the text, showing that readers were not merely mining this text for bits of information but were also drawn to the literary and dramatic contours of the work. Perhaps the widespread loyalty among scribes to the source texts indicates that medieval readers saw in Alfonsi's *Dialogi* a trustworthy and authoritative rendering of conversion, in all of its messy complexity.

Notes

1. "I took upon myself the name of the apostle, that is, Peter, out of reverence for and as a remembrance of this same day. Moreover, my spiritual father [godfather] was Alfonsus, the glorious emperor of Spain, who received me at the sacred font. This is why I took for myself the name Petrus Alfonsi." Petrus Alfonsi, *Dialogue against the Jews*, trans. Irven Michael Resnick, Fathers of the Church vol. 8 (Washington, DC: Catholic University of America Press, 2006), 40. English renderings of Alfonsi's works in this essay are quoted from Irven Resnick's translation. "Unde michi ob venerationem et memoriam eiusdem

diei et apostoli nomen, quod est Petrus, michi imposui. Fuit autem pater meus spiritualis Alfunsus gloriosus Hyspaniae imperator, qui me de sacro fonte suscepit, qua re nomen eius prefato nomini meo apponens, Petrus Alfunsi michi nomen imposui." Petrus Alfonsi, *Diálogo contra los judíos*, ed. John Victor Tolan et al., Larumbe 9 (Huesca: Instituto de Estudios Altoaragoneses, 1996), 6.

2. Because of the relative dearth of sources related to Jewish conversion on the Muslim-Christian frontier during this period, the scholarship on responses to Jewish conversion to Christianity and Islam in the community of origin or the new religious community is relatively sparse. Piero Capelli has speculated that disputes within Jewish communities about the nature and legitimacy of rabbinic authority may have motivated some Jewish intellectuals to convert from Judaism to Christianity between the twelfth and fifteenth centuries in Iberia. See Piero Capelli, "Jewish Converts in Jewish-Christian Intellectual Polemics in the Middle Ages," in *Intricate Interfaith Networks in the Middle Ages*, ed. Ephraim Shoham-Steiner (Turnholt: Brepols, 2016), 33–83. In contrast, there is a large and growing body of scholarship examining changing views of converts to and from Judaism in the wake of the First Crusade among Ashkenazi Jews. Ephraim Kanarfogel and Simha Goldin have charted a significant shift in attitudes as expressed in cultural and halakhic terms beginning in the twelfth century about whether baptism—even under coercion—fundamentally altered the convert's nature. See Ephraim Kanarfogel, "Changing Attitudes toward Apostates in Tosafist Literature, Late Twelfth-Early Thirteenth Centuries," in *New Perspectives on Jewish-Christian Relations: In Honor of David Berger*, ed. Elisheva Carlebach and Jacob J. Schacter (Leiden: Brill, 2012), 297–327; and "Approaches to Conversion in Medieval European Rabbinic Literature: From Ashkenaz to Sefarad," in *Conversion, Intermarriage, and Jewish Identity*, ed. Adam Mintz and Marc D. Stern (Brooklyn: KTAV and Urim, 2015), 217–57, which primarily focuses on conversion into Judaism in Ashkenaz. Also Simha Goldin, *Apostasy and Jewish Identity in High Middle Ages Northern Europe: "Are You Still My Brother?,"* trans. Jonathan Chipman (Manchester: Manchester University Press, 2014).

3. For a catalogue of manuscripts, see John V. Tolan, *Petrus Alfonsi and His Medieval Readers* (Gainesville: University of Florida Press, 1993), 182–98.

4. There is by now a sizable body of scholarship on Petrus Alfonsi. I include here only the works that have most influenced my thinking. Charles S. F. Burnett, "Las obras de Pedro Alfonso: problemas de autenticidad," in *Estudios sobre Pedro Alfonso de Huesca*, ed. María Jesus Lacarra, Colección de Estudios Altoaragonesas, 41 (Huesca: Instituto de Estudios Altoaragoneses., 1996), 313–48; Amos Funkenstein, "Basic Types of Anti-Jewish Polemics in the Later Middle Ages," *Viator* 2 (1971): 373–82; Leor Halevi, "Lex Mahometh: Carnal and Spiritual Representations of Islamic Law and Ritual In a Twelfth Century Dialog by a Jewish Convert to Christianity," in *The Islamic Scholarly Tradition: Studies in History, Law, and Thought in Honor of Professor Michael Allan Cook*, ed. Asad Q. Ahmed, Behnam Sadeghi, and Michael Bonner (Leiden: Brill, 2011), 315–42; Steven F. Kruger, *The Spectral Jew: Conversion and Embodiment in Medieval Europe*, Medieval Cultures, vol. 40 (Minneapolis: University of Minnesota Press, 2006); Irven M. Resnick, "The Falsification of Scripture and Medieval Christian and Jewish Polemics," *Medieval Encounters* 2, no. 3 (1996): 344–80; Irven M. Resnick, "The Priestly Raising of the Hands and Other Trinitarian Images in Petrus Alfoni's Dialogue against the Jews," *Medieval Encounters* 13, no. 3 (2007): 452–69; Irven M. Resnick, "La portée historique du *Dialogue contre les juifs* de Petrus Alfonsi," *Les cahiers du judaïsme* 25 (2009): 83–101; Bernard Septimus, "Petrus Alfonsi on the Cult at Mecca,"

Speculum 56, no. 3 (1981): 517–33; Ryan Szpiech, *Conversion and Narrative: Reading and Religious Authority in Medieval Polemic*, The Middle Ages Series (Philadelphia: University of Pennsylvania Press, 2013); Ryan Szpiech, "Rhetorical Muslims: Islam as Witness in Western Christian Anti-Jewish Polemic," *Al-Qantara* 34, no. 1 (2013): 153–85; and Tolan, *Petrus Alfonsi and His Medieval Readers*.

5. Joseph Godfrey breaks these categories down along slightly different lines: "[A] belief is primarily examined as a belief-that, the holding of a proposition to be true. Faith is understood to be a human response to God, essential for salvation. ('Faith' is also used to name a taking of the word of another; or to name a firm assertion or conviction or intention that has a less firm basis; or as an antonym to reason; or to name the divine gift connecting people to God; or to name a set of practices that one may persevere in, as in 'keep the faith.') Trust is understood as an element in human interactions (often unnoticed until it is betrayed), as a relationship the role of which is contested in political, commercial, and intimate life, especially when compared to explicit agreements such as contracts." Joseph J. Godfrey, *Trust of People, Words, and God: A Route for Philosophy of Religion* (Notre Dame: University of Notre Dame Press, 2012), 14.

6. While this text easily lends itself to psycho-historical or psychoanalytical reading, it is not my intention to undertake that project here.

7. Petrus Alfonsi, *Dialogue against the Jews*, 39–40. "Cum itaque divine miserationis instinctu ad tam excelsum huius fidei gradum pervenissem, exui pallium falsitatis et nudatus sum tunica iniquitatis et baptizatus sum. . . . Hora etiam baptismatis preter ea, quae premissa sunt, credidi beatos apostolos et sanctam ecclesiam catholicam." Petrus Alfonsi, *Diálogo contra los judíos*, 6.

8. Petrus Alfonsi, *Dialogue against the Jews*, 41. "Hunc igitur libellum composui, ut omnes et meam cognoscant intentionem et audiant rationem, in quo omnium aliarum gentium credulitatis destructionem propisui, post hec Christianam legem omnibus prestantiorem esse conclusi. Ad ultimum etiam omnes cuiuslibet Christiane legis adversarii obiectiones posui positasque pro meo sapere cum ratione et auctoritate destruxi." Petrus Alfonsi, *Diálogo contra los judíos*, 7.

9. Petrus Alfonsi, *Dialogue against the Jews*, 41. "Librum autem totum distinxi per dialogum, ut lectoris animus promptior fiat ad intelligendum. In tutandis etiam Christianorum rationibus nomen, quod modo Christianus habeo, posui, in rationibus vero adversarii confutandis nomen, quod ante baptismum habueram, id est Moysen." Petrus Alfonsi, *Diálogo contra los judíos*, 7.

10. Philosophers are mostly interested in the social dynamics of trust, focusing on the mechanics of trust between individuals. This yields a body of literature that neglects socially or culturally transmitted values that apply to categories or classes of people. Sociologists, on the other hand, do focus on groups, but mainly from the perspective of cost/benefit assessment, where the recognition of risk becomes the tipping point at which distrust—a response that finds clear expression—replaces unspoken trust. To bridge this gap, Edna Ullman-Margalit distinguishes clearly between trust and cooperation. See Edna Ullmann-Margalit, "Trust Out of Distrust," *The Journal of Philosophy* 99, no. 10 (October 2002): 532–48; Thomas W. Simpson, "What Is Trust?," *Pacific Philosophical Quarterly* 93, no. 4 (December 2012): 550–69; and Linda Trinkaus Zagzebski, *Epistemic Authority: A Theory of Trust, Authority, and Autonomy in Belief* (New York: Oxford University Press, 2012). The most satisfying treatment of social expression of trust is Steven Shapin, *A Social History of*

Truth: Civility and Science in Seventeenth-century England (Chicago: University of Chicago Press, 1994).

11. The accusation that Jews converted for personal gain was not uncommon. Guibert of Nogent, for example, offers the fortune-hunting Jewish apostate as an example of one who is thoroughly undeserving of divine grace. He compares the insincere Jewish convert unfavorably to faithless clerics who administer the Eucharist: "To be sure, countless bishops and men of secondary office have celebrated mass before the people without believing in the inner truth of these sacraments. When they performed these rites and did not understand the value of what, to all appearances, they regularly did . . . they made something heavenly? Not really. . . . As they enunciated the holy words, there was no faith in their minds to accompany their outward deeds. Faith alone is what brings about the secret spiritual transformation. But in this respect this gift from heaven is especially splendid, for it does not abandon people who receive it, although it does escape their false priests. . . . For comparison, if a Jew undergoes baptism with a mind bent on financial gain, as so often happens, surely he does not receive remission for his sins? The Holy Spirit who has the power to sanctify baptism, cannot indulge even the least sin of someone who falsely and malevolently engages with such purity." Guibert of Nogent, "On the Relics of Saints," *Monodies and On the Relics of Saints: The Autobiography and a Manifesto of a French Monk from the Time of the Crusades*, trans. Joseph McAlhany and Jay Rubenstein (New York: Penguin Classics, 2011), 229–30.

12. "Each act of distrust would be predicated upon an over all framework of trust, and, indeed, all distrust presupposes a system of takings-for-granted which make *this instance* of distrust possible. Distrust is something which takes place on the *margins* of trusting systems." Shapin, *A Social History of Truth*, 19. It's important to note, though, that this view addresses a self-consciously rational worldview; in the world of Christian theology, the Fall renders human society only marginally governed by a regime of trust.

13. Morrison is not talking about Petrus Alfonsi's *Dialogi* or texts of this sort, but about more conventional conversion accounts, in which the author struggled with a set impediments in order to achieve greater spiritual perfection. Karl F. Morrison, *Understanding Conversion* (Charlottesville: University of Virginia Press, 1992), xiv.

14. Morrison, *Understanding Conversion*, 8.

15. Hermannus quondam Iudaeos, or Herman the Jew, another twelfth-century convert from Judaism to Christianity, composed a detailed account of the theological doubts and social conflicts that led to his conversion. The oldest copies of this manuscript are held in Premonstratensian monasteries in northwestern Germany. For the most recent discussion of this work, see Jean Claude Schmitt, *The Conversion of Herman the Jew: Autobiography, History, and Fiction in the Twelfth Century*, trans. Alex J. Novikoff, The Middle Ages Series (Philadelphia: University of Pennsylvania Press, 2010). Also see Jeremy Cohen, "The Mentality of the Medieval Jewish Apostate: Peter Alfonsi, Hermann of Cologne, and Pablo Christiani," in *Jewish Apostasy in the Modern World*, ed. T. Endelman (New York: Holmes and Meier, 1987), 20–47; Karl F. Morrison, *Conversion and Text: The Cases of Augustine of Hippo, Herman-Judah, and Constantine Tsatsos* (Charlottesville: University Press of Virginia, 1992); G. Niemyer, *Hermannus quondam Judeaus, Opusculam de conversione sua*, Monumenta Germaniae Historica: Die Deutschen Geschichtsquellen des Mittelalters 500–1500; Quellen zur Geistesgeschichte des Mittelalters, 4 (Weimar: H. Bohlaus Nachfolger, 1963); and Avrom Saltman, "Hermann's Opusculum de Conversione Sua: Truth and Fiction," *Revue Des Études Juives* 147, nos. 1–2 (1988): 31–56.

16. "People rush into holy orders all over the place, and, without awe, without stopping to think, men appropriate for themselves the ministry which awes angelic spirits. They are not even afraid to grab the signs of the kingdom of heaven or to wear the imperial crown; them avarice reigns over, ambition commands, pride dominates, iniquity sits in, luxury lords over, and perhaps, were we to dig under the wall as the prophet Ezekiel suggests, within these very walls we should see vile abominations, horrors in the house of God. Beyond fornication, adultery and incest, there are even some who have given themselves up to shameless acts.... Would that when someone hints that human spirits are given to such abominable passion he could be called a liar." Marie-Bernard Saïd, trans., *Bernard of Clairvaux, Sermons on Conversion*, Cistercian Fathers Series, 25 (Kalamazoo, MI: Cistercian Publications, 1981), 72–73. Bernard of Clairvaux makes this point repeatedly in various guises throughout the sermon.

17. For example, see Guibert, *Monodies; and, On the Relics of Saints*, 29–35.

18. Petrus Alfonsi, *Dialogue against the Jews*, 43. "[P]erfectissimus adheserat amicus... qui a primaeva aetate meus consocius fuerat et condiscipulus." Petrus Alfonsi, *Diálogo contra los judíos*, 8.

19. David Berger, "Mission to the Jews and Jewish-Christian Contacts in the Polemical Literature of the High Middle Ages," *The American Historical Review* 91, no. 3 (1986): 576. For additional discussion of increased missionary activity among Jews by Christians, see Robert Chazan, *Daggers of Faith: Thirteenth-Century Christian Missionizing and Jewish Response* (Berkeley: University of California Press, 1989).

20. Petrus Alfonsi, *Dialogue against the Jews*, 41. "Librum etiam in titulos duodecim divisi, ut quod lector quisque desiderat citius in illis inveniat." Petrus Alfonsi, *Diálogo contra los judíos*, 7.

21. A.J. Minnis, *Medieval Theory of Authorship: Scholastic Literary Attitudes in the Later Middle Ages* (London: Scholar Press, 1984), 7–39.

22. Each of these near contemporary works includes a prologue introducing the author, a putative rationale for penning the text, and an introduction to the characters in the debate. Gilbert Crispin explains that he wrote his disputation down as instruction for other monks because Jews who had witnessed a previous debate ultimately converted to Christianity as a consequence. Gilbert Crispin, *Gisleberti Crispini Disputatio Iudei et Christiani et Anonymi Auctoris Disputationis Iudei et Christiani Continuatio*, ed. Bernhard Blumenkranz, Stromata Patristica et Mediaevalia, fasc. 3 (Ultraiecti/Antiverpiae: In Aedibus Spectrum, 1956), 28. On the other hand, Peter Abelard opens his *Diagogus inter Philosophum, Iudaeum et Christianum* with a frame narrative about three men he saw in a dream. Peter Abelard, *Ethical Writings: His Ethics or "Know Yourself" and His Dialogue between a Philosopher, a Jew, and a Christian*, trans. Paul Vincent Spade (Indianapolis: Hackett, 1995), 59; and Petrus Abaelardus, *Dialogus Inter Philosophum, Iudaeum et Christianum*, ed. Rudolf Thomas (Stuttgart-Bad Cannstatt: Friedrich Frommann, 1970), 41.

23. Petrus Alfonsi, *Dialogue against the Jews*, 47. "Unde si bonum tibi videtur, singulis sententiis singulos ascribamus titulos, ut unoquoque alterna sermonis ratione dimenso ad alium ordinatim accedamus." Petrus Alfonsi, *Diálogo contra los judíos*, 12. The interjections generally appear near the start and finish of various chapters.

24. Though Alfonsi states that he provided the characters with names that accord with his own names and that he wrote as a Christian, he never claims identity with either of the characters.

25. Anna Sapir Abulafia, "Jewish-Christian Disputations and the Twelfth-Century Renaissance," *Journal of Medieval History* 15, no. 1 (1989): 105-25.

26. Petrus Alfonsi, *Dialogue against the Jews*, 105. "Quod loqueris sanum sapientibus rationabilem et iustam parit intelligentiam." Petrus Alfonsi, *Diálogo contra los judíos*, 57.

27. Petrus Alfonsi, *Dialogue against the Jews*, 146. "Sed cum paternam reliqueris fidem, miror, cur Christianorum et non pocius Sarracenorum, cum quibus semper conversatus atque nutritus es, delegeris fidem . . . libros legisti, linguam intelligis. . . . Lex est siquidem larga de presentis vitae deliciis multa servans mandata, in quo ostenditur divina circa eos fuisse dilectio maxima, pariterque suis cultoribus gaudia repromittit ineffabilia." Petrus Alfonsi, *Diálogo contra los judíos*, 91.

28. Halevi, "Lex Mahometh."

29. Petrus Alfonsi, *Dialogue against the Jews*, 161-63; Petrus Alfonsi, *Diálogo contra los judíos*, 100-3. On the development of this discourse more generally, see John V. Tolan, *Saracens: Islam in the Medieval European Imagination* (New York: Columbia University Press, 2002).

30. Petrus Alfonsi, *Dialogue against the Jews*, 273. "M.: Multum certe suae tibi deus dedit sapientiae et te magna illustravit ratione, quem vincere nequeo, immo tu obiectiones meas confutasti ratione.
"P. . . . Quod si tu, quod credimus, ipse etiam crederes et baptizari te faceres, eandem Spiritus Sancti illustrationem haberes, ut, quae vera sunt, cognosceres et, quae falsa, respueres. Nunc autem quoniam super te pietatem habeo, dei misericordiam imploro, ut Spiritus sui plenitudine te illustret et finem meliorem quam principium tibi prestet. Amen." Petrus Alfonsi, *Diálogo contra los judíos*, 193.

31. For example, the disputation in Hermannus quondam Judaeos's *Opusculum* is singularly ineffective as a means of demonstrating the truth of Christianity to the doubting young man. Morrison, *Conversion and Text*, 81-85.

Bibliography

Abulafia, Anna Sapir. "Jewish-Christian Disputations and the Twelfth-Century Renaissance." *Journal of Medieval History* 15, no. 1 (1989): 105-25.

Berger, David. "Mission to the Jews and Jewish-Christian Contacts in the Polemical Literature of the High Middle Ages." *The American Historical Review* 91, no. 3. (1986): 576-91.

Burnett, Charles S. F. "Las obras de Pedro Alfonso: problemas de autenticidad." In *Estudios sobre Pedro Alfonso de Huesca*, edited by María Jesus Lacarra, 313-48. Colección de Estudios Altoaragonesas, 41. Huesca: Instituto de Estudios Altoaragoneses, 1996.

Capelli, Piero. "Jewish Converts in Jewish-Christian Intellectual Polemics in the Middle Ages." In *Intricate Interfaith Networks in the Middle Ages*, edited by Ephraim Shoham-Steiner, 33-83. Turnholt: Brepols, 2016.

Chazan, Robert. *Daggers of Faith: Thirteenth-Century Christian Missionizing and Jewish Response*. Berkeley: University of California Press, 1989.

Cohen, Jeremy. "The Mentality of the Medieval Jewish Apostate: Peter Alfonsi, Hermann of Cologne, and Pablo Christiani." In *Jewish Apostasy in the Modern World*, edited by T. Endelman, 20-47. New York: Holmes and Meier, 1987.

Crispin, Gilbert. *Gisleberti Crispini Disputatio Iudei et Christiani et Anonymi Auctoris Disputationis Iudei et Christiani Continuatio.* Edited by Bernhard Blumenkranz. Stromata Patristica et Mediaevalia, fasc. 3. Ultraiecti/Antiverpiae: In Aedibus Spectrum, 1956.

Funkenstein, Amos. "Basic Types of Anti-Jewish Polemics in the Later Middle Ages." *Viator* 2 (1971): 373–82.

Godfrey, Joseph J. *Trust of People, Words, and God: A Route for Philosophy of Religion* Notre Dame: University of Notre Dame Press, 2012.

Goldin, Simha. *Apostasy and Jewish Identity in High Middle Ages Northern Europe: "Are You Still My Brother?"* Translated by Jonathan Chipman. Manchester: Manchester University Press, 2014.

Guibert of Nogent. *Monodies and On the Relics of Saints: The Autobiography and a Manifesto of a French Monk from the Time of the Crusades.* Translated by Joseph McAlhany and Jay Rubenstein. New York: Penguin Classics, 2011.

Halevi, Leor. "Lex Mahometh: Carnal and Spiritual Representations of Islamic Law and Ritual in a Twelfth Century Dialog by a Jewish Convert to Christianity." In *The Islamic Scholarly Tradition: Studies in History, Law, and Thought in Honor of Professor Michael Allan Cook*, edited by Asad Q. Ahmed, Behnam Sadeghi, and Michael Bonner, 315–42. Leiden: Brill, 2011.

Kanarfogel, Ephraim. "Approaches to Conversion in Medieval European Rabbinic Literature: From Ashkenaz to Sefarad." In *Conversion, Intermarriage, and Jewish Identity*, edited by Adam Mintz and Marc D. Stern, 217–57. Brooklyn: KTAV and Urim, 2015.

———. "Changing Attitudes toward Apostates in Tosafist Literature, Late Twelfth–Early Thirteenth Centuries." In *New Perspectives on Jewish-Christian Relations; In Honor of David Berger*, edited by Elisheva Carlebach and Jacob J. Schacter, 297–327. Leiden: Brill, 2012.

Kruger, Steven F. *The Spectral Jew: Conversion and Embodiment in Medieval Europe.* Medieval Cultures, vol. 40. Minneapolis: University of Minnesota Press, 2006.

Minnis, A. J. *Medieval Theory of Authorship: Scholastic Literary Attitudes in the Later Middle Ages.* London: Scholar Press, 1984.

Morrison, Karl F. *Conversion and Text: The Cases of Augustine of Hippo, Herman-Judah, and Constantine Tsatsos.* Charlottesville: University Press of Virginia, 1992.

———. *Understanding Conversion.* Charlottesville: University of Virginia Press, 1992.

Niemyer, G. *Hermannus Quondam Judeaus, Opusculam de conversione sua.* Monumenta Germaniae Historica: Die Deutschen Geschichtsquellen des Mittelalters 500–1500; Quellen zur Geistesgeschichte des Mittelalters, 4. Weimar: H. Bohlaus Nachfolger, 1963.

Petrus Abaelardus. *Dialogus Inter Philosophum, Iudaeum et Christianum.* Edited by Rudolf Thomas. Stuttgart-Bad Cannstatt: Friedrich Frommann, 1970.

———. *Ethical Writings: His Ethics or "Know Yourself" and His Dialogue between a Philosopher, a Jew, and a Christian.* Translated by Paul Vincent Spade. Indianapolis: Hackett, 1995.

Petrus Alfonsi. *Diálogo contra los judíos.* Edited by John Victor Tolan et al. Larumbe 9. Huesca: Instituto de Estudios Altoaragoneses, 1996.

———. *Dialogue against the Jews.* Translated by Irven Michael Resnick. Fathers of the Church, vol. 8. Washington, DC: Catholic University of America Press, 2006.

Resnick, Irven M. "The Falsification of Scripture and Medieval Christian and Jewish Polemics." *Medieval Encounters* 2, no. 3 (1996): 344–80.
———. "La portée historique du *Dialogue contre les juifs* de Petrus Alfonsi." *Les cahiers du judaïsme* 25 (2009): 83–101.
———. "The Priestly Raising of the Hands and Other Trinitarian Images in Petrus Alfonsi's Dialogue against the Jews." *Medieval Encounters* 13, no. 3 (2007): 452–69.
Saïd, Marie-Bernard, trans. *Bernard of Clairvaux, Sermons on Conversion*. Cistercian Fathers Series, vol. 25. Kalamazoo, MI: Cistercian, 1981.
Saltman, Avrom. "Hermann's *Opusculum de Conversione Sua*: Truth and Fiction." *Revue des études juives* 147, nos. 1–2 (1988): 31–56.
Schmitt, Jean Claude. *The Conversion of Herman the Jew: Autobiography, History, and Fiction in the Twelfth Century*. Translated by Alex J. Novikoff, The Middle Ages Series. Philadelphia: University of Pennsylvania Press, 2010.
Septimus, Bernard. "Petrus Alfonsi on the Cult at Mecca." *Speculum* 56, no. 3 (1981): 517–33.
Shapin, Steven. *A Social History of Truth: Civility and Science in Seventeenth-Century England*. Chicago: University of Chicago Press, 1994.
Simpson, Thomas W. "What Is Trust?" *Pacific Philosophical Quarterly* 93, no. 4 (2012): 550–69.
Szpiech, Ryan. *Conversion and Narrative: Reading and Religious Authority in Medieval Polemic*. The Middle Ages Series. Philadelphia: University of Pennsylvania Press, 2013.
———. "Rhetorical Muslims: Islam as Witness in Western Christian Anti-Jewish Polemic." *Al-Qantara* 34, no. 1 (2013): 153–85
Tolan, John V. *Petrus Alfonsi and His Medieval Readers*. Gainesville: University of Florida Press, 1993.
———. *Saracens: Islam in the Medieval European Imagination*. New York: Columbia University Press, 2002.
Ullmann-Margalit, Edna. "Trust Out of Distrust," *The Journal of Philosophy* 99, no. 10 (2002): 532–48.
Zagzebski, Linda Trinkaus. *Epistemic Authority: A Theory of Trust, Authority, and Autonomy in Belief*. New York: Oxford University Press, 2012.

NINA CAPUTO, Associate Professor in the Department of History at the University of Florida, is a scholar of medieval Jewish history and interfaith relations in medieval Europe. She is author of *Nahmanides in Medieval Catalonia: History, Community, Messianism* and *Debating Truth: The Barcelona Disputation of 1263, a Graphic History* (illustrated by Liz Clarke), and editor (with Andrea Sterk) of *Faithful Narratives: Historians, Religion, and the Challenge of Objectivity*.

10 A Return to Credibility? The Rehabilitation of Repentant Apostates in Medieval Ashkenaz

Rachel Furst

ON THE THIRTEENTH of ʾAv in the year 5058 (1298), a wave of anti-Jewish violence sweeping through Franconia and the neighboring vicinities reached the city of Würzburg. Incited by a German nobleman named Rindfleisch, who had been stirring up crowds throughout the summer with allegations of host desecration, the citizens of Würzburg joined gangs of murderous knights to massacre nearly 900 Jews, according to contemporaneous accounts, earning the city the moniker "ʿIr Ha-Damim" (City of Blood). In addition to 800 Jewish residents of the city, the Nürnberger Memorbuch records the names of 100 visiting Jews who were caught up in the deadly violence;[1] together, they comprised the largest group of victims from among the 130 German Jewish communities that were affected by these events, known as the Rindfleisch Massacres.[2] Among the unfortunate visitors was Simeon ben Jacob, a resident of Worms who had come to Würzburg to pay and collect business debts.[3] Following the massacre, three witnesses reported that they had seen Simeon's dead body, and on the basis of these testimonies, the Jewish court in Worms declared Simeon's wife a widow and granted her permission to remarry, which she soon did.

Sometime later, the father of Simeon's widow, the scholar Rabbi Yakar Ha-Kohen, appeared as his daughter's legal representative before a second Jewish court in Speyer. His intention was to collect her *ketubah* payment (i.e., the value of her marriage contract) from Simeon's estate, only part of which had been allocated to her in Worms.[4] But this time, the widow's claim was contested by Simeon's heir, apparently his son from a previous marriage, who was represented by his own agent, a well-known scholar by the name of Rabbi Yedidyah ben Israel of Nürnberg.[5] In the name of the heir, Rabbi Yedidyah asserted that the witnesses to Simeon's death in Würzburg were invalid because they had been apostates living as Christians at the time of the massacre, which discredited their testimony even though they subsequently repented. Therefore, he maintained, the widow had no legal claim to her *ketubah* monies and indeed could not properly be considered a widow at all. This charge was designed to afford the heir himself access to the dead man's assets, but if substantiated, Rabbi Yedidyah's assertion had the further potential not only to deny the widow her pension but also to void her new marriage and render that relationship highly transgressive. A protracted court battle ensued, involving judges, scholars, and rabbinic decisors from across Germany, Austria, and as far away as northern Spain.

The testimony of the witnesses, the original court ruling from Worms, and three sets of counterclaims written and presented by the representatives of the widow and the heir have been preserved in *Sefer Zikhron Yehudah*, an anthology of responsa collected by Rabbi Judah ben Asher of Toledo, son of the famous Rabbi Asher ben Yehiel (known as "Rosh," c. 1250–1327).[6] The learned opinions of several prominent scholars that were solicited by the court in Speyer and the ultimate ruling of the Speyer *beit din* were recorded there as well. As one of the judges on the Speyer court, it is likely that Rabbi Asher brought this complete file with him when he emigrated from Germany to Spain several years after the case in question, and thus the records made their way to the hands of his son, Rabbi Judah.[7] Indeed, the dossier also contains a long responsum penned by Rabbi Asher himself when the orphan's agent subsequently appealed the ruling of the court in Speyer, as well as the text of that passionately argued and long-winded appeal.[8] In addition to the materials collected in the dossier and published by Rabbi Asher's son, another response to the case was composed and published elsewhere by Rabbi Hayim ben Isaac "'Or Zaru'a" of Wiener Neustadt, and later Mainz;[9] and yet another by Rabbi Solomon ben Abraham ibn Adret of Barcelona.[10] This collection of materials comprises one of the most complete surviving Jewish court files from medieval Ashkenaz, which renders it extremely valuable for understanding the way that judicial institution functioned, procedurally and politically.[11] It also demonstrates that this case captured the attention of many prominent thirteenth-century Jewish scholars and raises questions as to why it did so.

On the surface, the legal battle between Simeon ben Jacob's widow and his heir was a case of contested property, the sort of case that typified Jewish court business in medieval Ashkenaz, at least as far as we can ascertain from the surviving records. But in this instance, the case hinged on the status of witnesses who were liminal Jews—that is, Jews who had lived as non-Jews, and then as Jews again—and so it quickly became a case about the parameters of credibility for witnesses in Jewish courts, the relative weight of knowledge versus legally sanctioned authority, and who was a Jew, or at least who was allowed to speak as one. The rhetorical tone of the legal opinions previously mentioned indicates that for the scholars and jurists involved, this case was an opportunity to stake out the borderlines of the Jewish community and to define its attitude toward those who traversed those boundaries. Indeed, it seems as though the scholars whose legal opinions were solicited by the Speyer *beit din*, as well as those who responded on their own initiative, were drawn to this case precisely because of its urgency: apostasy and especially the treatment of repentant apostates was a formidable challenge for the Jewish communities of Germany and Northern France in the late thirteenth and early fourteenth centuries, as several historians have convincingly demonstrated.[12]

This chapter joins a growing body of scholarship that elucidates the complicated and often ambivalent attitude of medieval Jews toward coreligionists who failed to live up to the Ashkenazi ideal of martyrdom in the face of religious persecution. Through a close reading of the materials in the case file from Speyer, it will also examine the ways in which competing attitudes toward establishing the legal credibility of witnesses in Jewish courts reflected medieval Jews' struggles to negotiate internal attrition as well as the theological and political threat of a rival religion. Death claims in Jewish law bring the distinction between knowledge and authority into sharp relief, and the added element of religiously, socially, and legally marginal witnesses involved in the legal battle between Simeon ben Jacob's widow and his heir forced the advocates, judges, and jurists involved with this case to grapple head on with questions of truth, trust, and the law.

To appreciate the legal maneuvers and social sensitivities of thirteenth-century German-Jewish scholars, a bit of historical context as well as Talmudic background is in order. As the unexpected violence of the First Crusade gave way to official, legislated anti-Jewish policy during the course of the twelfth century, Western Europe witnessed an intensification of Christian efforts to convert the Jews in their midst. And despite the popularization of the *kiddush ha-Shem* (martyrdom) ideal amongst the Jews of medieval Ashkenaz, which demanded religious fealty to the point of death, apostasy was a reality of medieval Jewish life, in Northern Europe as well as in Spain. Scholars have estimated that in German-speaking lands, voluntary Jewish conversions reached their peak in the mid-thirteenth century.[13] Simultaneously, missionary zeal and religiously inspired violence culminated, on more than a few occasions, in the coerced baptism of unwilling individuals and even whole communities. Although many of these conversions were short-lived, the return or relapse of Jewish converts became a charged issue for both Jews and Christians.

In an oft-quoted article published in the 1950s, Jacob Katz contended that the attitude of medieval German and French Jewish jurists toward apostates in general and repentant apostates in particular was remarkably accepting, especially when contrasted with the rulings of eastern European authorities of later generations.[14] Furthermore, he argued that the application of the Talmudic statement "ʾAf ʿal pi she-hata, Yisraʾel hu" (in loose translation, "A sinful Jew is still a Jew") to converts by the eleventh-century French authority Rabbi Solomon ben Isaac (hereafter, Rashi) typified the stance of Ashkenazi authorities to Jews who abandoned Judaism and certainly to those who returned to the Jewish fold.[15] Rashi's use of the axiom assumes that Jewishness is inborn and inviolable. According to Katz, this understanding informed Ashkenazi rulings that a marriage contracted by an apostate was a valid marriage, that it was prohibited to lend to an apostate at interest, and that an apostate who repented was allowed to participate in ritual life and even serve as prayer leader, just as he had before his conversion.[16]

Yet in recent years, historians have challenged Katz's assessment, arguing that Rashi's approach was not universally accepted.[17] They have demonstrated that over the course of the Middle Ages, circumstances in Germany and France, including a tightening of Church policy concerning relapsed converts and those who assisted them, led Rashi's successors to reconsider and adapt Jewish legal positions regarding apostates in a variety of halakhic realms. Many authorities ruled that mourning customs were not to be observed by family members on the death of an apostate.[18] Female apostates were assumed to be motivated by sexual, as well as religious, infidelity and consequently were often precluded from returning to preexisting marriages and normative roles within the Jewish community.[19] And although baptism was formally of no halakhic significance, by the thirteenth century, popular practice—and the rulings of several prominent scholars—demanded that the returning convert undergo a purification rite reminiscent of a (re)conversion ceremony.[20]

By contrast, the attitudes of medieval scholars toward the legal requirements for witnesses in Jewish courts remained relatively constant. Jewish law requires that two adult male witnesses provide testimony in any civil or criminal case that carries punitive consequences; indeed, the Talmudic sages understood this requirement to be a tenet of biblical law.[21] Thus, they barred women from testifying in such cases, as well as minors, slaves, the mentally disabled, and non-Jews[22]—anyone who was not considered a full-fledged member of the community from a legal vantage point. Some adult males were also disqualified, among them serious violators of Torah law and particularly those who were subject to capital or corporal punishment for their transgressions.[23] The Talmudic sages, as well as later medieval authorities, debated the acceptability of testimony provided by individuals who were known to flout sexual regulations (*he-hashud ʿal ha-ʿarayot*) or to categorically deny the validity of certain religious strictures (*mumar le-hakhʿis*), but all agreed that individuals who committed financial violations (*rasha de-hamas*) and those who gave in to uncontrolled cravings (*mumar ʾokhel neveilot le-teʾavon*) thereby lost their credibility to serve as witnesses, ostensibly because they had proven themselves untrustworthy and of dubious moral character.[24] Medieval authorities barred all of these transgressors from testifying,[25] with few exceptions.[26] To the minds of medieval rabbinic decisors, Jewish converts to Christianity had flagrantly violated Torah law merely by professing another faith and surely violated many tenets of halakhic Judaism in the course of their lives as Christians. Thus, regardless of whether or not they believed apostates retained their inherent Jewishness, it was self-evident to medieval scholars that such individuals could not serve as witnesses in Jewish courts. With regard to testimony, the real question for medieval decisors concerned converts who ultimately renounced their adopted faith and rejoined the Jewish community. Did such penitents thereby regain credibility to testify about events they had witnessed while Christian?

A responsum attributed to Rashi, in which the author distinguished between the credibility of individuals who had agreed to baptism under duress and those who had done so willingly, set the tone for subsequent discussions. Although the precise circumstances of the case Rashi addressed in the following lines are unclear, his ruling was rarely challenged by his successors:

> And [regarding what] you asked, whether their testimony is testimony in light of [the fact] that they were coerced [to live as non-Jews] at the time. I respond to that: it all depends on the witnesses [themselves]. If it was established in court that the witnesses behaved in accordance with the law of Moses in secret and were not suspected of willfully committing those transgressions which the non-Jews coerced them to do [publicly], and among themselves they were God-fearing and lamented and grieved over their coercion and begged forgiveness—the testimony of people of that type should be accepted, and their testimony is valid. But if it was established that they behaved with abandon, [committing] transgressions that they were not coerced [to commit]—[in such a case,] even though they subsequently repented righteously, with all their hearts and all their souls and all their strength, they are not credible to testify now [regarding] what they saw in those days. . . . This is the principle: anyone who is qualified at both "beginning" and "end" is qualified; and [anyone] who is unqualified at either "beginning" or "end" is unqualified. And these witnesses, they were unqualified at the beginning.[27]

According to Rashi, a forced convert did not lose his basic credibility and, when he returned to the Jewish community, was allowed to serve as a credible witness on all matters. In contrast, converts known to have violated Jewish law without being coerced to do so were certainly encouraged to repent, but their penitence did not fully rehabilitate their legal credibility. As Katz himself pointed out, Rashi's seemingly clear distinction between coerced and deliberate transgression actually underscores the slippage between the two: according to Rashi, willing apostates were those who ultimately yielded to the religion that was forced on them. Although he was willing to clear the names of apostates who brought proof of their attempts to observe *halakhah* privately during their time as Christians, Rashi did not clarify on a practical level how one might determine whether a particular transgressive act was undertaken willingly or coercively. Consequently, as I will discuss further, one of the most intensely contested facets of the Simeon ben Jacob case concerned the nature of the repentant witnesses' apostasy.

Later scholars' skepticism concerning testimony provided by former apostates seemed to stem largely from their general suspicion of such individuals: that they had not truly repented and that they were, in fact, shady characters and opportunists who inhabited a gray zone between religions, appearing one day as Jews and the next day as Christians. An oft-quoted ruling by Rabbi Meir ben Barukh of Rothenburg (c. 1220–93) was penned in response to just such a person, whose claim to have encountered a man who had been presumed dead threatened to render that man's wife an eternal straw-widow:

> And [such a] transgressor is forever disqualified, until it becomes clear that he repented completely. . . . And certainly this abominable one, and others like him, who immerse [in purifying waters] with a forbidden creature in their hands—and it is well-known that they present themselves as Jews only so that they might be given [alms] to eat as well as an opportunity to steal and to commit all their abominations—he is certainly disqualified from testifying.[28]

As Rabbi Meir's words suggest, some decisors—possibly reflecting popular sentiment—adopted a stance toward those who had once chosen or succumbed to baptism that amounted to "guilty until proven innocent."[29]

In spite of rabbinic concerns about the trustworthiness of such marginal figures, the Jewish courts were acutely dependent on the testimony of individuals living outside the Jewish community in cases such as that of Simeon ben Jacob. Often, the only witnesses to instances of highway robbery and roadside accidents, not to mention anti-Jewish violence such as the Rindfleisch Massacres, were non-Jews or apostates living as non-Jews—and their testimony constituted the only evidence of a man's death, which was needed, for example, to release his wife from the bonds of her marriage and enable her to remarry.[30]

Motivated by the anguish of women trapped in dead marriages and by the breakdown of social order that was likely to result from what were often psychologically, emotionally, and financially untenable situations, the Talmudic sages had long previously adopted a policy toward these "chained women" (ʿagunot in halakhic parlance) that they themselves termed "lenient," thus emphasizing the responsibility of jurists and judges to seek solutions on these women's behalf. Specifically, the sages mandated a relaxation of the usual laws governing testimony and evidence, in the hopes that this would increase the number of confirmed deaths and thereby resolve many ʿagunah cases. For example, the Mishnah states clearly that certain individuals normally disqualified from testifying in a court of Jewish law—including women, slaves, and minors—are nonetheless credible to report a man's death and thereby free his widow to remarry. Similarly, the Mishnah asserts that various types of testimony and evidence—the testimony of a single witness, testimony obtained through hearsay, written (as opposed to oral) testimony, circumstantial evidence—that would normally be barred from a court of law were nonetheless accepted by the sages as a means of determining a husband's death and releasing his widow.[31] Yet in spite of their markedly lenient attitude in this realm and the legal safeguards they put in place to avoid disastrous mistakes,[32] the sages were not willing to accept testimony from just anyone. As a rule, the Talmudic rabbis accepted testimony on behalf of ʿagunot from individuals who had violated rabbinic law, much as they accepted this type of testimony from women, but they were less clear about the acceptability of testimony from individuals who had violated Torah law itself.[33] In considering the validity of apostates' testimony in ʿagunah situations, medieval scholars were mindful of the fact that the sages deemed even non-Jews to be potentially valid sources of information concerning a person's demise. Surely, argued some scholars, the word of a converted Jew was not less credible than the word of a non-Jew. But others pointed out that a non-Jew was considered credible only if he did not realize the legal significance of his words or intend for them to bear any legal weight—in Talmudic parlance, if he "spoke in innocence" (*hesiah lefi tumʾo*).[34] A converted Jew—or any other Jewish transgressor—may, then, be less credible than a non-Jew, for as someone familiar with the Jewish legal system, he might indeed fabricate an innocent-sounding remark in order to malign Jewish law and its adherents or to manipulate the law to his own advantage.[35] In light of this concern and their general skepticism regarding the trustworthiness of individuals who had converted to Christianity, some medieval scholars barred apostates (including those who subsequently repented) from testifying even in ʿagunah situations.

With these attitudes and legal traditions in mind, let us now return to the court case surrounding the death of Simeon ben Jacob. For most of the judges involved and the legal scholars consulted, the case essentially hung on whether the Würzburg witnesses had apostatized voluntarily or under duress. Before examining the positions expressed by the adjudicators, however, I want to consider how the legal representatives themselves constructed the case and what their arguments suggest about their own attitudes toward the credibility of apostates.

Rabbi Yakar Ha-Kohen, the widow's father and representative, initially attempted to build his daughter's case on her own credibility. In the first of his three written arguments, after briefly asserting the witnesses' qualifications, he proposed assessing the facts in accordance with the Talmudic model in which a woman arrives in court to report her husband's death. The Mishnah rules that in such a case, the woman herself is credible and her report is admitted;[36] consequently, she is free to remarry, and she is also granted her *ketubah* monies.[37] Thus Rabbi Yakar argued that since the *beit din* in Worms had already heard testimony concerning Simeon ben Jacob's death and granted his widow permission to remarry, she subsequently arrived in the Speyer court (albeit by proxy) as though bearing the report of her husband's death, and on the basis of her report alone, the Speyer court should release her *ketubah*, irrespective of other witnesses or evidence. Both the heir's representative and the scholars who issued rulings on the case dismissed Rabbi Yakar's line of reasoning, insisting that a wife's credibility to report her husband's death is limited to cases in which she herself witnessed his demise,[38] and by all accounts, Simeon's widow had not been with him in Würzburg when he was killed. Although he failed to convince anyone to treat Simeon's widow as a woman reporting her own husband's death, the legal maneuver attempted by Rabbi Yakar is significant because it suggests that he perceived the widow, who was not an eyewitness, to be more solidly credible than any of the three apostates who had actually seen Simeon's body—or at least that he thought others might find her to be so.

In a second maneuver (or act of desperation), Rabbi Yakar argued that proof of Simeon's death lay in the fact that his name was included on a list of martyrs that had been recited since the massacre in communities across the region.[39] The liturgical recitation constituted, to his mind, what other medieval jurists might have called "fama," or proof by reputation.[40] If anyone in the various communities believed Simeon to be alive, surely they would have protested his inclusion on such a memorial list. Yet as the heir's representative and several of the consulted scholars pointed out, liturgical memorializing following a massacre was hardly solid proof—on more than one occasion, someone on a memorial list had suddenly walked through the door.[41] Indeed, given that he did not offer any halakhic rationale for this form of evidence, Rabbi Yakar's use of the memorial list in his opening arguments seems more like an attempt to divert attention from the apostate witnesses than to provide a serious alternative to their testimony.[42]

As a last resort, the widow's representative called on his three witnesses—the repentant apostates Seligman, Jonathan, and an unnamed young man—each of whom claimed to have seen Simeon's dead body lying on the ground in front of a certain house. These three witnesses had also testified to seeing the dead bodies of numerous other Würzburg victims whose wives had been released and remarried on the basis of their reports. To shore up their credibility, Rabbi Yakar noted that the Worms court had already accepted their testimonies (in the presence, as it turns out, of the heir's representative, himself) and also brought character witnesses to attest to the lineage and upstanding comportment of Seligman and Jonathan prior to the violence. Rabbi Yakar conceded that the anonymous third witness was indeed an unknown entity but argued that if there was no way to ascertain his piety prior to the violence or thereafter, at least there was no reason to question his religious conduct. Although Rabbi Yakar maintained throughout that the testimony of his three witnesses was valid and certainly admissible for the purposes of releasing an 'agunah, the fact that he grasped at dubious arguments concerning the widow's credibility to report her husband's death and questionable sources of evidence, such as the memorial lists, suggests, at the very least, that he was unsure whether the judges and jurists would share his assessment of the witnesses' legitimacy. Similarly, the fact that he did not introduce the third witness in his first or second written arguments, but only in his third, intimates that he himself questioned the efficacy of that young man's deposition.

The orphan's representative, on the other hand, engaged in an open campaign both to discredit the widow and to invalidate the three witnesses. Rabbi Yedidyah ben Israel's argument, which set the tone for the subsequent debate between judges and jurists, was that regardless of their current religious observance and affiliations, the witnesses had unquestionably been deliberate transgressors at the time of the events in question and were consequently not to be trusted, then or forevermore. He claimed to have witnesses that Seligman had violated Jewish law willingly even after the violence had subsided, though these witnesses never actually made an appearance.[43] He also claimed that both Seligman and Jonathan had incriminated themselves by admitting that they had lived as non-Jews even when it was no longer a matter of life and death. In a subsequent appeal to the Speyer judges who ruled in favor of the widow, Rabbi Yedidyah wrote:

> Your [own] eyes see that it was testified regarding Seligman and Jonathan that all the days they lived among the non-Jews after they apostatized they did not refrain from any transgressions committed among the non-Jews, whether in private or in public, and they worshipped idols and they ate all of their impurities—and they themselves admitted [this] and asked for atonement. And Jonathan told me himself that he remained among the non-Jews for more than half a year. . . . And according to your [own] words, since you concede that a thief according to Torah law is disqualified from testifying on behalf of a [married] woman, they are both disqualified, Seligman and Jonathan—for it has been testified that they were absolute non-Jews [*goyim gemurim*], and so they admitted themselves.[44]

Even more tellingly, Rabbi Yedidyah insisted that the anonymous witness could not hide behind his anonymity and had surely violated Torah law as well, despite any evidence of the sort. To his mind, the very fact that the witness survived the massacre in which 900 professing Jews had been killed "proved" that he must have renounced his Jewish identity. Indeed, with reference to that witness, Rabbi Yedidyah boldly contended, "And I know that he is one of those who denied the essence [of Jewish faith] and ate non-Jewish meat with appetite, for if it were not so, how was he saved when Simeon ben Jacob was killed?"[45]

Rabbi Yedidyah seems to have taken his role as a legal representative seriously: each of his written arguments ends with a restatement of his claims on behalf of his orphan client, and much of his energy was invested in discrediting his opponent, the widow, in a manner designed to cast doubt on the sincerity of her own claims. What is more, neither the tenor of Rabbi Yedidyah's arguments nor his legal stance match the forgiving approach he adopted in other cases of apostasy that were submitted to him for adjudication, suggesting that the rhetoric he employed in the Simeon ben Jacob case reflected, first and foremost, his skills as a lawyer.[46] Nonetheless, the intensely polemical tone of Rabbi Yedidyah's attacks on the character and credibility of the three witnesses suggests that his positions ran deeper than a temporary role would normally elicit. It is possible that the death of Rabbi Yedidyah's own children, grandchildren, and other relatives at the hands of the Rindfleisch killers in nearby Nürnberg affected his approach to the case in question.[47] In light of his personal loss, it may have been particularly difficult for him to countenance granting former apostates full legal credibility, together with the belonging and trust that such status implied.

Rabbi Yedidyah's arguments were ultimately rejected by all of the judges and jurists involved, and the Jewish court in Speyer accepted the witnesses' testimony, released the widow, and granted her the *ketubah* payments she requested. But Rabbi Yedidyah's claims are significant nonetheless because they lent expression to a deep suspicion of and resentment toward repentant apostates among the rabbinic elite and not exclusively among the laypeople, although this is a distinction that some historians have proposed.[48] Indeed, most of the legal opinions rendered by the Speyer judges and by the other scholars who were consulted on the matter also betray a certain reserve concerning the credibility of those who apostatized. To clarify this point, let us examine the responsum of Rabbi Hayim ben Isaac ʿOr Zaruʿa. Afterward, I will turn to the ruling and arguments of Rabbi Asher ben Yehiel, who adopted a very different stance.

Rabbi Hayim argued forcefully in favor of accepting the testimony concerning Simeon ben Jacob's death, but the legal foundation for his argument was the claim that ʿ*agunah* cases demand reliable information but not authoritative speakers. The word *be-berur*—clearly, or certainly—appears over and over in his responsum, to emphasize that there is no doubt as to the truth of the witnesses' statements. Yet despite his confidence in the veracity of the reports, Rabbi Hayim refused to grant former apostates "kosher" or authoritative status. In a break with the tradition attributed to Rashi, he ruled that reports of a man's death need not stem from witnesses who were valid at the time of the reported events:

> The coerced ones who returned and testified upon their return that while they were still among the non-Jews they saw R. Simeon son of R. Jacob murdered, lying before the entrance to his home. It appears that they are reliable [*neʾemanim*], even if it becomes clear that they ate non-kosher meat with appetite—because now they have returned and they are surely qualified [*kesherim*], now they are reporting the truth. And for this we don't require them to be [religiously] qualified from the beginning ... here we don't require [actual] testimony, only to know that this is the truth, as they have spoken now ... here, when he testifies now, after he has returned, [regarding] what he saw in his waywardness, and now he is surely speaking the truth, even though at the

time he witnessed [the event] he was not qualified—it appears that he is reliable, because we do not require the testimony of a valid witness, for even the [married] woman herself is reliable to say that her husband has died. . . . This is the *halakhah* here, because even invalid individuals are reliable to testify as witnesses that her husband died, and even she herself [is reliable] . . . for we do not require him to be qualified at both beginning and end.[49]

Rabbi Hayim's responsum reflects a certain bifurcation between formal credibility and trust. To his mind, there was no reason to doubt the accuracy of the information provided by the former apostates, even if their transgressions had been "voluntary" or self-motivated. At the time they testified to Simeon ben Jacob's death, they had already returned to the Jewish community, and this step itself deemed their reports reliable. To act on reports of a man's death and free his widow to remarry, a court needs to be reasonably certain that the information is reliable, but it is not necessary for the court to obtain formal testimony from two *halakhically* valid witnesses. Indeed, even invalid witnesses, such as the widow herself, may provide the information. Thus, while he was not willing to grant the former apostates' reports the status of formal testimony, Rabbi Hayim maintained that the information they provided was unquestionably true and, as such, sufficient to release Simeon ben Jacob's widow from her marital bonds. In this vein, he declared:

> But here [i.e., in this case], where he testifies now, after having repented, about what he saw during his [time of] waywardness—and now he is certainly telling the truth—even though at the time he witnessed the events he was not valid [*kasher*], it seems that he is [now considered] reliable, because [in this case] we do not require the testimony of a valid witness [ʿ*edut kasher*].[50]

In contrast, Rabbi Asher ben Yehiel insisted that the witnesses in the Simeon ben Jacob case were fully qualified to testify to the unfortunate man's death. His outspoken support for the apostates and his willingness to categorize all their behavior as coerced and therefore excusable was designed primarily to counter the impact of Rabbi Yedidyah's arguments and the aspersion he cast on the men involved, but its implications for the direction of future rulings as well as for the case at hand can hardly be overemphasized. In stark contrast to Rabbi Yedidyah's suggestion that anyone who had survived the massacre was to be considered guilty of willing apostasy until proven otherwise, Rabbi Asher insisted that there was no reason to assume that survivors of the persecution were guilty of anything but concession to fear:

> We must not disqualify them out of doubt, for the majority of those who apostatized did not eat non-kosher meat with appetite, rather apostatized out of fear of death, and this fear obligated them to behave in their [non-Jewish] ways so that they would not kill them, and it is all considered coercion. . . . And it

is slightly [troublesome] that they remained among the non-Jews after they had the opportunity to flee, but the sword of God slashes and the fire of God rages around them . . . therefore they did not know what was up and what was down, until they heard that God had remembered His people and given them respite—then they hurried to fear God. And there were those who remained for the sake of Heaven, to save their children, and not one of them acted with abandon, to eat non-kosher meat with appetite, for if they had done so willingly, why did they [subsequently] return and repent? And my master wrote that he has witnesses that they ate non-kosher meat with appetite, but we have still not seen or heard [this testimony]. And who could testify to this, for do they see into their hearts, such that they could testify that they did so with appetite? And even I who was not present there can testify that they ate non-kosher meat and performed other violations, and this they were obligated to do out of fear, and it is all considered coerced, as I have written—but there is no person who can testify that they did so with appetite.[51]

Coerced apostates, Rabbi Asher argued, were more than qualified to testify to events they had witnessed during their apostasy, and in fact their reports concerning the death of particular individuals during the massacres could be considered especially reliable. While living as Christians, the apostates' lives had not been in danger and, therefore, there was no reason for them to presume death rather than ascertain death, as other witnesses to wartime or similarly violent killings might have done.[52]

Rabbi Asher's accepting approach was surely connected to the nature of the case at hand: unlike Rabbi Yedidyah, who represented the more stringent approach to ʿagunah cases typical of medieval Ashkenazi scholars, Rabbi Asher was willing to bend the rules in accordance with what he understood to be the overarching goal of Talmudic leniencies in this realm.[53] In addition, the disastrous implications of rejecting the witnesses' testimony for Simeon ben Jacob's widow, who had already remarried, as well as for the other Würzburg widows who had relied on their reports, seems to have weighed heavily on him. Certainly, Rabbi Asher did not always defend repentant apostates, even when their apostasy had occurred under duress. He issued a harsh condemnation of married women who had consented to baptism to save their lives during a persecution, although he subsequently allowed them to return to their marriages without financial penalty.[54] Similarly, he warned that many individuals who apostatized under duress had likely violated Jewish law voluntarily prior to being coerced.[55] Nonetheless, his strong words of support for those who bowed to fear during the Rindfleisch Massacres established him as the champion of returning converts in the Simeon ben Jacob case, and for later rabbinic authorities, his ruling in this case set precedent for relying on the testimony of repentant apostates more broadly.[56]

In conclusion, the prolonged and passionate legal battle recounted in the court records from Speyer was not really about the demise of the ill-fated Simeon ben Jacob. No one genuinely disputed Simeon's death: even the orphan and his representative Rabbi Yedidyah were angling to inherit the dead man's estate. Nonetheless, the witnesses who reported this man's slaying became a lightning rod for debates concerning one of the most sensitive issues of the day: the legal and communal status of individuals who had abandoned their people and their faith in a moment of crisis. In spite of the real-life consequences for Simeon ben Jacob's widow and other women in similar circumstances, the credibility of these witnesses to stand in court and report facts that were agreed on by all was disputed by reputable scholars, highlighting the critical role of trust in negotiating the boundaries of community affiliation.

Medieval rabbinic scholars regularly denigrated voluntary converts to Christianity for being impelled by raw ambition, greed, and desires of the flesh.[57] The court materials we have seen from late thirteenth-century Speyer demonstrate that some scholars, such as Rabbi Yedidyah ben Israel, viewed the victims of forced conversion, including those who subsequently returned to the Jewish community, with similar skepticism and distrust. Regardless of the circumstances under which their conversions came about, any amount of sustained contact with the Christian majority or weakness in the face of conversionary pressure raised the suspicion that the individuals affected were of the same shady character as those who had made a deliberate choice.[58] Yet for other scholars, including Rabbi Hayim ben Isaac 'Or Zaru'a and especially Rabbi Asher ben Yehiel, the circumstances that brought about the brief and unwelcome encounter between forcibly baptized individuals and their Christian persecutors did not substantiate the mistrust it engendered on both a scholarly and popular level. Individuals who left the community lost legal credibility, along with other privileges of Jewish "citizenship." By virtue of the fact that they returned, however, the repentant Jewish converts demonstrated that they could supply trustworthy testimony about events they had witnessed during their encounter with the rival religion. Furthermore, their reports provided valuable insight as well as critical information that realigned them with their coreligionists in practice and in spirit.

Whether permanent or temporary, voluntary or coerced, conversion to Christianity disrupted the relationships at the heart of Jewish communal life, which were predicated on interlocking conventions of trust. Those who left the community lost their credibility, much as they lost other markers of belonging; however, the intensity of the debates concerning their ability to regain authoritative standing in the event that they rejoined the community suggests that at the heart of the matter was not the legal definition of credibility but rather the social convention of trust. Trustworthiness may not have been a Jewish trait per se, but its association with dependability and constancy meant that it was an attribute few medieval Jews would have correlated with converts.

Notes

An early version of this chapter was presented at the "Word of a Jew" seminar hosted by the Oxford Centre for Hebrew and Jewish Studies during the academic year 2013–14. Many heartfelt thanks to the conveners of that seminar, Nina Caputo and Mitchell Hart, and to my colleagues in the related research group for their warm collegiality, thoughtful feedback, and general encouragement. Thanks, too, to several additional colleagues with whom I discussed the contents of this chapter, and especially to Paola Tartakoff, whose perceptive comments sharpened both my analysis and my writing.

1. Siegmund Salfeld, *Das Martyrologium des Nürnberger Memorbuches* (Berlin: Verlag von Leonhard Simion, 1898), 43–48.

2. See Jörg R. Müller, "*Erez Gezerah*—'Land of Persecution': Pogroms against the Jews in the *Regnum Teutonicum* from c. 1280 to 1350," in *The Jews of Europe in the Middle Ages*, ed. Christoph Cluse (Turnhout: Brepols, 2004), 251–54; and Friedrich Lotter, "Die Judenverfolgung des 'König Rintfleisch' in Franken um 1298. Die endgültige Wende in den christlich-jüdischen Beziehungen im Deutschen Reich des Mittlealters," *Zeitschrift für Historische Forschung* 15 (1988): 385–422, especially 395–96.

3. See Salfeld, *Nürnberger Memorbuches*, 46 where "He-Haver R' Shim'on ben Ha-Rav R' Ya'akov Ha-Levi" is listed among the dead.

4. Presumably, her dead husband's assets were located in Speyer. Rabbi Yakar Ha-Kohen (also cited as Rabbi Isaac Yakar Ha-Kohen) did not leave a literary legacy, but he seems to have been a recognized scholar, as the Speyer judges refer to him, along with the orphan's representative, as "my [i.e., our] teacher."

5. Rabbi Yedidyah ben Israel was active during the late thirteenth and early fourteenth centuries as a scholar and rabbinical court judge in Speyer and Cologne. His father, Rabbi Israel, was a published tosafist, and his own son, daughter, and other relatives were killed during the Rindfleisch Massacres in Nürnberg in 1298. For more biographical details, see Zvi Avneri, ed., *Germania Judaica II: Von 1238 bis zur Mitte des 14. Jahrhunderts* (Jerusalem: Leo Baeck Institut, 1968), 606–7; Efraim E. Urbach, *Ba'alei Ha-Tosafot: Toldotehem, Hiburehem, Shitatam* (Jerusalem: Bialik Institute, 1980), 566–70; and Irving Agus, ed., *Teshuvot Ba'alei Ha-Tosafot* (New York: Yeshiva University Press, 1954), 233.

6. *Sefer Zikhron Yehudah* no. 92 (hereafter, ZY 92); I have primarily used the edition by Avraham Y. Havatzelet, ed., *She'elot U-Teshuvot Zikhron Yehudah* (Jerusalem: Makhon Yerushalayaim, 2005), 112–27. For biographical information on Rabbi Asher, see Urbach, *Ba'alei Ha-Tosafot*, 586–99; and Israel Ta-Shma, "Between East and West: R. Asher b. Yehiel and His Son R. Jacob," in *Creativity and Tradition: Studies in Medieval Rabbinic Scholarship, Literature, and Thought*, ed. Israel M. Ta-Shma, 111–26 (Cambridge: Harvard University Press, 2006).

7. Rabbi Eliyahu Mizrahi cited a tradition in this vein in his responsa from sixteenth-century Turkey; see *Responsa of Re-'Em* no. 95. It is not clear whether Rabbi Mizrahi himself possessed or consulted the "large piece of parchment" on which—according to his description—all the responsa from the case at hand were copied. See too Judah Galinsky, "On the Legacy of R. Judah ben Harosh, Rabbi of Toledo: A Chapter in the Study of Responsa of Sages from Christian Spain" (in Hebrew), *Pe'amim* 128 (Summer 2011): 197–98.

8. For all these documents, see ZY 92. Rabbi Asher's responsum is also printed in Yitzhak S. Yudlov, ed., *She'elot U-Teshuvot Le-Rabbenu 'Asher ben Yehiel* (Jerusalem: Makhon Yerushalayim, 1994), 498–500 (Additional Responsa no. 68). (The collection as a whole will be referenced hereafter as *Teshuvot Ha-Rosh*).

9. *Responsa of Rabbi Hayim ʾOr Zaruʿa* no. 91 (hereafter, Hayim OZ 91). See Menahem Avitan, ed., *Sefer Teshuvot Maharah ʾOr Zaruʿa* (Jerusalem: M. Avitan, 2002), 82–84.

10. Rabbi Solomon ibn Adret's response was actively solicited by Rabbi Yedidyah ben Israel in the course of disputing the Speyer court's ruling. See Aharon Zelzenik et al., eds., *Sheʾelot U-Teshuvot Ha-Rashba*, vol. 2 (Jerusalem: Makhon Yerushalayim, 1997), 33–35 (no. 32) (hereafter, Rashba 32).

11. The only surviving Jewish court records from medieval Ashkenaz are fragments preserved in rabbinic responsa. For discussion of Jewish courts during this era, see especially Moshe Frank, *Kehilot ʾAshkenaz U-Batei Dineihem* (Tel Aviv: Dvir, 1938); Simcha Goldin, *Ha-Yihud Ve-Ha-Yahad: Hidat Hisardutan Shel Ha-Kevutzot Ha-Yehudiyot Be-Yemei Ha-Beinayim* (Tel Aviv: Ha-kibbutz Ha-meuhad, 1997), 116–36; Efraim Kanarfogel, *The Intellectual History and Rabbinic Culture of Medieval Ashkenaz* (Detroit: Wayne State University Press, 2013), 37–80; and Rachel Furst, "Striving for Justice: A History of Women and Litigation in Medieval Ashkenaz," PhD dissertation (Jerusalem: Hebrew University, 2015).

12. See Efraim Kanarfogel, "Returning to the Jewish Community in Medieval Ashkenaz: History and Halakhah," in *Turim: Studies in Jewish History and Literature Presented to Dr. Bernard Lander*, ed. Michael A. Shmidman, 69–97 (New York: Touro College Press, 2007) and Efraim Kanarfogel, "Changing Attitudes toward Apostates in Tosafist Literature, Late Twelfth–Early Thirteenth Centuries," in *New Perspectives on Jewish-Christian Relations: In Honor of David Berger*, ed. Elisheva Carlebach and Jacob J. Schacter, 297–327 (Leiden: Brill, 2012); David Malkiel, "Jews and Apostates in Medieval Europe: Boundaries Real and Imagined," *Past and Present* 194 (2007): 3–34; and Paola Tartakoff, "Testing Boundaries: Jewish Conversion and Cultural Fluidity in Medieval Europe, c. 1200–1391," *Speculum* 90, no. 3 (2015): 728–62, and the copious literature cited therein. See too Edward Fram, "Perception and Reception of Repentant Apostates in Medieval Ashkenaz and Premodern Poland," *AJS Review* 21/2 (1996): 299–339; and Simha Goldin, *Apostasy and Jewish Identity in High Middle Ages Northern Europe: "Are You Still My Brother?"* (Manchester: Manchester University Press, 2014), especially 52–76.

13. See Alfred Haverkamp, "Baptized Jews in German Lands During the Twelfth Century," in *Jews and Christians in Twelfth-Century Europe*, ed. Michael A. Signer and John Van Engen, 255–310 (Notre Dame: University of Notre Dame Press, 2001); William C. Jordan, "Adolescence and Conversion in the Middle Ages: A Research Agenda," in *Jews and Christians in Twelfth-Century Europe*, ed. Michael A. Signer and John Van Engen, 77–93 (Notre Dame: University of Notre Dame Press, 2001); and Joseph Shatzmiller, "Jewish Converts to Christianity in Medieval Europe, 1200–1500," in *Cross Cultural Convergences in the Crusader Period: Essays Presented to Aryeh Grabois on His Sixty-Fifth Birthday*, ed. Michael Goodich, Sophia Menache, and Sylvia Schein, 297–318 (New York: Peter Lang, 1995). See too Tartakoff, "Testing Boundaries," 734.

14. Jacob Katz, "ʾAf ʿal pi she-hata, Yisraʾel hu," *Tarbiz* 27 (1958): 203–17. See too Jacob Katz, *Exclusiveness and Tolerance: Jewish-Gentile Relations in Medieval and Modern Times* (London: Oxford University Press, 1961), 67–81.

15. The statement itself is Talmudic; see BT Sanhedrin 44a. Rashi, however, was the first to apply it to apostates in the medieval sense of the term; that is, to individuals who abandoned Judaism in favor of an alternative religion or religious identity. See I. Elfenbein, *Teshuvot Rashi* (New York: Shulsinger Bros., 1943), 193–94 (no. 173).

16. For a thorough review of these positions, see also Gerald J. Blidstein, "Who Is Not a Jew? The Medieval Discussion," *Israel Law Review* 11 (1976): 369–90.

17. See especially Kanarfogel, "Changing Attitudes."

18. Rabbenu Tam even suggested that the appropriate response was to rejoice, because death, which prevented the individual from idol worship, was a blessing. See Rabbi Isaac ben Moses's *Sefer 'Or Zaru'a* (hereafter OZ), section 2, no. 428; and Katz, *Exclusiveness and Tolerance*, 73–74.

19. See Gerald J. Blidstein, "The Personal Status of Captive and Apostate Women in Medieval Jewish Law" (in Hebrew), *Annual of the Institute for Research in Jewish Law* 3–4 (1976–77): 35–116; Rachel Furst, "Captivity, Conversion, and Communal Identity: Sexual Angst and Religious Crisis in Frankfurt, 1241," *Jewish History* 22 (2008): 179–221; and Ephraim Kanarfogel, "Returning Apostates and Their Marital Partners in Medieval Ashkenaz," in *Contesting Inter-Religious Conversion in the Medieval World*, ed. Yaniv Fox and Yosi Yisraeli, 160–76 (London: Routledge, 2016).

20. Katz, *Exclusiveness and Tolerance*, 73; Yosef Hayim Yerushalmi, "The Inquisition and the Jews of France in the Time of Bernard of Gui," *Harvard Theological Review* 63, no. 3 (1970): 363–76; and especially Kanarfogel, "Returning to the Jewish Community."

21. They based their position on a reading of Deut. 19:15 ("A case can be valid only on the testimony of two witnesses or more") in light of Deut. 19:17 ("The two parties [literally, men] to the dispute shall appear before the Lord").

22. All rabbinic traditions agreed that women were prohibited from testifying, they only disagreed as to the source of the prohibition; see M Shev 4:1 and M RH 1:8, as well as Midrash Sifrei Deut. 190, BT Shev 30a, and JT Shev 5:1 (35b). For a fuller treatment of these different Talmudic traditions and their implications, see Eliezer Hadad, *'Al Ma'amadan Shel Nashim Be-Batei Din Rabaniim*, Policy Paper 100 (Jerusalem: Israel Democracy Institute, 2013), 33–37. For the disqualification of minors, see BT BB 155b; slaves, BT BK 88a; the mentally disabled, BT BB 128a; and non-Jews, BT Yev 47a and BT BK 15a.

23. See BT Sanh 27a and Maimonides, Mishneh Torah, Laws of Testimony 10:1–2. This disqualification was considered biblical, in accordance with Exodus 23:1. Other disqualified people include relatives of the litigants or of each other.

24. See BT Sanh 26b–27a and discussion of this source and its medieval renditions in Avraham (Rami) Reiner, "*Mumar 'Okhel Neveilot Le-Te'avon—Pasul? Mashehu 'Al Nusah U-Perusho Be-Yedei Rashi*," in *Lo Yasur Shevet Me-Yehudah*, ed. Y. Hacker and Y. Harel, 223–28 (Jerusalem: Mosad Bialik, 2011).

25. Maimonides, Laws of Testimony, Chapter 10; Piskei Ha-Rosh, Sanh 3:7–17; Tur HM 34.

26. Regarding the credibility of an individual who is suspected of sexual violations (hashud 'al ha-'arayot), see Tosafot on BT Sanh 26b s.v. "*He-hashud 'al ha-'arayot kasher le-'edut*"; Piskei Ha-Rosh Sanh 3:13; and the discussion in Reiner, "*Mumar 'Okehl Neveilot Le-Te'avon.*"

27. Rashi's ruling was quoted—and thereby preserved—in the writings of several medieval scholars: see ZY 92 (Havatzelet edition, 123); *Teshuvot Ba'alei Ha-Tosafot* no. 128; and Hayim OZ no. 45. Elfenbein did not include this ruling in his collection of Rashi's responsa, but Agus subsequently added it; see *Teshuvot Ba'alei Ha-Tosafot* no. 9. All translations of rabbinic texts are my own, unless indicated otherwise.

28. *Teshuvot Maimoniyot*, Nashim no. 10. See too the responsum by Rabbi Meir ben Barukh in Mordekhai Ket 306.

29. In addition to the materials cited herein, see *Teshuvot Ba'alei Ha-Tosafot* no. 128 for the sharply worded appeal of an unnamed scholar to Rabbi Yedidyah ben Israel concerning another case that involved repentant apostate witnesses: "And in all probability it is

impossible that they did not commit a single transgression willingly rather than under coercion."

30. According to Jewish law, a married woman regains her single (i.e., "available") status in one of two instances: either her husband has died or he has legally divorced her. A woman whose husband has disappeared or whose death cannot be ascertained remains legally married and forbidden to contract a new relationship, even if her husband has been missing for years and has long been taken for dead.

31. The basic laws concerning the release of ʿagunot are enumerated in Mishnah Yevamot and its related Talmudic passages. Alongside these relaxed rules of evidence, the Mishnah also highlights the severe consequences facing an ʿagunah who is insufficiently vigilant in determining the truth of her husband's plight: a woman who remarries only to discover that her first husband is still alive is forbidden to maintain either of the two relationships, and her children from the second marriage are branded bastards (mamzerim). Thus the sages lent expression to the underlying tension in their dealings with all ʿagunah cases: a desire to unshackle women from dead marriages tempered by an abiding sense of the gravity with which halakhah relates to all matters of personal status.

32. Reflecting on the unprecedented leniencies in the admission of testimony to release ʿagunot, the Babylonian Talmud suggests that the sages' policy relied on two suppositions: (1) that a person's death was difficult to falsify, as the truth was likely to come to light ("milta de-ʿavida le-ʾigluye"); and (2) that given the severity of the consequences, the ʿagunah herself would take extra care to ascertain the validity of the evidence before remarrying ("me-shum de-hi gufa dayka u-minseba"). See BT Yev 115a.

33. See discussion in BT RH 22a and BT Yev 25a–b.

34. BT Yev 121b. Thus Rabbi Hayim ben Isaac ʾOr Zaruʿa ruled that as long as a non-Jewish informant does not intend to ingratiate himself with the Jews by providing the information or does not seem to report the Jew's death with evil intentions, his report is considered to have been "spoken in innocence" and is legally admissible. By way of example, he cited the case of a Jew detained by local authorities: when the community went to the local lord to petition on this man's behalf, the lord dismissed them, saying, "He already died, and I commanded that he be thrown to the dogs." That information—spoken "in innocence"—was sufficient to render the unfortunate man's wife a widow and render her free to remarry; see Hayim OZ no. 76.

35. See the presentation of Rabbi Eliezer ben Joel Ha-Levi's position in OZ, sec. 1, no. 697; and see Hayim OZ 91.

36. M Ket 15:1.

37. See M Ket 15:3 and the attendant discussion in BT Yev 117a. This rule applies only if the woman asks for her ketubah funds after asking for permission to remarry, thereby demonstrating that the money is not her primary concern; were she to ask only for a financial settlement, her motives (and therefore her credibility) would be suspect. In other words, the rabbis doubted the trustworthiness of a woman who was more concerned about securing her financial future than she was about her (re)marital prospects.

38. And, according to Rabbi Jacob Tam, limited to cases in which the wife is the sole source of this information; see Mordekhai Yev 93. It is curious that neither the orphan's representative nor the other respondents cited this famous ruling.

39. ZY 92 (Havatzelet edition, 114). Rabbi Yakar further suggested that if a call for witnesses were issued, numerous people would come forward to testify to Simeon ben Jacob's inclusion on local hazkarat neshamot lists. Concerning medieval memorial lists and the

liturgical practices associated with them, see Solomon B. Freehof, "Hazkarath Neshamoth," *HUCA* 36 (1965), especially 183–84; Judah Galinsky, "Commemoration and *Heqdesh* in the Jewish Communities of Germany and Spain during the Thirteenth Century," in *Stiftungen in Christentum, Judentum und Islam vor der Moderne*, ed. Michael Borgolte, especially 195–97; and Elisheva Baumgarten, *Practicing Piety in Medieval Ashkenaz: Men, Women, and Everyday Religious Observance* (Philadelphia: University of Pennsylvania Press, 2014), 106–7.

40. Roman law, which was in wide use across most of southern Europe by the thirteenth century, assigned significant legal weight to common knowledge about a person or an event. Regarding *fama* as an actionable legal category, see Marie Kelleher, *The Measure of Woman: Law and Female Identity in the Crown of Aragon* (Philadelphia: University of Pennsylvania Press, 2010), 39–45; Daniel Lord Smail, *The Consumption of Justice: Emotions, Publicity, and Legal Culture in Marseille, 1264–1423* (Ithaca, NY: Cornell University Press, 2003), especially 233–40; and the various essays in Thelma Fenster and Daniel Lord Smail, eds., *Fama: The Politics of Talk and Reputation in Medieval Europe* (Ithaca, NY: Cornell University Press, 2003).

41. ZY 92 (Havatzelet edition, 115 and 117). Rabbi Yedidyah cited a specific instance in which a missing woman who had been publicly memorialized subsequently reappeared, alive. See too related comments in the response of Rabbi Azriel ben Yehiel, ZY 92 (Havatzelet edition, 117–18).

42. Interestingly, Rabbi Solomon ben Abraham Ibn Adret of Barcelona, who wrote his own responsum on the Würzburg case at Rabbi Yedidyah ben Israel's request, did provide a halakhic rationale for Rabbi Yakar's claim, although he resoundingly rejected it: according to Tosefta Yev 14:7, "there is no greater testimony" to a man's death than hearing his name invoked by a professional weeper (*mekonenet*). See Rashba 32.

43. ZY 92 (Havatzelet edition, 114). See too the subsequent response of Rabbi Asher ben Yehiel (Havatzelet edition, 125): "And you, sir, wrote that you have witnesses that they [i.e., Jonathan and Seligman] ate non-kosher meat with appetite; but we have still not heard or seen [them]."

44. ZY 92 (Havatzelet edition, 121). At least on a rhetorical level, Rabbi Yedidyah's assertion that the witnesses were *"goyim gemurim"* was the polar opposite of Rashi's insistence that converts were merely lapsed Jews; see *Teshuvot Ba'alei Ha-Tosafot* no. 9 and note 27 in this chatper.

45. ZY 92 (Havatzelet edition, 116). In the text itself, the victim is called "Dan ben Naftali," but that is merely an epithet for Simeon ben Jacob, much as Rabbi Yakar is called "Reuben" and Rabbi Yedidyah is called "Simeon."

46. See, for example, *Teshuvot Ba'alei Ha-Tosafot* nos. 126 and 127, as well as *Teshuvot Ha-Rosh* no. 32:5. The use of legal counsel by adult litigants was proscribed by many Talmudic sages and later authorities, and it was not a regular feature of Jewish courtrooms in Ashkenaz until the fifteenth century. Nonetheless, the case in question demonstrates that some representatives did function as outright advocates, even in earlier periods. For further discussion, see Furst, "Striving for Justice," Chapter 3, and the literature cited therein.

47. See note 5 in this chapter.

48. This, for example, was the explanation offered by Katz and Yerushalmi, and subsequently by others, to account for the existence and persistence of a ritual to "debaptize" returning apostates, although Jewish law did not mandate such practice. More recently, however, Kanarfogel has demonstrated that the custom was indeed discussed and given sanction by more rabbinic authorities than previously realized, suggesting that the "elite" were not immune to the assumptions and attitudes of the "masses." See Kanarfogel, "Returning to the Jewish Community," and the references cited therein.

49. Hayim OZ 91.

50. Hayim OZ 91.

51. ZY 92 (Havatzelet edition, 125). In a later text, written after he had emigrated to Spain, Rabbi Asher mentioned a "lengthy" responsum he had authored while still in Ashkenaz on the subject of repentant apostate witnesses; see *Teshuvot Ha-Rosh* no. 52:5. Apparently, he was referring to his responsum on the Simeon ben Jacob case (i.e., the responsum under discussion). Already in the sixteenth century, Rabbi Joseph Karo made the connection between these two texts; see *Beit Yosef* EH 17.

52. According to the Mishnah (M Yev 15:1), when a man dies during war, his wife loses her credibility to report his death, just as she does when there is marital strife in the background. During war, she is not suspect of fabricating his death, but given the circumstances and the ongoing danger to herself, she is suspect of leaving the scene of her husband's death before he draws his last breath and assuming that he died, even when she did not actually see him expire. Although the Talmud itself only discusses presumption of death in connection with the testimony of a wife concerning her own husband, the two legal representatives and several of the decisors in the Simeon ben Jacob case raised this question concerning apostate witnesses as well.

53. Indeed, Rabbi Asher cited authorities, such as Rabbi Kalonymos and Rabbi Eliezer of Verona, whose rulings regarding the release of ʿagunot were seldom relied on by scholars of the era; I thank my colleague at Ben Gurion University of the Negev, Avigdor Haneman, for this insight. See too *Teshuvot Ha-Rosh* no. 54:1, where Rabbi Asher explicitly distinguished between the testimony of repentant apostates for releasing an ʿagunah (which he accepted) and the testimony of repentant apostates in monetary matters (which he was more reluctant to use).

54. See *Teshuvot Ha-Rosh* no. 32:8. And see Blidstein, "Captive and Apostate Women," especially 100–02.

55. *Teshuvot Ha-Rosh* 54:1.

56. See *Beit Yosef* EH 17, *Shulhan ʿArukh* EH 17:6, and related commentaries.

57. See the sources and secondary literature cited in Tartakoff, "Testing Boundaries," 737 n. 33. Tartakoff argues that most voluntary converts, across medieval western Europe, were indeed "marginal figures—socially, economically, or ideologically—who turned to baptism primarily as a means of escaping personal difficulties," although her research demonstrates that in many cases, despair and not covetousness drove them into the arms of the Church. Rather than being ideologically motivated, many of these conversions were an attempt to avoid punishment or taxation, to evade Jewish communal censure, to marry Christian lovers (who were usually fellow Jewish converts to Christianity), or to escape poverty. See Tartakoff, "Testing Boundaries," 740–44.

58. In fact, Malkiel argues that much of the rabbinic literature from medieval Ashkenaz fails to distinguish clearly between forced and willing apostates, "reflect[ing] an ambivalence on the part of these scholars towards the coerced." See Malkiel, "Jews and Apostates," 10–16.

Bibliography

Agus, Irving, ed. *Teshuvot Baʿalei Ha-Tosafot*. New York: Yeshiva University Press, 1954.

Avitan, Menahem, ed. *Sefer Teshuvot Maharah ʾOr Zaruʿa*. Jerusalem: M. Avitan, 2002.

Baumgarten, Elisheva. *Practicing Piety in Medieval Ashkenaz: Men, Women, and Everyday Religious Observance*. Philadelphia: University of Pennsylvania Press, 2014.

Blidstein, Gerald J. "The Personal Status of Captive and Apostate Women in Medieval Jewish Law." [In Hebrew.] *Annual of the Institute for Research in Jewish Law* 3–4 (1976–77): 35–116.

———. "Who Is Not a Jew? The Medieval Discussion," *Israel Law Review* 11 (1976): 369–90.

Elfenbein, I. *Teshuvot Rashi*. New York: Shulsinger Bros., 1943.

Fenster, Thelma, and Daniel Lord Smail, eds. *Fama: The Politics of Talk and Reputation in Medieval Europe*. Ithaca, NY: Cornell University Press, 2003.

Fram, Edward. "Perception and Reception of Repentant Apostates in Medieval Ashkenaz and Premodern Poland." *AJS Review* 21, no. 2 (1996): 299–339.

Frank, Moshe. *Kehilot ʾAshkenaz U-Batei Dineihem*. Tel Aviv: Dvir, 1938.

Freehof, Solomon B. "Hazkarath Neshamoth." *HUCA* 36 (1965): 179–89.

Furst, Rachel. "Captivity, Conversion, and Communal Identity: Sexual Angst and Religious Crisis in Frankfurt, 1241." *Jewish History* 22 (2008): 179–221.

———. "Striving for Justice: A History of Women and Litigation in Medieval Ashkenaz." PhD dissertation. Jerusalem: Hebrew University, 2015.

Galinsky, Judah. "Commemoration and *Heqdesh* in the Jewish Communities of Germany and Spain during the Thirteenth Century." In *Stiftungen in Christentum, Judentum und Islam vor der Moderne*, edited by Michael Borgolte and Lohse Tillmann, 191–203. Berlin: Academie Verlag, 2005.

———. "On the Legacy of R. Judah ben Harosh, Rabbi of Toledo: A Chapter in the Study of Responsa of Sages from Christian Spain." [In Hebrew.] *Peʿamim* 128 (2011): 175–210.

Goldin, Simcha. *Apostasy and Jewish Identity in High Middle Ages Northern Europe: "Are You Still My Brother?"* Manchester: Manchester University Press, 2014.

———. *Ha-Yihud Ve-Ha-Yahad: Hidat Hisardutan Shel Ha-Kevutzot Ha-Yehudiyot Be-Yemei Ha-Beinayim*. Tel Aviv: Ha-kibbutz Ha-meʿuhad, 1997.

Hadad, Eliezer. *ʿAl Maʿamadan Shel Nashim Be-Batei Din Rabaniim*. Policy Paper 100. Jerusalem: Israel Democracy Institute, 2013.

Havatzelet, Avraham Y. *Sheʾelot U-Teshuvot Zikhron Yehudah*. Jerusalem: Makhon Yerushalayaim, 2005.

Haverkamp, Alfred. "Baptized Jews in German Lands during the Twelfth Century." In *Jews and Christians in Twelfth-Century Europe*, edited by Michael A. Signer and John Van Engen, 255–310. Notre Dame: University of Notre Dame Press, 2001.

Jordan, William C. "Adolescence and Conversion in the Middle Ages: A Research Agenda." In *Jews and Christians in Twelfth-Century Europe*, edited by Michael A. Signer and John Van Engen, 77–93. Notre Dame: University of Notre Dame Press, 2001.

Kanarfogel, Efraim. "Changing Attitudes toward Apostates in Tosafist Literature, Late Twelfth–Early Thirteenth Centuries." In *New Perspectives on Jewish–Christian Relations: In Honor of David Berger*, edited by Elisheva Carlebach and Jacob J. Schacter, 297–327. Leiden: Brill, 2012.

———. *The Intellectual History and Rabbinic Culture of Medieval Ashkenaz*. Detroit: Wayne State University Press, 2013.

———. "Returning Apostates and Their Marital Partners in Medieval Ashkenaz." In *Contesting Inter-Religious Conversion in the Medieval World*, edited by Yaniv Fox and Yosi Yisraeli, 160–76. London: Routledge, 2016.

———. "Returning to the Jewish Community in Medieval Ashkenaz: History and Halakhah." In *Turim: Studies in Jewish History and Literature Presented to Dr. Bernard Lander*, edited by Michael A. Shmidman, 69–97. New York: Touro College Press, 2007.

Katz, Jacob. "'Af 'al pi she-hata, Yisra'el hu." *Tarbiz* 27 (1958): 203–17.
———. *Exclusiveness and Tolerance: Jewish-Gentile Relations in Medieval and Modern Times*. London: Oxford University Press, 1961.
Kelleher, Marie. *The Measure of Woman: Law and Female Identity in the Crown of Aragon*. Philadelphia: University of Pennsylvania Press, 2010.
Lotter, Friedrich. "Die Judenverfolgung des 'König Rintfleisch' in Franken um 1298. Die endgültige Wende in den christlich-jüdischen Beziehungen im Deutschen Reich des Mittlealters." *Zeitschrift für Historische Forschung* 15 (1988): 385–422.
Malkiel, David. "Jews and Apostates in Medieval Europe: Boundaries Real and Imagined." *Past and Present* 194 (2007): 3–34.
Müller, Jörg R. "*Erez Gezerah*—'Land of Persecution': Pogroms Against the Jews in the *Regnum Teutonicum* from c. 1280 to 1350." In *The Jews of Europe in the Middle Ages*, edited by Christoph Cluse, 245–60. Turnhout: Brepols, 2004.
Reiner, Avraham (Rami). "*Mumar 'Okhel Neveilot Le-Te'avon—Pasul? Mashehu 'Al Nusah U-Perusho Be-Yedei Rashi*." In *Lo Yasur Shevet Me-Yehudah*, edited by Y. Hacker and Y. Harel, 223–28. Jerusalem: Mosad Bialik, 2011.
Salfeld, Siegmund. *Das Martyrologium des Nürnberger Memorbuches*. Berlin: Verlag von Leonhard Simion, 1898.
Shatzmiller, Joseph. "Jewish Converts to Christianity in Medieval Europe, 1200–1500." In *Cross Cultural Convergences in the Crusader Period: Essays Presented to Aryeh Grabois on His Sixty-Fifth Birthday*, edited by Michael Goodich, Sophia Menache, and Sylvia Schein, 297–318. New York: Peter Lang, 1995.
Smail, Daniel Lord. *The Consumption of Justice: Emotions, Publicity, and Legal Culture in Marseille, 1264—1423*. Ithaca, NY: Cornell University Press, 2003.
Tartakoff, Paola. "Testing Boundaries: Jewish Conversion and Cultural Fluidity in Medieval Europe, c. 1200–1391." *Speculum* 90, no. 3 (2015): 728–62.
Ta-Shma, Israel. "Between East and West: R. Asher b. Yehiel and His Son R. Jacob." In *Creativity and Tradition: Studies in Medieval Rabbinic Scholarship, Literature, and Thought*, edited by Israel M. Ta-Shma, 111–26. Cambridge: Harvard University Press, 2006.
Urbach, Efraim E. *Ba'alei Ha-Tosafot: Toldotehem, Hiburehem, Shitatam*. 5th ed. Jerusalem: Bialik Institute, 1986.
Yerushalmi, Yosef Hayim. "The Inquisition and the Jews of France in the Time of Bernard of Gui." *Harvard Theological Review* 63, no. 3 (1970): 363–76.
Yudlov, Yitzhak S., ed. *She'elot U-Teshuvot Le-Rabbenu 'Asher ben Yehiel*. Jerusalem: Makhon Yerushalayim, 1970.
Zelzenik, Aharon, et al., ed. *She'elot U-Teshuvot Ha-Rashba*. Vol. 2. Jerusalem: Makhon Yerushalayim, 1997.

RACHEL FURST is a research fellow in medieval Jewish history at Ludwig Maximilian University of Munich, where she also lectures on Jewish history and Jewish law.

11 The Jewish Physician as Respondent, Confidant, and Proxy

The Case of Marcus Herz and Immanuel Kant

Robert Leventhal

> "We should try to understand the History of Friendship, or Friendships."
> —Michel Foucault[1]

THE HISTORIES OF the philosophy and practice of friendship amply demonstrate that this most important form of achieved rather than ascribed or constrained human relatedness[2] is not, nor has it ever been, a clear, straightforward matter. The dilemmas, trials, frustrations, issues of trust, privacy and intimacy, competition and envy, and the tests of morality and justice, are well known to all who have genuinely engaged in its practice.[3] While the different forms of friendship articulated in antiquity by Aristotle and Cicero continued well into the seventeenth century, the eighteenth century marked a transformational moment: friendship became a private, intimate, and equal relationship between two individuals rather than a relationship based on inherited obligation, *Stand*, reciprocal service, self-interest, duty or loyalty.[4] In the German states of the eighteenth century, even as Jews and gentiles lived side by side in small towns and villages, and as Jews served the courts, friendship between Jews and Christians outside the parameters of mutually beneficial commercial or monetary interactions, duty, or service was exceedingly rare.

In the following, I will argue that Kant's negative remarks about Jews and Judaism notwithstanding, and with a full view of the dissonances, disparities, frustrations, and difficulties of their relationship, Marcus Herz and Kant managed to forge an extraordinary friendship based on a high degree of trust, judged within the framework of eighteenth-century German-Jewish relations and in the context of Kant's theory of "moral friendship" as well.[5] The use of the term "trust" might give us pause, as it, too, is an historical concept. For the purposes of this essay, I rely on Kant's own discussion of trust and friendship in the *Die Metaphysik der Sitten* (1797). The methodological justification for this is twofold: first, Kant's text crystallizes and reflects the transformation of the concept of friendship within the emerging semantics of individuality[6] in the eighteenth century mentioned above, and second, we remain historically sensitive to the common notions and practices articulated at the time. I argue that only when held up against an ahistorical, imaginary, and overly idealizing, rigid sense of friendship does their relationship fail, as some scholars have suggested. I thus navigate a third path between naïve affirmation and idealization on the one hand, and unwarranted devaluation and dismissal of their friendship on the other. Their friendship traversed multiple borderlands and boundaries in the almost thirty years of their correspondence: not merely Christian and Jewish, but mentor and disciple; the generational divide; philosophy and medicine, or the *Streit der Fakultäten*; theory and practice; the public and the private; Kant's critical system and Herz's unique and still underexplored, highly psychological, aesthetic, and experimental philosophy.[7] Finally, their friendship had to navigate a decisive rupture in the late 1780s, when two parallel developments called into question the central concerns, ideals, and values of the *Aufklärung*: first, the failure of meaningful reforms to absolutistic state power and the arbitrary authority of the princes that had been advanced by many key figures of the Enlightenment,[8] and second, the cultural swerve from the Enlightenment ethos of publicity, universalism, and reason, to which both Kant and Herz remained committed despite their differences, first to the growing sentimentalism of *Empfindsamkeit* and the tumultuous Sturm und Drang movement of the 1770s, and then, in the 1790s, the shift towards Romanticism, with its unbridled empowerment of the imagination, feeling, and immediacy against reason (*Vernunft*) and understanding (*Verstand*). I begin with the historical context and origins of their friendship, briefly discuss the existing scholarship and positions on their relationship, then proceed to the evolution of the friendship itself and its interpretation, specifically with regard to Kant's concept of moral friendship, closing with some remarks on what their friendship might be able to tell us about how we think about German-Jewish relationships and the history of philosophy more generally in this period.

In 1762, Marcus Naphtali Herz (1747–1803), a particularly bright young Jewish man from Berlin, arrived in Königsberg to become the apprentice of a wealthy Jewish merchant. Königsberg was the site of one of the most important and enlightened Jewish communities in all of Germany, the first place of the publication of the journal *Ha-Me'-assef* (*The Collector,* 1783–1812),[9] and the city of the Albertina, the Universität Königsberg, one of first and most significant institutions of higher learning in Brandenburg-Prussia accessible to Jews. In 1766, recognized by and with the support of the Jewish community of the city, Herz matriculated in the medical faculty at the Albertina, which had the highest percentage of

Jewish students of any institution of higher learning in the German territorial states:[10] in the period 1731–1800, seventy-five Jews enrolled in the faculty of Medicine.[11] Medicine was the only faculty open to Jews in the German territories, and access was restricted to a small number of Protestant universities.[12] Because Jews were barred from positions in the civil service, medicine was the most significant path for a Jew to move out of the traditional merchant-commerce milieu and enter into modern German literary-scientific society.[13] For the next four years, in addition to his courses in anatomy, physiology, and nosology at the Albertina, Herz attended courses in philosophy taught by Immanuel Kant (1729–1804). Herz participated in Kant's classes on logic, metaphysics, physics, mathematics, law, and morality, as did many other Jewish students: Jacob Hirsch, Marcus Samuel, Aaron Issac Joël, and Isaac Abraham Euchel. Herz became one of Kant's most brilliant students. After leaving Königsberg in 1770, Herz first returned to Berlin, where he studied at the Collegium Medico-Chirurgicum, one of the foremost medical training sites in Europe, and then matriculated at the Universität Halle, as many Jewish medical students did, where he received his doctorate in medicine in 1774.[14] He then returned to Berlin, where he became a close friend of Mendelssohn, served as chief physician at the Jewish Hospital, founded in 1755, mentored young Jewish medical students, and held lectures on philosophical and scientific topics in the home he shared with his wife Henriette Herz, whose salon was one of the most famous in Europe. In addition to his activities as a physician, Herz published important philosophical essays and monographs on Kant, aesthetics, empirical psychology, and anthropology.[15] Although Berlin did not have a university at the time, Herz was appointed professor of philosophy in 1787 by Friedrich Wilhelm III; he was the first Jew to receive this title, and the only Jew to receive it in Brandenburg-Prussia until 1853. Although he was nominated and highly recommended to the Berlin-Brandenburg Academy of Sciences, Herz was repeatedly rejected because of his Jewish origins.

On March 31, 1770, Immanuel Kant was appointed professor of logic and metaphysics at the university, and, as was the custom in such appointments, called on to deliver an inaugural lecture. Kant chose his student Marcus Herz as "respondent" to defend the dissertation *On the Form and the Principles of the Sensible and Intelligible World*.[16] The respondent was tasked with the defense of the dissertation against three opponents, in this case all gentile students at the Albertina. The defense took place on August 21, 1770, in the Aula of the University. For Herz as a Jew, this was a tremendous, even unheard of honor; for Kant, it was a provocative decision. Kant had to confront and overcome the strong objections of the Faculty Senate for designating a Jew to this role. Herz was apparently excluded from the festivities after the defense.[17] The title page of the dissertation attests to the importance accorded to the respondent: in print and in the lecture hall, Kant, the proponent, was essentially sharing the stage with Herz, his

DE
MVNDI SENSIBILIS
ATQVE
INTELLIGIBILIS
FORMA ET PRINCIPIIS.

DISSERTATIO PRO LOCO
PROFESSIONIS LOG. ET METAPH. ORDINARIAE
RITE SIBI VINDICANDO,

QVAM,

EXIGENTIBVS STATVTIS ACADEMICIS,
PVBLICE TVEBITVR
IMMANVEL KANT.

RESPONDENTIS MVNERE FVNGETVR
MARCVS HERTZ, Berolinensis,
Gente Ivdaevs, Medicinae et Philosophiae Cvltor,

CONTRA OPPONENTES

GEORGIVM WILHELMVM SCHREIBER, reg. bor. art. stvd.
IOHANNEM AVGVSTVM STEIN, reg. bor. i. v. c.
ET
GEORGIVM DANIELEM SCHROETER, elbing. s. s. theol. c.

IN AVDITORIO MAXIMO
HORIS MATVTINIS ET POMERIDIANIS CONSVETIS
DIE XX. Avg. A. MDCCLXX.

REGIOMONTI,
Impensis Io. Iac. Kanteri.

The title page of Kant's Inaugural Dissertation of 1770, *On the Form and the Principles of the Sensible and Intelligible World*, with Marcus Herz from Berlin listed as the respondent, Jew, and student of medicine and philosophy. Courtesy of the Thüringer Universitäts- und Landesbibliothek, Jena.

defendant.[18] Herz made two trips to Königsberg to visit his teacher and mentor Kant, the first in 1772 and a second, with Moses Mendelssohn, in 1777. They remained in correspondence until 1797. Their correspondence is generally regarded as the most important exchange for an understanding of Kant's development, particularly in the eleven years between the inaugural dissertation of 1770 and the publication of the *Critique of Pure Reason* in 1781.[19]

There are several competing narratives regarding the relationship between Herz and Kant. The biographical sketches written directly after Kant's death by L. Borowski, R. B. Jachmann, and E. A. C. Wasianski dismiss Herz's importance in general, and his significance for Kant and his development in particular.[20] According to these accounts, Herz was merely a disciple of the great master in his formative years; there is no recognition of Herz as a philosopher in his own right, no recognition of his cultural accomplishments, nor any sense of their intellectual bond. While they are of historical interest, one can reasonably discount these depictions, written by Protestant theologians primarily interested in apologetics. Historical Kant scholars, above all Lewis White Beck and German-Jewish historians, including Schulte, Feiner, Hertz, Lowenstein, and Meyer, and the newer biographies of Kant—by Ritzel, Keuhn, Dietzsch, and Geier—adopt a largely affirmative position. Generalizing on this view, Herz was Kant's most brilliant student and went on to become Kant's chief interlocutor and sounding board in the critical "silent years" in which Kant was working out his ideas for his mature transcendental-critical philosophy.[21] Herz was also Kant's public representative in Berlin, particularly in the late 1770s, when he held several series of extremely well-attended and enthusiastically received lectures on various aspects of the Kantian philosophy in his home, one of the most sought-after salons in Berlin.[22] However, without in-depth examination of his philosophical output and his contributions to epistemology, psychology, and aesthetics, Herz is all too often categorized as a "Kantian" and thereby relegated to the voice of the master.[23] Finally, because of his relationship to the illustrious Kant, Herz served, in this view, as a model for many Jews to embrace the natural-scientific-medical *Laufbahn* and to enroll at the Albertina or at one of the other universities where Jews could gain admittance.

For many literary and cultural critics, however, the relationship between Kant and Herz was characterized by increasing disillusionment, mutual misunderstanding, frustration, and resentment. According to Martin Davies, not only does his relationship to Kant suffer on this account, but Herz himself, rendered once again a mere disciple, embarks on a "flawed path of metaphysics," "elides" the subjective and the objective, and "digresses" from Kant's revolutionary critical-transcendental path.[24] Davies goes on to argue, "Herz derived only bitterness from Kant's essentially enlightened, humanistic thinking. Instead of moving with the current or cultural revolution, Herz found himself in the bewildering circumstance of remaining with the reaction against it."[25] Herz developed an *"ontological anxiety* [my emphasis] caused by Kant's critical examination of rationalist metaphysics . . . at times voiced as frustration and resentment."[26] The basis of Herz's misapprehension of Kant is to be found, according to Davies, in the "philosophical premises of the politics of German-Jewish assimilation."[27] While it is true that Herz was never able to embrace Kant's mature critical philosophy, their difference had less to do with the politics of German-Jewish assimilation than with profound differences of philosophical temperament and Herz's unwillingness to accept Kant's transcendental idealism, utterly foreign to his anthropological-psychological approach to epistemology, aesthetics, and morality.

An even stronger critical assessment has been offered by Peter Fenves, who asserts that "a careful evaluation of Kant's relation to Marcus Herz is necessary for any thoughtful consideration of Kant's relation to Judaism,"[28] but then attacks the relationship as one of Kant's "contempt" toward his former student because Kant allegedly dismissed Herz's *Versuch über den Schwindel* (1791), having his servant place it aside with an acerbic comment that he did not suffer from vertigo and therefore did not need it. Against Manfred Kuehn's weak explanation that Kant was not terribly interested in empirical psychology, Fenves concludes, "The reason for Kant's surprising *contempt for his former student* and *apparent friend* [my emphases] has to lie elsewhere. That it has something to do with his ambivalence towards the Jews-Palestinians, which seemed to have intensified with age, cannot be seriously doubted."[29] While Fenves's analysis points up some interesting paradoxical aspects of Kant's theory of friendship as presented in "The Doctrine of Virtue" section of the *Metaphysics of Morals*—especially that respect entails a form of mastery and surveillance—the argument concerning Herz and Kant's friendship with him seems flawed in two ways: first, even if it is true that Kant "contemptuously dismissed" Herz's study on vertigo in the privacy of his home, one cannot conclude from this event alone that their friendship was merely "apparent." Secondly, it is methodologically spurious to suggest that, because of Kant's well-known, largely negative public attitude toward Jews in general,[30] his relationship with Herz could not be anything but deceptive, without the respect and equality required by ideal moral friendship, which is precisely what Fenves suggests.[31] The narratives of Jeffrey Librett, Michael Mack, and Ritchie Robertson are equally derogatory. Librett barely touches on Herz, and Mack does not discuss the relationship, leaving us to surmise how they might devalue it from what they argue concerning the problematic gentile figurations of the Jew as "the embodiment of the heteronymous" and Judaism as "materialistic."[32] Robertson is unequivocal in his judgment: "Biographical documents suggest a whole series of ill-requited attachments between Jews and Germans in real life. An eighteenth century example is the sad relationship based on mutual misunderstanding between the Berlin physician and philosopher Marcus Herz and his mentor Immanuel Kant."[33]

The first moment or aspect of this relationship I see embodied in the term "respondent." By this, I do not simply mean Kant's appointment of Herz to the position of defendant at the inaugural lecture in 1770. As Jacques Derrida poignantly implies, this term brings us into close proximity with both the response of the Other and the responsibility toward the Other.[34] Kant's choice of Herz for the defense of the Inaugural Dissertation of 1770 itself implied an enhanced level of trust. The correspondence gives ample evidence that Kant relied on and trusted Herz to provide him with criticism, suggestions, and commentary on his emerging and then, in 1781, nascent critical system. Of all the people Kant was hoping to be able to count on—he specifically mentions Johann Heinrich Lambert and Moses Mendelssohn—it was Herz to whom, during the 1770s, he actually communicated the structure and specific arguments of his burgeoning system. Herz's letter of July 9, 1771, outlined the differences evident in his own critical commentary on Kant's inaugural dissertation presented in his *Observations on Speculative Philosophy*, published in 1771, which contained a number of *Auschweifungen*, or digressions, from his mentor, as Herz himself puts it.[35] In his reply of February 21, 1772, to Herz, Kant presented the fundamental questions and arguments that guided his thinking during the incubation period of the first *Critique*: "On what ground," Kant asks, "is there the basis for any relation whatsoever between the representation and the object?"[36] The idea of passive synthesis—the proposal that something in the human mind simply responds in a synthetic manner to the manifold of experience—is quickly dismissed as inadequate. Kant then puts forth the decisive point fundamental to his entire critical-transcendental approach:

> The pure concepts of the understanding cannot be abstracted from the sensations of the senses, nor can they express the receptivity of our representations through the senses, but rather must have their origin in the nature of the soul itself.[37]

Herz had grasped Kant's precritical philosophy of the Dissertation and its problems better than any other reader. His *Observations on Speculative Philosophy* of 1771 demonstrate a penetrating and highly critical understanding of his teacher's work. Now he was being called on to comment on and offer criticism of the central idea of Kant's magnum opus. The fact that, among all of his many correspondents, Kant imparted the emerging critical system to Herz alone implies that Kant trusted Herz as no other in the decisive phase of working through the difficult arguments of what was to become the *Critique of Pure Reason*. Rather than viewing the mentor-disciple relationship merely as an obstacle to an open and candid airing of views, the textual evidence suggests that it was precisely

Herz's position as loyal disciple/student that allowed their correspondence to serve as such a proving ground for his thought. To no other person did Kant so fully impart the overall structure and the specific arguments of the critical architecture at length as it unfolded. When the first *Critique* appears in 1781, Kant writes to Herz:

> The book contains the result of all the manifold investigations that began with the concepts, which we, under the name of *mundi sensibilis und intelligibilis*, discussed, and it is a very special occasion, to present to the same insightful man for his judgment, who found it worthy enough to work on my ideas and was so perceptive to plumb the depths of my thought, the total summation of my philosophical efforts of the last years.[38]

It is notable that Kant uses the first-person plural to designate the subject of their discussions. With the publication of the *Critique of Pure Reason* in 1781, Kant sent four copies to Herz in Berlin, one for Herz himself and three for personal distribution to Mendelssohn, Lambert, and Johann Georg Sulzer. In the letter of May 11, 1781, Kant expresses his eagerness—one might even say anxiousness—to receive from Herz a positive review of the first *Critique*. To be sure, the urgency with which he writes appears somewhat demanding: "From the man who, of all of my students whom fortune has sent me, grasped my thoughts and ideas most exactly and quickly, alone can I hope that he will [also] arrive at an understanding of my system, which would alone make possible a decisive judgment concerning its value."[39] One can certainly read this as flattery and solicitude in the expectation of a positive review of Kant's newly minted masterpiece. What appears significant, however, is that Kant also reveals his need for Herz's approbation: it is evident from the letter that Kant was struggling with the new approach and that he was in effect relying on Herz to provide him with an additional perspective to affirm his own sense of the validity of the critical system. When Kant does not receive the hoped-for letter of review from Mendelssohn, he confides his deep disappointment to Herz: "That Herr Mendelssohn has put aside my book is quite disappointing to me, but I hope that it will not remain so. He is among all whom in this world could enlighten, the most important man, and it is to him, to Herr Tetens, and to you, my dear friend, above everyone else, that I look to."[40] The language and tone of these letters from around the time of the appearance of the first *Critique* exhibit a confidential and intimate trust between Kant and Herz quite unlike any we have from Kant's other correspondence, and indeed quite rare for correspondence between Germans and Jews in the 1780s.

Among the ideals or virtues ascribed to the ideal of friendship in the European Enlightenment, trust was perhaps the single most important factor. The defining moment of this crucial transformation in the history of modern friendship finds its most succinct formulation in Kant's determination of what he referred to as "moral friendship" in his *Lectures on Ethics* and in the *Metaphysics of Morals* (1797): "Moral friendship is the complete confidence of two persons in disclosing to one another their secret thoughts and feelings, so far as such disclosure is compatible with mutual respect."[41] The criteria of intimate communication and openheartedness, along with benevolent love with respect to others (*die Liebe des Wohlwollens gegen Andere*), equality, reciprocal possession (*wechselseitiger Besitz*), and the love for mutual pleasure (*die Liebe zu dem wechselseitigen Wohlgefallen*), together prescribe a particularly modern form of friendship based on trust and confidence (*Vertrauen*), and intimacy (*Vertraulichkeit*), rather than mere reciprocal concern, mutual association (*wechselseitige Gesellschaft*), need, obligation, or common taste.[42] As David Garrioch has stated, "The ideal that many people attempted to realize was that of the intimate friend, a very personal and exclusive relationship that was a very long way from the Ciceronian ideal of virtuous friendship as a basis of political life."[43] Mutual trust, or the ability to keep something in confidence, not merely reliance, would have to be assumed for any such relationship of true moral friendship. For Kant, the intimate disclosure of one's innermost thoughts and feelings presupposes that each person in the relationship be able to receive such intimate communications in a spirit of trust. As Kant writes, "The closest friendship demands that this understanding and trusted friend should also feel bound not to impart secrets confided to him to any other."[44] To trust meant to be able to entrust one's innermost, secret thoughts and feelings to another without any fear that the other might disclose these to anyone else or to use them for any purpose whatsoever. But it also entailed not intruding on the other to divulge something that had been entrusted to her. This absence of fear Kant refers to as total or complete trust:

> If he finds a man of understanding with whom he need not fear this danger but can unburden himself in *complete trust* [my emphasis]—a man who in addition shares his ability to judge things in a similar manner—he can give voice to his thoughts; he is not fully alone with his thoughts and enjoys a freedom that he must do without in among the masses, where he must close himself off in himself.[45]

From the *Lectures on Ethics* in the early 1770s to the 1790s, however, Kant grappled first with the balance of love and respect required of such a moral friendship, then increasingly with the equally delicate measure of intimacy and respect. Thus the sentence from *The Metaphysics of Morals* (1797) defining "moral friendship" accentuates "insofar as such disclosure is compatible with reciprocal mutual respect."[46] This shift is decisive, for it seems to impose limits on the degree of intimacy possible and desirable in such a friendship. At the very least, it suggests a boundary of intimacy that can only be negotiated by an intensification of reciprocity, a deepening of trust, the sense being that if one's confidant does not reveal as much of herself, one might lose the respect of the other by revealing oneself too much. In fact, Kant explicitly questions the ability to find the perfect balance of the two due to the "natural antagonisms" inherent in human nature, and offers only the delimitation of intimacy (*Vertraulichkeit*) as necessary to the maintenance of respect (*Achtung*):

> For one can consider the former [love] as attraction (*Anziehung*), and the latter [respect] as repulsion (*Abstoßung*), and if the principle of the first requires increasing closeness, the latter seems to suggest holding one another at an appropriate distance, which the limitation of intimacy expresses in the rule that even the best of friends should not make themselves too familiar with one another.[47]

It is remarkable that at this point in the discussion of moral friendship, Kant refers back to the relation between the "higher" (*Höhere*) and the "lower" (*Niedrige*) partners. He states that complete disclosure might cause the higher one to be injured in her pride (*gekränkt sein*) and to defer (*aufschieben*) the requisite respect for a moment (*für einen Augenblick*), and suggests further that such an injury of respect might damage such a relationship beyond repair (*unwiederbringlich*), even though the external relation is brought back into the pre-existing balance.

Why does Kant issue a differential of the higher and the lower when, according to his own theory, moral friendship relies on the equality of the two persons? For Kant, one simply cannot escape from the possibility of a loss of respect, the sense that one will fall in the other's estimation. This introduces a sense of anxiety concerning the maintenance of equality and reciprocity so important to moral friendship, which, at least at first sight, seems to signal an inherent fear at odds with the former exposition of complete trust. The important question that emerges from Kant's discussion of moral friendship and the necessary equilibrium of intimacy and respect is, therefore, that given the "natural antagonism" of human nature and the moral fact that people will always feel a certain degree of anxiety in the face of the danger of losing respect, how does one trust in order to be able to trust? That is, how is the trust required for moral friendship first warranted or grounded? Kant, I would argue, can only respond by asserting, first, that such trust must be based on judgment and respect, and second, that one cannot be intimidated by such constant danger (*beständiger Gefahr*) and must, within limits, risk losing respect for the other or losing respect oneself for the greater potentiality of what moral friendship has to offer. Moral friendship thus now appears far less stable and more vulnerable than it does in Kant's bold positive utterances about the moral virtue and social value of friendship. The fragility of the delicate balance between intimacy and respect in Kant's theory of friendship, and the resultant tentative nature of trust (for one must continue to trust in order to trust, and will not go on trusting if the presumed reciprocity and respect has been injured, as Kant asserts) provide a prism through which we might view Kant's most important friendship. Kant and Herz both recognized and respected the limits and shortcomings of the other. Their differences of age, status, religion, and philosophical temperament notwithstanding, they continued to maintain a strong relationship of mutual trust and intimacy, the very definition of moral friendship.

The second rubric in my title refers to the manifold ways in which Kant takes Herz into confidence and divulges quite personal, private aspects of his state of mind and body—mood, health (particularly digestion), sociability, and attitude—in great physiological and psychological detail. Kant in fact shared his most intimate fears and concerns regarding his body and health with Herz. Most of these communications concern what was referred to in antiquity and the eighteenth century as dietetics and what we have come to designate as care of the self.[48] As a student of medicine and then as physician, Herz was, for Kant, the person—aside from Kant's personal physician in Königsberg—to whom he would turn in all matters of health and well-being. Kant's hypochondria and his response to it have been well documented.[49] We have the stunning pathography of Harmut and Gernot Böhme—*Das Andere der Vernunft*—to thank for a most perspicacious look into the hidden recesses of Kant's tortuous inner regime of defense, renunciation, fear of the Other, repudiation of the sensual world, and rejection of all forms of heteronomy.[50] Despite, or even perhaps precisely because of Kant's debilitative, severe psychic constitution, his demanding nature and plaintive appeals, Herz countered each of Kant's medical and psychological crises with steady empathy and care. Numerous letters attest to Herz's ongoing concern regarding Kant's health, as well as Kant's reliance on and solicitation of Herz's advice in medical matters. We find such an exchange at the beginning of their correspondence. Kant wrote to Herz of the stress and dysthymia he was experiencing: "I have been in the last days very indisposed, and the burdens of the *collegien* that have been placed on me have not allowed me to seek any repose, nor reply to letters as I have promised."[51] Herz not only voices his concern, but also counsels him as to how he might mitigate the strain: "Is it not possible for you to lessen the pressure of your *Collegien*? If you were to lecture only half of the afternoon and in a less agitated manner? . . . If you think it could be valuable for me to consult with your physicians there, be so good as to write me in detail concerning the entire state of your body, how happy I would be if I could be the smallest instrument to your well-being."[52] The intimacy of their communication extends into the late 1780s. On August 20, 1787, Kant describes his digestive dysfunctions at length and in minute detail, his "bloating in the cardiac opening," "obstructions," "insufficient bowel movements," and "constipation."[53] Kant writes of his high reactivity to medication of any kind and asks Herz to prescribe something for him in a small dosage. Certainly, Herz as the disciple turned physician played a role in enabling this sort of intimacy, yet Kant was under the care of the Jewish physician Aaron Isaac Joël (1747–1813) in Königsberg whom he trusted.[54] In addition, this intimate tone did not only issue from Kant; it flowed both ways. In the famous letter of November 25, 1785, Herz waxes nostalgic regarding his university days in Königsberg until their powerful, sudden ceasura: "But those times are gone, now everything is different. The life of the practicing physician is the most disruptive and exhausting for the mind and the body."[55] Herz and Kant did away with formalities, as Kant had suggested to Herz in the letter of February 21, 1772: "I count on your lasting affinity and friendship just as you can always be assured of mine . . . between us, the guarantee of the candid concern that each demonstrates towards the other must replace the need for mere formalities."[56]

Kant and Herz both made good on this. Kant expressed unease and displeasure openly to Herz and explicitly reproached him when Herz likened him to Lessing in the introduction to his *Versuch über die Verschiedenheit des Geschmacks* of 1776.[57] He communicated his frustration when Herz constantly urged Kant to send him lecture notes of his students and his disappointment concerning the absence of an in-depth response to Kant's first *Critique*. Herz was less forthcoming, to be sure, but did communicate his dismay at Kant's turn away from classical metaphysics, and openly admitted his inability to follow Kant on the critical path after 1781.[58] In 1786, Herz attempted to reassure Kant that he was not a mere defector (*Abtrünniger*), but rather, referring to the intersection of philosophy and medicine, "a renegade, who still wears your uniform, and seeks to perform your service by other means . . . I love wandering around in the borderlands of the two territories, Philosophy and Medicine."[59] Remarkable about this passage is not Herz's genial interdisciplinary self-positioning, but Herz's argument that philosophers (Kant!) ought to visit such "borderlands." "It would be good," Herz writes, "if these borderlands were visited diligently by *philosophers* [my emphasis], practical teachers, and artists."[60] This pointed remark shows clearly that Herz did not refrain from self-assertion and critique on what was surely for them both an important disciplinary question of the limits and bounds of philosophy.

The third and final term in my title expresses the vital function Herz served as Kant's social, cultural, intellectual, and philosophical agent, delegate, messenger, and proxy in Berlin. Rather than a mere functionalization of Herz—the argument that Kant was merely using Herz to disseminate his philosophy to the Berlin intelligentsia, a project which Herz, as we know, despite all of his medical responsibilities, took very seriously—the correspondence suggests the assignation and acceptance of a high degree of responsibility in a spirit of trust far exceeding any mere operational or functional definition. Herz served as mediator between members of the Berlin *Aufklärung* and Kant in Königsberg; he also served as a conduit between the Jewish community of Berlin and the journal *Ha-Ma'assef* (*The Collector*), founded by Isaac Abraham Euchel (1756–1804), who translated parts of Kant's *Critique* into Hebrew and whom Kant also supported, albeit unsuccessfully, in a bid for lecturer at the Albertina.[61] Most importantly, beginning in 1777, with Kant's blessing and encouragement, Herz held public lectures on Kant's philosophy based on their correspondence, a meeting in Königsberg in 1777 (with Mendelssohn), and copies of notes from Kant's students being sent to Berlin on a regular basis. Herz writes to Kant (November 24, 1778):

> I announce today for the twentieth time lectures on your philosophical teachings with an applause that has far exceeded all of my expectations. The number of my listeners increases daily—it has already risen to about thirty—people of some standing and learned people in the professions, professors of medicine, privy counselors, mining advisors, etc. among which also our Minister [Minister of Education, Secretary of State, and later Minister of Justice Karl Abraham Zedlitz] who is always the first in my room and the last to leave.[62]

We know that Herz held these public lectures in his home on (Kantian) logic and metaphysics, philosophical encyclopedia (introduction to philosophy), ontology, and Kant's two favorite topics of the 1770s, psychology and anthropology. Decisive here is not only the evident success of the lectures academically and the extremely difficult task of rendering Kant's ideas and arguments accessible, which Kant himself often found elusive, but the tremendous degree of trust placed in Herz, a Jew, in this crucial cross-cultural knowledge transfer, especially with Kant's full recognition of the profound philosophical differences between them. In a letter of January 1779, Kant wrote to Herz, "The unexpected success of your lectures does not reside in the astuteness and insight in which I have good reason to place absolute trust (*Vertrauen*), but in the popularity, in regard to which, for me, such an undertaking would be worrisome and frightening."[63] Herz as proxy and proponent was clearly able to fulfill a desideratum of Kant's, making the new critical philosophy comprehensible to a broader literate public. And one could plausibly argue that these lectures served as a medium through which Herz was able to immerse himself in Kant's new system. However, contrary to much of the extant scholarship, Herz was not a Kantian.[64] After his commentary on Kant's dissertation in 1771, *Observations on Speculative Philosophy*, Herz went on to publish numerous important works, read by Jews and Christians alike, on aesthetics, empirical psychology, medicine, experimental philosophy, and psychopathology that departed significantly from the arguments of his mentor, both precritical and critical.[65]

Apart from Kant's biographers and the historians of the *Haskalah* who have written affirmatively on the relationship between Kant and Herz, enlisting their bond as a sign of a productive and mutually beneficial relationship between Jews and Christians in the late eighteenth century, suspicion and disavowal by other critics, sometimes quite severe, have sought to deny and dismiss any real friendship or trust between them. Fueled in part by Kant's negative reading of Judaism in his *Religion within the Limits of Reason Alone* and *Anthropology* and his negative statements concerning the Jews, and in part by real, unmistakable dissonances and tensions in each man and in their relationship, the skeptics have declared the relationship to have been, in the final analysis, one of estrangement, bitterness, mutual misunderstanding, and resentment.[66] These are strong terms. Psychoanalytic explanations to the effect that Herz was somehow unable to emancipate himself from his mentor, that Kant was a mere vehicle for Herz to gain access to Berlin society, or that Herz derived existential security from his letters to Kant, or conversely, that Kant could not tolerate Herz's intellectual and disciplinary autonomy, merely used Herz as a disseminator, and had contempt for his former student and his work and writings, simply do not stand the test of rigorous examination of the entire corpus of the correspondence. A careful study of the friendship between Kant and Herz shows an utterly human, fallible, and vulnerable bond of trust and mutual respect between the two, one that cannot be reduced to a utilitarian quid pro quo, as some have suggested, or, on the other hand, idealized as a form of German-Jewish symbiosis. It was a friendship that was not immune from the vicissitudes and asymmetries of the time and place in which they lived and wrote, nor from the oppositions and tensions enumerated above.

Kant's views on Judaism and the Jews have often been enlisted to diminish or even dismiss his friendship with Herz. How could Kant have maintained a close friendship with a Jew, given his negative remarks concerning the Jews and Judaism?[67] As Susan Meld Shell has shown, Kant's relation to Judaism and the Jews was complex and evolved over time.[68] In *Religion within the Limits of Reason Alone* (1783), Kant argued that Judaism was essentially a constitution, not a religion: "Judaism is really not a religion at all, but merely the union of a number of people who, since they belonged to a particular stock, formed themselves into a commonwealth under purely political laws."[69] As he grew older, Kant's negative position regarding the Jews only seemed to intensify. In the *Anthropology* (1800), Kant asserted that the Jews were a nation of deceivers and cheaters, principally because of their history as merchants, diaspora, and their long-standing practice of moneylending.[70] The contradiction between Kant's stated public views concerning the Jews, his support and mentoring of young Jews at the Albertina, and his lifelong relationship with Herz should neither be glossed over nor used as an argument to denigrate or second-guess Kant's trust and friendship. His general characterizations of the Jews as a nation in the context of scholarship and as a writer in the public sphere must be carefully differentiated from the private realm of his intimate relationships and the role he played in the education, mentoring, and support of his Jewish students, extraordinary for the time. The paradox between Kant's public views towards Jews, of which Herz was certainly aware, and his moral friendship with Herz is symptomatic of the deep schism in the late eighteenth century between the public and the private.[71] More pointedly, however, prejudice and friendship do not exclude one another.

Additionally, there has been a tendency to subsume the Jewish philosophy of the late eighteenth century under the heading of Kantianism. However, we should treat with caution the argument, first advanced by Jürgen Habermas years ago but still eerily present,[72] that Kant and Kantianism were the indispensable "philosophical instrument" (*philosophisches Handwerkzeug*) with whose assistance "the magnificent independent Jewish spirit sought to take possession of its religious and social fate,"[73] as if it were Kant who led the way for the *Maskilim* to modernity; as if Kant and Kantianism would emancipate the Jews from their own (self-imposed) exile. Herz and Solomon Maimon, whom Kant described as his sharpest critic,[74] both offered serious objections to Kant's mature critical philosophy, and while there is a well-researched tradition of Jewish Kantianism, the metonymic reduction of Jewish philosophy in need of or dependent on Kant or Kantian philosophy requires a critical reinvestigation. The ambivalence of Habermas's thesis is apparent: on the one hand, Kant and Kantianism served as the mere empowering instruments for the Jews to embrace their own emancipation; on the other hand, Kantianism was the necessary link without which the Jews would have remained alienated to their true purpose, according to Kant: assimilation and social-political integration.[75]

To do justice to Herz, his friendship to Kant, and his specific role in the Berlin *Haskalah* 1770–1800, one must consider Kant's influence on his student: formidable, to be sure. Yet it would be a mistake to reduce Herz to a mere appendage to Kant or view him as the mouthpiece of Kantianism in Berlin. His decisive contributions extended far beyond Kant. Any considered judgment would have to include not merely his philosophical and medical works in their own right, but his position in the Berlin *Haskalah* community and Jewish public sphere more generally; as a mentor to Jewish medical students, as well as an esteemed mediator in Jewish-German scientific relations and knowledge transfer; as the most highly regarded Jewish physician in all of Germany, and as a royally appointed professor of philosophy; and finally, as one of the most prolific public intellectuals and writers in the last quarter of the eighteenth century. Herz was able, as Shmuel Feiner and Natalie Naimark-Goldberg put it so eloquently regarding Jewish physicians in Berlin in general at this time, "to contribute to a wider scientific discourse by publishing books and essays for a European public."[76] This requires that we rewrite the friendship and trust between Herz and Kant as something decidedly more powerful, more nuanced, and more complex than either apologists or skeptics would have us believe.

Notes

1. Michel Foucault, "Sex, Power, and the Politics of Identity," in *Ethics: Subjectivity and Truth. The Essential Works of Michel Foucault*, vol. 1, ed. Paul Rabinow (New York: The New Press, 1994), 171.
2. Anthropologists, sociologists, and psychologists tend to view friendship as an achieved rather than ascribed or assigned relation, meaning that it does not naturally occur simply because of familial, group, tribal, ethnic, class-caste, or national ties. On this, see Liz Spencer and Ray Pahl, *Rethinking Friendship: Hidden Solidarities Today* (Princeton, NJ: Princeton University Press, 2006); and Amit Desai and Evan Killick, *Ways of Friendship: Anthropological Perspectives* (New York: Berghahn, 2013).
3. The many *aporias* of friendship have been beautifully articulated in Jacques Derrida, *The Politics of Friendship* (New York: Verso, 2006).
4. David Garrioch, "From Christian Friendship to Secular Sentimentality: Enlightenment Re-Evaluations," in *Friendship: A History*, ed. Barbara Cain (Ithaca, NY: Cornell University Press, 1993), 165–214.
5. Kant's theory of "moral friendship" as presented in his *Doctrine of Virtue* (1797), part 2 of *The Metaphysics of Morality*. Kant, AA 6:471: "Moralische Freundschaft [. . .] ist das völlige Vertrauen zweier Personen in wechselseitiger Eröffnung ihrer geheimen Urtheile und Empfindungen, so weit sie mit beiderseitiger Achtung gegen einander bestehen kann." All references to Kant from the *Akademie-Ausgabe* (*Gesammelte Schriften*), using the abbreviation *AA*.
6. Niklas Luhmann, "Individuum, Individualität, Individualismus," in *Gesellschaftstruktur und Semantik. Studien zur Wissenssoziologie der modernen Gesellschaft*. Band 3 (Frankfurt: Suhrkamp, 1989), 149–258.
7. Robert Leventhal, "Ästhetische Dimensionen der psychologischen Fallgeschichte: Zu einer Ästhetik der Abweichung und Grenzüberschreitung am Beispiel Marcus Herz" in *Kleine anthropologische Prosaformen der Goethezeit*. Hg. Alexander Košenina/Carsten Zelle (Hannover: Wehrhahn, 2011), 191–229.
8. Including the disastrous "General-Privilegium" decreed by Friedrich II concerning the Jews in 1750, which placed further restrictions on the size of the community, commerce, trade, inheritance, the right to own property, and movement in Prussian lands.
9. *The Collector* was founded by Isaak Abraham Euchel and the *Gesellschaft hebräischer Literaturfreunde* and was the most important journal of the Jewish *Haskalah*.
10. Steffan Dietzsch, *Immanuel Kant. Eine Biographie* (Leipzig: Reclam, 2003), 173.
11. Monika Richarz, *Der Eintritt der Juden in die Akademische Berufe: Jüdische Studenten und Akademiker 1678–1848* (Tübingen: J. C. B. Mohr [Paul Siebeck], 1974), 189; Dietzsch, *Immanuel Kant*, 173: "Die Albertina hatte die höchste Frequenz studierender Juden aller vergleichbaren deutschen Universitäen jener Zeit."
12. Richarz, *Der Eintritt der Juden in die Akademische Berufe*, 28–29.
13. Dietzsch, *Immanuel Kant. Eine Biographie*, 181, 188. Shmuel Feiner and Natalie Naimark-Goldberg, *Cultural Revolution in Berlin* (Oxford: The Bodleian Library, 2011), 61.
14. W. Kaiser and A. Völker, "Berolina iubilans: Berlin physicians as Halle doctoral candidates (V). Marcus Herz (1747–1803)," *Zeitschrift fur die Gesamte Innere Medizin und Ihre Grenzgebiete* 1, no. 42 (21) (1987): 618–23.

15. Herz has only recently been studied as a philosopher in his own right. See Martin L. Davies, *Identity or History? Marcus Herz and the End of Enlightenment* (Detroit: Wayne State, 1996); Christoph Maria Leder, *Die Grenzgänge des Marcus Herz* (Münster: Waxmann, 2007); Stephanie Buchenau, "'Der Grund zu allen liegt in Ihnen': le Kantisme de Marcus Herz," in *Haskalah et Aufklärung. Philosophes juifs des Lumières allemandes. Revue Germanique Internationale* 9 (2009): 53–67; and Stephanie Buchenau, "Marcus Herz: Kritik und Religion," in *Aufklärung und Religion. Neue Perspektiven.* Hg. Michael Hoffmann/Carsten Zelle (Hannover: Wehrhahn, 2010), 223–42.

16. *De mundi sensibilis atque intelligibilis et principiis* (Königsberg: Jacob Kanter, 1770).

17. Manfred Keuhn, *Kant: A Biography* (Cambridge: Cambridge University Press, 2001), 189. Keuhn cites Davies, *Identity or History?*, 20, who in turn cited Haimann Jolowizc, *Geschichte der Juden in Königsberg* (Posen: Joseph Jolowizc, 1867), 92, and Hans Jürgen Krüger, *Die Judenschaft in Königsberg in Preussen, 1700–1802* (Marburg: Johann Gottfried Herder Institut, 1966). See also Dietzsch, *Immanuel Kant*, 109.

18. See Kevin Chang, "Kant's Disputation of 1770: The Dissertation and the Communication of Knowledge in Early Modern Europe," *Endeavor* 31, no. 2 (2007): 48.

19. Geier, *Kants Welt*, 143: "Vor allem sein Briefwechsel mit Herz ist ein Fundus, aus dem sich Kants Gedankenentwicklung und Stimmungswechsel in diesem Jahrzehnt rekonstruieren lässt." See also Ernst Cassirer, *Kants Leben und Werk* (Darmstadt: Wiss. Buchgesellschaft 1977), 130.

20. The accounts of L. E. Borowski, R. B. Jachmann, and E. A. C. Wasianski are contained Felix Gross, ed., *Immanuel Kant. Sein Leben in den Darstellungen von Zeitgenossen* (Darmstadt: Wissenschaftliche Buchgesellschaft, 1980; rpt. 2012).

21. This position stems largely from Joseph Grozinger, *Geschichte der jüdischen Philosophie und der jüdischen Philosophen von Mendelssohn biz zur Gegenwart* (Berlin: Philo Verlag, 1930), 102–4.

22. On the dual Berlin salon of Henrietta and Marcus Herz, see the still-classic study by Deborah Hertz, *Jewish High Society in Old regime Berlin* (New Haven: Yale University Press, 1988), especially 119–203.

23. See Davies, *Identity or History?*, 55; Dietzsch, *Immanuel Kant*, 133; Michael A. Meyer, *Die Anfänge des modernen Judentums: Jüdische Identität in Deutschand 1749–1824* (Munich: C. H. Beck, 2011), 66; Christoph Schulte, *Die jüdische Aufklärung: Philosophie, Religion, Geschichte* (Munich: C. H. Beck, 2002), 103–5. A notable exception is the dissertation by Jason Michael Peck, "From the Transcendental to the Particular: German Jewish Philosophy at the End of the Eighteenth Century," Diss., University of Minnesota, 2006.

24. Davies, *Identity or History?*, 31–37.

25. Davies, *Identity or History?*, 66.

26. Davies, *Identity or History?*, 67.

27. Davies, *Identity or History?*, 67.

28. Peter Fenves, *Late Kant. Toward Another Law of the Earth* (New York: Routledge, 2003), 185.

29. Fenves, *Late Kant*, 185.

30. For an account of Kant's relation to Judaism and the Jews, see Susan Meld Shell, "Kant and the Jewish Question," *Hebraic Political Studies* 2, no. 1 (Winter 2007): 101–36; Jonathan Hess, *Germans, Jews, and the Claims of Modernity* (New Haven: Yale University Press, 2002), 145–67; and the exhaustive analysis of Bettina Stangneth, "Antisemitische und Antijudaistische Motive bei Kant? Tatsachen, Meinungen, Ursachen," in *Antisemitismus bei*

Kant und anderen Denkern der Aufklärung, Hg. Horst Gronke (Würzburg: Königshausen & Neumann, 2001), 11–114.

31. Fenves, *Late Kant*, 123. This would require a lengthier discussion, but Kant's "euthanasia of Judaism" expressed in his later philosophy is nothing other than what Kant refers to as the true religion of reason. All institutional religions would ultimately suffer the same fate. Quite another matter is Kant's generalized statements concerning Jews-Palestinians, which, without downplaying their strong negativity, must be historically understood. In a word, it cannot be doubted that Kant, his negative comments notwithstanding, sought to support and further his Jewish students, and had respect for both the resilience of the Jews and the moral teachings of the Old Testament.

32. Michael Mack, *German Idealism and the Jew* (Chicago: University of Chicago Press, 2003), 4–41. Jeffrey Librett, *The Rhetoric of Cultural Dialogue* (Stanford: Stanford University Press, 2000) puts forth a similar argument of how the Jew is imagined in eighteenth-century German philosophy and letters.

33. Ritchie Robertson, *The Jewish Question in German Literature, 1743–1939* (New York: Oxford University Press, 1999), 362.

34. Jacques Derrida, "The Politics of Friendship," *American Imago* 50, no. 3 (1993): 379.

35. That Kant was not particularly pleased with Herz's publication is clear from his letter to Friedrich Nicolai dated October 25, 1772. Kant, *AA* 10:143. The digressions have been noted by Davies, *Identity or History?*, 56–65. Another reading of Herz's decisive "digressions" can be found in my article "Ästhetische Dimensionen der psychologischen Fallgeschichte: Zu einer Ästhetik der Abweichung und Grenzüberschreitung am Beispiel Marcus Herz."

36. Kant, *AA* 10:130: "Aus welchem Grunde beruhet die Beziehung desjenigen, was man in uns Vorstellung nennt, auf den Gegenstand?"

37. "Die reinen Verstandesbegriffen müssen also nicht von den Empfindungen der Sinne *abstrahiert* seyn, noch die Empfänglichkeit der Vorstellungen durch Sinne ausdrücken, sondern in der Natur der Seele zwar ihre Quellen haben." Kant, *AA* 10:130. Lewis White Beck brought attention to this decisive move, and the significance of Herz as interlocutor, in his seminal essay "Kant's Letter to Marcus Herz, February 21, 1772," in *Studies in the Philosophy of Kant* (New York: Bobbs-Merrill, 1965), 54–60.

38. Kant, *AA* 10:266.

39. Kant, *AA* 10:269.

40. Kant, *AA* 10:270. See also Frederick Beiser, *The Fate of Reason* (Cambridge: Harvard University Press, 1993), 172.

41. Immanuel Kant, "Die Metaphysik der Sitten," in *Gesammelte Schriften. Akademie-Ausgabe* 6: 471 (Berlin: Reimer, 1911f): "Moralische Freundschaft (zum Unterschiede von der ästhetischen) ist das völlige Vertrauen zweier Personen in wechselseitiger Eröffnung ihrer geheimen Urtheile und Empfindungen, so weit sie mit beiderseitiger Achtung gegen einander bestehen kann."

42. See Allen Wood, *Kant's Ethical Thought* (New York: Cambridge University Press, 1994), 278–80; Andrea Veltman, "Aristotle and Kant on Self-Disclosure in Friendship," *The Journal of Value Inquiry* 38 (2004): 225–39; and Stijn Van Impe, "Kant on Friendship," *International Journal of Arts & Sciences* 4, no. 3 (2011): 127–39.

43. Garrioch, "From Christian Friendship to Secular Sentimentality," 203.

44. Kant, "Die Metaphysik der Sitten," *AA* 6:472: "zumal da die engste Freundschaft es verlangt, daß dieser verständiger und vertraute Freund zugleich verbunden ist, ebendasselbe

ihm anvertraute Geheimniß einem anderen, für eben so zuverlässig gehaltenen ohne des ersteren ausdrückliche Erlaubniß nicht mitzutheilen."

45. Kant, "Die Metaphysik der Sitten," *AA* 6:472: "Findet er also einen, der Verstand hat, bei dem er in Ansehung jener Gefahr gar nicht besorgt sein darf, sondern dem er mit völligem Vertrauen eröffnen kann, der überdem auch eine mit der seinigen übereinstimmende Art die Dinge zu beurtheilen an sich hat, so kann er seine Gedanken Luft machen; er ist mit seinen Gedanken nicht vöig allein, wie im Gefängnis, und genießt eine Freiheit, die er in dem großen Haufen entbehrt, wo er sich in sich selbst verschliessen muß."

46. Kant, "Die Metaphysik der Sitten," *AA* 6:471: "so weit sie mit beiderseitiger Achtung gegeneinander bestehen kann."

47. Kant, "Die Metaphysik der Sitten," *AA* 6:470: "Denn man kann jene als Anziehung, diese als Abstoßung betrachten, und wenn das Prinzip der ersteren Annäherung gebietet, das der zweiten sich einander in geziemendem Abstande zu halten fordert, welche Einschränkung der Vertraulichkeit, durch die Regel: daß auch die besten Freunde sich unter einander nicht gemein machen sollen, ausgedrückt."

48. Michel Foucault, "Dietetics," in *The Use of Pleasure: The History of Sexuality*, vol. 2, trans. Robert Hurley (New York: Vintage, 1990), 95–116.

49. See Susan Meld Shell, *The Embodiment of Reason* (Chicago: University of Chicago Press, 1996), 284–86. Kant, *AA* 7:104: "Ich habe wegen meiner flachen und engen Brust, die für die Bewegung des Herzens und der Lunge wenig Spielraum läßt, eine natürliche Anlage zur Hypochondrie, welche in frühern Jahren bis an den Überdruß des Lebens gränzte."

50. Harmut und Gernot Böhme, *Das Andere der Vernunft: Zur Entwicklung der Rationalitätsstrukturen am Beispiel Kants* (Frankfurt: Suhrkamp, 1983).

51. Kant, *AA* 10:95.

52. Kant, *AA* 10:101.

53. Kant, *AA* 10:212. Kant tells Herz of his "*Blehungen im Magenmunde,*" "*Obstructionen,*" "*unzureichende Exoneration*" and "*zurük bleibende und sich anhäufende feces.[o]*"

54. Krüger, *Die Judenschaft in Königsberg in Preussen, 1700–1802*, 93. See also Jill Storm, "Culture and Exchange: The Jews of Königsberg, 1700–1820" (PhD diss., Washington University, St. Louis, 2010), 177, and Andreas Kennecke, *Isaac Abraham Euchel: Architekt der Haskala* (Göttingen: Wallstein, 2007), 85.

55. Kant, *AA* 10:425–26.

56. Kant, *AA* 10:135.

57. Kant, *AA* 10:198: "Eine Stelle in demselben liegt mir noch im Sinne, über die ich Ihrer partheyischen Freundschaft gegen mich ein Vorwurf machen muss. Der mir, in Parallel mit *Lessing* ertheilte Lobspruch, beunruhigt mich."

58. See Cassirer, *Kants Leben und Lehre* (1917; rpt. 1977), 130.

59. Kant, *AA* X: 431: "Ein Überläufer, der noch Ihre Uniform trägt, und bey andern Mächten, Ihren Dienst einzuführen sucht [...] ich liebe das Umherwandeln in den Gränzorten der beyden Länder, der Philosophie und der Medizin."

60. Kant, *AA* 10:432.

61. Kuehn, *Kant. A Biography*, 314.

62. Kant, *AA* 10:244.

63. Kant, *AA* 10:247.

64. In Herz's letter of April 17, 1789, he states, "Das System so ganz zu umfassen, es zu durchdringen, dazu hat mich mein praktisches Leben völlig unfähig gemacht." Kant *AA*

10:xxx. Numerous scholars label Herz a Kantian. See Thomas Broman, *The Transformation of German Academic Medicine, 1750–1820* (Cambridge: Cambridge University Press, 1996), 118; David Lowenstein, *The Berlin Jewish Community: Enlightenment, Family, and Crisis, 1770–1830* (New York: Oxford University Press, 1994), 105; Michael A. Meyer, *The Origins of the Modern Jew: Jewish Identity and European Culture in Germany, 1749–1824* (Detroit: Wayne State University Press, 1967; Meyer, *Die Anfänge des modernen Judentums*, 66; Schulte, *Die jüdische Aufklärung*, 165.

65. Davies's assertion that "Herz was no significant cultural innovator in his own right" (Davies, *Identity or History?*, 11) should be questioned not merely on the basis of his publications, teaching, and renown alone, but also on his achievement of a royal appointment to professor of philosophy and medicine (1787), the introduction of secular philosophy into Jewish culture (and the Jewish appropriation of such philosophy), and the cultural capital he brought to the *Haskalah* in general.

66. Davies, *Identity or History?*, 30–38.

67. Another attempt to come to terms with this problem is that of Christoph Maria Leder, *Die Grenzgänge des Markus Herz*, 212–13.

68. Shell, "Kant and the Jewish Question," *Hebraic Political Studies* 2, no. 1 (Winter 2007): 101–36.

69. Kant, *AA* 6:125.

70. Kant, *AA* 7:220. See also Stangneth, "Antisemitische und Antijudaistische Motive bei Kant? Tatsachen, Meinungen, Ursachen," 24–28.

71. Even in so-called enlightened absolutism, discerning who could be trusted and being able to rely on one's friends for secrecy and confidence were crucial.

72. Habermas, "Der deutsche Idealismus der jüdischen Philosophie," in *Philosophisch-Politische Profile* (Frankfurt: Suhrkamp, 1971), 37–66.

73. Habermas, "Der deutsche Idealismus," 45–46. Habermas reads Herz as an instance of the "inflection" of Jewish thought by Kant's critical-transcendental philosophy.

74. Kant, Letter to Herz, May 26, 1789, *AA* 11: 49.

75. It would not be a great stretch now, on the basis of current research, to reverse Habermas's argument with an article entitled "Die jüdische Philosophie des deutschen Idealismus," as the profound influence of Spinoza and the enormous contributions of Maimon, Benjamin, Rosenzweig, and Arendt have emerged from under the shadows of German thought and assumed their rightful place in the history of philosophy.

76. Shmuel Feiner and Natalie Naimark-Goldberg, *Cultural Revolution in Berlin. Journal of Jewish Studies*, Supplement Series 1 (Oxford: The Bodelian Library 2011), 61.

Bibliography

Batnitzky, Leora. *How Judaism Became a Religion: An Introduction to Modern Jewish Thought*. Princeton, NJ: Princeton University Press, 2011.

Beck, Lewis White. "Kant's Letter to Marcus Herz, February 21, 1772." In *Studies in the Philosophy of Kant*, 54–60. New York: Bobbs-Merrill, 1965.

Beiser, Frederick. *The Fate of Reason: German Philosophy from Kant to Fichte*. Cambridge: Harvard University Press, 1993.

Böhme, Harmut, and Gernot Böhme. *Das Andere der Vernunft: Zur Entwicklung von Rationalitätsstrukturen am Beispiel Kants.* Frankfurt: Suhrkamp, 1983.

Boulby, Mark. "Marcus Herz the Psychologist." *Journal für internationale Germanistik*, Reihe A, Band VIII 4 (1980): 327–31.

Broman, Thomas. *The Transformation of German Academic Medicine, 1750–1820.* Cambridge: Cambridge University Press, 1996.

———. "University Reform in Medical Thought at the End of the Eighteenth Century." *Osiris*. 2nd series, vol. 5, *Science in Germany: The Intersection of Institutional and Intellectual Issues*, 36–53. 1989.

Buchenau, Stephanie."'Der Grund zu allen liegt in Ihnen': le Kantisme de Marcus Herz." *Haskalah et Aufklärung. Philosophes juifs des Lumières allemande. Revue Germanique Internationale* 9 (2009): 53–67.

Cassirer, Ernst. *Kants Leben und Werk.* Darmstadt: Wiss. Buchgesellschaft, 1977.

Chang, Kevin. "Kant's Disputation of 1770: The Dissertation and the Communication of Knowledge in Early Modern Europe." *Endeavor* 31, no. 2 (2007): 45–49.

Davies, Martin L. *Identity or History? Marcus Herz and the End of Enlightenment.* Detroit: Wayne State University Press, 1996.

Derrida, Jacques. "The Politics of Friendship." *American Imago* 50, no. 3 (1991): 353–91.

———. *The Politics of Friendship.* New York: Verso, 2006.

Desai, Amit, and Evan Killick. *Ways of Friendship: Anthropological Perspectives.* New York: Berghahn, 2013.

Dietzsch, Steffen. *Immanuel Kant: Eine Biographie.* Leipzig: Reclam, 2006.

———. "Kant, die Juden, und das akademische Bürgerrecht in Königsberg." In *Königsberg. Beiträge zu einem besonderen Kapitel der deutschen Geistesgeschichte*, edited by Joseph Kohnen, 111–25. Frankfurt: Peter Lang, 1994.

Feiner, Schmuel. *The Jewish Enlightenment.* Philadelphia: University of Pennsylvania Press, 2004.

Feiner, Schmuel, and Natalie Naimark-Goldberg. *Cultural Revolution in Berlin. Journal of Jewish Studies.* Supplemental Series 1. Oxford: The Bodleian Library, 2011.

Fenves, Peter. *Late Kant: Towards Another Law of the Earth.* New York: Routledge, 2003.

———. "Politics of Friendship, Once Again." *Eighteenth-Century Studies* 32, no. 2, *Politics of Friendship* (1998/1999): 133–55.

Foucault, Michel. "Dietetics." In *The Use of Pleasure: The History of Sexuality*, vol. 2, translated by Robert Hurley, 109–16. New York: Vintage, 1990.

———. "Sex, Power, and the Politics of Identity." In *Ethics, Subjectivity, and Truth: Essential Works of Michel Foucault, 1954–1984*, edited by Paul Rabinow, translated by Robert Hurley, 163–73. New York: New Press, 1997.

Garrioch, David. "From Christian Friendship to Secular Sentimentality: Enlightenment Reevaluations." In *Friendship: A History*, edited by Barbara Caine, 165–214. London/ Oakville: Equinox, 2009.

Geier, Manfred. *Kants Welt. Eine Biographie.* Reinbek bei Hamburg: Rowohlt, 2003.

Goetschel, Willi. *Kant als Schriftsteller.* Wien: Passagen, 1990.

Graupe, Heinz Moshe. *The Rise of Modern Judaism.* New York: Robert E. Kreige, 1978.

Grayling, A. C. *Friendship.* New Haven: Yale University Press, 2013.

Gross, Felix, ed. *Immanuel Kant. Sein Leben in den Darstellungen von Zeitgenossen.* Darmstadt: Wissenschaftliche Buchgesellschaft, 1980. Reprint, 2012.

Habermas, Jürgen. "Der deutsche Idealismus der jüdischen Philosophie." In *Philosophisch-Politische Profile*, 37–66. Frankfurt: Suhrkamp, 1971.

Hansen, Leeann. "From Enlightenment to *Naturphilosophie*: Marcus Herz, Johann Christian Reil, and the Problem of Border Crossings." *Journal of the History of Biology* 26, no. 1 (1993): 39–64.
Hertz, Deborah. *Jewish High Society in Old Regime Berlin*. New Haven: Yale University Press, 1988.
Hess, Jonathan M. *Germans, Jews, and the Claims of Modernity*. New Haven: Yale University Press, 2002.
Jolowicz, Heimann. *Geschichte der Juden in Königsberg*. Posen: Joseph Jolowicz, 1867.
Kant, Immanuel. *Gesammelte Schriften*. Hrsg. von der Königlich-Preussischen Akademie der Wissenschaften zu Berlin. Berlin: Riemer, 1922.
Kennecke, Andreas. *Isaac Abraham Euchel: Architekt der Haskala*. Göttingen: Wallstein, 2007.
Kisch, Guido. *Forschungen zur Rechts-, Wirtschafts- und Sozialgeschichte der Juden. Ausgewählte Schriften*. Zwei Bände. Sigmaringen: Thorbecke, 1978–79.
Krüger, Hans Jürgen. *Die Judenschaft in Königsberg in Preussen, 1700–1802*. Marburg: Johann Gottfried Herder Institut, 1966.
Kuehn, Manfred. *Immanuel Kant: A Biography*. Cambridge: Cambridge University Press, 2001.
Leder, Christoph Maria. *Die Grenzgänge des Marcus Herz*. Münster: Waxmann, 2007.
Leventhal, Robert. "Ästhetische Dimensionen der psychologischen Fallgeschichte: Zu einer Ästhetik der Abweichung und Grenzüberschreitung am Beispiel Marcus Herz." In *Kleine anthropologische Prosaformen der Goethezeit*. Hg. Alexander Košenina/Carsten Zelle, 191–229. Hannover: Wehrhahn, 2011.
Librett, Jeffrey S. *The Rhetoric of German-Jewish Dialogue: From Moses Mendelssohn to Richard Wagner and Beyond*. Stanford: Stanford University Press, 2000.
Lowenstein, David. *The Berlin Jewish Community: Enlightenment, Family, and Crisis, 1770–1830*. New York: Oxford University Press, 1994.
Luhmann, Niklas. "Individuum, Individualität, Individualismus." In *Gesellschaftsstruktur und Semantik. Studien zur Wissenssoziologie der modernen Gesellschaft*, 149–258. Band 3. Frankfurt: Suhrkamp, 1989.
Mack, Michael. *German Idealism and the Jew: The Inner Anti-Semitism of Philosophy and German Jewish Responses*. Chicago: University of Chicago Press, 2003.
Marcucci, Silvestro. "'Moral Friendship' in Kant." *Kant-Studien* 90 (1999): 434–41.
Meyer, Michael A. *The Origins of the Modern Jew: Jewish Identity and European Culture in Germany, 1749–1824*. Detroit: Wayne State University Press, 1967.
Meyer, Michael A. *Die Anfänge des modernen Judentums: Jüdische Identität in Deutschand 1749–1824*. Munich: C. H. Beck, 2011.
Paton, H. J. "Kant on Friendship." In *Friendship: A Philosophical Reader*, edited by Neere Kapur Badwhar, 133–54. Ithaca, NY: Cornell University Press, 1993.
Peck, Jason Michael. "From the Transcendental to the Particular: German-Jewish Philosophy in the Late 18th Century." PhD diss., University of Minnesota, 2006.
Richarz, Monika. *Der Eintritt der Juden in die akademischen Berufe. Jüdische Studenten und Akademiker in Deutschland 1678–1848*. Tübingen: J. C. B. Mohr, 1974.
Ritzel, Wolfgang. *Immanuel Kant: Eine Biographie*. Berlin: Walter de Gruyter, 1985.
Robertson, Ritchie. *The Jewish Question in German Literature, 1743–1939*. New York: Oxford University Press, 1999..
Shell, Susan Meld. *The Embodiment of Reason: Kant on Spirit, Generation, and Community*. Chicago: University of Chicago Press, 1996.
———. "Kant and the Jewish Question." *Hebraic Political Studies* 2, no. 1 (2007): 101–36.

Schulte, Christoph. *Die jüdische Aufklärung: Philosophie, Religion, Geschichte.* Munich: C. H. Beck, 2002.
Sorkin, David. *The Transformation of German Jewry, 1780–1840.* Oxford: Oxford University Press, 1987.
Spencer, Linda, and Ray Pahl. *Rethinking Friendship: Hidden Solidarities Today.* Princeton, NJ: Princeton University Press, 2006.
Stangneth, Bettina. "Antisemitische und Antijudaistische Motive bei Kant? Tatsachen, Meinungen, Ursachen." In *Antisemitismus bei Kant und anderen Denkern der Aufklärung.* Hg. Horst Gronke 11–114. Würzburg: Königshausen & Neumann, 2001.
Storm, Jill. "Culture and Exchange: The Jews of Königsberg, 1700–1820." PhD diss., Washington University, St. Louis, 2010.
Sutcliffe, Adam. *Judaism and Enlightenment.* Cambridge: Cambridge University Press, 2003.
Van Impe, Stijn. "Kant on Friendship." *International Journal of Arts & Sciences* 4, no. 3 (2011): 127–39.
Veltman, Andrea. "Aristotle and Kant on Self-Disclosure in Friendship." *The Journal of Value Inquiry* 38 (2004): 225–39.
Vorländer, Karl. *Kant: Der Mann und das Werk.* Leipzig: F. Meiner, 1925.
Wood, Allen. *Kant's Ethical Thought.* New York: Cambridge University Press, 1994.
Yovel, Yirmiyahu. *Dark Riddle: Hegel, Nietzsche, and the Jews.* University Park: Penn State University Press, 1998.

ROBERT LEVENTHAL is Associate Professor of German Studies in the Department of Modern Languages at the College of William and Mary. He is author of *The Disciplines of Interpretation*, editor of the volume *Reading after Foucault*, and has written on Lessing, Herder, F. Schlegel, Kant, Moritz, Herz, Kafka, Bernhard, Wenders, Heidegger, Jewish identity, the history of humanistic disciplines, and, most recently, Herder's appropriation of Spinoza in Germany, 1770–1800.

Section Four
The Politics of Trust

12 Perspectives from the Periphery

The East India Company's Jewish Sepoys, Anglo-Jewry, and the Image of "the Jew"

Mitch Numark

AN EXAMINATION OF the historical record would undoubtedly disclose circumstances in which individual non-Jews trusted individual Jews. The more difficult question, one that transcends but inevitably includes the realm of individual experience and perception, is the identification of a place and time in which some cohesive segment of non-Jews trusted Jews—or a subset of Jews—as Jews *because they were Jews*. To address this question, one must examine the relationship between the Jews and non-Jews under consideration and situate Jews within the non-Jewish contexts that they inhabited. British India, on the periphery of the Jewish world, provides a place and perspective from which to examine trust and Jews whose implications, as this essay demonstrates, reverberate out from the British Empire's periphery to Britain itself.

There are a number of reasons an examination of India's Bene Israel Jews and nineteenth-century colonial Bombay—especially during the Company Raj—provides an even more complex case, place, and perspective from which to explore the question of trust and Jews. First, nineteenth-century Bombay was a place where non-Jewish Britons visited, worked, and administered, but they came from places and were reared in cultures enmeshed in traditions that stigmatized Jews. Second, Bombay-based Britons encountered, interacted with, and expounded ideas about not only a multitude of discrete and endogamous non-Jewish Indian communities but also at least two non-Ashkenazi Jewish communities—including the Bene Israel Jews, the largest community of "native" Jews in any nineteenth-century British colony—emically and etically considered distinct. Third, Bombay-based Britons both differentiated Bene Israel Jews from other Jews and identified specific non-Jewish communities as "the Jews of India" and equated them with British Jews. A consideration of Bene Israel Jews and Bombay therefore diversifies and enriches Jewish, South Asian, and British history and reveals an historical situation in which a distinctive Jewish community was considered trustworthy in a colonial context, in which, it is said, "the British saw deception and deceit everywhere,"[1] and in a realm conventionally disassociated with Jews of the time: military service.

Through an examination of Bene Israel Jews in the East India Company's Bombay army, this essay elucidates how the specificities of place, the particularities of subject, and the Indian experiences and encounters of Bombay-based Britons could generate representations that undermine the totalizing agentive and generative power attributed to colonial discourse. It uncovers Bene Israel Jews' actual presence in the Company's Bombay army and demonstrates that in contrast to the predominant depiction of Jews as unscrupulous and avaricious merchants, financiers, and moneylenders, nineteenth-century Britons consistently represented Bene Israel Jews as brave sepoys (native soldiers) and trustworthy native officers. These divergent representations were connected to Bene Israel Jews and British Jews' different occupational profiles, the former's involvement with and exemplary performance in a British-run army, and the latter's comparative absence from British army service and combat. This situation, in conjunction with an imperial vision linking colony and metropole within a unified British world, gave rise to a hitherto-unnoticed element of Jewish emancipation rhetoric in which British Jews sought to prove that they were or should be considered trustworthy, brave, and patriotic British soldiers, subjects, and citizens by pointing to India's Bene Israel Jews. The circumstances that fostered the depiction of Bene Israel Jews as soldiers rather than Shylocks are contextualized by illuminating the ways in which discrete non-Jewish Indian communities were identified with some of the occupations and stereotypes conventionally ascribed to Jews. By bringing together subjects that have been overlooked or treated separately, this essay reveals unrecognized connections between Bombay and Britain and elucidates unnoticed and rarely linked aspects of South Asian, Jewish, and British history. It concludes by suggesting that a consideration of Bene Israel Jews expands the horizons of the Jewish experience and complicates and provincializes conventional understandings of British images of Jews, if not "the Jew."

Bene Israel Jews began serving in the Bombay army in the middle of the eighteenth century. Labeled in Company recruitment documents as the "Native Jew Caste," Bene Israel Jews were explicitly recruited as Jews from as early as 1786.[2] Like other Indian communities the Company recruited into its military, Bene Israel Jews had a precolonial tradition of military service, specifically in the military forces of eighteenth-century Indian princes such as the Angrias of Colaba, the Sidis of Janjira, and the Peshwas.[3] The earliest sources on Bene Israel Jews refer to them as soldiers. Their recruitment into the Bombay army followed Bombay's 1755 annexation of Bankot, which was the first Company possession on the Konkan littoral and functioned as the army's major recruiting center.[4] Located directly south of what became Bombay Presidency's Kolaba District, Bankot's acquisition is also important with respect to Bene Israel enlistment. As the area of the Kolaba District encompassed most of the over one hundred towns and villages where Bene Israel Jews traditionally resided, it is not a coincidence that they began enlisting in the Bombay army five years after Bankot came under the Company's control.[5]

Nineteenth-century British accounts of Bene Israel Jews almost invariably mention their service in the Bombay army and regularly characterize them as good, brave, and loyal soldiers who frequently served as native officers. John Malcolm's 1816 *Short Account of the Rise, Progress, and Character of the Native Army in India* is an early and noteworthy example of this representation. "Jews have always been favourite soldiers in this [Bombay] army," declared Malcolm, "and great numbers of them attain the rank of commissioned officers." Here one of the most distinguished early nineteenth-century British generals, colonial officials (including the governor of Bombay), and authorities on India does something more than merely acknowledge the existence of Jews serving in the Bombay army: he reveals a preference for Jewish soldiers. Malcolm expanded on his brief description in a footnote quoting a Bombay officer who described Jews as "clean, obedient, and good soldiers, [who] make excellent non commissioned and commissioned officers until they arrive at an advanced age, when they often fall off and turn drunkards."[6]

Other distinguished British soldiers and officials in India expand on Malcolm's characterization of Bene Israel Jews as good and loyal soldiers and native officers. Major James Rivett-Carnac (governor of Bombay, 1839–41) wrote glowingly about the Bombay army's native Jewish soldiers in an 1833 letter to Isaac Lyon Goldsmid:

> As soldiers they are esteemed for bravery, subordination, and steady allegiance, and frequently have been raised to the rank of officers, possessing the confidence of their European superiors, and the respect of the native soldiery, composed of various religious persuasions. I know no class from which, in proportion to its extent, more have been selected for the responsible station of a native officer, than from the Jews I have met with in the Bombay army, either with reference to their qualifications in point of capacity and information, or the beneficial effects of their example for general good conduct and attachment to the Government which they serve. I have on all occasions also, in every station in which the Jews of India have come under my observation, found them industrious and inoffensive. . . . The general good feeling which among all denominations prevailed towards them in India, I attribute to the character which they have always sustained, as faithful subjects and useful members of society.[7]

Here one should not fail to notice the source of Rivett-Carnac's opinion: his personal encounters with and knowledge of Indian Jews and Bombay's Jewish sepoys. The significance of the inclusion of Rivett-Carnac's letter in Francis Henry

Goldsmid's 1833 *Arguments Advanced against the Enfranchisement of the Jews*, a text written to counter arguments put forward opposing the removal of Jewish disabilities, is examined below.

Rivett-Carnac's letter describing the loyalty and quality of the Bombay army's native Jews may have been solicited to support Goldsmid's effort to remove the disabilities affecting British Jews, but there are numerous other Company officials and officers who expressed similar sentiments about Bombay's Jewish sepoys without any apparent concern for either British Jewry's image or emancipation. As with John Malcolm, the following sample of Bombay officers and colonial officials' description of the trustworthiness and fighting ability of Bene Israel Jews were expressed explicitly in the context of and in relationship to India and the condition and composition of the Bombay army and its native troops, not the status of British Jews. For example, one Bombay officer insisted that "Musselmen and native Jews, though few in number, are certainly the most manly, clever, and 'European-like' of our sepoys." The Jews, he declared, were "generally very clever, well informed, and trustworthy men, and generally rise quickly to the rank of a native officer."[8] Lieutenant-Colonel Thomas Best Jervis, described recently as a Bombay army officer and official who "crusaded with the task of giving India 'useful knowledge,'"[9] observed that many native Jews "enter into the native army and are proverbially distinguished for their gallantry, fidelity and cleanliness."[10] According to Herbert Bartle Frere (commissioner of Sind and future governor of Bombay), Jews "were usually among the best soldiers in their corps."[11] A year before he was appointed commander-in-chief, the Bombay army's Major General Sir Hugh Rose in his report to the 1858–59 Royal Commission on the Re-Organization of the Army in India (known as the Peel Commission) distinguished Bene Israel Jews as a class from the other communities that comprised the Bombay army: "It is just to the Jews to state that they are universally allowed to be good, intelligent, and faithful soldiers; the only regret expressed by officers respecting them is, that they are so few in numbers."[12]

Nineteenth-century Protestant missionaries and Christian and Jewish travelers also noted the presence of "native" Jews in the Bombay army and commented on the positive opinion of them as soldiers. As the most prominent missionary in Bombay and the individual most associated with and considered as *the* authority on Bene Israel Jews, Reverend John Wilson must be discussed in this regard. In 1840, in the first published scholarly account of the Bene Israel Jews, he wrote: "Some of them, generally bearing an excellent character as soldiers, are to be found in most of the regiments of Native Infantry in the Bombay Presidency; and few of them retire from the service, without attaining to the rank as native officers."[13] These sentiments were repeated in his later publications.[14]

Prominent early nineteenth-century Christian travelers, such as the second Anglican bishop of Calcutta Reginald Heber and the German-Jewish convert to

Christianity Josef Wolff, discussed the Bombay army's Jewish sepoys.[15] Whereas Heber's *Narrative of a Journey through the Upper Provinces of India* is one of the most-cited Indian travelogues, Wolff's 1835 *Researches and Missionary Labours* is comparatively unknown. Like Heber, Wolff was an Anglican minister who encountered Jews in his travels in and outside of India. One crucial difference between these Anglican clergymen is the motivation propelling them to undertake their travels: Wolff's travels were explicitly undertaken to visit Jewish communities around the world and spread the Gospel. Wolff arrived in Bombay in 1833. Unsurprisingly, he met Bene Israel sepoys and remarked that they served "the English as volunteers in their armies, and are esteemed the best native soldiers."[16] Notwithstanding Wolff's encounters with many Jews around the world, germane to this study is that no Jews other than Bene Israel Jews are identified in his travelogue as soldiers.[17]

Even more remarkable is Reginald Heber's observation that the Bombay army is comprised of "no inconsiderable number of Jews."[18] Whereas Wolff's 1835 travelogue has been referenced in some works of Jewish history, neither Heber's Indian travelogue nor his Eastern European travel writing seem to have been examined in Jewish studies scholarship. This is unfortunate, because prior to taking up his episcopal see in India, Heber had traveled extensively throughout Eastern Europe and wrote much about its Jews and their occupations.[19] Some have argued that Heber's Eastern European travels had "prepared him for many things he was to come across in India" and served as a foretaste of his Indian travels.[20] Yet whereas Heber's Indian travelogue is indeed full of explicit comparisons and analogies to what he observed in Eastern Europe, his many encounters with European Jews in no way prefigured his observations about India's Jews. In comparison to his Indian travelogue, his European travel writing contains many more references to Jews. But unlike the Bombay army's Jews, Heber identified no Jews in Europe as soldiers. The lens of anticipation and expectation do not always supersede the realities of experience and the recognition of difference.

Until its abolition in 1858, the East India Company governed Britain's Indian territories. The Company's territories in India were divided into three presidencies (Bombay, Madras, and Bengal), each of which maintained its own army. As Douglas Peers has observed, "the differences between the three armies were for the most part pragmatic responses to local conditions." Like the other armies, the Bombay army developed its own peculiar "well-protected traditions" that in some crucial respects distinguished it from the Bengal army.[21] Space does not permit a detailed examination of the ways in which the Bombay army's distinctive origins, composition, traditions, and policies both distinguished it from the Bengal army and elucidate reasons it employed Bene Israel Jews as soldiers. But one crucial factor must be mentioned: namely, only the Bombay army had a substantial number of Jews in its ranks in part because Bombay was British India's only region that had a substantial Jewish population, and that population consisted overwhelmingly of Bene Israel Jews. In 1837, the presidency's Bene Israel Jews comprised at least seventy-six percent of India's Jews.[22]

One feature that distinguished the Company's Bengal army from the Bombay army—and elucidates the specific context in which Bene Israel Jews could be promoted to the Bombay army's native officer ranks in numbers far out of proportion to their population—is the different systems and principles that governed promotion. Whereas promotion in the Bengal army was based on seniority, in the Bombay army it was based primarily on merit. Sir Patrick Cadell, author of the most comprehensive history of the Bombay army, explicitly linked the overrepresentation of Jews in the native officer ranks to the army's meritocratic system of promotion.[23] Although H. S. Kehimkar's assertion that Bene Israel Jews "constituted almost half of the number of native officers of each Regiment of the Bombay Presidency for nearly a century and a half"[24] is most likely an exaggeration, it is clear that a large number of Bene Israel Jews attained the rank of native officer.[25]

Reliable and official statistics from the 1820s to the 1850s enumerate Bene Israel Jews in the Bombay army. Such information is often presented in the form of lists and tables indicating the number or percentage of the different castes in the army. "Jew" is the designation of one of the five to ten castes almost invariably listed. The adjutant general of the Bombay Army's August 26, 1828, enumeration of the castes in the different Bombay regiments indicates that not only were there 270 native Jews in the army but also that every Bombay native regiment (apart from two) included Jews.[26] By 1842, the number of native Jews in the army rose to 327.[27] An 1840 letter from an anonymous Bombay officer noted that there were thirty to thirty-five Jewish soldiers in the 4th, 21st, and 24th Bombay Native Infantry (BNI) regiments, but the 19th, with its seventy to eighty Jews, had the largest number of Jews in any regiment. All other BNI regiments had between three and fifteen Jewish sepoys. He also noted that there were many Jews in his own regiment, including five or six native officers and the senior noncommissioned officer.[28] Almost two decades later, at the end of 1858, at a time in which there were only 590 Gurkhas in the Bengal army's regular forces, Bene Israel Jews accounted for 370, or about 1.1 percent, of the Bombay army's 33,965 native soldiers.[29]

From a purely numerical perspective, the number of Bene Israel Jews in the Bombay army in any given year was comparatively insignificant. But their number in the army is less important here than their representation. In the context of Bombay Presidency's numerous communities, the Bene Israel community was miniscule. Nevertheless, it contributed an integral, visible, and valued portion of the Bombay army's native troops, especially the native officer and noncommissioned officer ranks. One indication of this—evident in the army's classificatory practice, which elucidates a meaning beyond the specific informational content of the classification—is the regular presence of the category "Jew" as one of the castes that comprised the army. Like other Bombay officers, the statistician Colonel W. H. Sykes noted the manner in which such a small community was valued: "The Jews [in the army], although small in number, are valuable, from their steadiness and ability."[30] The few hundred Bene Israel sepoys serving in the Bombay army in any given year is also significant insofar as in 1837, nearly twenty percent of the Bene Israel community is estimated to have "depended for their livelihood on professional military service."[31]

Surely the consistent representation of Bene Israel Jews as soldiers was partly based on the fact that soldiering was a common nineteenth-century Bene Israel occupation. This occupation—distinctive in degree for a Jewish community of the time qua a Jewish community—is reflected in the British-Jewish historian and social scientist Joseph Jacobs's 1891 *Studies in Jewish Statistics*, which examined the different countries where Jews lived and their "principal trades." Only in India is soldiery listed as a principal Jewish occupation, and Bene Israel Jews, as opposed to India's other Jews, are specifically identified as the soldiers.[32] Non-Jews also identified Bene Israel Jews' military occupation as atypical for a Jewish community of the time. As the premier British military periodical noted, "Natives of the Jewish persuasion are to be found in the Bombay army, probably the only instance in which Jews, as a class, adopt the soldier's profession."[33]

Over the course of the nineteenth-century European Jews increasingly served in the military forces of European states.[34] Even so, keeping in mind the caution required when generalizing about the attitudes of large collectivities, it would be difficult to argue that nineteenth-century non-Jewish Europeans associated contemporary European Jews with military service, attributed to Jews a penchant for soldiering, or trusted Jews *as Jews* to perform their duties as soldiers to the extent to which Bombay-based Britons associated, praised, and trusted Bene Israel Jews with and for their military service. For all the apologetic literature European Jews produced trumpeting Jews' military service,[35] European Jews' increasing participation in European states' armed forces did not erase the widespread gentile perception that Europe's recently emancipated or conscripted Jews were effeminate, nonmilitary, questionably loyal cowards, physically unfit for military service, who "could never become good soldiers."[36] By contrast, before Britain's Indian armies were restructured in the late nineteenth century into largely Punjabi-comprised entities,[37] Bene Israel Jews did not need to produce apologetic literature trumpeting their military service in Bombay because their usefulness as soldiers, bravery in battle, and loyalty was widely recognized. Criticism of Bene Israel Jews certainly existed, but it centered on their inclination to drink, not cowardice nor their inability or fitness to be good soldiers.[38] Whatever praise from gentiles nineteenth-century European Jews may have received for their military service, it would have been surely eclipsed by the numerous other characteristics attributed to and occupations associated with Europe's Jews. No counter-discourse existed identifying the Bene Israel Jews with the characteristics and occupations associated with Europe's Jews.

The recognition of Jewish sepoys as an integral part of the Bombay army was not only institutionalized in its classification of them as Jews but also in the form of the oath of fidelity to the Company and the regiment recruits swore to on entering the Bombay army and that was administered "according to the mode of their [the recruits'] religion."[39] More specifically, in Bombay regiments, the oath of fidelity's Hindustani and Marathi term for God was modified to account for the army's religious diversity; thus, for "Hindoos, 'Bhugwan;' for Jews, Christians, and Mussulmans, 'Khooda.'"[40] The furlough days Bene Israel Jews were allowed to be absent from their duties also instantiates how their service as Jews in the Bombay army was recognized. An illustrative example can be gleaned from the 8th BNI regiment's 1846 regulations stipulating that Jewish sepoys would receive twenty-one furlough days to celebrate nine different Jewish holidays and fast days, many of which Bene Israel Jews had only recently begun to observe, such as Simcha Torah and Tisha B'Av.[41] Not until the middle of the 1880s did British Jews in the regular British army receive furlough days for Jewish holidays.[42] Jews in the 8th BNI regiment also received ten to seventeen more leave days for marriages than any other class of native soldier.[43] In the British Christian-run Bombay army, being a Jew was not a disadvantageous burden. On the contrary, in the Company's military, a sepoy's conversion to Christianity, including the Christianity of the established British churches, would have almost certainly resulted in persecution and dismissal.[44]

The furlough days permitting Bene Israel sepoys to be absent from their duties points to one aspect and consequence of their Bombay army service: the Hebraization of Bene Israel Jews. For example, in 1796, Commandant Samaji Hassaji Divekar built Shaar Harahamim, the first Bene Israel *masjid* (synagogue), as a direct consequence of his Bombay army service. Other Bene Israel soldiers also played crucial roles in establishing and maintaining synagogues and other Jewish institutions and organizations. Bene Israel sepoys were the principal benefactors of the Bene Israel Benevolent Society. Bombay army veterans comprised most of Shaar Harahamim's *choglas* (councilors) in the 1830s. In 1844, while a soldier in Aden, Abraham Isaac Galsukar acquired from Yemenite Jews the first Sefer Torah Bene Israel Jews possessed. Subedar Major Mossaji Israel (Koletkar), celebrated by many as a hero of the 1857–58 Indian Rebellion (the Mutiny), played a crucial role in Thane's Shaar Hashamayim synagogue, which was built in 1879, the year he retired from the army. When another Bene Israel hero of the Mutiny, Subedar-Major Moses Benjamin, retired from the army, he became Shaar Harahamim's chief warden and treasurer.[45] The Bombay army, therefore, played a vital role in enabling the religious and organizational, but not occupational, transformation of Bene Israel Jews into a Diaspora Jewish community like other Jewish communities.

The inclusion of Rivett-Carnac's letter about the Bombay army's Jews in Goldsmid's 1833 *Arguments Advanced Against the Enfranchisement of the Jews* represents an early example of an element of nineteenth- and early twentieth-century Anglo-Jewish discourse: the explicit use of Bene Israel soldiers as evidence of the British monarch's Jewish subjects' loyalty and their willingness to fight on behalf of British interests. The manner in which the experience of Bene Israel Jews was used as a demonstration of and a model for the integration of Jews within Britain reveals a hitherto-unnoticed component of Jewish emancipation rhetoric and Anglo-Jewish history. This, in turn, elucidates two broader phenomena: British Jews and Bene Israel Jews' connected histories and the impact of the British Empire, India, and the East India Company on the lives and identities of Anglo-Jewry.

One practical and profound example of the impact of India and the Company on Anglo-Jewry is the 1744 case *Omychund v. Barker*, which removed any uncertainty about a Jew's testimonial competency in English courts by establishing the authoritative precedent that a Jew's testimony in court was valid if the Jewish witness swore an oath on the Pentateuch or Old Testament.[46] One arresting aspect of the case is that Barker's counsel argued (unsuccessfully) that Omychund's testimony was inadmissible in part because "if a Jew, who accepted the Old Testament but not the New Testament, could not be a witness, then *a fortiori* a Hindu, who accepted neither, could [also] not be a witness."[47] Yet it was the ruling in a case involving the admissibility of a Hindu's testimony in an English court that established the principle that "all persons who believe in a supreme being, who will punish them if they swear falsely, are competent witnesses, and should take the oath in the form binding on them according to the tenets of their religion"[48] and consequently legitimized English Jews' hitherto uncertain testimonial competency. In the context of English courts, the decision in *Omychund v. Barker* meant that—in principle if not in practice—the word of a Jew could be trusted.

A striking element of F. H. Goldsmid's 1833 *Arguments Advanced against the Enfranchisement of the Jews* is that it was written partly to demonstrate the patriotism and loyalty of British Jews but does not include any British Jews among the many different Jewries in the text that manifest their patriotism and loyalty through military service.[49] Derek Penslar has argued that "military service played a major role in eighteenth-and nineteenth-century debates about the emancipation of Jews" even in the case of Britain, which did not have a draft.[50] Without a strong record of their own military service and criticized for not fighting for Britain, British Jews pointed someplace else to demonstrate not only that Jews were patriots who fought for their countries, but also that they fought for Britain. In 1833, Goldsmid answered this charge by pointing to British India, where, unlike in Britain itself, "Jewish inhabitants are admitted to the same privileges with the rest of the natives" and consequently "distinguished for their fidelity and good conduct as citizens, officers, and soldiers; and form a most valuable portion of the native troops."[51]

Whereas the Bombay army counted and classified its Indian Jewish soldiers as Jews from as early as 1786, Jews were not formally recognized or counted in the British army proper as Jews until the 1880s. Before 1886, Jews could join the British army, but "they were denied any corporate identity as Jews owing to the fact that no religion other than Christianity was recognised in the services, for the purposes of public worship."[52] When the British army began to count Jews, how many were there? An answer comes from the *Jewish Chronicle*, which was invariably eager to highlight Jewish military service and achievement. It reported on the official number of Jews in the British army's rank and file from 1886 to 1890: 1886, three; 1887, one; 1888, five; 1889, sixteen; 1890, eighteen. Even if, as the *Jewish Chronicle* was keen to point out, only 25 percent of the army's Jews registered as Jews, the point is clear: before the Second Boer War (1899–1902), a miniscule percentage of British Jews earned their livelihood from soldiering.[53]

In the eighteenth and nineteenth centuries, British Jews were inextricably associated with occupations largely foreign to and not associated with Bene Israel Jews: commerce, moneylending, finance, and trade, especially peddling and the selling of old clothes.[54] The identification of Jews with peddlers was so strong that some Britons found it difficult "to separate the idea of Jews from pedlars who cry 'old clothes.'"[55] Non-Jewish moneylenders were denominated as Jews because they were moneylenders.[56] Likewise, "stockjobber," a derogatory term "virtually synonymous with financial trickery, amorality and avarice,"[57] also became a synonymous term for Jew.[58] The occupational profile and proclivities of Jews and their difference from the supposed "productive" occupational inclination of Saxons was expressed in Robert Knox's much-discussed 1850 *Races of Man*. Not insignificantly, Knox explicitly based his characteristics of Jews on observations of them in London and Europe. Reflecting popular ideas of Jews, he asked rhetorically: "But where are the Jewish farmers, Jewish mechanics, labourers?"[59] To be sure, the image of Jews as parsimonious, deceitful, money-grubbing Shylocks and their association with peddling, moneylending, and other means of livelihood often regarded as disreputable, dishonorable, unmanly, unproductive, and parasitical occupations was widespread, deeply rooted, and maintained a resonance in European thought and history. William Cobbett, a British proponent of such ideas, spewed invective against Jewish cupidity and insisted that British Jews were an alien, anti-English people "that never work" and were obsessed with extracting money from Christians, usually in some underhanded manner.[60] During Parliamentary debates on the removal of Jews' disabilities, Cobbett inquired if it was even possible to "produce a Jew who ever dug, who went to plough, or who ever made his own coat or his own shoes, or who did anything at all, except get all the money he could from the pockets of the people."[61]

When Parliament began to debate the removal of British Jews' disabilities, F. H. Goldsmid tackled the notion that Jews "have always been employed in trade, in money-getting, and are fit for no other occupation" by arguing that in England, trade should not be deemed a crime, and that the occupations associated with Jews were a natural consequence of their history, treatment, and the prohibitions placed on them.[62] One can interpret the inclusion of the material on the Bombay army's Jews in Goldsmid's publication as an effort to publicize evidence that would disabuse the British public of the idea that Jews were innately unproductive, unpatriotic cheats unwilling to engage in activities, such as military service, that would be useful to the state.[63]

Whereas F. H. Goldsmid and others in Britain argued that the British Jews' history and their practical exclusion from the soldiering profession and government office both generated the image of British Jews as unpatriotic and nonmartial and funneled them into occupations some considered unproductive,[64] contemporaneous British missionaries, colonial officials, and army officers in India—some of whom, in contrast to Goldsmid, possessed firsthand knowledge of Bene Israel Jews—could have also challenged conventional notions about Jewish vocations and proclivities by referring to Bene Israel Jews' occupations other than soldiering and by pointing out that in Bombay, the peddlers and moneylenders were not Jews. Bombay-based Britons identified Bene Israel Jews not only as soldiers but also as carpenters, "cultivators of the soil," and oil pressers. Oil pressing was so associated with Bene Israel Jews that they were referred to as *Teli* (Oil-pressers), *Teli Lok* (Oil-pressing people), *Israel Teli* (Israel Oil-pressers), and *Shaniwar Teli* (Saturday Oil-pressers).[65] One revealing example of the association of India's largest Jewish community with oil pressing is the entry for the word "Jew" in the most important nineteenth-century English-Marathi dictionary. Complied by and under the supervision of two Bombay army officers, the dictionary contains one definition of "Jew" that would be utterly foreign to conventional British ideas of Jews: *Shaniwar Teli*.[66] Apropos Bene Israel Jews' occupations and the extent to which they differed from English Jews' occupations, one British visitor to Bombay wrote in 1850 that Bombay's Jews "obtain for the most part an honest livelihood, as house-builders, carpenters, and cultivators of the soil. That a Jew should be thus employed may appear singular to many who are familiar with their history, their known dislike to anything like manual labour; for who ever heard, among ourselves, of a Jewish farmer, or a Jewish carpenter?"[67] Lest this be mistaken, there is no indication of any irony in this visitor's astonishment at the sight of a "Jewish carpenter." Later in the nineteenth century, the missionary J. Henry Lord, who had labored amongst London's Jews before relocating to Bombay, marveled at the "new sight to see persons of the Jewish race engaged in the quiet pursuits of husbandry," specifically the cultivation of coconut and areca palms. Lord linked the vocation of these Jewish agriculturalists not to British Jews, but rather to Biblical Jews and the Jews of the First Aliyah in Ottoman Palestine.[68]

Bombay-based Britons' identification of Bene Israel Jews as oil pressers, carpenters, agriculturalists, and soldiers served to publicize information about the livelihood of living Jews, instantiating the postulation that Jews' occupations were a by-product of their history and treatment. The implication was that when treated differently—as they were in the Konkan and British India—Jews were corrigible and therefore could become productive and useful to Britain in ways besides the domains of finance and commerce.

Bene Israel Jews remained a prominent example of Jewish military service to Britain even after British Jews themselves had begun to be recognized and accommodated in the British army as professing Jews. Examples of this incorporation can be found in the section on "Jews in the British Army and Navy" in the 1901–6 *Jewish Encyclopedia*'s "Army" entry and in the *Jewish Chronicle* article "Anglo-Jewish Warriors of Bygone Days."[69] Such consideration was also expressed in what can be deemed the quintessential effort on the part of the Anglo-Jewish establishment at self-representation: the 1887 Anglo-Jewish Historical Exhibition. The exhibition may have ignored the growing number of East End Jewish immigrants, but it included Jews much further east: in India. Virtually all the pieces dealing with Jewish military service to Britain are found in the Indian Jewry section of the exhibit, which was not entitled "Indian Jews," but rather "Beni Israel."[70] Bene Israel Jews continued to occupy a place in accounts of Jewish military service to Britain for several reasons. First, in comparison to some European states, British Jews enlisted, were conscripted, and experienced combat as Jews in the British army at a late date. Second, by the late nineteenth century, a British Empire Jewish identity existed. Third, at that time, India, Britain's Indian armies, and the British Empire maintained a purchase and popularity in the British imagination and in domestic politics and society. Fourth, into the twentieth century, immigrants and native-born British Jews continued to be criticized as disloyal, unpatriotic, non-British aliens who shirked military service.[71]

Bene Israel Jews' place in accounts of Jewish military service to Britain reveals the extent to which British Jews were thinking about themselves as British and Jewish imperially. If a British Empire Jewish identity did not exist earlier, it certainly existed in the late nineteenth century and connected Jews in the colonies (even native and actual "Oriental" Jews) to Jews in the metropole (including Ashkenazi Jews portrayed as "Oriental") within a unified British Jewish world. Even after the 1857–58 Indian Rebellion—interpreted as the event that reinforced the notion of Indian difference—the existence of the British Empire, British India, and the Bombay army broadened the outlook, scope, and identity of Anglo-Jewry to encompass India's "native" Bene Israel Jews and connect Jewish Bombay to Jewish Britain. This branch of a transnational British Jewish imperial network was built on, informed by, and existed within the connections and structures uniting the British Empire's different regions. While the link that bound Britain's Jews and India's Jews together was informed by traditional ideas of Jewish kinship connecting Jews in distant locations together within the notion of Jewish peoplehood, it also transcended those notions in the way in which the link became formal, concrete, and exclusive—manifested institutionally in the Chief Rabbinate of the British Empire and represented visually, materially, and conceptually in the *Jewish Chronicle*, the *Jewish Year Book*, and the Anglo-Jewish Historical Exhibition. This is not to say that British Jews and Anglo-Jewish institutions neither supported nor identified with Jews beyond the British Empire's borders. Even so, the Chief Rabbinate of the British Empire, the Anglo-Jewish Historical Exhibition's "Beni Israel" display and its map of the Empire's Jewish congregations, the explicit incorporation of Indian Jews in *Jewish Chronicle* articles about Anglo-Jewish military service, and the *Jewish Year Book's* separate enumeration, classification, and lists of the Empire's Jews and institutions clearly distinguished the British Empire's Jews from other Jews.[72] Notwithstanding the imaginative element of it, the existence of the "Jews of the British Empire" enabled Anglo-Jewry to identify with Jews in other parts of the world in a manner that would neither call their patriotism into question nor reinforce the idea that British Jews could not be both British and Jewish. It therefore served to confute the claim, which garnered renewed popularity in the 1870s and 1880s, that British Jews could not be true British patriots because as Jews they maintained "a tribal bond, tribal aspirations, and tribal feelings" toward other Jews in part because Judaism was perceived as a religion of race and caste.[73]

Before July 26, 1858, when Lionel de Rothschild took the oath of abjuration on the Old Testament without the declaration "on the true faith of a Christian" and took his seat in the Commons as a professing Jew, the symbolic value of the Company's Jewish soldiers and the loyalty attributed to and the trust reposed in Bombay's Bene Israel sepoys was especially salient. Thus, an 1847 *Jewish Chronicle* article argued that excluding Jews from sitting in Parliament contradicted and opposed what was already occurring in India: Jews were already taking "charge of the secular interests of the empire."

> In one portion of India, our native army is largely recruited from among the Jews, who, in that part of the world, fight and die for the honour of England as fearlessly and faithfully as Mohammedan or Hindu—more faithfully or fearlessly they could not. And if we entrust the defence of the empire to the Jew, why should he not take his share in the legislation of the empire? He helps to support the state, why should he not enjoy the power and honours it has to bestow?[74]

Here the utility of Jews to Britain and the British Empire is not represented in terms of their eschatological significance or financial influence and connections, but rather in their military service.

Bene Israel Jews' military service was used as part of the argument to remove British Jews' disabilities and demonstrate that Jews could be trusted to defend British interests and fulfill their duties to the state. However, other features of the East India Company also elucidate how the state of affairs and bureaucratic organization of the colony was deemed worthy and relevant to deliberate on in connection to the affairs, policies, and organization of the British state at home. In particular, the Company and the Company Raj informed the discourse surrounding the removal of Jews' disabilities in Britain, explicitly referenced in domestic British debates about Jews' political, occupational, and educational rights and opportunities, and considered as a model for an inclusive religious diversity that would not be realized in Parliament until 1858.

From 1833 to 1858, British Jews and non-Jews had highlighted an inconsistency: positions were opened to and sometimes filled by professing Jews in the Company's government and military while they were excluded as professing Jews from obtaining comparable and even less prestigious and important positions in the British government and military at home. Similar arguments were voiced about Jews' ability to attend and graduate from the Company's educational institutions in England—Haileybury College and Addiscombe Military Seminary—when at the same time professing Jews were not able to obtain a degree from England's two ancient universities.[75] The implication of the inconsistency was clear: if Jews were trusted to hold positions in British India's army and administration, then they should have the right to be treated as full citizens in Britain. W. D. Christie expressed this sentiment in an 1845 speech in the Commons in which he declared that a British Jew might "become a member of the Supreme Council of India—he might, for a time, be the acting Governor-general of India; and the honourable baronet opposite meant to make a battle about a beggarly bill for allowing Jews to be Aldermen in this country."[76] Twelve years before the 1845 Jewish Municipal Relief Act, which allowed Jews to occupy municipal offices without taking the oath "on the true faith of a Christian,"[77] the principle that Jews should not be excluded from military and public office in India was established in Article 87 of the 1833 East India Company Charter Act.

> No native of the said territories, nor any natural-born subject of His Majesty resident therein, shall by reason only of his religion, place of birth, descent, colour, or any of them, be disabled from holding any place, office or employment under the said company.[78]

At the time, the Company's Court of Directors interpreted the Act to mean "that there shall be no governing caste in British India; that whatever other tests of qualification may be adopted, distinctions of race or religion shall not be of the number."[79]

British Jews were among the beneficiaries of the 1833 Charter Act. Sir Barrow Herbert Ellis, a colonial official in India, realized in 1869 Christie's 1845 pronouncement that a Jew might become a member of the Supreme Council of India; in addition, Cecil Roth identified the Bengal army's Lionel Gomez da Costa and the Bombay army's Edmund Helbert Ellis (B. H. Ellis's brother) as the first professing British Jews to obtain commissions in a British army.[80] Modifications to E. H. Ellis's standardized cadet form to account for his Judaism demonstrates the Company's willingness to alter the official documents to allow British Jewish cadets to enter into its military service as officers.[81] The Ellis brothers' entrance into the Company's political and military branches shows how the Company enabled sons of a stockjobber—a stereotypical Jewish profession—to enter professions that, as F. H. Goldsmid noted in 1830, British Jews were excluded from in Britain.[82] In 1848, Goldsmid used the 1833 Charter Act to argue that Parliament had already established a precedent for the nonexclusion of Jews from holding public and political office.[83] W. P. Wood echoed this position in his February 7, 1848, House of Commons speech, in which he argued that "religious opinions should not be used as a qualification or disqualification for political offices" and that the 1833 Act meant that "the Governor-General might be a Mahometan, and the Members of the Council might be Mahometans too." He concluded his speech "by calling on the House to follow the example which it had already set in India" and make concessions that would allow professing Jews to sit in Parliament.[84] Here one finds the Company not only informing domestic British debates about British Jews, but also deliberately being used as a model for the compositional transformation of Parliament in a liberal direction.

Not only were Bene Israel Jews overrepresented and valued as soldiers in the Company's Bombay army but they were also seen as exceptionally trustworthy sepoys. The trust the British reposed in Bene Israel sepoys is exemplified during the cataclysm the British considered as the most traumatic event in Victoria's Empire and the ultimate act of Indian and sepoy betrayal: the 1857–58 Indian Rebellion, or Sepoy Mutiny/Revolt.

In contrast to the Bengal army, Bombay army sepoys overwhelmingly remained loyal to "the Company Bahadur" during the Rebellion. Some, however, did not. On July 31, 1857, 140 Maratha sepoys of the 27th Bombay Native Infantry regiment stationed at Kolhapur rose in revolt and attacked the homes of their British officers, killing some of them.[85] The conspirators had initially planned to begin the uprising ten days later, on August 10, which was rumored to be the day on which new rifle cartridges would be issued. But the August 10 date was foiled when the regiment's Bene Israel native adjutant Jamedar Moosaji Israel

(Koletkar) attempted to send "away his family, whose presence was regarded as a security for his fidelity, if not for his co-operation." This action signaled to the would-be mutineers that Israel "was about to betray them." They were right. On the evening of July 31, Israel "ran to give warning [to the British officers] barely in time to permit the ladies to fly from their houses before the Sepoys came up, and poured volleys into them."[86] In his testimony to the Peel Commission, Major General Sir Hugh Rose detailed Jamedar Israel's conduct at Kolhapur and argued that it demonstrated the trustworthiness and value of the Bombay army's Jewish soldiers: "A Jew was the only native officer in the late 27th regiment Bombay native infantry who informed its [British] officers of the intended mutiny of the regiment, and by so doing saved their lives."[87]

Reverend John Wilson wrote a short account of Mossaji Israel's actions at Kolhapur. His account largely corresponds to General George Le Grand Jacob and Major General Hugh Rose's versions of the event. All highlighted and had the effect of demonstrating Bombay's Jewish sepoys' fidelity to their British officers and the Company Bahadur. One significant difference in the explication of the event is that in Wilson's account alone, Israel's "family," and not just his mother, is attacked not in revenge for betraying the mutineers but rather because as "Israelites," Jewish soldiers and their families were "instinctively viewed as entirely incapable of co-operation with them in their murderous designs." To illustrate this, he mentioned that there were only eight Bene Israel sepoys in the 27th BNI regiment when it disbanded and, as he added, "no charge was brought against any of their number." The loyalty and actions of the 27th BNI regiment's Jews instantiated Wilson's broader claim that "implicit, and fully justified, confidence was exercised in the Bene Israel sepoys during the Indian military mutiny of 1857–58."[88]

Anglo-Jewry publicized Bene Israel Jews' loyalty and service during the Mutiny to call attention to Jewish military service to the British Empire. As an 1875 *Jewish Chronicle* article on Bene Israel Jews proudly proclaimed, "It is they who have furnished to our Indian army many of those brave and loyal soldiers who have valiantly assisted us in our struggles in India, and faithfully stood by our side when treason lurked all around us, and our power in India trembled in the balance."[89] This treason was commonly represented in the most bloodthirsty and savage terms, especially in the popular depiction of lustful, beastly, and mutinous sepoys salivating at the opportunity to ravage British women and thereby betray their "unmanly character."[90] A few examples from the *Jewish Chronicle* illustrate the way in which Anglo-Jewry publicized Bene Israel Jews' military service during the Mutiny. Subedar Jacob David Bargawker, for instance, "did important service during the Indian Mutiny in 1857–58 . . . by giving timely warning to the British officers of the mutinous spirit among several men in his corps . . . and a serious disaster was thereby averted." At Deesa, Moses Benjamin's "integrity and trustworthiness led to his being specially selected (though then only a noncommissioned officer) for the responsible duty of watching over the wives and families of the European officers during the troublous time of the Mutiny of 1857."[91] In an era of muscular Christianity and the Christian heroes of the Mutiny, British Jewry found among India's native, Oriental, and "colonized" Bene Israel Jews muscular Jewish heroes of the Mutiny entrusted with the duty to protect British women and children.

To appreciate fully the Bombay context that enabled Bene Israel Jews to be represented in a manner so radically different from the conventional representations of Jews, one must keep in mind that not all Jews in the Bombay Presidency were Bene Israel Jews. A handful of European Jews, Yemenite Jews, and Cochin Jews resided in Bombay City. But apart from Yemenite Jews in Aden—part of Bombay Presidency—and Bene Israel Jews, only Baghdadi Jews could be said to have constituted a community.

An 1874 study on the Poona District's castes written by the colonial administrator W. F. Sinclair is revealing in that it elucidates how the characteristics attributed to Bene Israel Jews were not attributed to Bombay Presidency's Jews indiscriminately. Bene Israel Jews, Sinclair maintained, still manifested a "warrior-spirit," and many were "honorably distinguished for intelligence and honesty, and in the native army a greater number of them rise to commissions than of any other race, proportionably [sic] to the number of recruits." He added tellingly, "These Indian Jews seem to have no great aptitude for trade." This observation suggests that Bene Israel Jews represented some sort of deviation from the norm. Importantly, in the same section of the text, he also observed that there were a few Baghdadi Jews in the district who, in contrast to the Bene Israel, "conform much more to our European idea of the race, being keen men of business, and little given to entering the military or administrative service of Government."[92]

There is another facet of European perceptions of and encounters in India that may have indirectly contributed to the depiction of India's largest Jewish community as radically different from the predominant British representations of Jews: namely, there were other "Jews" in India that conformed much more to the "European idea of the race." More important than Baghdadi Jews are the discrete non-Jewish Indian communities—Jains, Banians, Bohras, Marwaris, and Parsis—particularly prominent in Bombay recurrently equated with or identified as Jews and associated with some of the occupations, predilections, and characteristics Europeans attributed to Jews. It is perhaps not incidental that it took an apparently "Crypto-Jew," Garcia da Orta, to disabuse the Portuguese of the idea that Parsis were Jews and to identify Parsis as "Gentiles (heathens), who came from Persia."[93] Nevertheless, the literal or figural identification of Parsis as "the Jews of India" persisted. For example, Mrs. E. F. Chapman argued that India's

Parsis were like Europe's Jews in "their aptitude for business, their enterprise, and their commercial prosperity, as well as by their loyalty to the Government of the country, although, like the Jews, the Parsis are seldom if ever to be found in the ranks of the army."[94]

When described in more favorable terms, these Indian non-Jewish "Jews" could be identified innocuously or even positively as "keen men of business" possessing an "aptitude for trade."[95] But when expressed in more unpleasant terms, the same non-Jewish communities could be represented as cunning, crafty, defrauding, and parsimonious usurers and avaricious seekers of lucre. Jean-Baptiste Tavernier observed that in business, Banians were "a thousand times worse than the Jews" and "so subtle and skillful in trade that, as I have elsewhere said, they could give lessons to the most cunning Jews."[96] At the end of the eighteenth century, Edmund Burke echoed Tavernier and declared that

> a Gentoo banian is a person a little lower, a little more penurious, a little more exacting, a little more cunning, a little more money-making, than a Jew. There is not a Jew in the meanest corner of Duke's Place in London that is so crafty, so much a usurer, so skillful how to turn money to profit, and so resolved not to get any money but for profit, as a Gentoo broker of the class I have mentioned.[97]

Here Burke represented a non-Jewish community as more stereotypically "Jewish" in occupation and inclination than Jews.

More than merely describing non-Jewish Indian communities in terms similar to the language Europeans used to depict Jews, Britons explicitly denominated Jains, Bohras, Marwaris, and Parsis as "the Jews of India." In early nineteenth-century Bombay, Bohras seemed to have been the community most commonly identified with the characteristics and occupations Britons in Britain attributed to Jews. James Forbes, a Bombay-based Company employee, described Bohras as "considerable traders in commercial towns" and "the chief travelling merchants in Guzerat and the western parts of India; [where] they go about like the Jews in Europe with boxes of different commodities." According to Forbes, Britons in Bombay considered Bohras as "sort of Mussulman Jews."[98] Walter Hamilton's popular *East-India Gazetteer* identified Bohras as "Jews in features, manners, and genius . . . and are every where [sic] noted for their address in bargaining, minute thrift, and constant attention to lucre."[99] In the same work in which Heber mentioned the Bombay's Jewish sepoys, he also noted that Bohras were considered as "usurers and oppressors," and that they were "held in the same estimation for parsimony that the Jews are in England."[100] Likewise, in one text in which Wolff recounted how Bene Israel Jews were "esteemed the best native soldiers," he also described Bohras as "the most stingy people in India."[101]

Apart from Protestant missionaries, Bombay army officers were the Britons who interacted most with Bene Israel Jews and were among those who contrasted their military service from the non-Jewish Indian communities identified with the occupations and stereotypes that in Britain were associated with Jews. In the same paragraph in which Lieutenant Edward Moor observed that in Bombay, "the pressers and dealers in oil are *Jews;* to the exclusion nearly, if not wholly, of every other description of men" and that in the Bombay army, Jews "are of all ranks, from the drummer to the commissioned officer, and are very clean, good soldiers," he also noted that Bohras "follow in India the habits of the lower classes of Jews in England. In Bombay, where they are very numerous, and rarely respectable, they go about the town, as the dirty Jews do in London, early and late, carrying a bag, and inviting, by the same nasal tone, dishonest servants and others, to fill it with pilfered clothes, empty bottles, old iron, &c."[102] Another Bombay army officer distinguished Parsis' mercantile inclinations and absence from the army from Bombay's "native" Jews, who as soldiers were "really good men, and, I should say, "staunch to the backbone" on occasion!"[103] Unlike Bohras, Parsis, and British Jews, Bene Israel Jews were depicted as brave and reliable soldiers, not traders, usurers, and peddlers possessing a penchant for moneymaking.

Nineteenth-century Bombay-based Britons' references to Bene Israel Jews do not convey a sense of incredulity about either the existence of contemporary Jewish soldiers or the soldiery ability and unsurpassed loyalty of the Bombay army's Jews. Such a perspective is striking if one considers the historian of Anglo-Jewry Sharman Kadish's somewhat exaggerated but nevertheless substantive observation that the "image of the Jew as soldier jarred in the eyes of both Jews and non-Jews, certainly until the creation of the State of Israel in 1948."[104] What made the image of Bene Israel Jews so different from the conventional European representations of Jews during the same period? Surely part of the reason Bene Israel Jews were associated with military service and praised for their soldiering ability in such a matter-of-fact fashion is linked to the peculiarities of the Bene Israel and a common feature of most of the individuals who authored the descriptions: Britons who had lived and worked in Bombay, and several who had encountered, served with, and knew about the Bombay army's Jews. Here the experiential, geographical, and cultural context and the specific Jewish community in question are undeniably crucial factors. Whether or not living in Bombay and personal experience with or knowledge of Bene Israel Jews necessarily modified stereotypes about Jews Britons brought to India, what is indisputable is that the Bene Israel Jews were clearly perceived as a species of Jew substantially different from the rich and poor Ashkenazi and Sephardic Jews eighteenth and nineteenth-century Britons encountered on London's streets, in the stock exchange, in Europe and the Middle East, in literature, on stage, and in the papers, and discussed, praised, or ridiculed in pubs and clubs.

Accounts of Bohras, Banians, and Parsis demonstrate that the conventional European discourse on "the Jews" clearly informed representations of certain South Asian communities, but not the largest community of actual Jews in India. A consideration of the ways in which Bene Israel Jews were represented demonstrates that essentialist notions of "the Jews" did not ineluctably shape British conceptions of Jews. Practitioners of colonial discourse analysis have done much to alert scholars to the problems and complexities of European representations of non-European peoples and "Others" closer to home. In many cases, these scholars have rightly highlighted the ways in which representations could produce as well as reflect the content of that which they sought to represent. However, for all the power and influence attributed to abstract essentialist representations and Orientalist discourse, the case of Bene Israel Jews shows the limitations of this perspective. Conventional representations of the Other, Indians, Jews, or "the colonized" were not necessarily immutable cognitive mechanisms invariably informing and inevitably configuring that which is represented. Instead, British conceptualization and representation of Bene Israel Jews seems to have been based on direct experience or indirect awareness of the specific context and Jewish community in question. Any theoretical framework, insightful as it may be, divorced from the particularities of time, place, and the specific subject of investigation inevitably diminishes the heterogeneity of the human experience and conceals the specificities and the distinctiveness of historical circumstance.

Some British Christians explicitly and systematically argued that Bombay's Jewish sepoys' performance in combat against Sikhs and Afghans provided sufficient evidence that Jews as a people, not just Indian Jews or Bene Israel Jews, possessed innate "moral and military qualities."[105] Nevertheless, it would overstate the case to contend that the reputation and reports of Jewish sepoys swayed large sections of the British public at home either that living Jews possessed innate moral and military qualities or of the utility of Jews to Britain beyond the domain of finance and commerce. British Jews, however, enthusiastically received information about the Bombay army's Jews and used it to promote the image of the martial and trustworthy Jewish soldier fighting for the British Empire. Keen to distance themselves from negative images of "the Jews," British Jews deliberately identified with India's "native" and "colonized" Bene Israel Jews on the periphery of both the Jewish and the British worlds. This identification, buttressed by the imperial connection, enabled British Jews to demonstrate their patriotism and utility to the nation without recourse to commerce and finance—activities often tainted as unproductive, unpatriotic, and peculiarly Jewish—and for specific representational and political purposes publicize what some of the most respected British soldiers, Christian missionaries, and colonial officials encountered in India: Jewish subjects of Victoria who were not unscrupulous Shylocks and villainous Fagins but brave soldiers and faithful fighters.

Notes

I thank Todd Endelman, Mitch Hart, Derek Penslar, Mitra Sharafi, and Albion Urdank for their suggestions.

1. Thomas Metcalf, *Ideologies of the Raj* (Cambridge: Cambridge University Press, 1995), 41.
2. Walter Fischel, "Bombay in Jewish History in the Light of New Documents from the Indian Archives," *Proceedings of the American Academy for Jewish Research* 38–39 (1970–71): 125–26.
3. Haeem Samuel Kehimkar, *History of the Bene Israel of India* (Tel Aviv: Dayag, 1937), 78–84, 188–91; Brenda Joseph Ness, "The Children of Jacob: The Bene Israel of Maharashtra," (PhD diss., University of California, Los Angeles, 1996).
4. Patrick Cadell, *History of the Bombay Army* (London: Longsman, 1938), 61–62.
5. Kehimkar, *History of the Bene Israel*, 78–84, 190–91.
6. John Malcolm, "Origin and State of the Indian Army," *Quarterly Review* 18, no. 36 (May 1818): 402–3. This publication is essentially a third-person version of Malcolm's first-person "Short Account of the Rise, Progress, and Character of the Native Army of India," written in 1816 and published in John Malcolm, *The Government of India* (London: John Murray, 1833), 209.
7. Rivett Carnac to I. L. Goldsmid, April 29, 1833, in Francis Henry Goldsmid, *The Arguments Advanced Against the Enfranchisement of the Jews*, 2nd ed. (London: Richard Bentley, 1833), 44–45.
8. Quoted in *Colburn's United Service Magazine* (February 1850): 295–98.
9. Stephen Wade, *Spies in the Empire: Victorian Military Intelligence* (London: Anthem, 2007), 23–24.
10. T. B. Jervis, "Statistics of the Western Coast of India: Extracted from a Memoir of the Konkun Drawn Up in 1823–1830," *Oriental Christian Spectator* 2, no. 12 (December 1841): 532–47.
11. Papers Received from H. B. E. Frere, Esq., Commissioner in Sind, November 8, 1858, Parliamentary Papers (*PP*): *Papers Connected with the Re-organization of the Army in India* (hereafter, *PCRAI*), 1859, VIII (2541), 46.
12. Papers Received from Major-General Sir Hugh Rose, February 24, 1859, *PP:PCRAI*, 71.
13. John Wilson, "Abstract of an Account of the Beni-Israel of Bombay," *Oriental Christian Spectator* 11, no. 1 (1840): 29.
14. See, for example, John Wilson, *The Bene Israel of Bombay: An Appeal for their Christian Education*, 2nd ed. (Edinburgh: Thomas Constable, 1865), 10–11; and John Wilson, "The Beni-Israel of Bombay," *Indian Antiquary* 3 (November 1874): 321–23.
15. M. A. Laird, *Bishop Heber in Northern India: Selections from Heber's Journal* (Cambridge: Cambridge University Press, 1971), 293; Josef Wolff, *Researches and Missionary Labours among the Jews, Mohammedans, and Other Sects* (London: J. Nisbet, 1835), 494–95.
16. Wolff, *Researches and Missionary Labours*, 494–95.
17. A Bukharin rabbi did inform him that before the messiah appeared, "Russia shall force her Jewish subjects to become soldiers." Wolff, *Researches and Missionary Labours*, 202.

18. Heber quoted in Laird, *Bishop Heber*, 293.
19. Amelia Heber, ed., *Life of Reginald Heber*, vol. 1 (London: John Murray, 1830).
20. Laird, *Bishop Heber*, 1–39; K. K. Dyson, *A Various Universe: A Study of the Journals and Memoirs of British Men and Women in the Indian Subcontinent, 1765–1856*, 2nd ed. (Delhi: Oxford University Press, 2002), chap. 4.
21. Douglas Peers, *Between Mars and Mammon: Colonial Armies and the Garrison State in India 1819–1835* (London: I. B. Tauris, 1995), 73–75.
22. H. G. Reissner, "Indian-Jewish Statistics (1837–1941)," *Jewish Social Studies* 12, no. 4 (1950): 349–66.
23. Cadell, *History of the Bombay Army*, 201; Peers, *Between Mars and Mammon*, 85–86, 104n104.
24. Kehimkar, *History of the Bene Israel*, 218.
25. See Anthony Pamm, *The Military Services of the Bene Israel of India and the Honours and Awards Granted to them (1750–1918)*, unpublished manuscript dated 1992, National Library of Israel. I thank Andrew Esensten for obtaining a copy of this manuscript.
26. J. H. Aitchison, "Abstract Statement of the Cast and Country of the Men of the Native Calvary and Regiments of the Line Composing the Bombay Army, 26 August 1828," Bombay Military Consultations, September 11, 1828, British Library/Oriental and India Office Collections/P/359/8.
27. W. H. Sykes, "Vital Statistics of the East India Company's Armies in India: European and Native," *Journal of the Statistical Society of London* 10, no. 2 (1847): 102.
28. *Jewish Intelligence*, February 1852, 45–46.
29. Papers Received from Col. P. Melvill, December 18, 1858, *PP: PCRAI*, 217–20; David Omissi, *The Sepoy and the Raj: The Indian Army, 1860–1940* (London: Macmillan, 1994), 7.
30. Sykes, "Vital Statistics of the East India Company's Armies," 102.
31. H. G. Reissner quoted in Shirley Isenberg, *India's Bene Israel: A Comprehensive Inquiry and Sourcebook* (Berkeley: Judah Magnes Museum, 1988), 162. As late as 1881, Bombay Presidency's seven thousand Bene Israel Jews comprised 1.2 percent of the Bombay army's infantry, which shows that they were overrepresented in the infantry at a level twenty-seven times greater than their representation in the population.
32. Joseph Jacobs, *Studies in Jewish Statistics: Social, Vital and Anthropometric* (London: D. Nutt, 1891), chaps. 4–5.
33. Nomad, "The Governor's Guard: A True Tale of Sepoy Superstition," *Colburn's United Service Magazine* 3 (May–October 1889): 214n.
34. Derek Penslar, *Jews and the Military: A History* (Princeton: Princeton University Press, 2013).
35. Penslar, *Jews and the Military*, chaps. 2–3.
36. See, for example, Todd Samuel Presner, *Muscular Judaism: The Jewish Body and the Politics of Regeneration* (New York: Routledge, 2007), 187–88.
37. Structural changes in Britain's Indian armies in the late nineteenth century made military service less attractive to Bene Israel Jews. Isenberg, *India's Bene Israel*, 160–207; Joan Roland, *Jews in British India: Identity in a Colonial Era* (Hanover, NH: University Press of New England, 1989), chaps. 1–2. Only in the late nineteenth century does one find Bene Israel Jews producing apologetic literature touting their military service to the British Empire. H. S. Kehimkar's histories are prime examples of such writing.
38. See, for example, John Briggs, *A Letter on the Indian Army* (London: Harrison, 1857), 13–15; "The Bombay Army," *Asiatic Journal* 22, no. 85 (1837): 9–11; *Jewish Advocate* (February 1852): 43.

39. Edward Moor, *A Compilation of All the Government and General—Government—General—Brigade and Garrison Orders* [. . .] (Bombay: Courier and Gazette Presses, 1801), XXXII; John Aitchinson, *General Code of Military Regulations in Force under the Presidency of Bombay* (Calcutta: Mission School Press, 1824), 518. On the ritual, meaning, and importance of the Company's sepoys' oath of loyalty and the fidelity it sought to instill, see Philip Mason, *A Matter of Honour: An Account of the Indian Army, Its Officers and Men* (New York: Holt, 1974).

40. Papers Received from Col. P. Melvill, December 18, 1858, *PP: PCRAI*, 208.

41. *Standing Orders of the Eighth Regiment, N. I.* (Bombay, 1846), 26.

42. This only occurred after the Board of Deputies of British Jews lobbied the War Office for the accommodation. Michael Clark, *Albion and Jerusalem: The Anglo-Jewish Community in the Post-Emancipation Era, 1858-1887* (Oxford: Oxford University Press, 2009), 131–32.

43. *Standing Orders of the Eighth Regiment*, 27.

44. Penelope Carson, *The East India Company and Religion, 1698-1858* (Woodbridge: Boydell Press, 2012), 169–94.

45. Kehimkar, *History of the Bene Israel*, 78–84, 190–91; Isenberg, *India's Bene Israel*, 314–19; *Jewish Chronicle*, February 6, 1880, 6; *Times of India*, September 8, 1886; E. M. Jacob, "History of 'Shaar Harahamim' ('Gate of Mercy') Synagogue," in *Religious and Cultural Heritage of the Bene-Israels of India* (Bombay: E. M. Jacob, 1984), 1–9; Monique Zetlaoui, *Shalom India: Historie des Communautes Juives en Inde* (Paris: Imago, 2000), 217; *Jewish Encyclopedia* (New York: 1901–6), s.v. "Moses Benjamin," "Samuel Isaac Jawlikar."

46. On the case and its significance, see C. J. W. Allen, *The Law of Evidence in Victorian England* (Cambridge: Cambridge University Press, 1997), 50–52; Richard Willen, "Rationalization of Anglo-Legal Culture: The Testimonial Oath," *British Journal of Sociology* 34, no. 1 (1983): 109–28; David Michels and David Blaikie, "Matters of Faith and Conscience: A Turning Point in the Taking of Oaths in Canada," in *L'etat Canadien et la Diversite Culturelle ed Religieuse, 1800-1914*, ed. Lorraine Derocher et al. (Quebec: University of Quebec Press, 2009), 54–56; and M. C. N. Salbstein, *The Emancipation of the Jews in Britain: The Question of the Admission of the Jews to Parliament, 1828-1860* (Rutherford: Fairleigh Dickinson University Press, 1982), 46–47. And for a specific discussion of issues of trust in this case, see Mitchell Hart's essay in the present volume.

47. Douglas Edlin, *Judges and Unjust Laws: Common Law Constitutionalism and the Foundations of Judicial Review* (Ann Arbor: University of Michigan Press, 2010), 74–77.

48. H. S. Q. Henriques, *The Jews and the English Law* (Oxford: Horace Hart, 1908), 177–83, 309.

49. Goldsmid, *Arguments Advanced Against the Enfranchisement of the Jews*.

50. Penslar, *Jews and the Military*, 7–11.

51. Goldsmid, *Arguments Advanced Against the Enfranchisement of the Jews*, 21–22n.

52. Sharman Kadish, *"A Good Jew and a Good Englishman": The Jewish Lads' & Girls' Brigade, 1895-1995* (London: Vallentine Mitchell, 1995), 5–59.

53. *Jewish Chronicle*, October 27, 1899, 12.

54. Todd Endelman, *The Jews of Georgian England 1714-1830* (Ann Arbor: University of Michigan Press, 1999), chaps. 3–7; Endelman, *The Jews of Britain, 1656 to 2000* (Berkeley: University of California Press, 2002), chaps. 1–4.

55. Endelman, *Jews of Georgian England*, 181–82.

56. Don Herzog, *Poisoning the Minds of the Lower Orders* (Princeton: Princeton University Press, 1998), 302–3.

57. C. S. Monaco, *The Rise of Modern Jewish Politics* (New York: Routledge, 2013), 22–23.

58. Jonathan Karp, "Can Economic History Date the Inception of Jewish Modernity?," in *The Economy in Jewish History: New Perspectives on the Interrelationship between Ethnicity and Economic Life*, ed. Gideon Reuveni and Sarah Wobick-Segev (New York: Berghahn Books 2010), 29.

59. Robert Knox, *Races of Men* (Philadelphia: Lea & Blanchard, 1850), 44–46, 130–32.

60. Herzog, *Poisoning the Minds*, chap. 7; 302–3; Endelman, *Jews of Georgian England*, chap. 3.

61. Cobbett quoted in Polly Pinsker, "English Opinion and Jewish Emancipation (1830–1860)," *Jewish Social Studies* 14, no. 1 (1952), 55–56.

62. Francis Henry Goldsmid, *Remarks on the Civil Disabilities of British Jews* (London: Henry Colburn and Richard Bentley, 1830), 17–19.

63. Goldsmid, *Arguments Advanced Against the Enfranchisement of the Jews*, 21–22n, 41–46.

64. Goldsmid, *Civil Disabilities of British Jews*, 17–19; *Voice of Jacob*, October 28, 1842, 56.

65. See, for example, Edward Moor, *Hindu Infanticide* (London: J. Johnson, 1811), 168; Wilson, "Account of the Beni-Israel of Bombay," 28–29; Arthur Crawford, *Our Troubles in Poona and the Deccan* (Westminster: Archibald Constable, 1897), 238–40; and *Gazetteer of the Bombay Presidency*, vol. 11, *Kolaba and Janjira* (Bombay: Government Press, 1883), 85–86.

66. James Molesworth and Thomas Candy, *A Dictionary, English and Marathi* [. . .], 2nd ed. (Bombay: Ganpat Krishnaji, 1873), 453.

67. Henry Moses, *Sketches of India* (London: Simpkin, 1850), 263–64.

68. J. Henry Lord, "The Beni-Israel in the Villages around Bombay," *Bombay Diocesan Record* 2 (July 1885–December 1886), 75. Rice constituted nineteenth-century Bene Israel Jews' main cash crop. Isenberg, *India's Bene Israel*, 160.

69. *Jewish Encyclopedia*, s.v. "Army"; *Jewish Chronicle*, December 9, 1904, 19.

70. *Catalogue of Anglo-Jewish Historical Exhibition, 1887: Royal Albert Hall* (London: William Clowes, 1887).

71. On this last point see, for example, Endelman, *Jews of Britain*, 152–86.

72. Joseph Jacobs, ed., *Jewish Year Book* (London: Greenberg, 1898), 26–130.

73. Clark, *Albion and Jerusalem*, chap. 5; David Feldman, "Englishmen, Jews, and Immigrants in London, 1865–1914: Modernization, Social Control, and the Paths to Englishness," in *Jewish Settlement and Community in the Modern Western World*, ed. Ronald Dotterer, Deborah Dash Moore, and Steven Cohen (Selinsgrove: Susquehanna University Press, 1991), 98–100.

74. *Jewish Chronicle*, December 10, 1847, 343.

75. *Voice of Jacob*, October 28, 1842, 56; *Jewish Chronicle*, April 18, 1845, 143; April 25, 1845, 147; July 21, 1843, 205; May 28, 1858, 189; Dec. 10, 1847, 343; July 11, 1856, 656; June 11, 1858, 204.

76. *Jewish Chronicle*, April 18, 1845, 143.

77. Salbstein, *Emancipation of the Jews in Britain*, 52; Endelman, *Jews of Britain*, 103.

78. T. A. Heathcote, *The Military in British India: The Development of British Land Forces in South Asia, 1600–1947* (Manchester: Manchester University Press, 1995), 110.

79. H. H. Dodwell, "Imperial Legislation and the Superior Government, 1818–1857," in *The Cambridge History of the British Empire*, ed. H. H. Dodwell, vol. 5 (Cambridge: Cambridge University Press, 1932), 9–11.

80. C. E. Buckland, *Dictionary of Indian Biography* (London: Swan Sonneschein, 1906), 137; *Albion and Jerusalem Jewish Chronicle*, April 25, 1845, 147; October 27, 1871, 9; Cecil Roth, "The Jews in Defence of Britain: Thirteenth to Nineteenth Centuries," *Transactions of the Jewish Historical Society of England*, vol. 15, 1939-1945 (London: Edward Goldston, 1946), 23.

81. Cadet Papers 1 to 100 (1849-50), British Library/Oriental and India Office Collections/L/MIL/9/222.

82. Goldsmid, *Civil Disabilities of British Jews*, 18-19.

83. Francis Henry Goldsmid, *Reply to the Arguments Advanced Against the Removal of the Remaining Disabilities of the Jews* (London: John Murray, 1848), 51-53.

84. Charles Egan, *The Status of the Jews in England* (London: R. Hastings, 1848), 76-78.

85. Cadell, *History of the Bombay Army*, 200-204.

86. George Le Grand Jacob, *Western India Before and During the Mutinies*, 2nd ed. (London: Henry King, 1872), 146-77.

87. Papers Received from Major-General Sir Hugh Rose, February 24, 1859, *PP: PCRAI*, 71-77.

88. Wilson, *Bene-Israel of Bombay*, 11n.

89. *Jewish Chronicle*, November 19, 1875, 548.

90. Peter van der Veer, *Imperial Encounters: Religion and Modernity in India and Britain* (Princeton: Princeton University Press, 2001), 57-89.

91. *Jewish Chronicle*, September 11, 1908, 11; January 4, 1895, 12; December 10, 1897, 30.

92. W. F. Sinclair, "Notes on Castes in the Puna and Solapur Districts," *Indian Antiquary* 3 (1874): 337-38.

93. J. Gerson da Cunha, "The Origin of Bombay," *Journal of the Bombay Branch of the Royal Asiatic Society*, extra number (1900): 109-11.

94. Mrs. E. F. Chapman, *Sketches of Some Distinguished Indian Women* (London: W. H. Allen, 1891), 113-14.

95. See, for example, "Parasnath as a Civil Sanatarium," *Calcutta Review*, 47, no. 94 (1868): 130-32; W. W. Hunter, *A Statistical Account of Bengal*, vol. 9 (London: Trubner, 1876), 252-54.

96. Valenine Ball, ed., *Travels in India by Jean Baptiste Tavernier*, vol. 1 (London: Macmillan, 1889), 136; William Crooke, ed., *Travels in India by Jean Baptist Tavernier*, vol. 2, trans. V. Ball (London: Macmillan, 1889), 183-84.

97. *Works of the Right Honorable Edmund Burke*, vol. 10, 8th ed. (Boston: Little, Brown, 1884), 382.

98. James Forbes, *Oriental Memoirs*, vol. 1, 2nd ed. (London: Richard Bentley, 1834), 470-71.

99. Walter Hamilton, *East-India Gazetteer*, vol. 1, 2nd ed. (London: W. H. Allen, 1828), 601.

100. Heber quoted in Laird, *Bishop Heber*, 312.

101. Joseph Wolff, *Travels and Adventures of the Rev. Joseph Wolff* (London: Saudners, Otley, 1861), 468-78.

102. Moor, *Hindu Infanticide*, 168.

103. *Colburn's United Service Magazine and Navel and Military Journal* (February 1850): 296.

104. Kadish, "A Good Jew and a Good Englishman," 57.

105. *Jewish Intelligence*, March 1855, 65-68. *Jewish Intelligence* was the London Society for Promoting Christianity Amongst the Jews' main periodical.

Bibliography

Aitchinson, John. *General Code of Military Regulations in Force under the Presidency of Bombay.* Calcutta: Mission School, 1824.
Allen, C. J. W. *The Law of Evidence in Victorian England.* Cambridge: Cambridge University Press, 1997.
Anonymous. "Parasnath as a Civil Sanatarium." *Calcutta Review* 47, no. 94 (1868).
Ball, Valenine, ed. *Travels in India by Jean Baptiste Tavernier.* Vol. 1. London: Macmillan, 1889.
Briggs, John. *A Letter on the Indian Army.* London: Harrison, 1857.
Buckland, C. E. *Dictionary of Indian Biography.* London: Swan Sonneschein, 1906.
Burke, Edmund. *Works of the Right Honorable Edmund Burke.* Vol. 10. 8th ed. Boston: Little, Brown, 1884.
Cadell, Patrick. *History of the Bombay Army.* London: Longsman, Green and Co., 1938.
Carson, Penelope. *The East India Company and Religion, 1698–1858.* Woodbridge: Boydell, 2012.
Catalogue of Anglo-Jewish Historical Exhibition, 1887: Royal Albert Hall. London: William Clowes, 1887.
Chapman, E. F. *Sketches of Some Distinguished Indian Women.* London: W. H. Allen., 1891.
Clark, Michael. *Albion and Jerusalem: The Anglo-Jewish Community in the Post-Emancipation Era, 1858–1887.* Oxford: Oxford University Press, 2009.
Colburn's United Service Magazine. February 1850.
Crawford, Arthur. *Our Troubles in Poona and the Deccan.* Westminster: Archibald Constable, 1897.
Crooke, William, ed. *Travels in India by Jean Baptist Tavernier.* Vol. 2. Translated by V. Ball. London: Macmillan, 1889.
Dodwell, H. H. "Imperial Legislation and the Superior Government, 1818–1857." In *The Cambridge History of the British Empire,* vol. 5, edited by H. H. Dodwell, 1–19. Cambridge: Cambridge University Press, 1932.
Dyson, K. K. *A Various Universe: A Study of the Journals and Memoirs of British Men and Women in the Indian Subcontinent, 1765–1856.* 2nd ed. Delhi: Oxford University Press, 2002.
Edlin, Douglas. *Judges and Unjust Laws: Common Law Constitutionalism and the Foundations of Judicial Review.* Ann Arbor: University of Michigan Press, 2010.
Egan, Charles. *The Status of the Jews in England.* London: R. Hastings, 1848.
Endelman, Todd. *The Jews of Britain, 1656 to 2000.* Berkeley: University of California Press, 2002.
———. *The Jews of Georgian England 1714–1830.* Ann Arbor: University of Michigan Press, 1999.
Feldman, David. "Englishmen, Jews, and Immigrants in London, 1865–1914: Modernization, Social Control, and the Paths to Englishness." In *Jewish Settlement and Community in the Modern Western World,* edited by Ronald Dotterer, Deborah Dash Moore, and Steven Cohen, 95–116. Selinsgrove: Susquehanna University Press, 1991.
Fischel, Walter. "Bombay in Jewish History in the Light of New Documents from the Indian Archives." *Proceedings of the American Academy for Jewish Research* 38–39 (1970–71): 119–44.

Forbes, James. *Oriental Memoirs*. Vol. 1. 2nd ed. London: Richard Bentley, 1834.
Kolaba and Janjira. Vol 11 of *Gazetteer of the Bombay Presidency*. Bombay: Government Press, 1883.
Gerson da Cunha, José. "The Origin of Bombay." Vol 20 of *Journal of the Bombay Branch of the Royal Asiatic Society*. Mumbai, India: Royal Asiatic Society, 1900.
Goldsmid, Francis Henry. *The Arguments Advanced Against the Enfranchisement of the Jews*. 2nd ed. London: Richard Bentley, 1833.
———. *Remarks on the Civil Disabilities of British Jews*. London: Henry Colburn and Richard Bentley, 1830.
———. *Reply to the Arguments Advanced Against the Removal of the Remaining Disabilities of the Jews*. London: John Murray, 1848.
Hamilton, Walter. *East-India Gazetteer*. Vol. 1. 2nd ed. London: W. H. Allen, 1828.
Heathcote, T. A. *The Military in British India: The Development of British Land Forces in South Asia, 1600–1947*. Manchester: Manchester University Press, 1995.
Heber, Amelia, ed. *Life of Reginald Heber*. Vol. 1. London: John Murray, 1830.
Henriques, H. S. Q. *The Jews and the English Law*. Oxford: Horace Hart, 1908.
Herzog, Don. *Poisoning the Minds of the Lower Orders*. Princeton, NJ: Princeton University Press, 1998.
Hunter, W. W. *A Statistical Account of Bengal*. Vol. 9. London: Trubner, 1876.
Isenberg, Shirley. *India's Bene Israel: A Comprehensive Inquiry and Sourcebook*. Berkeley: Judah Magnes Museum, 1988.
Jacob, E. M. *Religious and Cultural Heritage of the Bene-Israels of India*. Bombay: E. M. Jacob, 1984.
Jacobs, Joseph, ed. *Jewish Year Book*. London: Greenberg, 1898.
———. *Studies in Jewish Statistics: Social, Vital and Anthropometric*. London: D. Nutt, 1891.
Jervis, T. B. "Statistics of the Western Coast of India: Extracted from a Memoir of the Konkun Drawn Up in 1823–1830." *Oriental Christian Spectator* 2, no. 12 (1841): 532–47.
Kadish, Sharman. *"A Good Jew and a Good Englishman": The Jewish Lads' & Girls' Brigade, 1895–1995*. London: Vallentine Mitchell, 1995.
Karp, Jonathan. "Can Economic History Date the Inception of Jewish Modernity?" In *The Economy in Jewish History: New Perspectives on the Interrelationship between Ethnicity and Economic Life*, edited by Gideon Reuveni and Sarah Wobick-Segev, 23–42. New York: Berghahn, 2010.
Kehimkar, Haeem Samuel. *History of the Bene Israel of India*. Tel Aviv: Dayag, 1937.
Knox, Robert. *Races of Men*. Philadelphia: Lea & Blanchard, 1850.
Laird, M. A. *Bishop Heber in Northern India: Selections from Heber's Journal*. Cambridge: Cambridge University Press, 1971.
Le Grand Jacob, George. *Western India Before and During the Mutinies*. 2nd ed. London: Henry King, 1872.
Lord, J. Henry. "The Beni-Israel in the Villages around Bombay." *Bombay Diocesan Record* 2 (July 1885–December 1886).
Malcolm, John. "Origin and State of the Indian Army." *Quarterly Review* 18, no. 36 (1818): 385–423.
———. *The Government of India*. London: John Murray, 1833.
Mason, Philip. *A Matter of Honour: An Account of the Indian Army, Its Officers and Men*. New York: Holt, 1974.

Metcalf, Thomas. *Ideologies of the Raj*. Cambridge: Cambridge University Press, 1995.
Michels, David, and David Blaikie. "Matters of Faith and Conscience: A Turning Point in the Taking of Oaths in Canada." In *L'etat Canadien et la Diversite Culturelle ed Religieuse, 1800–1914*, edited by Lorraine Derocher et al., 51–69. Quebec: University of Quebec Press, 2009.
Molesworth, James, and Thomas Candy. *A Dictionary, English and Marathi, Compiled for the Government of Bombay* [. . .]. 2nd ed. Bombay: Ganpat Krishnaji, 1873.
Monaco, C. S. *The Rise of Modern Jewish Politics*. New York: Routledge, 2013.
Moor, Edward. *A Compilation of All the Government and General—Government—General—Brigade and Garrison Orders* [. . .]. Bombay Army. Bombay: Gazette, 1801.
———. *Hindu Infanticide*. London: J. Johnson, 1811.
Moses, Henry. *Sketches of India*. London: Simpkin, 1850.
Ness, Brenda Joseph. "The Children of Jacob: The Bene Israel of Maharashtra." PhD diss., University of California, Los Angeles, 1996.
Nomad. "The Governor's Guard: A True Tale of Sepoy Superstition," *Colburn's United Service Magazine* 3, 214n (May–October 1889).
Omissi, David. *The Sepoy and the Raj: The Indian Army, 1860–1940*. London: Macmillan, 1994.
Pamm, Anthony. *The Military Services of the Bene Israel of India and the Honours and Awards Granted to them (1750–1918)*. Unpublished manuscript. National Library of Israel, 1992.
Peers, Douglas. *Between Mars and Mammon: Colonial Armies and the Garrison State in India 1819–1835*. London: I. B. Tauris, 1995.
Penslar, Derek. *Jews and the Military: A History*. Princeton, NJ: Princeton University Press, 2013.
Pinsker, Polly. "English Opinion and Jewish Emancipation (1830–1860)." *Jewish Social Studies* 14, no. 1 (1952): 51–94.
Presner, Todd Samuel. *Muscular Judaism: The Jewish Body and the Politics of Regeneration*. New York: Routledge, 2007.
Reissner, H. G. "Indian-Jewish Statistics (1837–1941)." *Jewish Social Studies* 12, no. 4 (1950): 349–66.
Roland, Joan. *Jews in British India: Identity in a Colonial Era*. Hanover, NH: University Press of New England, 1989.
Roth, Cecil. "The Jews in Defence of Britain, Thirteenth to Nineteenth Centuries." *Transactions of the Jewish Historical Society of England*. Vol. 15, 1939–1945 (London: Edward Goldston, 1946): 1–28.
Salbstein, M. C. N. *The Emancipation of the Jews in Britain: The Question of the Admission of the Jews to Parliament, 1828–1860*. Rutherford: Fairleigh Dickinson University Press, 1982.
Sinclair, W. F. "Notes on Castes in the Puna and Solapur Districts." *Indian Antiquary* 3 (1874).
Sykes, W. H. "Vital Statistics of the East India Company's Armies in India: European and Native." *Journal of the Statistical Society of London* 10, no. 2 (1847): 100–131.
van der Veer, Peter. *Imperial Encounters: Religion and Modernity in India and Britain*. Princeton, NJ: Princeton University Press, 2001.
Wade, Stephen. *Spies in the Empire: Victorian Military Intelligence*. London: Anthem Press, 2007.
Willen, Richard. "Rationalization of Anglo-Legal Culture: The Testimonial Oath." *British Journal of Sociology* 34, no. 1 (1983): 109–28.

Wilson, John. "Abstract of an Account of the Beni-Israel of Bombay." *Oriental Christian Spectator* 11, no. 1 (1840).
———. "The Beni-Israel of Bombay." *Indian Antiquary* 3 (1874).
———. *The Bene Israel of Bombay: An Appeal for their Christian Education.* 2nd ed. Edinburgh: Thomas Constable, 1865.
Wolff, Josef. *Researches and Missionary Labours among the Jews, Mohammedans, and Other Sects.* London: J. Nisbet, 1835.
———. *Travels and Adventures of the Rev. Joseph Wolff.* London: Saudners, Otley, 1861.
Zetlaoui, Monique. *Shalom India: Historie des Communautes Juives en Inde.* Paris: Imago, 2000.

MITCH NUMARK is Associate Professor in the Department of History at Sacramento State in California. His specialization is the history of the British Empire in South Asia, including the Jews of South Asia.

13 Between Honor and Authenticity
Zionism as Theodor Herzl's Life Project

Derek Jonathan Penslar

A LIFE PROJECT IS a set of goals and practices that endow a person's life with meaning and direction. It is both more specific and more all encompassing than careerist ambition, a desire to accumulate wealth or objects, or a yearning for personal fulfilment through romantic relationships. A life project transcends these pedestrian aspirations in its devotion to a cause, belief, or ideology, yet is nourished by the same psychological needs and drives that underlie all human behavior.

From the mid-1890s onward, Zionism became Theodor Herzl's life project. To put it more accurately, at this time, Zionism became the latest manifestation of Herzl's ongoing project to attain both honor and authenticity. These two concepts—honor and authenticity—overlap, yet are distinct and at times contradictory. Herzl's yearnings to achieve them and attempts to reconcile the tensions between them were manifest in his writings over the course of his lifetime. In this regard, there was no clear distinction between writings produced before or after his turn to Zionism, or those specifically about the Zionist cause and those about other subjects. This chapter's exploration, therefore, reflects my general view that a biography of Herzl must be holistic. It should not create hard boundaries between pre-Zionist and Zionist periods of his life or between the different genres of his writing—plays, feuilletons, fiction, political tracts, and journalism. Herzl never gave up literature for politics, and his political activity was intensely literary.

The terms "honor" and "authenticity" require a certain amount of unpacking before we can proceed. This volume centers around the concepts of trust and keeping one's word, concepts that are associated with the bases for stable interpersonal relations, which assume a reliability of performance and exchange. If person A places her trust in person B, person B's sense of obligation to perform as expected may be motivated by purely instrumental and utilitarian factors. But socioeconomic obligations are often underpinned by more than mere instrumentality; they depend as well on an individual's sense of honor—that is, a belief that self-worth depends on following a certain code of behavior even when it is not convenient or personally beneficial to do so. Honor is usually associated with qualities such as resolve, courage, self-sacrifice, and loyalty (e.g., "Meine Ehre heisst Treue," the SS's notorious motto). Honor is also often associated with honesty and fair play (e.g., in gaming or sports), but codes of honor can demand reticence, holding one's tongue, or even outright dissemblance as long as such behavior is altruistic, not self-serving. Simply put, honor does not demand a constant, unremitting display of transparency toward others.

Nor does honor necessarily demand authenticity. "Authenticity" is a fraught term with deep philosophical roots in the thought of, among others, Kierkegaard, Nietzsche, Heidegger, and Sartre, and it is especially tempting to relate Herzl to his contemporary Nietzsche's concept of the authentic self. The intellectual historian Jacob Golomb has attempted to do so, although the Oxford literary scholar Ritchie Robertson has disputed this comparison.[1] Direct evidence of Nietzschean influence on Herzl is scant. Herzl owned most of Nietzsche's books but made few references to Nietzsche in his diaries and letters. (In the fall of 1895, he bristled at the notion that he was a Nietzschean, dismissing the philosopher as a "madman.") Herzl's aesthetics and morality, unlike Nietzsche's, were supremely conventional, and the mechanistic utopia of Herzl's novel *Altneuland* (*Old New Land*) provides little room for Nietzschean individualism. Golomb's evidence for Nietzschean influence on Herzl is either circumstantial (resemblances between motifs in the two men's writings) or hearsay (e.g., the judgment of Herzl's cousin Raoul Auernheimer, a literary journalist who lovingly prepared a two-volume selection of Herzl's feuilletons after Herzl's death). Rather than proclaim Herzl to be a Nietzschean, I would place both men within a broad swathe of fin de siècle central European writers who championed authenticity in the form of self-awareness and purposefulness. As we shall see, as difficult as it was for Herzl to perceive himself as a man of honor, it was even more difficult, in fact impossible, for him to achieve authenticity. The very act of striving toward these two affective states, however, fueled his Zionist passion and sustained him during the nine years during which he irrevocably transformed the Jewish world.

* * *

The study of Theodor Herzl's affective state is both enriched and challenged by the vast corpus of his writings. In addition to hundreds of pieces published in his lifetime, Herzl kept a diary between 1882 and 1885, and some six thousand letters written by Herzl over the course of his life have survived. (The diary and letters were published in a seven-volume German edition between 1983 and 1996.) The most commonly cited source by Herzl's biographers has been what he called his "Zionist diaries," composed between the time of his turn to Zionism in 1895 and his death in 1904. (Several abridged versions of the diaries have been published, and a complete English-language version appeared in 1960.) The diaries begin with a brief autobiographical sketch and contain some highly revealing passages from June of 1895, when Herzl experienced a manic episode during which he wrote hundreds of pages, some of it lucid and brilliant, some of it truly mad, and out of which came much of the text of his famous pamphlet of 1896, *Der Judenstaat* (*The Jewish State*). The Zionist diaries constitute both a public and private text: on the one hand, they are an expression of Herzl's innermost feelings, with flashes of self-awareness and revealing passages of internal dialogue, and on the other hand, they provide a record of his self-presentation to the world. In the first entry from 1895, Herzl writes of "the honesty inherent in this diary—which would be completely worthless if I played the hypocrite with myself."[2] Yet from early on, he hoped that someday his diaries would be published as a record of "what I had to put up with, who have been the enemies of my plan, and, on the other hand, who stood by me."[3]

Shlomo Avineri has called the diaries a Bildungsroman, an account of encounters with the world, the passage from innocence to experience and from fantasy to pragmatism.[4] In fact, the diaries are more superficial than a bildungsroman or a classic autobiography, which Marcus Mosley, in his definitive study of modern Jewish life-writing, nicely describes as a study in the self's becoming and fashioning. Autobiography privileges perception and feeling over action; childhood receives disproportionate attention as the time when the self and its relation with the world are established.[5] Herzl's diaries, on the other hand, do not tell the story of his personal formation; they are an account of action in real time. Nonetheless, if read critically and carefully and alongside other writings by Herzl to serve as points of confirmation and contrast, the Zionist diaries provide a useful lens through which to ascertain Herzl's affective state, especially given the diaries' generous helpings of self-aggrandizement, depression, hypochondriasis, and self-pity. In this sense, the diaries maintain the spirit of the pioneer of life-writing Jean-Jacques Rousseau, whose *Confessions* proclaim, "I suffered before I learned to think."[6]

Understanding Herzl requires engaging not only his own writings but also a vast body of scholarly literature on Herzl's life, thought, and Zionist activities. Biographies of Herzl number in the hundreds; leaving aside hagiographies and other propagandistic works, there are at least ten major biographies that any serious scholar of Herzl must consult.[7] Although some biographies focus on Herzl's Zionist writings and present him as a serious political thinker as well as leader, others, particularly those of Desmond Stewart, Amos Elon, and Ernst Pawel, take a more psychological approach. I am indebted to these works, and especially to Peter Lowenberg's insightful article of 1971 that subjected Herzl to a posthumous psychoanalysis.[8] My own approach to Herzl is somewhat more psychological than psychoanalytical. Freudian categories, I fear, may obscure more than they reveal. Like Lowenberg, I believe that Herzl suffered from a profound lack of psychic stability and made a life project of compensating for that lack. But whereas Lowenberg sees Herzl's turn to Zionism and claims to political leadership as constituting that life project, I believe that the project took multifarious forms and that Herzl's literary, journalistic, and Zionist careers were entirely intertwined.

Unlike other biographies of Herzl, my own book in progress situates Herzl as a Zionist leader by drawing on the scholarly literature on leadership, charisma, and the psychology of political leaders. I have written elsewhere of Herzl's charisma as a relational construct that depends as much on the social context in which the charismatic leader lives as on the individual himself.[9] Here, however, I want to focus on Herzl's interiority, in particular the striving of this deeply troubled individual to construct a stable persona with a will to live and to engage the world. Most of Herzl's biographers have focused on his troubled relationship with his own Jewishness. His encounters with antisemitism were hurtful and humiliating; the ensuing sense of humiliation and shame catalyzed an internalization of antisemitism and a harsh critique of his fellow Jews. But the psychic origins of Herzl's life project lay not in Jewishness or antisemitism as such, or certainly not in them alone. Anterior to Herzl's construction of "the Jews" and his own Jewish self-ascription was an ongoing struggle to find meaning in life and to win recognition, which was the only way he could allay chronic and powerful depression.

Herzl was a darkly unhappy man, given to the blackest of moods. Although he never seriously planned to end his own life, he did suffer from bouts of depression—at nineteen, and then again at twenty-three, when his theatrical career appeared stalled, his love life was in tatters, and he had resigned from his student fraternity due to its increasing antisemitism. Herzl's turn to Zionism, taken to give his life meaning and purpose, offered no immediate cure for Herzl's ailment. Herzl fell into a depression again in 1896, when, after only a few months of Zionist activity, he had not yet attained a charter for Palestine from the Ottoman Sultan. In that same year, Herzl published a feuilleton about an unhappily married man, on the verge of drowning himself, who is saved thanks to a chance encounter with an eccentric inventor. An innkeeper tells the miserable would-be suicide:

> Despair is a precious substance, from which the most wonderful things may be generated: courage, self-denial, resolution, sacrifice.... To the stubbornest I recommend self-realization in a great task, and they have achieved the most.... As I look back in the past, it seems to me that all of the great men of history were once at the river's edge and turned back so that their despair bore fruit. All discoverers, prophets, heroes, statesmen, artists—yes, all philosophers also, for one never philosophizes better than when staring death in the face.[10]

Depression—and the determination to overcome it—has indeed been common among great leaders, and there are intriguing parallels on this point between

Herzl and Winston Churchill, whose psyche was trenchantly analyzed by Anthony Storr in his classic essay of 1989, "Churchill's Black Dog." Had Churchill "been a stable and equable man," writes Storr, "he could never have inspired the nation." Churchill's triumphant moment in 1940, like Herzl's in 1896, came about only because "all his life, he had conducted a battle with his own despair that made it possible to convey to others that despair can be overcome."[11] Churchill's 1897 novel *Savrola* begins almost identically to Herzl's *Altneuland*, with a thirty-something man steeped in melancholy, overcome by work and worry, jaded, nervous, and emotionally enervated. As young men, Churchill and Herzl alike were consumed by shame (for Churchill, over his boyhood frailty and cowardice; for young Herzl, over his rejection from military service on medical grounds, contraction of gonorrhea from a prostitute, and evasion of fighting duels while a university student). Both men catapulted between self-deprecation and self-aggrandizement; Churchill was writing very much in a Herzlian mode when he claimed that "We are all worms. But I do believe that I am a glow-worm." Both men were preoccupied by thoughts of death, and both were hypochondriacs. At the same time, both men had the most vivid of imaginations and escaped into colorful fantasies, be they Churchill's watercolors or Herzl's utopian visions. Storr's description of what painting meant for Churchill nicely elucidates the pageantry and chivalry that fills so much of his writings: "The counterpart to the gloomy, subfusc world of the depressive is a realm of perpetual excitement and action in which colors are richer and brighter, gallant deeds are accompanied by heroes, and ideas are expressed in language replete with simile, ornamented with epithet, and sparkling with mellifluous turns of phrase."[12] For such men, the aspiration to political leadership stems from something deeper than ambition for power or material gain. Rather, the belief in one's heroic mission is a means of fulfilling deep-seated psychic needs. And it was precisely because Herzl and Churchill were not balanced, rational men that they could inspire the public in times of crisis that corresponded to the perpetual sense of imminent catastrophe with which they lived on a daily basis.

Neither man was warm, had the common touch, or spoke easily and informally. Yet psychically, Herzl was in many ways more fragile than Churchill. He was a desperately lonely man, stuck in a catastrophic marriage to a woman even more mentally unbalanced than himself. Herzl had some youthful, rather mechanical dalliances, and he appears to have felt a volcanic, albeit ephemeral, erotic attraction to his wife, Julie, whose kisses set him afire when the two first met in 1886 and who gave birth to their first child scarcely eight months after their wedding.[13] Yet the marriage to Julie quickly soured, and after that, Herzl never found (or, apparently, sought) sexual satisfaction with individuals of either gender. He was too narcissistic to be capable of mature, conjugal love, or even of sustained platonic friendship. His only true friend, the journalist Heinrich Kana, committed suicide in 1891. Tellingly, when Herzl received the news of Kana's suicide, he abandoned Julie, who was five months pregnant, and decamped for Italy and France, returning to Vienna only during the final weeks of the pregnancy and then fleeing to Spain two months after his son Hans was born. On these misery-induced European trips, Herzl wrote outstanding travel feuilletons, which cemented his good reputation with the editors of the *Neue Freie Presse* and won him the position as that newspaper's Paris correspondent. Not surprisingly, peripatetic, brokenhearted men litter his novel *Altneuland:* the protagonist (and Herzl's alter ego) Friedrich Lowenberg, the crusty Prussian aristocrat Kingscourt, and even Kingscourt's Tahitian servant have all loved and lost, and now prefer to seek the companionship of men, circumnavigating the globe by ship and sojourning for decades on an isolated South Pacific island.

Loneliness was both a source and product of Herzl's melancholy temper, but shame drove him to seek honor. Shame over what he perceived as physical weakness and cowardice led Herzl to exalt allegedly Prussian aristocratic values such as manliness, stolidity, strength of character, self-discipline, direct speech, and decisiveness. Herzl juxtaposed these qualities against those of Jews, who even in his most mature writings are often depicted in stereotypically antisimetic terms (e.g., as crass and venal). Herzl was wont to portray Jewish women in a particularly grotesque way, as bedecked with jewels and displaying fallen décolletage. Herzl's finest play, *Das Neue Ghetto* (*The New Ghetto*, 1894), is filled with unpleasant Jewish characters but also features a corrupt, aristocratic mine owner who, at the play's end, fights a duel with and kills the hero, Jacob Samuel (clearly an alter ego, as Jacob was Herzl's father's name). Over the course of the play, Jacob has come to realize that it is both impossible and dishonorable to assimilate into Christian society, and that Jews must learn how to, in his words, "bow without subservience, and stand tall without truculence." Paradoxically, Herzl's yearning to behave with honor led him to exempt himself from his infamous proposal of 1893 that Jews undergo a mass conversion to Christianity to put an end to antisemitism. Herzl saw himself as remaining Jewish out of what he called "filial loyalty and manly pride"; to invoke terminology made famous by Hannah Arendt, Herzl would always be the proud pariah, and never the parvenu.

The sense of being a pariah caused Herzl to claim a bond with the hapless Captain Alfred Dreyfus. He did not do so at the time of Dreyfus's first trial in December 1894. In his dispatches for the *Neue Freie Presse*, Herzl did not assume Dreyfus's innocence or protest the verdict. Dreyfus did not appear in Herzl's private writings until November 1895, and the reference is only to the accusation of treason, not to any miscarriage of justice. But by 1899, Herzl had changed his tune. As Jacques Kornberg has written, in that year Herzl invented a genealogy of his conversion to Zionism that inaccurately placed the writing of *The New Ghetto* as occurring after and having been inspired by Dreyfus's first trial. In fact, Herzl completed the play more than a month before the trial, although, to be fair to his recollection, the pretrial publicity, which began in early November, was extensive and vitriolic, and could well have unsettled him. It is also possible to read Herzl's narrative as a canny act of self-invention at a time when the Dreyfus trial had ballooned into the Dreyfus Affair, Emile Zola's "J'Accuse…!" had galvanized the world, and the fortunes of Zionism stood to benefit if the movement's leader could claim to have foreseen the tragic import of the arrest, show trial, and brutal punishment of an army officer for no other reason than his Jewish faith. But Herzl clearly identified with Dreyfus's love of the state and sense of duty. He claimed that any Jew who had advanced so far as to become an officer on the General Staff would never betray his country; it was "psychologically impossible." Writing as much about his own frustrated ambitions for military service as about Dreyfus, Herzl argued that "because they were deprived of the honors of citizenship for such a long time, the Jews have a desire for the honors of citizenship that frequently borders on the pathological, and in this respect a Jewish army officer is a Jew raised to the nth degree."[14]

For Herzl, Zionism was at least as much about the attainment of individual and collective Jewish honor as it was about the rescue of impoverished and persecuted masses and their transportation to a safe haven. This striving for dignity helps account for the bitterness with which Herzl attacked assimilationist anti-Zionists, most notoriously in his essay "Mauschel" of 1897. The title refers to a venerable German pejorative for the language of Jews, depicted as a perversion of pure German, inextricably linked with sharp dealing, cheating, and insincerity. The infinitive "mauscheln" connotes duplicitous speech that conceals dishonorable behavior. Employing the proper noun Mauschel (akin to "kike"), Herzl declaims: "In poverty Mauschel is a despicable schnorrer; in wealth he is an even more despicable show-off." The distinction between the good Jew and the wicked Mauschel is that the latter has no honor: "After all, in civilized countries only the honor of the Jews is being attacked. Mauschel shrugs his shoulders. What is honor? Who needs honor? If business is all right and one's health is good one can live with the rest." Herzl concludes that "no true *Jew* can be an anti-Zionist; only Mauschel is one."[15]

Although Herzlian Zionism certainly aspired to restore Jews to their ancient homeland, Herzl envisioned that Jews would continue to live outside of the future Jewish state. The Jewish state's very existence would endow Jews the world over with a sense of honor, and once the state was in place, Jews would be respected by gentiles as a normal people, grounded in a territory that, to the Jews' even greater credit, would be developed in an exemplary fashion and seen as a "rampart of Europe against Asia, an outpost of civilization against barbarism."[16] Jews would no longer be rootless cosmopolitans whose exceptionality stimulates chronic and ultimately destructive anxiety in gentiles (the "ghost-like apparition of a living corpse, as described by Lev (Leon) Pinsker in his pamphlet of 1882, *Auto-Emancipation*,[17] which in so many ways adumbrated the work of Herzl).

When Herzl testified in 1902 before the Royal Commission on Alien Immigration, he made clear that his Zionist vision left plenty of room for Jews to remain in place. Asked if he demanded that every Jew leave England or even the entirety of Europe, Herzl replied, "You must leave that to every man for himself, and he must decide whether he will assimilate or not, whether he will go to another nation or belong to his sister nation. I say it is not right to influence a man to do it, except by putting arguments before him, or by letting the forces work [sic]."[18] On one level, this quotation refers to the rights of free humans to choose where they wish to live. But the full meaning of the quotation emerges when comparing it with a key theme in Herzl's novel *Altneuland*, published in the year after his testimony before the royal commission. In the novel, poor and persecuted Jews have moved to a utopian society, but the very acts of immigration and social creation have caused gentiles to appreciate Jews to the point that they beg them not to leave. Once the New Society, as the Jewish community of Palestine is called, has been created, Jews in diaspora may stay abroad, or they may, if they wish, convert to Christianity, doing so out of pure belief, without any instrumental intent. Jews in diaspora no longer need to act out of shame or opportunism; they are endowed with complete freedom and untainted honor.

One of the last scenes in *Altneuland*, and the most momentous, takes place in Jerusalem, on the Sabbath eve, in the rebuilt Temple, where the novel's hero Friedrich Lowenberg reflects on Jewish honor. Lowenberg reflects on

> the time when the Jews had been ashamed of everything that was Jewish, when they believed that they looked more aristocratic when they hid their Jewishness, by this very concealment showing themselves to be slaves or freedmen in spirit. How could they wonder that they were despised, when they themselves despise their own origins? They had crawled after the strangers, and so they were rightly repulsed.... All around him Friedrich could see the signs of how it had come about. Jewry had a look so different now because it was no longer ashamed of itself.... The strong, the free, the successful had also returned home—and they received more than they gave. Thinking these thoughts, Friedrich suddenly, in a flash, solved the meaning of the Temple.... Only here had the Jews again developed a free commonwealth in which they could work for the good of mankind.... In the ghetto they were without honor, without rights, without justice, without defence—when they left the ghetto, they ceased to be Jews. Yet a man, to be a man, must have both freedom and the feeling of community. Only when the Jews had both, could they rebuild the house of the Invisible and Almighty God.[19]

Herzl reprises the reference to the divine in the novel's last sentence, when a venerable rabbi invokes God as the source of the Jews' salvation in their old-new land. This is but a melodramatic flourish; Herzl was no believer, and his writings had featured a brisk anticlericalism dating back to his charming essay of 1891 on Lourdes, in which he was sympathetic to the desperate pilgrims who seek cures at the shrine but dryly insulted the clerics and merchants who grew rich off of the suffering of others. Herzl hinted at his own search for salvation not in the deity but in art when he wrote, "There should be a beloved Lady in every dark wood, in all human despair. And verily, she is there. Everywhere where a warm heart searches for a pretext to continue beating—she is there One or another. For there is more than one, Bishop: Poetry, art, philosophy, (true) labor are such dear women, rich in pain."[20] Yet Herzl's anticlericalism went hand in hand with a secularized religiosity, not only because of his typically Viennese love of tradition and ceremony, but also because the essence of Jewishness, in Herzl's opinion, lay in Jews' origins as a religious community. As he put it baldly, "We recognize ourselves as a nation by our faith (Wir erkennen uns als Nation am Glauben)."[21] Religion was a container, not content; a carrier wave, not a signal. Herzl drew a distinction between the hypocrisy of organized religion, embodied in the novel's villain, the xenophobic Rabbi Geyer, and the shared history of the Jews as a religious community. For a Jew to deny his religion would be an act of supreme dishonor.

Altneuland is replete with long monologues that closely resemble theatrical soliloquies. This is no surprise, as a dramatic, performative quality penetrated all of Herzl's professional activity—as a Zionist, a journalist, and, of course, a playwright. Just as Herzl would read the entire scripts of his plays to prospective producers, directors, and cast members, so did he read lengthy memoranda or early versions of his pamphlet *Der Judenstaat* to current or would-be supporters of the Zionist cause. Herzl saw nothing dishonorable about performance per se, as long as its motives were sincere and its outcome beneficial. In his play *Die Glosse* (The glosarry) (1895), one Philippus of Montaperto, a lawyer in thirteenth-century Bologna, wins back his straying wife by dramatically reciting to her a Roman marriage code. In *Altneuland*, the act of recitation has the power to inspire as well as educate; the engineering and managerial expert Joe Levy proclaims the technological wonders of the New Society via a gramophone recording played at a Passover seder. Like the Haggadah, the recitation is long, somewhat tedious, and absolutely central to a narrative of Jewish enslavement and liberation.

There is no necessary contradiction between performance and honor. Rituals by which honor is asserted or reaffirmed are performative acts. As Herzl wrote to Kana in 1883, "It seems that you have still not found the key to my character, perhaps because I make a show of presenting myself as wide open. I do not always speak the truth, not even often. Yet I am a sincere animal. (And if I do often lie, I never do so if there is no apparent advantage in it.)"[22] Being authentic, that is, true to oneself, does not necessarily demand transparency and absolute truthfulness toward the world. But there is a fine line between maintaining a duality between internal and external self-representation to preserve personal honor and simply lying to others to promote self-interest. Sincerity and hypocrisy were key elements in much of Herzl's journalistic writings. An epigraph in his feuilleton collection *The Book of Folly* (1888) taken from Jonathan Swift's *Tale of a Tub* speaks of "the sublime and refined point of felicity, calling the possession of being well-deceived, the serene and peaceful state of being a fool among knaves."[23] Criticism of stultifying social norms and the exposure of hypocrisy were staples of the era's literature (e.g., the psychologically fraught plays of Henrik Ibsen, or the thunderous polemics of Max Nordau). This critique takes a rather simplistic form in Herzl's story "The Mind Reader" (1887), about a man whose mind-reading powers expose him to the falseness in human speech and the contradictions between what we truly think and what we say. The mind reader concludes from his observations that "in the beginning everyone is good, or, as I would put it, genuine. . . . Then something intervenes, it may be only the passage of time, and they become ungenuine."[24] Similarly, the story "A Good Deed" (1888) is about the often impure intentions that lie behind beneficial action.

From childhood, Herzl's affect was aloof, poised, and defensive. These characteristics were intensified during his adolescence by an unrequited schoolboy crush on a teenaged girl named Madeleine Herz, who was the daughter of family acquaintances, and by his sister Pauline's death in 1878. Pauline's death devastated Herzl, yet he kept those feelings private and, in his autobiographical sketch of 1898, focused entirely on his mother's grief, to which he attributed his family's move from Budapest to Vienna shortly after Pauline died. Some level of concealment or displacement of personal feeling is to be expected in any kind of public life-writing, so this statement in and of itself is not surprising, any more than Herzl's misrepresentations about the effects of the Dreyfus trial on his Jewish consciousness, or his claim in 1898 that he left a pleasant job as a state attorney in Salzburg out of a realization that as a Jew, he would never be promoted to the judiciary. (In fact, he resigned after completing the minimum term of service to pursue his theatrical career.) Authenticity can survive a bit of creative storytelling; but it demands a high level of self-awareness, and in this regard Herzl was sorely lacking.

Herzl was apparently unaware that he developed a posthumous love for his sister that fused fraternal and erotic elements, so much so that in *Altneuland*, his alter ego, Friedrich Lowenberg, marries the virtuous Miriam, an avatar of Pauline Moreover, Herzl did not find anything untoward about a romantic infatuation he developed at the age of twenty-six with Madeleine Herz's thirteen-year-old niece, whom Herzl had held in his arms as an infant. (Madeleine herself had died tragically two years after Pauline.) Shortly after this episode, Herzl met the beautiful eighteen-year-old Julie Naschauer, with whom he exchanged flirtatious kisses that aroused his desire but also an inexplicable self-disgust and self-hatred—what he described as a "wild nausea"—that drove him to consider suicide. Torn between eros, repulsion, and fear of sexual maturity and marital responsibility, Herzl cut off ties with Julie and buried himself in his work until the spring of 1887, when debilitating tension headaches compelled him to take a long restorative trip abroad. In the fall, with some theatrical and journalistic successes under his belt and apparently feeling somewhat better about his masculinity, Herzl returned to Julie, and two years later they entered into their disastrous marriage.

In his youth, Herzl had been frank, even ribald, in writings to his friend Kana about his sexual encounters (as a result of which he contracted gonorrhea). There is more than a touch of adolescent boasting in these writings, but what is most striking about them is their underlying tone of anxiety. After a particularly graphic comparison of writing a novel with prolonged intercourse, Herzl concludes, "I'll tell you one thing—and here I am speaking from personal experience—both a love affair and a novel can drain you."[25] Although Herzl would eventually write his novel *Altneuland* —a work that would be his greatest solace as his Zionist diplomatic efforts went awry—he gave up on erotic love, marital or otherwise, and contented himself with fantasies of virginal and unattainable girls.

This obsession mars one of his most mature and revealing stories, "The Reading Glasses" (1902). This is an epistolary account addressed to an unknown recipient from a middle-aged man who has acquired his first pair of reading glasses and dwells on their melancholy import: "Reading lenses are the border, the watershed. From here on the water flows to the other side. One must leave this. The glasses are the official beginning of old age."[26] As Herzl puts it even more bluntly, first we lose our looks, then our passion, and reading is our only remaining pleasure. The character reflects that as we age, our eyes lose the ability to see things at close range, but our distance perception remains sharp. This is an obvious metaphor for the ability of older people to perceive what really matters in life and to ignore petty matters. The composer of this letter is wearing his new lenses while he writes in a hotel salon. He sees—or rather, he perceives—a young woman entering the room; because of the lenses, he cannot see her, but he catches the scent of her perfume and hears the rustle of her dress. He abandons all ambition to flirt with her or to hide the glasses in her presence so as to conceal his age. These reflections appear rather mature, but as the story approaches its end, the letter writer notes that this blurry-faced woman in the salon reminds him of a fourteen-year-old girl whom he had loved in his youth. It is unclear if Herzl is reminiscing about Madeleine or her niece, but in either case, he appears to be hiding in memories rather than embracing the present, which is the opposite of the story's explicit directive.

Herzl explored a more virile form of erotic authenticity in another late story, "Epaphroditus," which was closely adapted from Plutarch's *Life of Sulla*.

In Herzl's rendering, the Roman dictator steps down from power to enjoy private life and its simple sensual pleasures; he dies in the arms of his enemy's mistress. There is more than a hint of identification with the charismatic self-made dictator who was surrounded by scheming enemies, and of wish fulfilment in the beauteous mistress and the death that grants him peace. (In this story, the mistress is a developed woman, not a nymphet, but Herzl, perhaps still bearing the scars of his relationship with Julie, cannot separate erotic union from destruction.) Herzl adds to Plutarch's tale a story in which a centurion upbraids Sulla for walking unarmed in the public square. The centurion sees this behavior as a sign of weakness, yet for Sulla, in Herzl's rendering, walking in public, unarmed or, as he puts it, "exposed," is the highest expression of masculine strength. This paean to exposure of vulnerability reminds us of Herzl's notorious plea of 1894 to his friend Arthur Schnitzler to submit Herzl's play "The New Ghetto" to theatres under a pseudonym lest the play be rejected out of hand because of its author's Jewish origins. At the time, Herzl wrote to Schnitzler that having finished the play, he longed "to hide, to go underground": "In the special instance case of this play I want to hide my genitals more than any other time."[27]

In his journalistic writings and plays, Herzl praised authenticity, but it was difficult for him to achieve it in real life. For him, Zionism became a means by which he could expose his genitals—that is, his circumcised penis—by proclaiming attachment to the people who bore that mark, and who, thanks to Zionism, would do so with pride and dignity. In the first entry in Herzl's Zionist diary in 1895, he compared Jews to seals who, after ages of living entirely in the sea, have, due to Darwinian selection, come to look like fish. If they were to return to dry land, however, their fins would soon turn back to feet. Leaving aside the implications of this metaphor—seals live their lives both in water and on land, so perhaps Jews are meant to live in both diaspora and their own country—the point here is that for Herzl, Zionism provides an opportunity to be authentic, but only by assuming a role—that of the proud, dissimilating Jew.

Herzl had a somewhat easier time writing with honesty, sophistication, and self-awareness about parental love as opposed to adult romantic relations. Several of Herzl's feuilletons offer engaging meditations on the brevity of his children's childhood and on the pleasures of the nursery. As one might expect given the era and the journalistic genre in which Herzl was writing, these accounts could be saccharine, but he writes with keen insight about the wonders of child development and the inability of adults to comprehend or to appreciate that magical experience. Herzl is particularly interested in how his children learn to speak and write. He describes his preliterate youngest child, Trude, as living in a paradise of the imagination, yet profoundly disquieted by her siblings' ability to write, which for Herzl is the most essential sign and catalyst of maturation.[28] The wistful tone of these essays reminds us that Herzl almost certainly had a happy childhood: he was beloved by his parents, was kept at home and educated by tutors until his early teens, and once in school, he had friends, although he tended place himself above them as their leader. These sentimental feuilletons should not blind us, however, to the fact that Herzl was an absent father, whose observations of his children's growth came at distant intervals akin to time-lapse photographs. Herzl's diaries regularly note his son Hans's birthday but at times mistake his age. Considerably more disturbing than paternal absence or absent-mindedness is the ease with which the feuilletons about childhood cross the line from wistful to melancholy, and from melancholy to macabre. For example, in one feuilleton, Herzl has a waking nightmare of his daughter's death; in another, stray and pet birds die with regularity and are buried in the garden.[29]

These gloomy, gothic ruminations pale in comparison, however, with the feverish fantasy of a Herzlian royal dynasty that Herzl envisioned for the future Jewish state in his diary entries of June of 1895. Herzl wrote that his father Jacob would be the first senator of the Jewish state and his son Hans would be its doge. Herzl envisioned a coronation ceremony with cuirassiers, artillery, and infantry, "marching in gold-studded gala uniforms." "The doge himself will wear the garb of shame of a medieval ghetto Jew: the pointed hat, the yellow badge.... Only inside the temple we wrap a princely cloak about his shoulders and place the crown on his head."[30] Herzl wrote that the grandeur of his vision, and the prospect of crowning his own son as doge, caused him to burst into tears.

In retrospect, it appears that he was experiencing a manic episode, and at the time, he feared for his own sanity. The bond between genius and insanity crops up frequently in Herzl's published writings, as in an essay of 1895: "The imaginations of a madman are much more colouful, wild, majestic and frightful than those of Shakespeare, even of Ponson du Terrail."[31] In a Zionist essay of 1897, Herzl quotes from the French writer, Pierre-Jean de Béranger: "How long must an idea wait, like an unknown maid for her bridegroom! / Fools call her mad. The wise man tells her: 'Hide.' / But then, far from the crowd / a lunatic, who still believes in tomorrow / meets her and marries her, and she becomes fecund / for the happiness of all mankind."[32]

Herzl's psychological disturbances call into question the possibility of his authenticity. How could he have a lucid, realistic view of himself given his narcissism and his delusions of grandeur? (Herzl told his first biographer, Reuven Brainin, that as a child he dreamed of conversing with Moses and being called the Messiah. Whether Herzl actually had the dream or not is less important than the fact that he told the story at all.) And even if Herzl were considered sane, can we apply concepts of authenticity, or honor, to a political leader? Politicans, whether by their psychological makeup, the demands of the positions that they assume, or both, frequently engage in devious and manipulative behavior. They are often egotistical and even egomaniacal. They flatter, wheedle, and compromise, but they also bully and threaten. They can inspire trust, but they are seldom entirely trustworthy. Yet Herzl's search for honor and authenticity drove him into, of all things, politics. Regardless of his choice of occupation, Herzl would have encountered obstacles to achieving personal authenticity given his own fragmented psyche. He would have found it difficult to maintain a belief in his own honorability given that he was flooded with shame. Becoming a Zionist leader, however, made his quest into a quagmire.

Herzl's behavior as a Zionist leader was hardly a model of integrity and sincerity. He could not abide criticism from his lieutenants and surrounded himself in the Vienna Zionist Executive with sycophants. Herzl could be petulant, even savage, toward his opponents and arrogant, willful, and secretive toward his allies. Nor was Herzl averse to playing internal foes against each other, as when he encouraged the founding of the religious-Zionist Mizrahi as a counter to the cultural Zionist Democratic Faction, whose members attacked him relentlessly.[33]

Herzl's diplomatic activity was consistently opportunistic. When he began in 1896 to seek the favor of the Ottoman sultan, Herzl ensured that the *Neue Freie Presse* would present the Ottoman government in a favorable light regarding the Armenian question. In his contacts with the Ottomans, Herzl avowed that an imperial charter to Jews to settle Palestine would help the empire to maintain its independence and territorial integrity, yet at the same time, he courted the European powers, particularly Britain and Germany, one of which, he hoped, would proclaim a protectorate over Palestine on behalf of the Jews. In international diplomacy, however, opportunism is hardly dishonorable, and the only difference between Herzl and his interlocutors was that they had more power and played the diplomatic game more effectively than he did. Moreover, Herzl appears to have genuinely believed that he could form a syndicate of Jewish bankers who would raise vast loans for the Ottoman Empire and could, once a charter for Palestine had been granted to the Zionists, settle the empire's ballooning debt. Although Herzl was a great apologist for European colonialism and happily hitched the fortunes of Zionism to the European powers' global expansion, he had a clear-headed understanding of European colonialism's limitations as well as its strengths. In a colorful feuilleton written in Egypt in 1903, Herzl gushed that the Egyptians should feel fortunate to be occupied by the British, but he also observed the nationalist sentiments of educated Egyptian youth and predicted that Britain's days in Egypt might be numbered.[34]

There appears to be a stark contrast between Herzl's private and public statements about his diplomatic methods and political goals. At the outset of his Zionist activity, Herzl's private statements were bellicose, and he displayed no compassion toward the native population of what would become a Jewish state. At his first meeting with Baron Maurice de Hirsch, Herzl preached that the Jews "must be made strong for war, eager for work, virtuous."[35] In a diary entry of 1896,

Herzl mused that the Zionists should wait to establish colonies until they have a Jewish army to defend them; over time, the colonies would gain a critical mass, and the army would ensure that they could not be dislodged.[36] In a diary entry from the previous year, Herzl wrote cursorily and blithely about expelling natives from the territory of the future Jewish state. The processes of expropriation and removal, he wrote, must be carried out "discreetly and circumspectly."[37] Taken together, these private statements have led the historian Benny Morris to claim that if Herzl had had access to formidable military power, he would have taken Palestine by force.[38]

After 1896, however, such aggressive language disappeared from Herzl's diary and correspondence. In public, Herzl consistently assumed a pacific posture, and he never spoke openly about the use of military force against the Ottoman Empire or expelling the Palestinian Arabs. Should we grant greater weight to his earlier, as opposed to his later, diary entries and letters, or to his private, as opposed to his public statements? Many of the private comments that Herzl made during his manic episode in June 1895 and the first turbulent months of Zionist activity were not confessions so much as fantasies, the products of an at times unbalanced mind. Later, and especially in public, Herzl put himself together, as it were; his carefully constructed, measured, and calculated statements, when made over and over again over time, were no less authentic than the private cries of a tortured and unfocused psyche. Herzl was psychologically exoskeletal, constructed from the outside in.

Thus emerges the centrality of Herzl's novel *Altneuland*. On one level, the novel was a propaganda piece, an attempt to present Zionism to the world as an attractive and honorable enterprise. Reflecting Herzl's neurotic need for approval from gentile society, the Prussian aristocrat Kingscourt's praise of *Altneuland*'s New Society is expressed throughout the novel. Tellingly, in an interfaith seder toward the end of the novel, there is no rabbi or imam, yet there are Orthodox, Catholic, and Protestant clerics in attendance. The novel is set in Palestine, but its audience—and its author—were firmly placed in Europe. Yet this novel was much more than a public relations exercise; it was the apple of Herzl's eye, written over more than two years when he could steal time away from the double demands of his position at the *Neue Freie Presse* and the crush of Zionist diplomatic, organizational, and journalistic work. Writing the novel gave Herzl a sense of purpose, and no small amount of solace, in the face of fruitless Zionist diplomatic activity. Its plot is clumsy and melodramatic, its dialogue is stilted, and its characters are one-dimensional; it is shot through with Eurocentrism, paternalism, misogyny, adolescent wish fulfilment, and mawkishness. It is also utterly sincere. And it depicts a community that is not a sovereign state, that has no defined borders and no army, and in which Arabs have not only not been expelled but have been welcomed into *Altneuland*'s New Society.

Altneuland represented an intellectual breakthrough for Herzl in terms of social thought as well as geopolitical strategy. In the 1890s, Herzl sympathized with various forms of peaceful social reform, but there was also a deeply conservative, fatalistic side to his social thought, as seen in his story "Solon in Lydia" (1900). In this tale set in ancient Greece, a young man, Eukosmos, invents a machine that manufactures wheat out of air and promises to end all hunger. Aesop advises the King of Lydia to put the machine into action—and once he does, people grow lazy, self-indulgent, possessive, disruptive, and violent. Solon the lawmaker then urges that Eukosmos be killed. Herzl's anxieties about the corrupting effects of technology also emerged in a review of *Robinson Crusoe* that he published in the *Neue Freie Presse* in 1899. In the review, Herzl presented the heroic Crusoe as a model of manly behavior to be emulated by European boys growing up in the face of enervating urban amenities. Moreover, "Solon in Lydia's" message that inequity and the struggle to survive are necessary evils was in tune with a feuilleton that Herzl wrote in 1903 on a march of unemployed men in London. Observing the mass of impoverished humanity, Herzl felt great pity toward them yet wrote that the fear of falling into poverty and striving to avoid it are key to all social success.[39]

From the beginning, Herzl's Zionist writings featured a more benign and optimistic view of human nature than his journalistic pieces written for the general public. As early as 1896, he spoke of agricultural producers' cooperatives ensuring a technologically advanced and lucrative livelihood for the rural folk of the future Jewish state. In 1899, he envisioned a new society based on mutualism, a third economic system in between capitalism and socialism.[40] But until Herzl wrote *Altneuland*, such statements were rare, and social issues were at the periphery, not the center, of his Zionist consciousness. In *Altneuland*, however, the New Society not only solves the "Jewish Problem" but tackles the world's thorniest social, economic, and medical challenges. In this novel, his literary will and testament, Herzl put aside his social Darwinist sensibilities just as he bid farewell to his militaristic ones.

*   *   *

How do we make sense of a man as riven with contradictions as Herzl, a profoundly irrational man who couched his life project in the language of indisputable rational argument, who yearned for honor and was steeped in shame, who saw in Zionism the road to authenticity while not having any clear idea where that road would lead? People whose embrace of nationalism stems from deep psychological need, from feelings of shame, inferiority, or weakness, are liable to become martial, extremist, and maximalist. At the outset of his Zionist activity, Herzl started down that road, but then he reversed course. Zionism was his life project, but Herzl's needs were entirely internally focused on imagining a Jewish state that would enable him to live comfortably as a European. Thus he sufficed with a disarmingly modest concept of the Jewish nation:

> We are noticed, we are a group, a historical group of people who clearly belong together and have a common enemy; this seems to me an adequate definition of a nation. I do not think the nation must speak only one language or show uniform racial characteristics. This quite moderate definition of nationhood is sufficient. We are a historical group of people who clearly belong together and are held together by a common foe. That is what we are, whether we deny it or not, whether we know it or not, and whether we desire it or not.[41]

Herzl's Zionism was a reaction to arrested emancipation and social slights, not pogroms and existential threat; it was an expression of a search for purpose and a desire to be of consequence. During his first year or two of Zionist activity, Herzl flirted with fantasies of Jewish armed power, but after that, he invariably spoke in a softer political register, as in the following remarks at the beginning of the second Zionist Congress in 1898: "If there is such a thing as a legitimate claim to any piece of the Earth's surface then all the peoples who believe in the Bible must recognize the right of the Jews. And they can do so without envy or concern, for the Jews are not a political power and will never be one again." A few moments later, he added, "This land presumably cannot, and never will, become the property of any single great power, for it is the best-guarded land of all. It is carefully guarded not only by its present proprietor but by everyone else as well."[42] Herzl's wavering loyalties between the Ottoman Empire, Britain, and Germany did not contradict his firm belief that even under a protectorate, the holy places in Jerusalem would remain *extra commercium* under international law.[43] Ironically, the author of *Der Judenstaat* was vague, unsure, and supremely flexible about the form that the Jewish polity should take—it could be a sovereign state, or a vassal or satrapy, or an autonomous region. As Herzl said at a debate in Berlin in 1898, "Well what is a state? A big colony. What is a colony? A small state."[44]

For Herzl, not only the Jews' antiquity but also their relative small numbers and powerlessness ensured that the monotheistic world could safely leave the Holy Land in the hands of the Jews. They would guard and preserve it. Herzl felt supremely satisfied playing his favorite role—a good servant of the West, entrusted with the most precious terrain in the world, the *terra sancta*. If all Herzl had was military strength, he would have the honor of a warrior. But he wanted something more: the respect and trust of his fellow Europeans.

Notes

Many thanks to the members of the "Word of a Jew" working group at the Oxford Centre for Hebrew and Jewish Studies and to Anita Shapira and the participants in her Tel Aviv University scholars' forum for their helpful comments on an earlier version of this chapter.

1. Jacob Golomb, "Thus Spoke Herzl: Nietzsche's Presence in Herzl's Life and Work," *Leo Baeck Institute Year Book* 44, no. 1 (1999): 97–124; Jacob Golomb, *Nietzsche and Zion* (Ithaca: Cornell University Press, 2004). For Robertson's critical review of the latter, see *Journal of Nietzsche Studies* 3, no. 1 (2006): 71–72.

2. *The Complete Diaries of Theodor Herzl*, vol. 1, ed. Raphael Patai (New York: Herzl Press, 1960), 4.

3. See the autobiographical sketch published in the *Jewish Chronicle* on January 14, 1898, reproduced in Theodor Herzl, *Zionist Writings* (New York: Herzl Press, 1973–75), 1:19.

4. Shlomo Avineri, "Theodor Herzl's Diaries as a Bildungsroman," *Jewish Social Studies* 5, no. 3 (Spring/Summer 1999): 1–46.

5. Marcus Mosley, *Being for Myself Alone: Origins of Jewish Autobiography* (Stanford: Stanford University Press, 2006).

6. Mosley, *Being for Myself Alone*, 297.

7. Early biographies by Zionist activists who knew Herzl personally are palpably biased but are richly detailed, evocative, and colorful; see, for example, Reuven Brainin, *Hayei Hertsel* (New York: Asaf, 1919); and Jacob de Haas, *Theodor Herzl: A Biographical Study* (Chicago: Leonard, 1927). The first scholarly biography of Herzl was Alex Bein, *Theodore Herzl* (German ed., Berlin: Fiba-Verlag, 1934; Philadelphia: Jewish Publication Society, 1941). Subsequent biographies include André Chouraqui, *A Man Alone: The Life of Theodor Herzl* (Jerusalem: Keter, 1970); Desmond Stewart, *Theodor Herzl: Artist and Politician* (New York: Doubleday, 1974); Amos Elon, *Herzl* (New York: Holt, Reinhart and Winston, 1975); Ernst Pawel, *The Labyrinth of Exile: A Life of Theodor Herzl* (New York: Farrar, Straus, and Giroux, 1989); Steven Beller, *Herzl* (New York: Grove Weidenfeld, 1991); Jacques Kornberg, *Theodor Herzl: From Assimilation to Zionism* (Bloomington: Indiana University Press, 1991); and Shlomo Avineri, *Herzl: Theodor Herzl and the Foundation of the Jewish State* (London: Weidenfeld and Nicolson, 2013; originally published in Hebrew, Jerusalem: Zalman Shazar Center, 2008).

8. Peter Lowenberg, "Theodor Herzl: A Psychoanalytic Study in Charismatic Political Leadership," in *The Psychoanalytic Interpretation of History*, ed. Benjamin Wolman (New York: Basic Books, 1971), 150–91.

9. Derek J. Penslar, "Theodor Herzl: Charisma and Leadership," in *The Individual in History: Essays in Honor of Jehuda Reinharz*, ChaeRan Y. Freeze, Sylvia Fuks Fried, and Eugene R. Sheppard (Lebanon, NH: Brandeis University Press, 2015), 13–27.

10. Cited in Lowenberg, "Theodor Herzl," 172–73.

11. Anthony Storr, *Churchill's Black Dog and Other Phenomena of the Human Mind* (London: HarperCollins, 1989), 5

12. Storr, *Churchill's Black Dog*, 44.

13. Theodor and Julie married on June 25, 1889. Most biographies of Herzl list their daughter Pauline's birth date as March 25, 1890, but in fact she was born on March 4, as Herzl's own letters from March 5 confirm. Assuming Pauline was conceived on the Herzls' honeymoon, she was born in the thirty-sixth week of Julie's pregnancy, which made her slightly but not dangerously premature. The birth caught Herzl by surprise, which substantiates the hypothesis that Pauline was a bit premature. One wonders who first moved Pauline's birth date to full term, and why. I assume it was done to remove any suspicion of premarital sexual relations.

14. Theodor Herzl, "Zionism" (1899), in *Zionist Writings*, 2:113.

15. Herzl, "Mauschel," in *Zionist Writings*, 2:167.

16. Theodor Herzl, *The Jewish State* (New York: American Zionist Emergency Committee), 1946, 15, http://www.mideastweb.org/jewishstate.pdf (accessed July 27, 2018).
17. Leon Pinsker, "Auto-Emancipation," trans. D. S. Blondheim (New York: Federation of American Zionists, 1916).
18. Herzl, "The Tragedy of Jewish Immigration," in *Zionist Writings*, 2:192.
19. Theodor Herzl, *Altneuland—Old-New Land* (Haifa: Haifa Publishing Company, 1960), 186.
20. Theodor Herzl, "Der Herr Bischoff von Meaux" (1891), in *Feuilletons*, vol. 2, ed. Raoul Auernheimer (Vienna, 1911), 225.
21. Diary entry of June 9, 1895, in Theodor Herzl, *Briefe und Tagebücher*, ed. Johannes Wachten and Chaya Harel (Frankfurt: Propyläen, 1984), 2:90.
22. Herzl to Kana, July 4, 1883, in Theodor Herzl, *Briefe und Tagebücher*, ed. Alex Bein, Hermann Greive, and Julius Schoeps (Frankfurt: Propyläen, 1983) 1:135.
23. Jonathan Swift, *The Tale of a Tub and Other Works*, ed. Henry Morley (London: Routledge, 1889) 133
24. Cited in Bein, *Theodore Herzl*, 55–56.
25. Cited in Pawel, *Labyrinth of Exile*, 80.
26. Herzl, "Die Brille," in Herzl, *Feuilletons*, vol. 2, 285–95.
27. Cited in Kornberg, *Theodor Herzl*, 152.
28. Herzl, "Trudes Träne" (1899), in *Feuilletons*, vol. 1, 18–24.
29. "Die leere Kinderstube" (1896) and "Unter dem Lebensbaum" (1898), in Herzl, *Feuilletons*, vol. 1, 1–9, 10–17.
30. Among the entries for June 9, 1895, Herzl, *Complete Diaries*, vol. 1, 57.
31. "Ravachol!," in Herl, *Feuilletons*, 1:64. Pierre Alexis Ponson du Terrail (1829–71) was a popular French writer of tales of adventure and fantasy.
32. "Leroy-Beaulieu on Antisemitism," in Herzl, *Zionist Writings*, 1:116. Herzl was wont to compare himself to misunderstood inventors and other geniuses who are dismissed as madmen, yet who do, in fact, possess salvific powers. See Herzl's feuilleton of 1896, "Das lenkbare Luftschiff," reprinted in *Theodor Herzl oder Der Moses des Fin de siècle*, ed. Klaus Dethloff (Vienna: Hermann Böhlaus, 1986), 178–86.
33. David Vital, *Zionism: The Formative Years* (New York, 1982), 220.
34. "Die Reise nach Ägypten" (1903), in Herzl, *Feuilletons*, vol. 2, 227–47, esp. 235.
35. Herzl, *Complete Diaries*, entry of May 26, 1895, vol. 1, 21–22.
36. Herzl, *Complete Diaries*, entry of July 8, 1896, vol. 1, 412.
37. Derek Penslar, "Herzl and the Palestinian Arabs: Myth and Counter-Myth," *The Journal of Israeli History* 24, no. 1 (2005): 65–77.
38. "If Herzl had five divisions of marines at his command, I think he wouldn't have hesitated for a moment to send them to Palestine to defeat the Turks. Herzl and his successors in the Zionist movement employed persuasion and diplomacy mainly because they had no power to attain their goal any other way." In Morris's review of *Yigal Allon: Aviv Haldo* by Anita Shapira, *Haaretz*, April 26, 2004, http://www.haaretz.com/print-edition/business/he-tried-harder-1.120770.
39. "Winter" (1903), in Herzl, *Feuilletons*, vol. 1, 232–41, esp. 238.
40. Derek J. Penslar, *Zionism and Technocracy: The Engineering of Jewish Settlement in Palestine, 1870–1918* (Bloomington: Indiana University Press, 1991), 49.
41. "Judaism" (1896), in Herzl, *Zionist Writings*, 1:51.

42. "Opening Address at the Second Zionist Congress," in Herzl, *Zionist Writings*, 2:19–20.
43. "Leroy-Beaulieu on Antisemitism," in Herzl, *Zionist Writings*, 1:115.
44. "Who Fears a State?," in Herzl, *Zionist Writings*, 1:214.

Bibliography

Avineri, Shlomo. *Herzl: Theodor Herzl and the Foundation of the Jewish State*. London: Weidenfeld & Nicolson, 2013. Originally published in Hebrew, Jerusalem: Zalman Shazar Center, 2008.
———. "Theodor Herzl's Diaries as a Bildungsroman." *Jewish Social Studies* 5, no. 3 (Spring/Summer 1999): 1–46.
Bein, Alex. *Theodore Herzl*. Philadelphia: Jewish Publication Society, 1941.
Beller, Steven. *Herzl*. New York: Grove Weidenfeld, 1991.
Brainin, Reuven. *Hayei Hertsel*. New York: Asaf, 1919.
Chouraqui, André. *A Man Alone: The Life of Theodor Herzl*. Jerusalem: Keter, 1970.
Elon, Amos. *Herzl*. New York: Holt, Rinehart & Winston, 1975.
Golomb, Jacob. *Nietzsche and Zion*. Ithaca: Cornell University Press, 2004.
———. "Thus Spoke Herzl: Nietzsche's Presence in Herzl's Life and Work." *Leo Baeck Institute Year Book* 44, no. 1 (January 1, 1999): 97–124.
de Haas, Jacob. *Theodor Herzl: A Biographical Study*. Chicago: Leonard, 1927.
Herzl, Theodor. *Briefe und Tagebücher*. 7 vols. Edited by Alex Bein, Hermann Greive, Moshe Shaerf, Julius H. Schoeps, and Johannes Wachten. Frankfurt: Propyläen, 1983–1996.
———. *Complete Diaries*. 5 vols. Edited by Raphael Patai. New York: Herzl Press, 1960
———. "Das lenkbare Luftschiff." 1896. Reprinted in *Theodor Herzl oder Der Moses des Fin de siècle*, edited by Klaus Dethloff, 178–86. Vienna: Hermann Böhlau, 1986.
———. *Feuilletons*. Edited by Raoul Auernheimer. Berlin: Benjamin Harz
———. *Altneuland—Old-New Land*. Haifa: Haifa Publishing Company, 1960.
———. *Zionist Writings*. 2 Vols. New York: Herzl Press, 1973–75.
Kornberg, Jacques. *Theodor Herzl: From Assimilation to Zionism*. Bloomington: Indiana University Press, 1991.
Lowenberg, Peter. "Theodor Herzl: A Psychoanalytic Study in Charismatic Political Leadership." In *The Psychoanalytic Interpretation of History*, edited by Benjamin Wolman, 150–91. New York: Basic Books, 1971.
Morris, Benny. Review of *Yigal Allon: Aviv Haldo* by Anita Shapira. In *Haaretz*, April 26, 2004. http://www.haaretz.com/print-edition/business/he-tried-harder-1.120770.
Mosley, Marcus. *Being for Myself Alone: Origins of Jewish Autobiography*. Stanford: Stanford University Press, 2006.
Patai, Raphael, ed. *The Complete Diaries of Theodor Herzl*. New York: Herzl Press, 1960.
Pawel, Ernst. *The Labyrinth of Exile: A Life of Theodor Herzl*. New York: Ferrar, Strauss and Giroux, 1989.
Penslar, Derek J. "Herzl and the Palestinian Arabs: Myth and Counter-Myth." *The Journal of Israeli History* 24, no. 1 (2005): 65–77.
———. "Theodor Herzl: Charisma and Leadership." In *The Individual in History: Essays in Honor of Jehuda Reinharz*, edited by ChaeRan Y. Freeze, Sylvia Fuks Fried, and Eugene R. Sheppard, 13–27. Lebanon, NH: Brandeis University Press, 2015.

———. *Zionism and Technocracy: The Engineering of Jewish Settlement in Palestine, 1870–1918.* Bloomington: Indiana University Press, 1991.
Pinsker, Leon. "Auto-Emancipation." Translated by D. S. Blondheim. New York: Federation of American Zionists, 1916.
Robertson, Ritchie. Review of *Nietzsche and Zion* by J. Golomb. In *The Journal of Nietzsche Studies* 31, no. 1 (2006): 71–72.
Stewart, Desmond. *Theodor Herzl: Artist and Politician.* New York: Doubleday, 1974.
Storr, Anthony. *Churchill's Black Dog and Other Phenomena of the Human Mind.* London: HarperCollins, 1989
Swift, Jonathan. *The Tale of a Tub and Other Works.* Edited by Henry Morley. London: Routledge, 1889.
Vital, David. *Zionism: The Formative Years.* New York: Oxford University Press, 1982.

DEREK JONATHAN PENSLAR, the William Lee Frost Professor of Modern Jewish History at Harvard, is a comparative historian with interests in the relationship between modern Israel and diaspora Jewish societies, global nationalist movements, European colonialism, and postcolonial states. He is a Fellow of the Royal Society of Canada and President of the American Academy of Jewish Research.

14 The Most Trusted Jew in America
Jon Stewart's Earnestness

Shaina Hammerman

> Jon Stewart: If you were to change your name, to Anglicize it as some have done, what would it be?
> Jerry Seinfeld: Well, I'd have to keep the Seinfeld, I wouldn't want to offend my parents. So I'd have to go with "Jesus."
> —Jon Stewart interviews Jerry Seinfeld
> *The Daily Show with Jon Stewart*, April 5, 2004

> Here is what I . . . would love to see . . . find someone . . . in the pursuit of being a judge, an arbiter, and earning the trust of the audience over time as an oversight to the shenanigans of the political world.
> —Jon Stewart, describing his ideal news network
> *Charlie Rose*, September 29, 2004

On one of his final appearances as host of *The Daily Show*, Jon Stewart had friend and fellow comedian Louis C. K. as the featured guest.[1] Louis, as he's known to fans, recalled seeing Stewart perform stand-up at the Comedy Cellar in New York when both men were just starting out as comics. "You were so great," Louis told Stewart, "I was like, 'Who's this little Jew? He's funny.'" The famously quick-witted Stewart replied, "That was the original title of my act, 'Little Funny Jew.'" While Stewart was clearly making a joke, the "little funny Jew" was more than just a way for Louis to poke fun at his friend and for Stewart to play along. It was a persona that Stewart embraced strategically over the course of his sixteen years in the host's seat. Stewart's "little funny Jew" character contrasts starkly with his other persona as "the most trusted man in America," a label bestowed on him by *Time* magazine in 2009 and reiterated by other news outlets ever since.[2] As "most trusted," Stewart was the main source of news for a generation of viewers and shared his stage with some of America's and the world's most important newsmakers. While it may seem that the "little funny Jew" act would undermine his more serious role as "most trusted," it was in those Jewish moments that Stewart engendered trust.

Social scientists have traced the outcomes of Stewart's popularity, crunching numbers and analyzing voting patterns to determine if his show played a perceptible role in its audience's political behaviors. One comprehensive study is the 2011 *The Stewart/Colbert Effect: Essays on the Real Impacts of Fake News*, which, among other feats, tracks changes in political discourse and engagement based on viewership.[3] There is a nexus between the audience's trust in Jon Stewart's television persona and the ways Americans, especially young Americans, engage in politics. If I am correct in my claims that Stewart's "Jewish" act is what engenders that trust, then what follows here is about more than just an analysis of why certain types of jokes resonate with audiences. It is about how a certain variety of public Jewishness can produce real-life political outcomes.

As host of *The Daily Show*, Stewart shared his stage with dozens of prominent intellectuals, politicians, and other newsmakers. Outside the program, he was a guest on several serious news programs: CNN's *Crossfire*, *NOW with Bill Moyers* on PBS, *Charlie Rose* (also on PBS), *Larry King Live* (CNN), *FOX News Sunday*, and others. He challenged powerful policy makers and political candidates with questions that belied his supposed role as a jokester. He used his platform to influence policy as well, pushing for Congress to pass the 9/11 First Responders' Bill and urging lawmakers who came on his program to increase veterans' health benefits.[4] In 2006, Stewart interviewed former attorney general John Ashcroft, a polarizing figure who served in George W. Bush's administration. Although the interview was mutually respectful, Stewart presented thoughtful challenges to Ashcroft concerning the Bush administration's use of surveillance technology on American citizens, the way it politicized opposition to the Iraq war, and its defense of torture. Ashcroft later joked that he would "rather be waterboarded" than be interviewed by Stewart.[5]

How did a "little funny Jew" comic from New Jersey find a place among serious journalists, intellectuals, and politicians as America's "most trusted"? And how are these starkly contrasting labels related? Remarkably, attributing the title "most trusted newscaster" to someone who would deny that he is a journalist in the first place is part of how he earned the title. Playing down his own power—not just as a straight white man, but also as an exceptionally successful, wealthy entertainer—is part of a complicated strategy Stewart employed to engender trust with his audience and his adversaries, as well as with notable intellectuals, celebrities, and politicians.

Unlike other late-night comedy talk shows, Stewart's show was a site where audiences came for news as well as entertainment. Unlike other news programs, Stewart and his team of writers and correspondents brought levity—from toilet humor and cursing to carefully crafted puns and parody—to serious issues. During President Obama's campaign for a second term, Stewart asked him, "Do you feel you have a stronger affirmative case for a second Barack Obama presidency or a stronger negative case for a Romney presidency?"⁶ The question received laughs from the audience even though it was a thoughtful and serious inquiry, but not one that other journalists or talk show hosts would ask. *Daily Show* viewers trusted Stewart to inform, to ask powerful individuals tough questions, and to offer up challenging critiques of political policy and "legitimate" media responses to the news of the day. And *Daily Show* viewers trusted Stewart to balance the tough questions with a laugh.

Why was the honor "most trusted" given to someone who insists he was merely "sit[ting] in the back of the country and mak[ing] wisecracks"?⁷ This troublemaker persona doesn't appear to engender trust. Why was the honor given to a satirist and not to an earnest reporter—are audiences more likely to trust a comic than a newscaster? When and how did earnestness become a quality Americans *don't* trust? For me, these issues serve a larger question related to many others in this volume: What does it mean that Americans invest their public trust in a Jew? Is Stewart's brand of comic satire the only kind of political speak that Jews can be trusted with among the general public? Can only Jews be trusted to do this kind of satirical work?

Sig Altman compared the work of a stand-up comic to that of a salesman, a person who manufactures a kind of closeness or friendship with his audience in order to sell laughs.⁸ This perceived closeness is dependent on the comic's disclosure of something presumably personal about himself. And for Jewish comedians, this disclosure is produced by confessing his Jewishness, which is "meant to appear as a form of confiding."⁹ This is certainly true of Stewart. In a 2012 interview with NBA All-Star, sportscaster, and author Charles Barkley, Stewart leaned in and said, "I'm a Jew. I can't dunk. So we all have our limitations."¹⁰ The "limitation" of Jewishness is a strategy Stewart employed to build confidence with his interviewee and his audience. It is, as Altman described, "a confidence trick."¹¹ Used in this way, Jewishness comes across as a vulnerability that renders Stewart at once nonthreatening and relatable. When Stewart "confided" to guests or directly to his audience that he is Jewish, he was also giving them permission to laugh with him at Jewishness. The Jewish "reveal" only works as such if there is a tacit understanding that Jewishness should be perceived as a weakness, albeit one that may be kept secret. The self-irony that Jewish comics employ is unrelated to their actual position within American culture. Altman calls this phenomenon a "cultural lag," continuing:

> [The Jewish Comedian is] no longer a *Jewish* institution; he is a creation of the popular culture. And so there is a precariousness in that Jewishness. . . . That precariousness has to do with the dubious salesman's "sincerity" that is the stock attitude of the Jewish Comedian. If confiding that he is Jewish is part of that sincerity, then the way Jewishness is used reflects the dishonesty of that sincerity.¹²

Altman sees the content of stand-up comic Jewishness as empty. He bemoans the lack of a "struggle to understand and come to terms" with what Jewishness means.[13] In fact, he concludes that "self-irony may be a way of maintaining a sense of being Jewish," in addition to simply stating it.[14]

Writing in 1971, Altman touched on a mechanism of Jewish-American comedy that persists today: constructing Jewishness as the underdog position in spite of Jews' unquestionable success in American cultural, economic, political, and intellectual spheres. The "cultural lag" that enables Jewish comics to pretend their inferiority while implicitly acknowledging Jewish power may serve to explain "the comic quality of the word 'Jewish.'"[15] This comic quality and the cultural lag that preempts it must both be present in order to achieve the confidence effect. Stewart's secret ("I'm a Jew.") was one the audience and interviewee already knew. So while it was staged like a confession, it was merely a (re)statement of the obvious.

The Daily Show employed this strategy—reiterating a known truth—in its news reports as well. When Stewart aired a clip of President Bush at a press conference, viewers laughed, "not because Bush's statements were considered funny when he first said them or even when they were aired on the evening news, but because they have been transcontextualized into a comedically deconstructive frame."[16] Transcontextualization is a term coined by Linda Hutcheon to capture the way literary or artistic materials may be removed (intact) from their contexts to ironic or parodic effect.[17] Similarly, it is not, on its own, funny that Jon Stewart is Jewish. But it becomes funny when he announces his Jewishness while sitting across the table from Charles Barkley. The dissonance that leads to laughter here has to do with a host of assumptions that are contained within the confession. Stewart constructed Jewishness to mean "little funny Jew," that is, short, unathletic, effeminate, book smart but not streetwise, and so on. When the five-foot-seven Stewart was sitting across from the six-foot-five Barkley and bringing up something everyone already knows—that he is Jewish—it is funny because it makes Barkley and Stewart into an awkward odd couple, the big black athlete and the little funny Jew. Exposing his "limitations" as a Jew rendered those limitations irrelevant, or, more aptly, revealed them to never have been there to begin with. Stewart built trust with his audience and interviewee by "confiding" a Jewish vulnerability he created; he maintained that trust because the vulnerability he exposed was not a liability but an asset.

The "most trusted" epithet originated in 1972 when a survey was conducted across eighteen states asking respondents to compare the trustworthiness of several prominent politicians.[18] Inexplicably, newscaster Walter Cronkite's name was included in the survey, and he outranked Richard Nixon, George McGovern, and a spate of others, earning him the title "most trusted man in America." The title stuck with Cronkite throughout his career and was used as a promotional tactic for his newscast despite the fact that he was the only newscaster among a cast of famously *un*trustworthy politicians. That survey and the honorific "most trusted" became a touchstone for determining the success of later newscasters, which is how a 2007 Pew Research Poll came to be, asking respondents about the most trusted newscaster in America. Then the host of Comedy Central's *The Daily Show* for ten years, Jon Stewart ranked fourth—tied with "legitimate" TV journalists Tom Brokaw, Brian Williams, Dan Rather, and Anderson Cooper.[19] A similar 2009 *Time* magazine poll following Cronkite's death put Jon Stewart on top.[20] As his career as a fake news host came to a close (he left his fake anchor's desk on August 6, 2015), the "most trusted man in America" epithet was widely used to characterize Stewart's success and the success of satire in American political news in general.

Unlike Cronkite, Stewart is not a "real" journalist and takes great pains to remind his viewers as well as his adversaries that he is "merely" a comedian. "Remember," he announced during an interview, "we are not actual newspeople."[21] Similarly, in one of his most famous moments, which took place outside *The Daily Show* studios, Stewart appeared on the pundit shouting match program *Crossfire* on CNN. He badgered that show's hosts, insisting that their unproductive debates about left versus right were "hurting America." When they returned the jab, questioning Stewart's journalistic integrity, he reminded the hosts that "the show that leads into mine is puppets making crank phone calls."[22] In this surprising move of playing down his power, Stewart actually shored it up. In denying that he was a newscaster, or that he has the same responsibility to his viewers as a newscaster, Stewart got to report the news seemingly free of responsibility, making him more powerful than CNN, MSNBC, and especially FOX news anchors. Stewart's massive success as an entertainer and political force—he received two private invitations to Obama's White House to discuss policy—attest to the fact that he was nowhere near the "back of the country" but that he was on the front lines.[23] Getting to those front lines, however, depended on consistently pretending to be in the back. "Our show is obviously at a disadvantage," Stewart announced in a 2005 interview, comparing *The Daily Show* to straight news. "For one thing, we are fake. They are not. So in terms of credibility we are, well, oddly enough, actually about even. We're about even."[24] The punchline here calls out the major "legitimate" news networks for lacking credibility in their reporting, on level with a "fake" news show. But the joke also raises up *The Daily Show*'s trustworthiness to be on par with serious news outlets.

Stewart's humility and comic "objectivity" recall Cronkite's journalistic integrity and neutrality; Cronkite once proclaimed that he felt "no compulsion to be a pundit."[25] There is an irony behind Cronkite's denial of punditry and Stewart's antipundit rants. Both men earned their audience's trust precisely at those moments when their personal opinions and agendas, rather than their humor on the one hand or journalistic objectivity on the other, were center stage. For Cronkite, it happened when he presented a special on the Vietnam War in 1968, declaring, "We are mired in stalemate," legendarily ticking off President Johnson.[26] For Stewart, it happened when he faced the camera after national tragedies. When he returned to the show on September 20, 2001, following the attacks of 9/11, Stewart delivered a heartfelt nine-minute monologue showcasing his anger, his sadness, and his hope. Stewart gratefully recognized the privilege of working in "a country that allows for open satire." "I want to tell you why I grieve, but why I don't despair," he declared as he choked back tears.[27]

Both Cronkite and Stewart earned trust not because of their objective positions, but because of the strategic moments in which they opted to make the political personal. The tone of Stewart's 9/11 monologue was mournful and raw but also carefully balanced with levity. He explained that "they said go back to work, but there were no jobs for a man in the fetal position crying underneath his desk." Regaining his composure after letting out tears, Stewart joked, "Luckily, we can edit this." In both of these cases, Stewart was careful never to make a mockery of the tragedy, but to mock his own grieving. When he joked about editing out the crying, he called attention to the supposed embarrassment a man should feel at crying publicly. At the same time, he reiterated the raw, unedited, unmanufactured quality of the moment. The joke worked because the tears were real. Stewart returned from the commercial break "with his makeup refreshed" and declared, "Hey, you know what's nice? A good cry. I feel like Robin Williams in *Bicentennial Man*. I—I can feel love!"[28]

Here Stewart dispelled the complex yet straightforward string of emotions he conveyed during his extended monologue by repeating them ironically. He took great care in crafting a speech that balanced both sorrow and hope, and took equally great care in reintroducing comic levity—not by bringing levity to the tragedies of 9/11, but to the distressing image of a comedian (and a man) crying in public. He helped his viewers return to laughter by laughing *at him*.

Seemingly unrelated, Stewart's moments of confiding his Jewishness for a laugh produced the same effect as his earnestly confiding his private feelings about public events. They engendered trust from the audience because of their deeply personal, confessional style. The Jewish jokes maintain trust because of the tacit understanding that Jewishness is *not* the vulnerability Stewart pretended it to be. The jokes that peppered the 9/11 monologue and the one that followed it maintain trust *because they are also Jewish jokes*. Part of Stewart's "little funny Jew" persona entails playing up the effeminate quality of the Jewish man—the Jew he constructed was too short, too anxious, too emotional to dunk when talking to Charles Barkley or to hold back tears when talking about 9/11. But for the persona to work, it required Stewart to poke fun at himself. In his host's seat not two weeks after the attacks of September 11, Stewart had to assert his authority as a person worthy of his platform on national television and his vulnerability as a fearful citizen who had just witnessed massive trauma.

In moments of earnestness as well as in his comedy, this little funny Jew rendered himself an accessible everyman. Rather than presenting himself as a wealthy, educated, New York intellectual, Stewart played up his roots as a middle-class kid from New Jersey, identifying strongly with the music of Bruce Springsteen. Rather than supporting the world champion New York Yankees, Stewart declared his undying loyalty to the famously cursed New York Mets. Although he received an athletic scholarship to college for soccer, he played down his athleticism and played up his short stature, his physical inferiority, and his lactose intolerance, especially in front of tall, attractive, and powerful interview guests on the show. Oddly, it is the specificities of Stewart's Jewishness that made him into a relatable everyman figure. During his first year as host, he joked, "Ultra-Orthodox Jews believe themselves superior to other Jews, claiming the Word was handed to them directly, right before [God] handed us big noses and took away all our athletic ability."[29] Once again, he exposes his vulnerability as a member of a physically inferior people and everyone laughs. They laugh because Stewart, who received honorable mention in *People* magazine's "sexiest men alive" contests in 2005, 2010, and 2014, is sexy, smart, rich, and powerful.[30]

In his *New Yorker* profile of Stewart, Tad Friend captured a moment when a construction worker approached Stewart during lunch:

> "My sister *loves* you," he said to Stewart. "Could you sign a Christmas note to her?" . . . [Stewart] wrote a note and signed it in John Hancock–size cursive, and shook his fan's hand. When he left, Stewart leaned over and whispered, "You know, I did fuck his sister, and she was great." Then he wrung his right hand cautiously. "The guy has hands like a maul. He's going to come out on the street and go"—he sniffed his hand—"'Oil of Olay? What is he, a florist?'"[31]

In one short interaction, Stewart played two sides. A macho misogynist joke about the man's sister is spun into a little funny Jew joke about the construction worker being bigger and stronger than he is, about Stewart having soft, effeminate, nice-smelling hands. As in his interaction with Charles Barkley, Stewart fashioned himself into one half of an odd couple with the construction worker—he is diminutive, effeminate, unsexy next to the powerful, masculine man who wanted a handshake and an autograph. In the face of a compliment about being adored by a fan, Stewart first acknowledged his appeal to strangers, then redirected the notion of his own celebrity into a self-deprecating joke.

Friend described Stewart's persona after the encounter with the construction worker as "the timorous outsider." Stewart responded, "You mean the short, hairy, big-nosed, picked-on Jew?"[32] Even here in conversation with a reporter, Stewart worked Altman's "confidence trick." By transposing "the timorous outsider" into what sounds like an antisemitic stereotype, Stewart is "confiding" who he really is. The joke might have worked just as well had Stewart simply said, "You mean the Jew?"—this points to the same quality, and calls out the non-Jewish reporter Friend for his clumsy euphemism. But while "timorous outsider" might have been a euphemism for "Jew," Stewart took it to an extreme, self-deprecating (some might say self-hating) qualification of "Jew." Once again, the severity of the description calls attention to the way in which Stewart's Jewishness is not a liability, but an asset. In this joke, "Jew" isn't a secret that must be covered over with euphemism, it is permission to laugh, it is confessional and inviting, and it is a reminder that the construction worker's sister "*loves*" him.

Playing down his privilege, his celebrity, and his sex appeal enabled Stewart to "punch up"—to mock the powerful safely and help an audience feel as if he spoke for them. As the *New York Times* put it, Stewart is "a proud New Yorker and part of a long tradition of smart-aleck Jewish comedians adopting argumentative outsider approaches, while using a subway car full of ethnic voices to punch up jokes."[33] This is by no means a new phenomenon: jesters in the king's court could point out the king's hypocrisy only because this mockery came from the jester's lowly, nonthreatening status. Jesters and fools regularly possessed physical deformities or some other marginalized characteristic (e.g., being a bastard) that made their mockery harmless, as it came from a disreputable sphere of society. Vicki Janik offers a vivid description of the fool's role in the social order:

> They participate in events, yet they remain isolated observers ... fools question prevailing order, and their objectivity makes them at once comic individuals who are too removed to suffer and ironists who see existence as absurdity. Fools mock social structures, individual righteousness, passionate personal relationships, and the mutating and fragile underpinning of human thought—language itself. Fools, then, operate as antirulers, offering society skeptical, unencumbered viewpoints that scorn pride and challenge such concepts as logic, cause, reward, and solution. It is significant that nearly all cultures instinctively seek such disordering perspectives.[34]

Like Janik's fools, Stewart built himself into a "lowly" position in the social hierarchy so his satirical critique of power would come across as nonthreatening. Stewart's Jewishness was central to this construct. Janik's words illuminate the ways in which Stewart's act is an old one, that he fulfills a universal human demand. Although there has not been a Jewish king for Jewish fools to serve since the Hasmoneans, Jews have their own tradition of fools and jesters. Entrenched in sacred text, Jewish jesters were a requirement at weddings to entertain the bride and groom. Among Ashkenazi Jews, the *badkhan, badkhn-letz*, or *marshallik*—names for those participating in the institutionalized tradition of

Jewish comedy—traditionally used his platform for teaching in addition to entertaining: "The *badchan-letz* moved between the two realms of Jewish scholar-preacher and festive clown."[35] Stewart moved between these two realms as well. As with the 9/11 monologue, he carefully brought in the "little funny Jew" persona when things became too serious or preachy, and carefully maintained a reverence and seriousness at times when humor was inappropriate.

Stewart falls squarely into Janik's category of "the wise fool." This type is able to perceive and acknowledge his own weaknesses and desires *and* perceive and acknowledge the weaknesses and desires of others. Too much of the latter and he's a "trickster," too much of the former and he's simply a "victim."[36] Because he can see himself critically, he may be trusted to make critical observations about the world around him. Never too smart and serious to be a trickster and never too self-deprecating to be considered a victim, Stewart artfully straddled every pointed insight he had into politics and the media with a joke about his Jewish shortcomings.

Stewart's tactics of playing down privilege as a method of empowerment recall an anecdote recounted by the philosopher Pierre Bourdieu. In 1974, the mayor of a village in the region of Béarn in southwestern France, gave a speech during a ceremony honoring a poet from the region. The mayor addressed his audience in the regional dialect, Béarnais. A reporter for the local newspaper attended the event and described the mayor's choice to speak Béarnais as a "thoughtful gesture." In describing the use of Béarnais as "thoughtful," the mayor, his audience, and the newspaper reporter "must tacitly recognize the unwritten law which prescribes French as the only acceptable language for formal speeches in formal situations."[37] They must also recognize the mayor's command of proper French and acknowledge that had he wanted to, he could have delivered the same speech in French. Here, the mayor conveys his dominance by speaking a "lower" language.

The mayor is employing a "strategy of condescension," lowering himself to demonstrate his power—a strategy unavailable to those outside the dominant class. In speaking Béarnais in a public forum (with French language notably absent), the mayor at first glance appears to be negating the linguistic hierarchy that places French at the top. Instead, however, he is demonstrating the very existence of that hierarchy by confidently standing at the podium and speaking the local dialect. Confidence is a key component to employing strategies of condescension, which are "reserved for those who are sufficiently confident of their position in the objective hierarchies to be able to deny them without appearing to be ignorant or capable of satisfying their demands."[38] Jon Stewart's success, his trustworthiness, is due in part to his successful employment of these strategies. Just as the mayor demonstrates his dominance, his perfect Frenchness, by speaking Béarnais, the Jewish Stewart demonstrates his position at the top of the American cultural hierarchy by strategically calling attention to the fact that he is Jewish.

In regularly "coming out" as Jewish on his show, the master of parody, satire, and irony built trust with his audience by showing them how "real" he is. He also frequently referenced his middle-class origins in New Jersey. When he celebrates his musical idol—the middle-class hero and New Jersey native Bruce Springsteen—and adopts a middle-class New Jersey accent, he ultimately reminds his viewers that he is well educated, wealthy, and articulate. Like the mayor's Béarnais, this play with subdominance—middle-class identity, Jewishness—only works if everyone tacitly accepts Stewart's dominance. Like the mayor's use of the local dialect, Stewart's "Jewish" moments on-screen demonstrate how Jewishness may be used as a currency for cultural capital rather than a burden. It is Stewart's particular approach to Jewishness, the strategies of condescension he employs by coming out as Jewish, that engender trust. Audiences did not place their trust in a Jew, but in Louis C. K.'s "little funny Jew."

If we consider other forums for public trust—politicians and the "legitimate" news media, for example—it comes as no surprise that a satirist would garner the most votes in a poll. As Amber Day explains in her book about satire and parody, twenty-first-century Americans are so accustomed to contrived realities (i.e., "reality" TV, political personae, etc.), that public displays of earnestness become suspect. She explains:

> This pull toward the ironic . . . is directly related to the manufactured quality of contemporary public life . . . public discourse is designed as spectacle, though it rarely acknowledges itself as such. . . . In a highly stage-managed, mediatized discursive landscape, then, earnestness can seem suspect. It is the very quality that politicians and other overproduced public figures bend over backward attempting to convey, while there is something about the unabashedly personal, ironic, tongue-in-cheek perspective that appears refreshingly authentic.[39]

In this way, Jon Stewart's satire feels to audiences more honest than the honest, straightforward political speech of serious newscasters and politicians. Recall, for example, John McCain's campaign bus, the "Straight Talk Express." So much emphasis has been placed on "talking straight" and "telling it like it is" that the public recognizes these shows of sincerity as pure performance. Stewart's carefully selected moments of sincerity, like his 9/11 monologue, are also performance, a fact that gets lost in the assumption that the host is simply being himself, voicing his personal opinions, speaking directly to his viewers. Of his acting, Stewart once told a reporter, "I'm not good at playing earnestness, but I feel that I am an earnest person."[40] The implication here is that on his show, he is not acting; he is being himself, because "irony is becoming a new marker of sincerity."[41] The regular Jewish "confessions" support this impression. The man on the screen is a real person, expressing his genuine views.

It is partly possible for Stewart to be "most trusted" because so many other venues for public trust have been foreclosed. People of color, women, politicians, CEOs, military leaders, journalists, public intellectuals, and other celebrities have broken trust for various reasons or never had the possibility to engender it to begin with. Day explains that "the vast majority of the individual satirists . . . are both white and male. This is certainly not a coincidence . . . to make the materiality of one's particular body seemingly irrelevant has always been the privilege of white male propertied bodies."[42] Stewart's Jewishness allows him to code switch—to be both "normative" and "other" as it suits him, from sexy celebrity to "timorous outsider." Or these are two sides of the same coin. Stewart made himself into the everyman by highlighting his own vulnerability, in this case Jewishness. In fact, if becoming an everyman is dependent on making "one's particular body seemingly irrelevant," Stewart adopted a different tactic, drawing attention to his Jewish body as a maneuver to make himself relatable.

In a 2010 episode, Stewart staged a conversation with a yarmulke-wearing bagel hand puppet he called "Dr. Bagelman." Together, host and puppet watched clips from a Hamas-produced cartoon featuring extreme depictions of Israeli Jews as bloodthirsty child killers. Responding to the cartoons with his mouth (and the puppet's mouth) agape, Stewart put on his best gravelly Brooklyn accent, channeling Jewish comics of the Catskills era. "The last time I saw an antisemitic caricature that bad," said Dr. Bagelman, "it was your high school yearbook photo! Boom! Zing!"[43] Here, Stewart's "little funny Jew" act is held up against (1) the obscene caricatures of Israeli Jews produced by Hamas, and (2) the Borscht Belt bagel stereotype of American Jews. But to draw out the comedy from a decidedly disturbing example of antisemitism, Stewart compares the Hamas cartoon to the innocuous Dr. Bagelman stereotype and ultimately to himself, and his "little funny Jew"-ish looks. The joke works because of the distance between Stewart's (imagined) Jewish looks and the cartoon distortions, a distance expanded by Dr. Bagelman's exaggerated Jewishness. Stewart succeeds here in poking fun at Hamas, Jewish comedians, and himself. The result is a vulnerable charm. He is vulnerable because as a Jew he is victimized by the antisemitism of the cartoons. He is charming because through his act of modest self-mockery (perpetrated by a bagel!), he draws attention to how handsome, sophisticated, and smart he is.

Yes, he sat across the table from presidents and Nobel Prize winners, but when he pointed to his own inadequacies, Stewart made it seem as if any of his viewers could be in his seat. Avoiding being too transgressive, too intellectual, too angry, "figures like Jon Stewart . . . act as if they are responding as anyone would to the crazy situations at hand, speaking out loud what we are all thinking."[44] When Stewart mocked himself for being short and hairy, this was not just a particular physical feature of a particular man, but a feature of a "short, hairy

Jew." Stewart's power lay in being at once a handsome, wealthy, educated white man *and* a "short, hairy, big-nosed, picked-on Jew."[45]

Day categorizes Stewart with figures like the documentary filmmaker Michael Moore, and while she mentions Stewart's Jewishness as "one step removed from the dominant, which allows [him] to play up [his] outsider's eye for absurdity," she leaves the Jewish question there.[46] We might compare Moore with Stewart to see how their individual "one step removed" qualities operate. Now a successful filmmaker, Moore is far removed from his working-class youth in Flint, Michigan. He knows that a "man on the street" cannot simply walk into a CEO's office and question a company's policies as he did in *Roger & Me* and *Fahrenheit 9/11*. He knows that a meeting with a CEO requires being put on a schedule, wearing proper attire, and following certain business conventions.[47] However, in wearing his baseball hat and hoodie, naively attempting to speak with some powerful individual during the workday, and acting surprised when security guards ask for identification or escort him away from the building, Moore gets to maintain his status as one of *Time* magazine's 100 Most Influential People, with an estimated net worth of $50 million dollars, *and* stand in as everyman, a voice for the disenfranchised, disappearing working class.[48] This straddling act—a multimillionaire, influential filmmaker playing the naïve everyman—is the same mechanism at work with Stewart, but in his case, he straddles the wealth and influence with Jewishness.

There is a neatly parallel disparity between Moore's actual wealth and his pretended working-class status, and it is worth exploring why this dissonance works in moving his audiences. That disparity is muddled, however, when contrasting wealth, fame, and influence on the one hand with Jewishness on the other. Not only does Jewishness have uncomfortable ties to wealth and influence in antisemitic rhetoric, but American Jews have succeeded as a "model minority" in obtaining disproportionate access to money, education, and other influential sectors of American society (read: Hollywood). While it is easy to see how the designations of working-class and wealthy exist on a single economic spectrum of power, it is less clear where Jewishness fits in relation to cultural capital. Jewishness can be characterized as dominant (again, as a "model minority") and subdominant (as a historically victimized minority), but Jewishness also fits squarely in the middle. Jews are associated with middlebrow forms of entertainment (the Broadway musical and the sitcom as opposed to opera and art film), functioned as economic middlemen in Europe as moneylenders and tradesmen, and, as historian Yuri Slezkine artfully demonstrated, have been used as a metaphor the world over for the "mercurial" mobile middle classes.[49]

As a "little funny Jew," Stewart embodied a particular type within the cultural marketplace. Like one of his comic heroes, Woody Allen, Stewart made being small, nebbishy, and neurotic part of his shtick to get laughs. Of course, in addition to playing one on TV, Stewart is also a Jew in real life. But what kind of Jew is Stewart? Although I'd attribute less of his success to his actual Jewishness than to his "little funny Jew" persona, Stewart's Jewish childhood in New Jersey cannot be overlooked. Most significantly, the way in which Stewart's childhood is narrated contributes to fashioning his comic persona. Pick up any popular magazine, newspaper, or blog profiling Stewart—and in the months leading up to his retirement, there were dozens—and they're sure to have a sentence starting with, "Born Jonathan Stuart Leibowitz . . ." Or consider this gem from the online Jewish magazine *Tablet*:

> We've covered Jon Stewart quite a lot over the years—mostly because of his run as host of Comedy Central's *The Daily Show*, which comes to a close on Thursday night, while keeping in mind his wonderfully Jewy given name, Jonathan Stuart Leibowitz.[50]

This snarky Jewish blogger offers up Leibowitz as a badge of Jewish kinship and pride. *Moment* magazine, another Jewish publication, featured a story in 2008 with the title, "Meet Jonathan Stuart Leibowitz (aka Jon Stewart)."[51] When Jewish publications "out" Stewart, the tone differs from when publications like *The New Yorker* make the same move.[52] Nevertheless, this phrasing, the big reveal of the performer's given name, almost always operates as a kind of outing. Stewart's apparent authenticity (delivered in a cloak of ironic irreverence) and his seemingly direct relationship to his viewers ("meet me over at camera 3") go a long way to engender public trust. In disclosing that he uses a stage name, publications from *Time* to *Tablet* call into question this trust. What is he hiding? By all accounts, it appears that this quintessential Jewish comic, who regularly references his Jewishness as part of his act, changed his name to mask his Jewishness.

The name change may be part of a long-standing tradition of Jewish performers concealing their origins to avoid discrimination—but that stands in stark contrast to Stewart's systematic pointing out of his Jewishness. When Senator Chuck Schumer came on the show to salute Jon Stewart's "Jewish shtick," Stewart inquired coyly while suppressing a laugh, "How did you know I was Jewish? For years, I have gone out of my way to avoid displaying any of the stereotypical characteristics of our shared heritage." "Then Jon, you have failed spectacularly," Schumer joked. This exchange was followed by a montage of "Jewish" moments on *The Daily Show*, titled "*The Daily Show* remembers Stu Leibowitz, Let My People Laugh."[53] The montage featured fast-paced clips of Jon using Yiddish, announcing "Happy Yom Kippur!" and making other Jewish holiday jokes, and putting on his best Brooklyn Jewish mother voice. In fact, there can be no doubt that Stewart is fully out of the closet about his Jewishness and that since his early stand-up days, being Jewish was a key element to making his comedy work. "Jon Stewart takes over as the host of Comedy Central's *Daily Show* tomorrow night,"

Seth Margolis wrote for the *New York Times*, "but don't expect many changes in the nightly news parody. 'Except I'll be reading the news with a Yiddish accent,' Mr. Stewart warned, and proceeded to ad-lib the day's headlines sounding uncannily like Jackie Mason."[54] As a guest on Craig Kilborn's *The Daily Show*, a few months before he took over as host in January 1998, Stewart even joked that he would make some changes to the set, including replacing a wall-sized grid of television monitors with menorahs, thereby setting up his persona even before he took the host's seat.[55]

Donald Trump, the man Stewart's *Daily Show* loved to hate, took to Twitter in response to some of Stewart's regular mockery. "I promise you that I'm much smarter than Jonathan Leibowitz—I mean Jon Stewart @TheDailyShow. Who, by the way, is totally overrated," he tweeted in April 2013. When *The Daily Show* predictably responded with further mockery, Trump returned to Twitter the following week, ranting, "If Jon Stewart is so above it all & legit, why did he change his name from Jonathan Leibowitz? He should be proud of his heritage!" It is no accident that of all the possible rebuttals Trump could have affected against Stewart, he zeroed in on Jewishness, a source of trust and power. Trump called Stewart out for (1) being (secretly) Jewish, and (2) being a self-hating Jew. As Senator Schumer's appearance attests, there has never been any secrecy to Stewart's Jewishness, and referencing it has been one of the comedian's most reliable gimmicks. Trump, however, was only saying publicly what the magazine profiles allude to obliquely—that his name change implies Stewart has something to hide, that the thing he has to hide is being Jewish, that Jews should not be trusted.

In interviews, Stewart has provided at least three reasons why he changed his name. One recalls his second stand-up appearance at a Manhattan club and hearing the announcer trip over his name. "The host's hesitation to pronounce my name the first night bothered me," Stewart told a reporter. The second reason for the name change has to do with "some leftover resentment at [his] family."[56] Stewart is estranged from his father, who divorced his mother when he was twelve years old. Dropping his father's name may have solidified the distance he felt. Drawing on this line of reasoning, the official *Daily Show* Twitter account responded to Trump's tweets with "Can't an overrated Jew have a complicated relationship with his dad without being accused of hiding his heritage?" The final reason Stewart provides for the name change is a fear of antisemitism—he didn't want a name that was "tauntable." He recalls being mocked in middle school, with bullies calling him "Leibotits" or "Leiboshits." "I didn't grow up in Warsaw," Stewart told Friend of *The New Yorker*, "but it's not like it wasn't duly noted by my peers that that's who I was—there were some minor slurs."

Stewart is careful to insist that his name change had nothing to do with his being Jewish: "People assume I changed it because it was too Jewish, but I've never shrunk away from that. Half my act is devoted to being Jewish."[57] Yet all three of his given reasons for dropping Leibowitz fall under the auspices of Jewishness. His family, the foreign, unpronounceable quality of his surname, and the childhood antisemitic slurs are all related to being Jewish. Drop the name and you drop the foreignness. Stewart can joke all he wants about how Jews "can't dunk," how he's too short and hairy to be sexy—the jokes work because they don't matter. Changing his name was an expression of "a dialectic tension between the specific ('Jewish enough') and the universal (not 'too Jewish')." Dropping Leibowitz was part of what helped the funny little Jew from Jersey become the "little funny Jew" in the host's seat for sixteen years. The sexy, smart, pronounceably named Stewart wins his audience's trust by constantly coming out as Jewish—a move that only draws attention to the ways in which he is *not* stereotypically Jewish. The more he calls it out, the less it matters and the more vacuous it becomes. In other words, Trump was right. Stewart did drop Leibowitz to avoid coming off as too Jewish, even though he regularly performed "too Jewish" to the audience's delight.

Altman writes that "the role of the Jewish Comedian is . . . the only role in which the Jew appears *as* Jew in the popular culture, pinning on himself a label of identity, tacitly claiming a valid relevance of that identity to the comic point of view."[58] This claim feels like an overstatement in 2015, but it is worth considering the differences between the Jewish comic's confession of Jewishness and the way other public Jewish figures treat their Jewishness. And while we have explored how non-Jewish performers like Michael Moore play up vulnerabilities to engender trust, how will this work for Trevor Noah, the new host of *The Daily Show*? How has Noah constructed his comic persona? "So, Jon is a white, fifty-two-year-old Jewish guy who grew up in New Jersey," Noah said at a press event. "I am a thirty-one-year-old, half-black, half-white South African who's lived in America for a few years on and off. So the way we'd look at the same story will be completely different. . . . We have different access to certain jokes, to certain sides of a story."[59] Has Noah's blackness become a tool to generate trust the way Stewart's Jewishness has been?

Already in his stand-up act, Noah refers to being "born a crime" in apartheid-era South Africa to a white father and black mother. When he confesses, "I wanted to be black . . . that's all I ever wanted," he creates a distance between himself and (American) ideas of blackness. He talks about coming to America in order to be black, becoming "fluent in black American" only to be mistaken for Mexican.[60] By confessing that he "wanted to be black," Noah gets to disavow his own blackness. He gets to be both black and not-black, a strategy used by half-black, half-white comedians Key and Peele, not to mention President Obama. In this way, Noah may have inherited Stewart's capacity for code switching, for expressing both the particularities that produce vulnerability and the universal qualities of everyman. Or, as I have argued of Stewart's Jewishness, he may perform those particular vulnerabilities as a means to come across as a relatable everyman. Noah's ascension to the host's seat came just a year before Donald Trump's ascension to the White House as the roles of "truth," "trust," and "fake news" in public discourse have shifted in remarkable ways. It remains to be seen whether Noah will come to earn the kind of public trust Stewart had.

If it's not clear from the tone of this essay, I'm a fan of Stewart's comedy, *The Daily Show with Jon Stewart*, and its many offshoots. His Jewish jokes could be characterized as manipulative, his serious turns in the wake of national tragedies as inauthentic performance. But the reason Stewart's work is worth investigating is because he thrived on the dialectic tension his own persona generated. On the program, he embraced the balancing act between being "too Jewish" and "Jewish enough." He allowed that tension, like the political tensions his show lambasted, to produce something cathartic: laughter.

Notes

1. *Daily Show with Jon Stewart*, "Louis C.K.," aired August 5, 2015, on Comedy Central.
2. "Now That Walter Cronkite Has Passed On, Who Is America's Most Trusted Newscaster?" *Time*, 2009, http://www.timepolls.com/hppolls/archive/poll_results_417.html. See also Jason Likins, "Online Poll: Jon Stewart Is America's Most Trusted Newsman," *Huffington Post*, September 22, 2009, http://www.huffingtonpost.com/2009/07/22/time-magazine-poll-jon-st_n_242933.html.
3. Amarnath Amarasingam, ed., *The Stewart/Colbert Effect: Essays on the Real Impacts of Fake News* (Jefferson, NC: McFarland, 2011). See also S. Robert Lichter, Jody Baumartner, and Jonathan S. Morris, eds., *Politics is a Joke!: How TV Comedians Are Remaking Political Life* (Boulder: Westview Press, 2015).
4. Bill Carter and Brian Stelter, "In 'Daily Show' Role on 9/11 Bill, Echoes of Murrow," *New York Times*, December 26, 2010, http://www.nytimes.com/2010/12/27/business/media/27stewart.html?_r=0; Ed Mazza, "Jon Stewart's 'Daily Show' Segment Leads to Huge Change for Veterans," *Huffington Post*, March 25, 2015, http://www.huffingtonpost.com/2015/03/25/jon-stewart-veterans_n_6937380.html.
5. Amanda Terkel, "Ashcroft Compares Waterboarding to Being 'Interviewed by Jon Stewart,'" *ThinkProgress*, April 22, 2008, http://thinkprogress.org/politics/2008/04/22/22074/ashcroft-torture-stewart/.
6. *Daily Show with Jon Stewart*, "Barack Obama," aired October 18, 2012, on Comedy Central.
7. "The show in general we feel like is a privilege, even the idea that we can sit in the back of the country and make wisecracks. Which is really what we do, we sit in the back and throw spitballs." *Daily Show with Jon Stewart*, "Monologue: September 11, 2001," aired September 20, 2001, on Comedy Central.
8. Sig Altman, *The Comic Image of the Jew: Explorations of a Pop Culture Phenomenon* (Plainsboro, NJ: Associated University Presses, 1971), 165–67.

9. Altman, *Comic Image of the Jew*, 165.
10. *Daily Show with Jon Stewart*, "Charles Barkley," aired January 3, 2012, on Comedy Central.
11. Altman, *Comic Image of the Jew*, 165.
12. Altman, *Comic Image of the Jew*, 167.
13. Altman, *Comic Image of the Jew*, 167.
14. Altman, *Comic Image of the Jew*, 173.
15. Altman, *Comic Image of the Jew*, xvii.
16. Amber Day, *Satire and Dissent: Interventions into Contemporary Political Debate* (Bloomington: Indiana University Press, 2011), 73.
17. Linda Hutcheon, *A Theory of Parody: The Teachings of Twentieth-Century Art Forms* (New York: Methuen, 1985), 15; cf. Day, *Satire and Dissent*, 73.
18. Bob Garfield, interview with Ben Zimmer, *On the Media*, NPR, July 31, 2009, http://www.onthemedia.org/story/132451-too-good-to-check/transcript/; Jack Shafer, "Why I Didn't Trust Walter Cronkite," *Slate*, July 21, 2009, http://www.slate.com/articles/news_and_politics/press_box/2009/07/why_i_didnt_trust_walter_cronkite.single.html.
19. Michiko Kakutani, "Is Jon Stewart the Most Trusted Man in America?" *New York Times*, August 15, 2008, http://www.nytimes.com/2008/08/17/arts/television/17kaku.html.
20. Likins, "Online Poll."
21. Warren St. John, "The Week That Wasn't," *New York Times*, October 3, 2004, http://www.nytimes.com/2004/10/03/fashion/the-week-that-wasnt.html.
22. *Crossfire*, CNN, October 15, 2004.
23. Michael D. Shear, "Jon Stewart Met Privately with Obama at White House," *New York Times*, July 28, 2015, http://www.nytimes.com/2015/07/29/us/politics/jon-stewart-secretly-met-with-obama-at-white-house.html.
24. Bill Moyers, interview with Jon Stewart, *NOW with Bill Moyers*, PBS, July 11, 2003, http://www.pbs.org/now/transcript/transcript_stewart.html.
25. Douglas Martin, "Walter Cronkite, 92, Dies; Trusted Voice of TV News," *New York Times*, July 17, 2009, www.nytimes.com/2009/07/18/us/18cronkite.html.
26. Joseph Campbell, *Getting It Wrong: Ten of the Greatest Misreported Stories in American Journalism* (Berkeley: University of California Press, 2010), 2. The transcript of Cronkite's speech was rebroadcast after his death by Guy Raz's program, *All Things Considered*, "Final Words: Cronkite's Vietnam Commentary," NPR, July 18, 2009, http://www.npr.org/templates/story/story.php?storyId=106775685.
27. *Daily Show with Jon Stewart*, "Monologue: September 11, 2001."
28. *Daily Show with Jon Stewart*, "Monologue: September 11, 2001."
29. Jeremy Gillick, "Meet Jonathan Stuart Leibowitz (aka Jon Stewart): The Wildly Zeitgeisty *Daily Show* Host," *Moment*, November–December 2008, http://www.momentmag.com/meet-jonathan-stuart-leibowitz-aka-jon-stewart/.
30. Caryn Midler, "Sexy Geeks!" *People*, November 3, 2005, http://www.people.com/people/gallery/0,,1113899_1113955_950086,00.html; "Sexy at Every Age," *People*, November 29, 2010, http://www.people.com/people/archive/article/0,,20443728,00.html; Kiran Hefa, "The United States of Sexy," *People*, December 1, 2014, http://www.people.com/people/package/gallery/0,,20315920_20635373_21207512,00.html.
31. Tad Friend, "Is It Funny Yet? Jon Stewart and the Comedy of Crisis," *The New Yorker*, February 11, 2002, http://www.newyorker.com/magazine/2002/02/11/is-it-funny-yet.

32. Friend, 2002.

33. Jason Zinoman, "A Late-Night Host Seamlessly Mixing Analysis, Politics and Humor," *New York Times*, February 10, 2015, http://www.nytimes.com/2015/02/11/arts/television/jon-stewart-seamlessly-mixing-analysis-politics-and-humor.html.

34. Vicki Janik, introduction to *Fools and Jesters in Literature, Art, and History: A Bio-Bibliographical Sourcebook*, Vicki Janik, ed. (Westport, CT: Greenwood, 1998), xiv.

35. Ariela Krasney, "*Badchan* (Jester)," *Encyclopedia of Jewish Folklore and Traditions*, Raphael Patai, ed. (New York: Routledge, 2015), 61.

36. Janik, introduction, 3.

37. Pierre Bourdieu, *Language and Symbolic Power*, trans. Gino Raymond and Matthew Adamson, ed. John Thompson (Cambridge: Blackwell Publishers, 1992), 68.

38. Altman, *Comic Image of the Jew*, 165.

39. Day, *Satire and Dissent*, 3.

40. Friend, "Is It Funny Yet?"

41. Day, *Satire and Dissent*, 43.

42. Day, *Satire and Dissent*, 8–9.

43. *Daily Show with Jon Stewart*, "The Story Hole: Children's Cartoons from Hamas," aired February 2, 2010, on Comedy Central.

44. Day, *Satire and Dissent*, 10.

45. Friend, "Is It Funny Yet?"

46. Day, *Satire and Dissent*, 9.

47. See Day, *Satire and Dissent*, 118–20.

48. Sean Penn, "The 2005 Time 100: Michael Moore," *Time*, April 18, 2005, http://content.time.com/time/specials/packages/article/0,28804,1972656_1972696_1973072,00.html. On his net worth, see, Gavin Polone, "Hollywood Producer Slams Michael Moore for Goldman Sachs Hypocrisy," *The Hollywood Reporter*, November 11, 2011, http://www.hollywoodreporter.com/news/michael-moore-occupy-wall-street-goldman-sachs-257186.

49. Yuri Slezkine, *The Jewish Century* (Princeton: Princeton University Press, 2004), 4–39.

50. Jonathan Zalman, "Shalom, Jon Stewart: The Liberal Lion Steps Down as Host of *The Daily Show* after 16 Years," *Tablet*, August 6, 2015, http://www.tabletmag.com/scroll/192710/shalom-jon-stewart.

51. Gillick, "Meet Jonathan."

52. See Friend, "Is It Funny Yet?"

53. *The Daily Show with Jon Stewart*, "Let His People Laugh," aired July 23, 2015, on Comedy Central.

54. Seth Margolis, "SIGNOFF; Enough News to Keep 'Em Rolling," New York Times, January 10, 1999, http://www.nytimes.com/1999/01/10/tv/signoff-enough-news-to-keep-em-rolling.html.

55. Andy Greene, "Flashback: Jon Stewart Guests on Craig Kilborn's 'Daily Show,'" *Rolling Stone*, April 2, 2015, http://www.rollingstone.com/tv/videos/flashback-jon-stewart-guests-on-craig-kilborns-daily-show-20150402.

56. Friend, "Is It Funny Yet?"

57. Lisa Rogak, *Angry Optimist: The Life and Times of Jon Stewart* (New York: Macmillan, 2014), 42.

58. Altman, *Comic Image of the Jew*, 166.

59. Yvonne Villarreal, "Trevor Noah: Jon Stewart's a White 'Jewish Guy' from New Jersey; 'I'm Not,'" *LA Times*, July 29, 2015, http://www.latimes.com/entertainment/tv/showtracker/la-et-st-trevor-noah-addresses-daily-show-jon-stewart-legacy20150729-story.html.

60. Trevor Noah, *Live at the Apollo*, series 9, episode 1, aired November 22, 2013, on BBC.

Bibliography

Broadcast Media

All Things Considered. "Final Words: Cronkite's Vietnam Commentary." NPR, July 18, 2009. http://www.npr.org/templates/story/story.php?storyId=106775685.

Crossfire. Aired on October 15, 2004. CNN.

Daily Show with Jon Stewart. "Monologue: September 11, 2001." Aired September 20, 2001, on Comedy Central.

Daily Show with Jon Stewart. "The Story Hole: Children's Cartoons from Hamas." Aired February 2, 2010, on Comedy Central.

Daily Show with Jon Stewart. "Charles Barkley." Aired January 3, 2012, on Comedy Central.

Daily Show with Jon Stewart. "Barack Obama." Aired October 18, 2012, on Comedy Central.

Daily Show with Jon Stewart. "Let His People Laugh." Aired July 23, 2015, on Comedy Central.

Daily Show with Jon Stewart. "Louis C.K." Aired August 5, 2015, on Comedy Central.

Garfield, Bob. *On the Media*. Interview with Ben Zimmer. NPR, July 31, 2009. http://www.onthemedia.org/story/132451-too-good-to-check/transcript/.

Moyers, Bill. *NOW with Bill Moyers*. Interview with Jon Stewart. PBS, July 11, 2003. http://www.pbs.org/now/transcript/transcript_stewart.html.

Noah, Trevor. *Live at the Apollo*. Series 9, episode 1. BBC, November 22, 2013.

Published Sources

Altman, Sig. *The Comic Image of the Jew: Explorations of a Pop Culture Phenomenon*. Plainsboro, NJ: Associated University Presses, 1971.

Amarasingam, Amarnath, ed. *The Stewart/Colbert Effect: Essays on the Real Impacts of Fake News*. Jefferson, NC: McFarland, 2011.

Bourdieu, Pierre. *Language and Symbolic Power*. Translated by Gino Raymond and Matthew Adamson. Edited by John Thompson. Cambridge: Blackwell, 1992.

Campbell, Joseph. *Getting It Wrong: Ten of the Greatest Misreported Stories in American Journalism*. Berkeley: University of California Press, 2010.

Carter, Bill, and Brian Stelter. "In 'Daily Show' Role on 9/11 Bill, Echoes of Murrow." *New York Times*, December 26, 2010. http://www.nytimes.com/2010/12/27/business/media/27stewart.html?_r=0.

Day, Amber. *Satire and Dissent: Interventions into Contemporary Political Debate*. Bloomington: Indiana University Press, 2011.

Friend, Tad. "Is It Funny Yet? Jon Stewart and the Comedy of Crisis." *The New Yorker*, February 11, 2002. http://www.newyorker.com/magazine/2002/02/11/is-it-funny-yet.

Gillick, Jeremy. "Meet Jonathan Stuart Leibowitz (aka Jon Stewart): The Wildly Zeitgeisty *Daily Show* Host." *Moment*, November–December 2008. http://www.momentmag.com/meet-jonathan-stuart-leibowitz-aka-jon-stewart/.

Greene, Andy. "Flashback: Jon Stewart Guests on Craig Kilborn's 'Daily Show.'" *Rolling Stone*, April 2, 2015. http://www.rollingstone.com/tv/videos/flashback-jon-stewart-guests-on-craig-kilborns-daily-show-20150402.
Hefa, Kiran. "The United States of Sexy." *People*, December 1, 2014. http://www.people.com/people/package/gallery/0,,20315920_20635373_21207512,00.html.
Hutcheon, Linda. *A Theory of Parody: The Teachings of Twentieth-Century Art Forms*. New York: Methuen, 1985.
Janik, Vicki. Introduction to *Fools and Jesters in Literature, Art, and History: A Bio-Bibliographical Sourcebook*, edited by Vicki Janik, 1–25. Westport, CT: Greenwood, 1998.
Kakutani, Michiko. "Is Jon Stewart the Most Trusted Man in America?" *New York Times*, August 15, 2008. http://www.nytimes.com/2008/08/17/arts/television/17kaku.html.
Krasney, Ariela. "*Badchan* (Jester)." In *Encyclopedia of Jewish Folklore and Traditions*, edited by Raphael Patai, 60–62. New York: Routledge, 2015.
Lichter, S. Robert, Jody Baumartner, and Jonathan S. Morris, eds. *Politics is a Joke!: How TV Comedians Are Remaking Political Life*. Boulder: Westview, 2015.
Likins, Jason. "Online Poll: Jon Stewart Is America's Most Trusted Newsman." *The Huffington Post*, September 22, 2009. http://www.huffingtonpost.com/2009/07/22/time-magazine-poll-jon-st_n_242933.html.
Midler, Caryn. "Sexy Geeks!" *People*, November 3, 2005. http://www.people.com/people/gallery/0,,1113899_1113955_950086,00.html.
Margolis, Seth. "SIGNOFF; Enough News to Keep 'Em Rolling," *New York Times*, January 10, 1999. http://www.nytimes.com/1999/01/10/tv/signoff-enough-news-to-keep-em-rolling.html.
Martin, Douglas. "Walter Cronkite, 92, Dies; Trusted Voice of TV News." *New York Times*, July 17, 2009. www.nytimes.com/2009/07/18/us/18cronkite.html.
Mazza, Ed. "Jon Stewart's 'Daily Show' Segment Leads to Huge Change for Veterans." *Huffington Post*, March 25, 2015. http://www.huffingtonpost.com/2015/03/25/jon-stewart-veterans_n_6937380.html.
"Now That Walter Cronkite Has Passed On, Who Is America's Most Trusted Newscaster?" *Time*, 2009. http://www.timepolls.com/hppolls/archive/poll_results_417.html.
Penn, Sean. "The 2005 TIME 100: Michael Moore." *Time*, April 18, 2005. http://content.time.com/time/specials/packages/article/0,28804,1972656_1972696_1973072,00.html.
Polone, Gavin. "Hollywood Producer Slams Michael Moore for Goldman Sachs Hypocrisy." *Hollywood Reporter*, November 11, 2011. http://www.hollywoodreporter.com/news/michael-moore-occupy-wall-street-goldman-sachs-257186.
Rogak, Lisa. *Angry Optimist: The Life and Times of Jon Stewart*. New York: Macmillan, 2014.
"Sexy at Every Age." *People*, November 29, 2010. http://www.people.com/people/archive/article/0,,20443728,00.html.
Shafer, Jack. "Why I Didn't Trust Walter Cronkite." *Slate*, July 21, 2009. http://www.slate.com/articles/news_and_politics/press_box/2009/07/why_i_didnt_trust_walter_cronkite.single.html.
Shear, Michael D. "Jon Stewart Met Privately with Obama at White House." *New York Times*, July 28, 2015. http://www.nytimes.com/2015/07/29/us/politics/jon-stewart-secretly-met-with-obama-at-white-house.html.
Slezkine, Yuri. *The Jewish Century*. Princeton: Princeton University Press, 2004.

St. John, Warren. "The Week That Wasn't." *New York Times*, October 3, 2004. http://www
.nytimes.com/2004/10/03/fashion/the-week-that-wasnt.html.
Terkel, Amanda. "Ashcroft Compares Waterboarding to Being 'Interviewed by Jon Stewart.'"
ThinkProgress, April 22, 2008. http://thinkprogress.org/politics/2008/04/22/22074
/ashcroft-torture-stewart/.
Villarreal, Yvonne. "Trevor Noah: Jon Stewart's a White 'Jewish Guy' from New Jersey; 'I'm
Not.'" *LA Times*, July 29, 2015. http://www.latimes.com/entertainment/tv/showtracker
/la-et-st-trevor-noah-addresses-daily-show-jon-stewart-legacy20150729-story.html.
Zalman, Jonathan. "Shalom, Jon Stewart: The Liberal Lion Steps Down as Host of *The Daily
Show* after 16 Years." *Tablet,* August 6, 2015. http://www.tabletmag.com/scroll/192710
/shalom-jon-stewart.
Zinoman, Jason. "A Late-Night Host Seamlessly Mixing Analysis, Politics and Humor." *New
York Times*, February 10, 2015. http://www.nytimes.com/2015/02/11/arts/television/jon
-stewart-seamlessly-mixing-analysis-politics-and-humor.html.

SHAINA HAMMERMAN is author of *Silver Screen, Hasidic Jews: The Story of an Image*. She teaches Jewish studies, cultural history, and literature at the University of San Francisco and San Quentin State Prison.

Index

Abelard, Peter, 189, 197n22
Abraham (biblical), 21, 24, 26–31, 33n26
agunot ("chained women"), 206, 207, 217nn30–32, 219n53
Alfonsi, Petrus: biography, 181–82, 183, 191, 193; *Dialogi contra Iudaeos*, 181–83, 186–93; literary alter egos (Moses and Petrus), 183, 186–87, 188–93
Alfonso I of Aragon, 181
Alsatian Jews, 104–7, 125–26
American Jews, 300, 307–8; Jewish peddlers in North America, 139–40, 143–44, 146–48, 149, 150
Amnon of Mainz, 49n11
Amos, book of, 41–42, 51n19, 53n37
Anglo-Jewry. *See* British Jews
anti-Judaism, 2, 67, 75n41, 227, 235–36. *See also* antisemitism
antisemitism, 2, 6, 10n6, 160, 165–70, 279, 281, 307–8, 310–11. *See also* anti-Judaism
Arendt, Hannah, 120, 122, 130, 241n75, 281
Ashcroft, John, 298, 300
Asher ben Yehiel (Rosh), 39–41, 47, 50n18, 52n31, 53n37, 202, 210–13, 218n43, 219n51, 219n53
Ashkenazi Jews, 7, 41, 194n2, 202–4, 212, 215n11, 218n46, 219n51, 219n58, 258, 265, 304. *See also* Central European Jews
atheism, 86, 92, 107
Atkyns, John Tracy, 81, 82, 84–86, 97n12
Attinger, Johann, 163, 166
Auernheimer, Raoul, 277
Avodah Zarah, 39, 44, 50n15, 51n25

Banians, 263, 264, 266
Bargawker, Jacob David, 262
Barker, 81–82, 84, 91, 255
Barkley, Charles, 299, 300, 302, 303
Barrot, Odilon, 107, 112, 115n32
Bauer, Oswald, 168, 175n61

Bavaria, 158–64, 166–67, 173n37
Becher, Johann Joachim, 132n17
Behrens, Leffman, 121, 129, 133n35
Bene Israel Jews, 7, 247–66
Benjamin, Moses, 254, 262
Bermann & Oppenheimer, 164, 170
Bloch, Simon, 112
Bohras, 263, 264–65, 266
Bourdieu, Pierre, 305
Bracton, Henry de, 68, 84, 92
British Jews, 7, 64–67, 71, 82–84, 89–90, 94–96, 247–50, 254–62, 264–66
Burke, Edmund, 264
Bush, George W., 298, 300

C. K., Louis, 297, 306
cattle trade, 6, 158–70, 172n16, 172n18, 172n24, 173n35, 173n37, 174n49, 174n53
Central European Jews, 5–6, 119–30, 158–71. *See also* Ashkenazi Jews
Chamberlain, Houston Stewart, 167–68, 175n59
Chapman, E. F., 263
Charter of 1814, 102, 105
chirographs/chirographers, 68, 69, 72, 76n54
Christianity: Christian-Jewish relations, 3, 7, 150, 263; and Jewish conversion, 181–93, 194n2, 196n15, 197n22, 198n31, 204–7, 213, 219n57, 250–1, 254, 281, 283; and secularism, 112; superiority to other religions, 91, 96, 98n29, 256; and trustworthiness, 82–84, 86
Churchill, Winston, 280
Chute (advocate), 91
Cobbett, William, 256
commerce, Jewish, 5–6, 141, 169, 224, 237n8, 256, 258, 266; and Court Jews, 119–30; and oaths, 36–47, 83, 89. *See also* cattle trade; peddlers, Jewish; schmoozers/schmoozing

319

conversion, Jewish, 6–7, 150, 187–88, 194n2, 250, 254, 281, 283; accounts of, 196n13, 196n15, 197n22; and anxiety over interacting with Christians, 36, 38; anticipated by Christians, 91, 182, 188; and apostates or lapsed, 203–5, 207, 212–13, 218n44; forced, 48, 203, 213; of Herman the Jew, 38, 186, 196n15, 198n31; of Petrus Alfonsi, 181–93, 193n1; and ulterior motives, 196nn11–12, 183, 213, 219n57
Costa, Lionel Gomez da, 261
Count Herberstein, 128
Count Kinsky, 127
Count Lamberg, 125, 128
Count Trautmannsdorf, 125
Court Jews, 5–6, 119–24, 126, 128–30, 130n2, 132n15, 134n42
Crémieux, Adolphe, 102-113
Crispin, Gilbert, 189, 197n22
Cronkite, Walter, 300–302

Daily Show, The, 297–301, 309–12
Damascus Affair, 109, 111–12
Daniel, Hermann, 162
David (moneylender), 68–69
Derrida, Jacques, 228
Divekar, Samaji Hassaji, 254
Dreyfus Affair, 281–82, 285
Dupin, André, 107

East India Company, 7, 81, 247–52, 254–55, 259–62, 264
Eder, Heinrich, 170
Edward I, king, 77nn69–71
Egbert of Münster, 38, 49n12
1833 Charter Act, 260–61
Eleazar ben Judah, 41–42, 53n37
Elias, son of Abraham, 72
Elias, son of Benedict, 69–70
Eliezer of Verona, 219n53
Ellis, Barrow Herbert, 261
Ellis, Edmund Helbert, 261
Emperor Leopold I, 120, 121, 124, 125
Ephraim ben Jacob, 37–38, 48n6, 49n11, 66
Epstein, Avraham (Schmaiah), 54n45
Esau (biblical), 28, 30

Esther (megillah), 127–28
Euchel, Isaac Abraham, 224, 234, 237n9
Exchequer of the Jews, 62, 63, 65, 68, 73n1, 88

FitzHenry, Robert, 68
Forbes, James, 264
Fould, Benoit, 109, 111
Freising, Karl, 164
French Jews, 37–38, 43, 101–4, 106, 108, 109, 112, 203
French Revolution, 101–7, 109, 111–12
Frere, Herbert Bartle, 250
Friedlander, David, 169
Friend, Tad, 303–4, 310
friendship (theory of), 6–7, 20, 222–23, 227, 229–32, 237n2

Gabbay, Abraham, 62–63
gage, 62, 66, 68, 72, 73n8
Galsukar, Abraham Isaac, 266
Gambetta, Léon, 113
Gilbert of Benniworth, 69–70
Glikl of Hameln, 121, 130
Goldsmid, Francis Henry, 249–50, 255, 257, 261
Goldsmid, Isaac Lyon, 249
Gospels (Evangelists), 17, 71–72, 81–82, 84–86, 92–93, 55n50, 102
Gramminger, M., 163
Grunwald, Max, 168, 175n59
Guibert of Nogent, 184, 186, 196n11

Habermas, Jürgen, 236, 241n73, 241n75
Hale, Matthew, 81–82, 85, 87, 92
Hamor, 29–30
Haskalah, 234, 236, 237n9, 241n65
Hawkins, William, 87, 92–93
Hayim ben Isaac (Or Zaruah), 202, 210–211, 213, 217n34
Heber, Reginald, 250, 251, 264
Henry I, king, 87, 97n20
Henry II, king, 66, 74n34, 87, 88
Henry III, king, 71, 77nn70–72
Herman the Jew (Hermannus quondam Judaeus), 38, 186, 196n15, 198n31

Herz, Henriette, 224
Herz, Madeleine, 285, 286
Herz, Marcus: career, 223–26, 233–34; friendship with Kant, 7, 222–29, 232–36; and Habermas, 236, 241n73; *Observations on Speculative Philosophy*, 228, 234; philosophy, 223, 224, 226, 233–34, 241n65; respondent to Kant's dissertation, 224–25, 228
Herzl, Theodor: Dreyfus Affair, 281–82, 285; mental health, 278–80, 285, 286, 288, 290, 294n32; and *Neue Freie Presse*, 281, 289–91; Hans (son), 281, 288; Julie Naschauer (wife), 280, 281, 285, 286, 287, 295n13; Pauline (daughter), 280, 293n13; Pauline (sister), 285; Trude (daughter), 287; Zionism, 8, 276–79, 281–84, 287–92, 294n38
Herzl, Theodor, works of: *The Book of Folly*, 285; "Epaphroditus," 286; *The Glossary*, 284; "A Good Deed," 285; *The Jewish State (Der Judenstaat)*, 278, 284, 292; "Mauschel," 282; "The Mind Reader," 285; *The New Ghetto (Das Neue Ghetto)*, 281, 287; *Old New Land (Altneuland)*, 277, 280–81, 283–84, 285, 286, 290–91; "The Reading Glasses," 286; "Zionist diaries," 277–78
Hesiod, 19
Hindu oath, 83–85, 90, 91, 93
Hirsch, Jacob, 224
Hirsch, Maurice de, 289
Homer, 20

Indian Jews, 249, 252–53, 258, 259, 263, 266. See also Bene Israel Jews
Indian Rebellion of 1857, 254, 258, 261–63
Isaac ben Moses (Or Zaruah), 49n11
Isaac ben Samuel (Ri "the Elder"), 44, 55n50
Isaac of Southwark, 70
Isaac (biblical), 21, 26, 27–31
Isaac, son of Josce, 66
Isambert, François-André, 109
Islam, 182, 185, 191–93, 194n2
Israel (biblical), 21, 25–26, 28–29, 31, 41–42, 53n37
Israel, Moosaji (Moosaji Koletkar), 254, 261–62

Jacob ben Judah, 56n54
Jacob ben Meir (Rabbenu Tam), 40, 42–45, 47, 51nn23–24, 52nn27–29, 55–56n50, 216n18, 217n38
Jacob (biblical), 26, 28–30
Jacobs, Joseph, 253
Jacques, Amédée, 112, 113
Jephthah (biblical), 22, 24
Jerusalem, 31, 37, 292
Jervis, Thomas Best, 250
Jesus of Nazareth, 17
Jews. *See individual geographic designations*
Jewish Chronicle, 256, 258, 259, 262
Jewish emancipation, 2,144, 236, 283, 292; in Britain, 7, 94–96, 248–50, 253, 255–57, 260; in France, 103–4, 106; in Germany, 158, 161, 169
Jewish oath (*more judaico*), 4, 9, 87, 97nn17–18, 102; in England, 63–73, 73n17, 86–89, 95–97; in France, 102–8, 110–12, 114n12, 114n15; oaths on Christian saints, 37, 39–47, 51n19, 51n21, 53n37, 55n50; in *Omychund v. Barker*, 81–82, 86–89, 92–93, 255
Joel, Aaron Isaac, 224, 233
Jonathan (Würzburg witness), 208, 209, 218n43
Jornin, son of Abraham, 70, 71, 76n63
Judah ben Asher, 202

Kalonymos, Rabbi, 219n53
Kana, Heinrich, 280–81, 284, 286
Kant, Immanuel: anti-Judaism, 227, 235–36; development of thought, 228–29; friendship with Marcus Herz, 7, 222–29, 232–36; health, 232–33; theory of moral friendship, 222, 229–32
Kant, Immanuel, works of: *Anthropology*, 235; *Critique of Pure Reason*, 226, 228–29, 233, 234; *On the Form and the Principles of the Sensible and Intelligible World* (inaugural dissertation), 224, 225, 228, 234; *Metaphysics of Morals*, 223, 227, 230; *Religion within the Limits of Reason Alone*, 235
King Charles X, 106
King John, 67, 68, 88, 97n20
King Richard I, 87
Knox, Robert, 256

Lambert, Johann Heinrich, 228, 229
Landau, Ezekiel, 106
Landenberger (attorney), 169–70
Levi, Solomon ben Naftali Herz, 124
Liebeck, Aron, 168
Liebmann, Jost (Judah Berlin), 129
Locke, John, 86
Lord Chief Baron, 92, 94
Lord Chief Justice Willes, 92–93, 96
Lord Coke, 85, 88–89, 92–94
Lord, J. Henry, 257–58
Lot (biblical), 27–28
Luther, Martin, 4

Madox, Thomas, 90, 92
Maimon, Solomon, 236, 241n75
Malcolm, John, 249, 250
Manser of Huntingdon, 69
Martin de Pateshull, 75n40, 76n52
McCain, John, 306
meat market, 158–60, 162–63, 165–167, 173n35
Meir ben Baruch, 39–42, 44–47, 50n18, 51nn20–22, 52n31, 53n33, 53n37, 55n49, 206
Meir ben Yekutiel, 128
Mendelssohn, Moses, 224, 226, 228, 229, 234
Meyrot (serjeant), 71
migration, 6, 138–39, 141, 148, 283
Mishnah, 56n54, 206, 207, 217n31, 219n52
Mohammed Ali of Egypt, 109, 111
Montefiore, Sir Moses, 109
Moor, Edward, 265
Moore, Michael, 308, 311
Murray, William (Lord Mansfield), 83, 89–91, 94–95
Mutun, Bonevie, 67, 75n51, 76n52

Napoleonic Code, 103–5
Naschauer, Julie (Julie Herzl), 280, 281, 285, 286, 287, 295n13
Neue Freie Presse, 281, 289
Nietzsche, Friedrich, 277
9/11, 298, 302, 305, 306, 308
Noah, Trevor, 311–12
Nuremberg laws, 170

oaths (theory of). See under trust (theory of)
Obama, Barack, 298, 301, 311
Omychund v. Barker (Ramkissenseat v. Barker, et al.), 81–83; significance, 93–95, 255; Hinduism in, 90–93; medieval Jewish oath as precedent in, 85–86, 87, 88–90, 91, 92–93, 96
Oppenheim, David, 123, 128
Oppenheimer, Jud Suess, 129
Oppenheimer, Samuel, 120–21, 123, 129, 130, 134n48
Orta, Garcia da, 263

Palestine, 279, 289, 290, 294n38
Parsis, 263–64, 265, 266
Paul of Tarsus, 26
peddlers, Jewish, 6, 138–51, 152n4, 152n7, 161–62, 169, 256–57, 265
Peretz ben Elijah, 51n25, 52n28, 55n49
Peytevin of Bedford, 69
Pinsker, Leon, 283

R. G. Dun, 146–147, 152n6
Rabbenu Tam. See Jacob Ben Meir
Rabbi Baruch, 52n31
Ramkissenseat (witness), 81–82
Rashbam. See Samuel ben Meir
Rashi. See Solomon ben Isaac
religious freedom, 83–84, 103, 105–107, 114n12. See also secularism; tolerance
Rider, Dudley, 85–86
Ries, Aaron, 123–124, 125, 126
Rindfleisch Massacres, 201, 206, 210, 212, 214n5
Rivett-Carnac, James, 249–250, 255
Rose, Hugh, 250, 262
Rosh. See Asher ben Yehiel
Roth, Cecil, 261
Rothschild, Lionel de, 259
Rousseau, Jean-Jacques, 278

Samuel, Marcus, 224
Samuel ben Meir (Rashbam), 40, 43–44, 47, 52nn28–29, 55n47
Saul (biblical), 21–22
schmoozers/schmoozing, 161–62, 167–68, 172n24

Schnitzler, Arthur, 287
Schulhoff, Esther, 124, 129
Schumer, Chuck, 309, 310
Second Crusade, 37–38, 48n6
secularism, 101–2, 108, 110, 112–13. *See also* religious freedom; toleration
Selden, John, 89
Seligman (Würzburg witness), 208, 209, 218n43
Sephardic Jews, 11n8, 130–1n2, 131n12, 132n17, 181, 265
Shlomo bar Shimon, 52n32
Simeon ben Jacob, 201–3, 205–13, 217n39, 218n45, 219nn51–52
Simon, Jules, 112, 113
Sinclair, W. F., 263
Sinzheim, David, 106
Sizeranne, Henri Monier de la, 111
Solomon ben Isaac (Rashi), 42–43, 45, 47, 54nn44–45, 55n47, 203–205, 210, 215n15, 218n44
Solomon ibn Adret, 202, 215n10, 218n42
Sombart, Werner, 167–68
Sotah Ritual, 23, 30–31
Springsteen, Bruce, 303, 306
Stewart, Jon, 8; and Barack Obama, 298, 301, 311; as everyman, 303–5, 306; Jewishness and trust, 297–312; "most trusted" epithet, 301–3, 307; name change, 309–11
Sulzer, Johann Georg, 229
Sykes, W. H., 253

Talmud, by tractate: *Avodah Zarah* 39–40, 51n54; *Baba Metziah*, 51n21; *Bekhorot* 42–44; *Sanhedrin*, 44–46, 50n15, 207; *Shabbat* 56n54; *Shevuot*, 133n33; *Sota* 51n22; *Yevamot* 217nn31–32; 219n52; as source of authority and knowledge, 50n15, 192, 203–4, 206–7, 218n46
Taussig, Barukh, 124
Taussig, Samuel, 122–23, 124–26, 127, 128, 130
Tavernier, Jean-Baptiste, 264
tolerance, 1, 5, 82–86, 91, 93–96, 103, 109, 111–12. *See also* religious freedom; secularism

Torah, 43, 204, 207, 209, 254; swearing oaths on, 63, 66, 70–72, 73n17, 95, 103–5
Trenchaunt, Henry, 72
Trump, Donald, 310, 311, 312
trust (theory of), 1–10, 48n5, 122, 172n15, 195n5, 195n10, 196n12; and authenticity, 276–77; and commerce, 140–41; and conversion, 181–82, 184–85; and friendship, 7, 20, 222–23, 229–32; and hospitality, 20–21; institution-based trust, 6, 160–61, 164, 166–67, 170; and mistrust, 1–3, 119; and oaths (theory of), 3–5, 17–19; process-based trust, 159–161, 165, 166–67. *See also* Jewish oath
"trustworthy businessman," 6, 162, 165, 166–68, 169–70
Turbe, Comitissa, 62–63, 67
Turbe, Solomon, 62–63

usury, 166, 168

Vassall-Fox, Henry (Lord Holland), 94–95

Walter (herdsman), 72
War of the Spanish Succession, 124
Weber, Max, 167–68
Weisskopf, Solomon, 124, 125–26, 127–28
Wertheimer, Samson, 121, 128
Wilson, John, 250, 262
Wolff, Josef, 251, 264, 267n17
Wood, W. P., 261
World War I, 158–59, 161, 163, 166, 168, 170, 173n32
Wurzinger, Samson, 162
Wurzinger, Siegmund, 162

Yakar Ha-Kohen, 201, 207–8, 214n4, 217n39, 218n42, 218n45
Yedidyah ben Israel, 201–202, 209–213, 214n5, 215n10, 216n29, 218nn41–42, 218n44–45
Yiddish, 166, 167, 172n24, 309–10
Yorke, Philip (Lord Hardwicke), 81–82, 87

Zionism. *See under* Herzl, Theodor

www.ingramcontent.com/pod-product-compliance
Lightning Source LLC
Chambersburg PA
CBHW021343300426
44114CB00012B/1058